THE
BURMA ROAD
TO CAPITALISM

Economic Growth versus Democracy

MYA MAUNG

Westport, Connecticut
London

Library of Congress Cataloging-in-Publication Data

Maung, Mya, 1933–
    The Burma road to capitalism : economic growth versus democracy /
Mya Maung.
      p. cm.
    Includes bibliographical references and index.
    ISBN 0–275–96216–4 (alk. paper)
    1. Burma—Economic conditions—1948– 2. Burma—Foreign economic
relations. 3. Burma—Politics and government—1948– I. Title.
HC422.M382   1998
338.9591—dc21   97–43959

British Library Cataloguing in Publication Data is available.

Library of Congress Catalog Card Number: 97–43959
ISBN: 0–275–96216–4

First published in 1998

Praeger Publishers, 88 Post Road West, Westport, CT 06881
An imprint of Greenwood Publishing Group, Inc.

Printed in the United States of America

∞™

The paper used in this book complies with the
Permanent Paper Standard issued by the National
Information Standards Organization (Z39.48–1984).

10 9 8 7 6 5 4 3 2 1

Copyright Acknowledgments

The author and publisher gratefully acknowledge permission to quote from the following:

For the author's interview with Maung Aung. Used with permission of Maung Aung.

For the author's interview with Yin Yin May. Used with permission of Yin Yin May.

To my children,
Christopher, Michael, and Melanie Maung

and the students, freedom fighters, and the symbol of "Freedom for Fear,"
Daw Aug San Suu Kyi of Burma

Contents

Illustrations

FIGURES

TABLES

Preface

This study is a continuation of my research and studies that began rigorously in the aftermath of the 1988 mass political uprising against the 26-year military dictatorship of General Ne Win in Burma. The main thesis of my studies, including this one, has been that "a country's course of development is determined not by its initial conditions, but by the quality of its national economic management."[1] This is a variant of the development theory that stresses not so much factor-endowment or richness in natural resources, savings, and capital formation of a country but rather the "social capabilities" or human capital, such as improved health, education, knowledge, and skills in the allocation of resources among competing wants, to initiate and sustain economic growth or enable a traditional society of low productivity to make the transition to a modern society of high productivity.

Burma's course of development—or, rather, lack of development— exemplifies a case of reduced human capabilities and poor national economic management of a country that is commonly acknowledged to be rich in natural resources. The Burmese case clearly demonstrates that the abundance of natural resources does not make a country rich, and conversely, a lack of natural resources does not make countries poor, as testified by the spectacular economic success and growth of Japan, Hong Kong, South Korea, and Taiwan with little arable land, no natural resources, and overpopulation relative to land size. A common observation has been made by some foreign observers and investors as well as the military government and its lobbyists on Burma's great potential to become another Asian Tiger based on the richness of its natural resources and the inflow of foreign direct investments. This observation is a mistaken notion of what constitutes the real wealth and the development potential of a nation. As Reuven Brenner correctly assessed, "The ability to produce wealth is far more important than wealth derived from occasional high prices of exportable natural resources."[2] The ability to produce wealth and generate economic growth ultimately lies in the managerial capacity of a nation or human capital, which has been depressed and depleted in Burma under military rule of more than three decades.

It is commonly acknowledged that improvement in the state of technology broadly defined as human capital or social capability has been the key determinant in increasing the productivity of labor, land, and capital or total factor productivity in promoting economic growth. Improvement in the state of technology to generate economic growth calls for investment in education and "the spread and level of modern education and the industrial and commercial experience of people."[3] The history of the Industrial Revolution and economic transformation of the Western world was not a simple story of sudden discoveries of new resources and methods of production. It was also a story of accumulation of knowledge, innovation, evolution, revolution of thought, and changes in the sociopolitical systems during the prolonged period stretching from the Renaissance and Reformation through the age of reason and Enlightenment to the age of science.[4]

In the contemporary history of rapidly developing Asian countries, such as the newly industrializing countries or the Asian Tigers (Hong Kong, Singapore, South Korea, and Taiwan) and the Association of Southeast Asian Nations (ASEAN), one common factor attributable to their economic success has been improvement in the state of technology due to high investment in the formation of human capital. Recent theories, debates, and inquiries in determining the reasons for the so-called East Asian economic miracle have produced a conclusion that "although the Four Tigers accumulated capital and increased labor participation at a much faster rate than other economies, the increase in these two factors far from fully explains their exceptional growth; growth in productivity attributable to innovative technology also accounts for a significant fraction."[5] In particular, this improvement in the state of technology occurred under the outward-looking or open-door policy adopted by these countries since the end of World War II, absorbing and adapting not only capital but also technology from the advanced industrial societies, especially Western democratic countries. The reverse was true of Burma and other Asian countries that adopted socialism and inward-looking policy to depress the state of technology and economic growth.

The central hypothesis of my research has been the bleak prospects for economic growth and democratization of Burma due to the ineffective and repressive policies of the consecutive military regimes and the enormous damage inflicted on human capital for more than three decades. The main goal of national economic management of the military regimes has been to sustain the stranglehold on political power by empowering and enriching the military elite and its followers with no long-term objective of elevating the standard of living of the people. Discrimination against the educated or intellectuals continues to persist and depress the social capabilities of Burma for development. The depletion of human capital continues unabated as hundreds of thousands of migrant legal and illegal workers, including students, teachers, intellectuals, and professionals, have left Burma in search of freedom from both poverty and fear in the prosperous neighboring countries and the Western world. This is direct evidence of the lack of real economic development for the people in Burma today and, in tandem, the dismal prospects for sustainable economic growth of Burma.

Although it is commonly acknowledged that the statistical data and economic information of the Burmese government are highly unreliable, this study uses them to show their flaws and contradictions in light of the data and information given by outside observers and international organizations, such as the Asian Development Bank, the World Bank, the International Monetary Fund, the United Nations Development Programme, and the US government. However, the main sources of data came mostly from interviews and writings of Burmese students, intellectuals, journalists, cross-border traders, medical doctors, economists, and those who lived through the rule of force and fear under both General Ne Win and the military regime, the State Law and Order Restoration Council (SLORC). This book may be viewed as the "Voice of Burma" presented by the Burmese through me to express their sufferings and exercise their right to freedom of expression, which has been denied for more than three decades by the ominous military rulers of Burma.

It is the hope of the author that in addition to the central hypothesis other related subhypotheses advanced and conclusions drawn in this study are going to be investigated further for empirical verification by those who are truly interested and concerned with the plight of a nation that has been under siege by its own army for over three decades. The empirical data for the case studies presented in this book were gathered over the course of several years, especially during the two years in 1994 and 1995, while I was a visiting fellow at the Centre for International Studies, London School of Economics and Political Science in 1994 and at the East-West Center, Honolulu, Hawaii, in 1995. I visited the Thai-Burmese border outpost of Mai Sai, where I interviewed a number of Burmese cross-border traders, and Singapore and Malaysia, where I interviewed a number of Burmese migrant legal and illegal workers. Although I wish to acknowledge many Burmese at home and abroad who have helped me in providing information, all of them plead not to mention their names for fear of repercussion. This fact in itself can be taken as the evidence of the nightmare state of Burma.

NOTES

1. William E. James, Seiji Naya, and Gerald M. Meier, *Asian Development: Economic Success and Lessons* (Madison: University of Wisconsin Press, 1989), p. xvi. See also Mya Maung, *The Burma Road to Poverty* (New York: Praeger, 1991).

2. Reuven Brenner, "The Pursuit of Poverty," *Wall Street Journal*, November 14, 1995.

3. Moses Abramovitz, "The Elements of Social Capability," in Ben Ho Koo and Dwight H. Perkins, eds., *Social Capability and Long-Term Economic Growth* (New York: St. Martin's Press, 1995), p. 35.

4. Gerald M. Meier and Robert E. Baldwin, *Economic Development: Theory, History, Policy* (New York, John Wiley and Sons, 1963), p. 83.

5. Michael Sarel, *Growth in Asia, What We Can and What We Cannot Infer, Economic Issues 1* (Washington, DC: International Monetary Fund, 1996), p. 10.

Acknowledgements

I am deeply grateful to Professor Emeritus Joseph Silverstein of Rutgers University and Professors Ronald Findlay and Hugh T. Patrick of Columbia University for their comments, encouragement, and support of my work. Special thanks are due to my colleague and friend Professor George Aragon, who read every chapter of the book and gave penetrating comments, criticisms, and invaluable suggestions to improve the data presented in the study. Professor Edward Kane of my department also gave invaluable comments on the theoretical aspects of the study. I would also like to thank Professors Michael Leifer, James Mayall, Michael Yahuda, and James Putzel of the London School of Economics and Political Science and Drs. Charles Morrison, Muthiah Alagappa, Chung H. Lee, and Manuel Montes of the East-West Center, Hawaii, for their help, comments, and criticisms of the papers on "Democracy, Economic Growth and Asian Values" and "The Burmese Approach to Development: Economic Growth without Democratization," which I prepared and presented while I was a visiting fellow. I wish to acknowledge the help of the editor of *Burma Alert*, Mr. Harn Yawnghwe of the Associates to Develop Democratic Burma (ADDB), for securing funds for some of my research trips and participation in various seminars on Burma. Special thanks are due to Mrs. Barbara Viechnicki, the Assistant Dean for Administration of the School of Management, Boston College, for reading, commenting, and meticulous editing of my work. Lastly, I like to thank Maung Zaw Oo, a young Burmese final-year medical student who participated in the 1988 political uprising and fled to the Thai border and later to the United States, for his research and assistance given to me in gathering data and information on contemporary developments in Burma.

Introduction

The end of the Cold War and the collapse of the Soviet Union and former socialist and communist economic systems have led to the revival of capitalism and the adoption of free market economic systems as the key to rapid development. The road to capitalism paved with open-door market economy, marketization, privatization, liberalization, and free trade has become the accepted goal and policy in vogue of former socialist and communist states across the world, including China, Burma, Cambodia, Laos, and Vietnam. However, a new theory of development of what political scientists called "developmental authoritarianism" and some economists termed the "East Asian model" advocates economic freedom, or rather, an "open-door, market-oriented economic system" under the control and management of a "strong state," and rejects political freedom and principles of fundamental human rights.

The fundamental postulate of this theory is that economic development or growth determines social and political development or that economic growth promotes political freedom and democratization. The acceptance of this postulate is clearly reflected in the development policies and strategies of promoting economic growth at all costs, including human rights violations, adopted by authoritarian regimes such as China and Burma. It is also reflected in the foreign policies of industrially developed Asian and Western governments and multinational corporations that construe that economic dealings and human rights considerations are separate, on one hand, and engagement with an authoritarian regime or trade and investment promote economic growth and, in tandem, democratization, on the other. The "constructive engagement policy" of the Association of Southeast Asian Nations (ASEAN) in particular champions these presumptions and justifies engagement with a pariah state like Burma.

Taken to the logical extreme, such notions also endorse the prevalent view of many Asian authoritarian regimes and their leaders, such as Li Peng of China, Mahathir bin Mohamad of Malaysia, and Lee Kuan Yew of Singapore, that establishment of "stability and discipline" at all costs, including the short-term suppression of human rights, is *a prerequisite* of economic growth. In the context of economic backwardness or the poverty of Asia, the primacy of economic development over any other development has been stressed by the authoritarian governments of Asia to justify the rule of force and human rights abuses. In short, the full-stomach theory of development, popularly phrased in Burma as "one can meditate only if the stomach is full," has been extolled over the moral message that "man does not live by bread alone."

It is the view of this author that the postulates and presumptions of so-called developmental authoritarianism run counter to the fundamental principles of capitalism. The ideals of modern capitalism are derived from the moral ideals and principles of liberal democracy born out of the long historical struggle of peoples and nations against tyrannical and authoritarian governments. The "invisible hand" of Adam Smith's *Wealth of Nations*, about which so much has been written and extolled as the guiding principle of capitalism, is "the outcome of market activities, not the ultimate governor of economic affairs."[1] The benevolence of economic liberty or the efficiency of the "invisible hand" is advanced by Adam Smith on the basis of the requisite system of natural justice and the rule of law laid down in his *Theory of Moral Sentiments*. The advocacy of "invisible hand" is made as a direct critique and denunciation of the "visible hand" of an unjust mercantile state that denies not only freedom of enterprise but also freedom of life, liberty, and pursuit of happiness to its common citizens.

It will be argued that development of a nation is a human endeavor involving more than material prosperity or pure economic growth. In the words of Daw (Madam) Aung San Suu Kyi, the pro-democracy and foremost opposition leader to the military regime of Burma, the SLORC:

If material embetterment [economic growth], which is but a means to human happiness, is sought in ways that wound human spirit, it can in the long run lead to greater human sufferings. The vast possibilities that a market economy can open up to developing countries can be realized only if economic reforms are undertaken within a framework that recognizes human needs[2]

As the United Nations Development Programme (UNDP) prescribed, "Both state and market should be guided by the people" with "the two working in tandem, and people should be sufficiently empowered to exert effective control over both."[3] This view is also endorsed by Amartya Sen: "Political rights are important not only for the fulfillment of needs, they are crucial for the formulation of needs. The importance of political rights for the understanding of economic needs turns ultimately on seeing human beings as people with rights to exercise, not as parts of a "stock" or a "population" that passively exists and must be looked after"[4] — a view held by authoritarian rulers across the world.

The military regime of Burma, the State Law and Order Restoration Council (SLORC), which seized power on September 18, 1988, after killing thousands of unarmed demonstrators, has adopted the so-called East Asian model of economic growth, espousing the tenets of development authoritarianism to hang on to power. In May 1990, it held a multiparty election, which was won in a landslide by the opposition party of 1991 Nobel Peace laureate Daw Aung San Suu Kyi, the National League for Democracy (NLD). The election result was not honored, and since then the SLORC has managed to remain in power and legitimate its rule by adopting a policy of "open-door, market-oriented economy" in the name of "the Burmese Way to Capitalism" to successfully attract foreign direct investment from around the world and sustain its rule.

ASEAN and many outside observers have been endorsing the Burmese Way to Capitalism of the SLORC and viewed the Burmese junta as making "positive changes and steps towards democratization and economic progress." Among those who hold this view are the US Texaco, Unocal, and Pepsi-Cola officials and a number of lawmakers, including George Archer and Nancy Johnson, who were invited by the SLORC to visit Myanmar in 1993. Others are New York businesswoman Mariam Marshall Segal (nicknamed by Burmese dissidents as "the shrimp lady," who owned a joint venture fishing firm with the SLORC and is under indictment for fraud by the Hong Kong-based Peregrine Ltd. at the New York court) and former congressman Lester Wolf. The latest advocates of SLORC who recommended for the US recognition of the SLORC as the legitimate government of Burma and the resumption of aid are Mya Saw Shin, Alison Krupnick, and Tom L. Wilson in their report entitled *"Burma" or "Myanmar": U.S. Policy at the Crossroads.*[5] Two Burma scholars who have put forth positive views on the SLORC's economic achievements are John Badgley and Thant Myint U in their respective articles in the *Asian Survey* (February 1994) and *Far Eastern Economic Review* (March 10, 1994).

This study challenges the views of authoritarian Asian leaders and the SLORC's supporters by demonstrating that the Burmese case exemplifies the rule of force to establish sociopolitical stability and the adoption of "an open-door, market-oriented economy" policy to sustain political power by an illegitimate government. It shows that:

1. The postulates and presumptions of developmental authoritarianism are utterly perverse and wrong by showing that in Burma "stability and discipline," or the rule of force imposed upon the people by the military regime of Burma, the SLORC, since 1988, have promoted neither real economic growth nor human development.

2. On the contrary, human rights abuses and the role of a "strong state" in undertaking ostentatious economic reforms in Burma by the SLORC have been detrimental to real economic growth and genuine development for the people.

3. The rule of force and the denial of the fundamental human rights of the people of Burma by the present military regime have also created sociopolitical instability inside Burma, causing greater repression and lack of public confidence and economic security to stifle economic growth.

4. The outside world's trade, investment, and engagement with the Burmese military regime have enabled the military rulers to enlarge their economic base of power to sustain their rule and encouraged them not to undertake genuine economic and political reforms.

5. The management, structure, and functioning of the Burmese economic system have not changed significantly to generate sustainable economic growth. The quality and goals of national economic policies and the portfolio of military managers with a low level of education and intellectual mediocrity remain poor and unchanged. Specifically, the main obstacle of Burma's economic development has been the depletion of human capital or social capabilities due to the inept sociopolitical and economic policies of the military regime.

BURMA

Burma encompasses an area of 262,000 square miles or about the size of Texas, bounded by Bangladesh (about 200 miles) and India (about 910 miles) on the northwest and the People's Republic of China (about 1,360 miles) on the northeast. It also borders Laos (about 150 miles) and Thailand (about 1,200 miles) on the eastern frontier, overlooked by China from the north forming the famous poppy land of the "Golden Triangle." The approximately 1,200-mile western and southern coastline of Burma stretches along the Bay of Bengal and the Andamen Sea to the southernmost tip of Victoria Point on the northern entrance of the Strait of Malacca. In land size, Burma is the largest country in mainland Southeast Asia and the second largest country next to Indonesia among the Southeast Asian countries, including the island republics of Brunei, Indonesia, Malaysia, the Philippines, and Singapore, with a relatively low ratio of people to land (172 persons per square mile in 1995).

The exact or dependable statistical figures of Burma's contemporary population, its growth, demographic distributions, and ethnic compositions are not known due to a lack of reliable census data taken by the military government. The last census taken by the government was back in 1983. The estimates of Burma's population in 1995 vary between 44 million and 45 million. However, the consensus is that approximately three-fourths of the population live in rural areas and are engaged in agriculture and extractive industries for their livelihood. About three-fourths of its population are made up of the majority ethnic group called Bamahs, or Myanmahs in Burmese, most of whom live in, and politically control, central Burma. It should be noted that this so-called majority ethnic group of Bamahs includes a large number of people with mixed blood, the children of the inter-marriages between the majority Bamahs and other ethnic minority groups along with the Anglo-Burmese, the Indo-

Burmese, and the Sino-Burmese. The rest of the population is made up of seven main ethnic minority groups, the Arakanese, the Chins, the Kachins, the Karens, the Kayars or Karennis, the Mons, and the Shans, along with more than 100 other ethnolinguistic groups. The peripheral land areas, or what the British colonial administrators created and called "the frontier states" of the ethnic minority groups, account for more than half of Burma's land. Roughly 85 percent of the population are Buddhists. The religious minorities are Christians and Muslims, most of who are found among the ethnic minorities.

It is a country rich in natural resources: the vast fertile soil of the Delta formed by the Ayeyarwaddy (Irrawaddy) River in Lower Burma; evergreen forests that cover nearly 50 percent of the land, including the famed Burmese teak forest, estimated to account for 75 percent of the world's reserves; gold, silver, ruby, amber, jade stone, iron, copper, and other mineral mines of the northern states of Kachin and Shan (the most famous gems being the Burmese jade or jadeite and ruby); inland and coastal waters of bountiful fish and crustaceans; and oil and recently discovered offshore natural gas in the Gulf of Martaban in the Andamen Sea along the Tenasserim Peninsula. This richness of Burma was noticed by ancient travelers in naming the country the "Golden Land." Its ancient capital, Mandalay (spelled and pronounced Mundalay in Burmese), of the last two kings of the Konbaung dynasty, Mindoan Min and Thibaw Min, which is popularly associated with Rudyard Kipling's poetical phrase "On the Road to Mandalay where the flying fishes played," was called the Gem City by Nineteenth Century foreign visitors from the West.

Historically, Burma was and still is considered one of the richest lands in natural resources that have yet to be fully developed or exploited. The richness in untapped natural resources and relatively large size of land to population provide a high potential for economic development, which has been the common observation of all interested foreign visitors to Burma from ancient times to the present. The sacred Sanskrit and Pali names of ancient Burma as *Suvarnabhumi* (*Thuwana Bhumi* in Burmese) and *Suvanna Chumi* or *Sonabhumi* connote Burma as "the Golden Frontier Country" or "the Golden Land." The mentioning of Burma by Claudius Ptolemaeus in *Chryse Regio* as part of Chersonesus Aurea in A.D. 160 seemed to confirm the richness of the precolonial economy of Burma with gold, precious stones, and other natural resources.[6] Some authors even identified it with the "Orphir of Solomon." As Dr. Mason wrote:

Few countries in the world are so rich in minerals as Burma; in none, perhaps, do those riches lie so dormant. Mergui has tin equal to Cornwall; in Tavoy iron could be made equal to the Swedish; the copper and antimony of Moulmain are good; the gold of Shwegyeen is not inferior to the Australian; and the lead of Taungoo Mountains has no superior in the hills of Missouri.[7]

In A.D. 1550, De Cruz said that "there be great richness in this county," and in A.D. 1569, Caesar Frederick wrote, "For people, dominions, gold and silver, the King of Bramas far excelled the power of the Great Turk in treasure and strength."[8]

It is stressed that the richness of Burma in natural resources is not constant over Burma's historical course of exploitation of natural resources and commercialization of extractive industries that stretched many centuries from the ancient Burmese kingdoms, through the British colonial rule, to the independent Burmese governments. Evidence of the depletion of natural resources can be found not only in the continued overcutting of trees and deforestation of Burma but also in the withdrawal of more than a dozen foreign oil companies, which embarked on ambitious joint venture oil exploration projects with the military government, beginning in 1993 after no significant find of onshore oil. Wanton squandering of the Golden Land by putting up depletable or already more or less depleted natural resources, such as teak, timber, oil, natural gas, gems, minerals, and fisheries, for sale to aggressive foreign investors for shortterm profit and foreign exchange by the military regime has been continuing with no end in sight, resulting in ecological rape and environmental damage.

ANCIENT BURMA

The emergence of the first historically recorded Burmese kingdom of Pagan dynasty in A.D. 1044 marked the beginning of the nation-state called "Myanmah Pyi," which literally means "the Country of Myanmahs" (the country of the majority ethnic group). It should be pointed out that the term Myanmar (the new name of Burma given by the present military rulers of Burma in 1989) itself refers not to the country but to the majority ethnic group designated in Burmese as Bamahs (in speaking) or Myanmahs (in writing). In ancient Burma, the official name of each Burmese kingdom does not use that term but instead uses the royal capital city such as the Pagan kingdom, or Paukkan Pyi (the country of royal city at Pagan or Paukkan), the Ava (Innwa) Pyi or Kingdom and so on. According to Dr. Than Tun, a well-known Burmese scholar and authority on ancient history of Burma, the usage of the word *Myanmah* in reference to the ethnic majority race appeared in A.D. 1190, while the usage of the term *Myanmah Pyi* in reference to the country of *Myanmahs* appeared in A.D. 1332. in the stone inscriptions of the Pagan dynasty, the first Burmese kingdom founded in the Eleventh century by King Anawya-hta or Anawrahta[9].

Between the founding of the Pagan dynasty and that of the last Koanbaung Dynasty of Burmese kings in A.D. 1752, Burma's political history was a saga of continual power struggle at the "center" and warfare among city states in central Burma as well as between the central Burmese kingdom and the kingdoms of the Arakanese, Mons, and Shans. At various intervals of time, the Burmese kingdoms fell at the hands of the ethnic minority rulers and foreign invaders, Chinese and Siamese. The fall of the Pagan Dynasty in A.D. 1312 occurred at the hands of the invading Kublai Khan army. During the four centuries following the fall of the Pagan dynasty, two Shan dynasties ruled Upper

Burma, and two other dynasties of Burmese kings, Toungoo and Ava, emerged to subdue the minority rulers. The famous king of the Toungoo dynasty, Bayintnaung (1551–1581), subdued the minority kingdoms of Arakan, Mon, and Shan, as well as marched twice to Siam and conquered its royal capital city of Ayuhtiya. His successor, Nanda Bayin, followed suit and mounted a fruitless attack on Siam, which eventually resulted in the fall of the Toungoo dynasty at the hands of the counterattacking Siamese army in collaboration with the Arakanese.[10]

During the 133 years of the Koanbaung dynasty (1752–1885), Burmese kings invaded and ravaged the land and people of the Arakanese, Mon, and Shan kingdoms. Externally, the Koanbaung dynasty was at war with the British and the kingdoms of Assam and Siam. The famed Burmese king of Ava kingdom, Sinbyushin (1763–1778), invaded the kingdom of Siam and destroyed its royal capital city of Ayuhtiya. Geopolitically, the rest of the minor ethnic minority groups—the Karens, Kayars or Karennis, Kachins, Chins, Nagas, Was, and many other hill tribes—remained relatively isolated from the mainstream of this ancient Burmese Buddhist society and polity. Throughout the history of precolonial Burma, the savagery and atrocity of the continuous wars fought between the majority Burmese kings and the minority rulers had left deep wounds of hate and mistrust among their leaders. In short, ancient Burma was a warring state internally and externally, producing a fragmented social order of mistrust, hate, and fear or ethnophobia among various ethnic groups and xenophobia for the Burmese. The legacy of wars between the central Burmese government and a number of ethnic minority rebel groups persists in independent Burma since 1948.

BURMA OR MYANMAR?

The British interest in the rich forests and natural resources of Burma in direct conflict with that of the French precipitated three different Anglo-Burmese wars fought over a span of 61 years under the reigns of three different Burmese Konbaung kings: Bagyidaw Min (1819–1838), Pagan Min (1846–1852), and Thibaw Min (1878–1885). The British colonial rule over Lower Burma lasted nearly a century (1852–1948), which ultimately ended in 1948, when Burma obtained its independence. For many generations before and after the ultimate British annexation or colonization of the entire country in 1886, the country was known as Burma. In 1989, like the new name of Campuchia given to Cambodia by the Khmer Rouge or Pol Pot regime, the new name of Myanmar was given to Burma by the military regime, the SLORC, which seized power in 1988. Not only the country but also names of the cities were changed. For example, the capital of Burma known for many generations as Rangoon is now called Yangon.

Like the racial origin of the majority ethnic group of Burma, the etymological root of the word "Bamah" or "Myanmar" as a country is dual in reference to the impact of India and China on the configuration of Burmese civilization and culture. According to the best-known legend, the Burmese racial and cultural heritage was traced to the Indian king, Abiyazah of Satkyah caste, who founded the Tagaung dynasty in Upper Burma. Another kingdom was supposedly founded at Pyi, or Thayai Khityah, as the Burmese call it, in Lower Burma by the descendants of Abiyazah. According to a well-known authority on ancient Burma, J. G. Scott "Hence when Tharé Kettara [Thayai Khitayah] came to an end through civil wars, or outside invasion, the remnant that came to found Pagan were the people from Brahma—the Mranma, Bama—Burmese."[11] However, other historians traced the racial and cultural origin of the Burmese to Tibet and the northwestern region of China. Burmese prose writers and poets refer to the country as Myan Taing, derived from what the Chinese writers refer to ancient Burma as "Mien Tien," which may be considered as the origin of the term "Myanmar."

After Burma gained independence from British colonial rule in 1948, the democratically elected government of the late U Nu adopted the name Union of Burma, which was retained until 1974, when the military regime of General Ne Win changed it to the Socialist Republic of the Union of Burma. This name was retained until 1988 and was unofficially changed to the Union of Burma during 1988 and to the Union of Myanmar, or Myanmar for short, officially in June 1989 by the SLORC, causing confusion and difficulties for some Westerners to pronounce the name properly. This change of name, made by the military regime without a national referendum, was obliged to be accepted by the United Nations. With the exception of the US government, the new name of Myanmar has been widely accepted and used by various countries around the world and international organizations, including the United Nations and its agencies and Amnesty International.

"Burma," which is apparently named after the majority ethnic race of Bamahs, or more correctly, *Bamah lumyo* in Burmese, by the British, is never used by the Burmese to signify their country. Instead, the Burmese call their country *Bamah Pyi* or *Naing-gan* (in speaking) or *Myanmah Pyi* or *Naing-gan* (in writing). The word "Bamah" or "Myanmah," pronouncing the ending "mah" softly as when addressing one's mother in English, refers to the majority ethnic group, while "Pyi" or "Naing-gan" means country. Hence, the term "Myanmar" or "Myanmah" Naing-gan adopted by the SLORC signifies the country of the majority ethnic race, *Bamahs* or *Myanmah lumyo*. Politically, it implies the suzerainty of the majority Bamahs or Myanmahs over the major ethnic minority groups, such as the Arakanese, the Kachin, the Karen, the Mon, and the Shan, which have been waging war against the rule of the majority Bamahs since Burma gained independence from the British in 1948.

AN OVERVIEW OF MILITARY DICTATORSHIP AND ECONOMIC GROWTH

Burma gained independence from the British colonial rule on January 4, 1948. The civilian political party responsible for obtaining independence was the Anti-Fascist People's Freedom League (AFPFL), which was formed in the immediate years following World War II under the leadership of General Aung San. General Aung San was the founding father of independent Burma from British rule and the father of Daw Aung San Suu Kyi, the 1991 Nobel Peace laureate and the foremost opposition leader to the military regime, the SLORC. General Aung San was also the leader of the famous Thirty Comrades, *Yebaw Thoangyate*, who left Burma for military training in Japan to fight for Burma's freedom from the British rule at the onset of World War II. General Ne Win, the dictator who ruled Burma for 26 years from 1962 to 1988, was a member of this group.

General Aung San and his comrades eventually turned against the Japanese occupation of Burma and formed the Burma Independence Army (BIA) and later the Burma National Army (BNA) during World War II. It was the first time since the British annexed Burma in 1886 that a Burmese army came into existence. The Burmese army founded by General Aung San joined the returning Allied forces and successfully liberated Burma from the fascist Japanese rule. At the end of World War II General Aung San assumed the civilian political leadership, while General Ne Win remained in the Burmese army as the British returned to rule Burma in 1945. From 1945 to 1947, General Aung San served as the president of the AFPFL and succeeded in mobilizing the people and uniting nationalist political leaders, including the leaders of the Burma Communist Party (BCP) and ethnic minorities, to demand independence from the British government. In 1946, General Aung San and the AFPFL succeeded in negotiating and demanding independence from British rule by mobilizing the people for a potential armed revolt if independence was not granted within two years. Under the governorship of Sir Hubert Rance, a new Governor's Executive Council or cabinet was formed whereby General Aung San was appointed the deputy chairman of the council or the de facto prime minister of Burma.

On July 19, 1947, General Aung San and six members of his cabinet were killed by the assassins of disfranchised U Saw, who was the last premier of colonial Burma. U Nu, who was one of the leaders of the AFPFL, succeeded General Aung San and successfully negotiated and signed the agreement with the British government for Burma's independence on January 4, 1948. Burma was named the Union of Burma under the premiership of the late U Nu, the one and only democratically elected prime minister of independent Burma. The immediate years following independence were beset with political power struggles, communist and ethnic minority insurgency that ultimately led to the dawn of military rule over Burma in 1958, when U Nu gave power to General Ne Win to form a caretaker government, which ruled the country for 18 months.

In 1960, a democratic election was held, and U Nu and his Pyidaungsu political party won in a landslide. In March 1962, General Ne Win staged a coup and seized power and established his dictatorship and imposed an iron rule for the next 26 years from 1962 to 1988. General Ne Win and his commanders formed the Revolutionary Council (RC) government and established a single-party political system with the formation of the Burma Socialist Programme Party (BSPP), designed after the Sino-Soviet model. In 1974, after drawing up a constitution, Burma was renamed the Socialist Republic of the Union of Burma, and Burma was made into a reclusive socialist state cut off from the outside world, especially the West.

Pursuing the dream of a utopian socialist economy of proportional development, equality, and justice for all, the Sino-Soviet model of a planned socialist economy was adopted by nationalizing all private enterprises and industries and imposing direct controls on production, distribution, trade, and finance. The highly inefficient dual economy, with a formal/official economy comprising 22 state corporations and more than 50 state enterprises, combined with the informal/unofficial economy of a nationwide black market, propelled Burma down the road to poverty. On December 11, 1987, the Socialist Republic of the Union of Burma under the management of General Ne Win and his commanders applied for, and officially gained, the economically degrading status of one of the 41 least developed countries in the world granted by the United Nations. The three criteria of the United Nations for granting this status were a country with less than $200 per capita income, less than 10 percent contribution of manufacturing to gross domestic product (GDP), and less than 20 percent national literacy. The last criterion was not met by Burma. Burma in 1987 remained a highly literate country, as it has been for many generations, but became one of the least-developed and poorest nations in the world.

THE STATE LAW AND ORDER RESTORATION COUNCIL (SLORC)

Public discontent against the unjust government and the impoverishment of the people led to a massive political uprising led by students in March 1988. Ne Win formally resigned from the chairmanship of the BSPP and nominally gave up the political throne in July 1988. From March to September 1988, the revolt against the military rulers and the BSPP continued. A series of confrontations between the pro-democracy demonstrators and the government security forces resulted in bloodshed and killings unprecedented in the modern history of Burma. In the name of "law and order" and "saving the country from abyss," General Saw Maung and the Burmese army staged a counterfeit military coup on September 18, 1988, killing some 10,000 unarmed demonstrators who demanded democracy and freedom from the 26-year dictatorship of General Ne

Win. The coup was counterfeit because the same entourage of Ne Win headed by General Saw Maung engineered the takeover of power.

With General Saw Maung as chairman, a 19 member military junta was created with the name of the State Law and Order Restoration Council (SLORC), along with a 9 member military cabinet to govern Burma. The formation and organization of SLORC replicated the Revolutionary Council (RC) created after the military coup of 1962. Two months after the 1988 September coup, on November 7, the SLORC issued Order No. 4/88 to form the Department of General Security Administration (DGSA) under the Ministry of Home and Religious Affairs. Under the DGSA, the former security unit of People's Council (PC) was reorganized and renamed Law and Order Restoration Council (LORC). Thousands of these councils were formed on the district, township, and village level to execute various government orders and projects of development. These LORCs, together with the People's Police Force, Special Bureau of Investigation (SBI), and the army, enforced tight security across the country to establish stability and discipline.

In order to quell the continued public protest against the military rule and halt the democracy movement, the SLORC introduced a multiparty democratic system and promised to hold a multiparty democratic election in 1990. On May 27, 1990, SLORC held the promised election after allowing over 200 political parties to be formed for the first time in 26 years and putting the foremost opposition leader Daw Aung San Suu Kyi under house arrest in July 1989. At the same time, U Nu, the late civilian prime minister deposed by General Ne Win in 1962, was also put under house arrest, and U Tin Oo, an ex-general who was purged by General Ne Win in 1975 and the chairman of Daw Suu Kyi's opposition party, the National League for Democracy (NLD), was imprisoned for a term of seven years with hard labor. All three leaders were declared ineligible to run in the elections.

To the surprise of many observers (particularly the SLORC, which hoped to install the party it backed, the National Unity Party), the official returns of the elections announced on June 30 revealed the landslide victory of candidates from the NLD, which captured over 80 percent of the constituencies by winning 392 out of the total 485 seats contested. The NLD leaders requested unsuccessfully to talk with SLORC for the transfer of power and the formation of a new government. Remnant NLD leaders and outspoken candidates were arrested and given long-term jail sentences. The election result was not honored, and the SLORC continues to rule against the will of the Burmese people in direct violation of Article 21 of the UN Universal Declaration of Human Rights: "The will of the people shall be the basis of the authority of government."

After the May 1990 election, the SLORC began to systematically erase the election outcome and stall the transfer of power to the winners by mandating the drafting of a catch-22 constitution and holding a national referendum to approve the constitution drafted by all 27 parties that won seats in the election, but not by the majority winner of the election, the NLD. July 27, 1990, was a day of reckoning for the Burmese voters when SLORC issued the infamous Declaration No. 1/90, which bluntly stated that "the SLORC, Defense Forces, is not bound by any constitution" and that it is "ruling the country with martial law" and is "a government recognized by the countries of the world and the United Nations." At the same time, the powerful chief of military intelligence, Khin Nyunt, also warned that "any attempt to form an interim government or General Assembly by the NLD candidates will be forcefully dealt with."

THE BURMA ROAD TO POVERTY

From a historical perspective, the economic performance of independent Burma may be viewed as a transition from revival and sustained economic growth in the 1950s under the management of the civilian government to stagnation in the two decades of 1960s and 1970s and to accelerated depression in the 1980s under military management. The real GDP growth rate of Burma from 1949 to 1960 under the development programs and the eight-year Pyidawtha Plan of the U Nu government (1952–1960) averaged 5.9 percent, with an average annual per capita real GDP growth rate of 4.7 percent.[12] During the same period, Burma had a balance of trade surplus for most of the years, with annual rice exports of 1.5 million tons, reaching 2 million tons in 1960 in recapturing two-thirds of the prewar level of rice exports.

By contrast, the economic performance of the military command economy of Burma shows a downward spiral in the annual growth rate of real GDP, plunging from an average growth rate of about 5 percent between 1962 and 1965 to a negative 6 percent in 1966. The average annual growth rate of real GDP between 1966 and 1974 remained stagnant at about 3 percent. Beginning in 1975, however, the government sought after, and received, massive foreign aid from the West by adopting some ostentatious liberalization measures. The growth rate of GDP was boosted with billions of dollars poured into Burma by a multinational consortium of donors, the Burma AID Group headed by the United States, the World Bank, the International Monetary Fund, the Asian Development Bank, and many Western nations, including Japan and Australia. The average annual growth rate of real GDP between 1975 and 1980 was around 6 percent. However, this externally stimulated growth rate could not be sustained, and by the mid-1980s the growth rate of real GDP plunged less than 1 percent.[13] In 1987, the bottom of the economy fell out as the growth rate of real GDP plunged to a negative rate of 4.2 percent, and socialist Burma became one of the least-developed countries in the world, with less than $200 per capita income. In 1988, the real GDP growth rate plunged further to a negative 11.4 percent, precipitating the mass political uprising.[14] Hence, it may be concluded that for the entire period from 1962 to 1988, the average annual growth rate of real GDP was no more than 3 percent. During the same period, Burma suffered from chronic trade deficit almost every year.

NOTES

1. Patricia H. Werhane, *Adam Smith and His Legacy for Modern Capitalism* (New York: Oxford University Press, 1991), p. 21.

2. Aung San Suu Kyi, "Empowerment for a Culture of Peace and Development," address to a meeting of World Commission on Culture and Development delivered by Corazon Aquino, Manila, November, 21, 1994, p. 8.

3. The UNDP, *Human Development Report 1993* (New York: Oxford University Press, 1993), p. 53.

4. Amartya Sen, "Freedoms and Needs," *The New Republic* (January 10 & 17, 1994): 38.

5. See Mya Saw Shin, Alison Krupnick, and Tom L. Wilson in their report entitled *"Burma" or "Myanmar": U.S. Policy at the Crossroads* (Washington, DC: Bureau of Asian Research, October 1995).

6. Charles J. F. Smith-Forbes, *British Burma: Its People, Native Manner, Customs and Religion* (London: Spottswood, 1878), p. 22.

7. Ibid., p. 20.

8. Ibid., pp. 20–21.

9. U Than Tun, *Ancient Burmese History: Studies in Burmese History No. 1* (in Burmese) (Rangoon: Mahah Dagon Press, 1964), pp. 185–186

10. See D.G.E. Hall, *Europe and Burma: A Study of European Relations with Burma to the Annexation of Thibaw's Kingdom 1886* (New York: Oxford University Press, 1945), p.6.

11. J. G. Scott (Shwe Yoe), *Burma: From the Earliest Time to the Present Day* (London: T. Fisher Unwin, 1924), p. 22

12. See Mya Maung, *Burma and Pakistan: A Comparative Study of Development* (New York: Praeger, 1971), p. 51

13. See for detail Mya Maung, *The Burma Road to Poverty* (New York: Praeger, 1991), pp. 136–142.

14. Ibid., p. 291.

1

Democracy, Economic Growth, and Asian Values

It is often in the name of cultural integrity as well as social stability and national security that democratic reforms based on human rights are resisted by authoritarian governments. It is insinuated that some of the worst ills of western society are the result of democracy, which is seen as the progenitor of unbridled freedom and selfish individualism. It is claimed, usually without adequate evidence, that democratic values and human rights run counter to the national culture, and therefore to be beneficial they need to be modified—perhaps to the extent that they are barely recognizable. The people are said to be as yet unfit for democracy, therefore an indefinite length of time has to pass before democratic reforms can be instituted.[1]

Since the September 18, 1988, military coup, the military regime of Burma, the SLORC, adopted the "Burmese Way to Capitalism," which is a variant or an emulation of the East Asian approach to development that envisions an open-door market economy of growth and prosperity under the control and management of "the strong or hard state." It is based on the theory that democracy, because of its inherent instability, is inimical to economic development for Third World countries, or "what a country needs is discipline more than democracy," and that "the exuberance of democracy leads to indiscipline and disorderly conduct which are inimical to development."[2] This philosophy is articulated by Lee Kuan Yew of Singapore and has been endorsed and publicly expressed by many authoritarian leaders of Asia, including Li Peng of China and Mahathir bin Mohamad of Malaysia. As Lee asserted:

All people of all countries need a good government. A country must first have economic development, then democracy may follow. With a few exceptions, democracy has not led to development because the government did not establish the stability and discipline necessary for development.[3]

The essence of this argument is that economic development precedes and supersedes any other development, including democracy, and that economic development, in turn, necessitates the establishment of "stability and discipline." Accordingly, a good government is one that can establish stability and discipline to bring about economic development. The argument also advances the thesis that the flowering of democracy is a function of economic growth rather than the other way around.

To reinforce and justify this argument, the relativity theory of values was expounded by Lee: "What is a good government? This depends upon the values of a people. What Asians value may not be what Americans and Europeans value. Westerners value freedoms and liberties of the individual."[4] In particular, he emphasized that Asians attach more value to social order, family, and social welfare than to individual freedom or civil liberties to justify the role of a strong authoritarian state in governing and developing a society. Lee's two closely intertwined tenets were embraced and echoed by the emissary of the SLORC, Burma's foreign minister Ohn Gyaw at the United Nations (UN) General Assembly meeting in New York on September 27, 1996:

We firmly believe that the international community should take a more holistic approach to the questions of human rights and not be preoccupied with individual rights and freedom. Any government, institution or individual seeking to promote human rights should bear in mind the significance of national and regional peculiarities as well as the stage of economic development. In Myanmar and other developing countries poverty remains an obstacle to the full enjoyment of these rights.[5]

The view that democracy or political liberty and economic growth are negatively correlated to each other and the need for "the strong or hard state" in promoting economic development go back a long way in the development literature. As Amartya Sen pointed out:

It is true that some relatively authoritarian states (such as Lee's Singapore, South Korea under military rule and more recently China) have had faster economic growth than some less authoritarian states (such as India, Costa Rica and Jamaica). But the overall picture is more complex than such isolated observations might suggest. Systematic statistical studies give little support to the view of a general conflict between civil rights and economic performance.[6]

Indeed, a serious empirical research conducted by 11 economic institutes with respect to the relationship between freedom and prosperity of some 102 countries over 20 years revealed overwhelmingly a positive instead of a negative correlation between the two.[7]

Conceiving the crises of Eastern European countries as examples of premature introduction of democratic reforms, Malaysia's prime minister, Mahathir bin Mohamad, recommended the establishment of stability and discipline to promote economic development and the natural evolution of democracy. He also suggested that "authoritarian rule cannot be sustained once a country achieves prosperity through a free market economy. Sooner or later a prosperous people will demand more freedom. And the government must give in."[8] However, in both prosperous and economically depressed Asian countries prosperity achieved through an open-door market economy controlled by the state has not persuaded the ruling elite to give in to the demand for more freedom by its disadvantaged and impoverished citizens. The crackdown of pro-democracy groups and dissidents continues in China, South Korea, Indonesia, Malaysia, Singapore, and Thailand to contradict the theory of Mahathir.

The case of Singapore, which was labeled by Korean political leader Kim Dae Jung as "a near-totalitarian police state"[9] based on its historical record of relentless crackdown on dissent and dissidents, exemplifies that prosperity does not necessarily make the ruling elite give in to the demand for more freedom by its citizens, negating, in fact, the theory of the Malaysian prime minister. The real reason for the advocacy of stability and emphasis on the need for tight discipline by Singapore leaders is that it is an island city-state with limited territory and vulnerability to Malaysia and Indonesia. Furthermore, the economic success of Singapore has not been singularly due to "strict discipline and stability" enforced by the state but to a number of factors, among which the most important are the smallness of its size (622 square kilometers), a fairly small and homogeneous population (Chinese making up two-thirds of its three million population) with no pressure or opposition groups, liberalization of labor laws, direct foreign investments of multinational corporations, and its strategic geoeconomic location as a transit seaport for foreign trade between the East and the West.[10]

The same is true of China, which to some seems to have achieved phenomenal economic growth by opening the economy to the outside world but which continues to deny greater political freedom and fundamental human rights to its people, as was exemplified by the 1989 Tiananmen Square massacre of pro-democracy demonstrators and continued suppression of political dissent. However, the rapid economic growth that China achieved by successful repression of public dissent has produced intensification of social tensions, creation of new sources of public discontent, and proliferation of corruption that could very well lead to political instability and greater repression. Contrary to the presumption of Singaporean and Malaysian political leaders, the Burmese case contradicts the hypothesis that "stability and discipline" imposed by an autocratic regime promote economic development and, in tandem, democratization.

STABILITY, DISCIPLINE, AND RELATIVITY OF ASIAN VALUES

To address the Chinese, Singaporean, and Malaysian political leaders' contentions, it is necessary to define and understand the meaning of "stability" and "discipline," which are construed as a *prerequisite* of economic development. Contemporary research on these subjects identifies the term "stability" with "sociopolitical stability," which is signaled by the absence of political riots, strikes, demonstrations, assassinations, and frequent turnovers of governments or executives.[11] In the context of Chinese, Burmese, and Singaporean historical records, the term "discipline" implies the imposition of authoritarian force, control, and penalties on the people who demand and exercise their fundamental human rights.

The insistence of authoritarian Asian leaders that the Western idea of democracy or good government as "the government of the people, by the people, and for the people" is alien to the Asian value systems in general is a myth. In reality, the fact is that Asian values are not homogenous. The claim of certain Asian leaders that Asians in general place family or social welfare over and above individual liberty and welfare ignores the fact that this exaggerated and distorted Chinese neo-Confucian value system is not universal among diverse Asian cultural systems. One cannot find such value orientation in either the Indic or highly individualistic Buddhist culture of Burma and other Southeast Asian countries. The very disastrous failures in adopting and experimenting with the Marxist values, philosophy, and socialist system to create a classless society of equality and justice for all by the so-called family-and-society value-oriented Asian countries, including Ne Win's Burma, Mao's China, Pol Pot's Cambodia, and Sukarno's Indonesia, should drive home the fact that man and society by nature are both individualistic and social in their nature and value orientation.

Samuel P. Huntington advanced the thesis that the fundamental source of conflict between the East and the West in the post-Cold War era is the "clash of civilizations" or value systems.[12] Against this thesis, David I. Hitchcock argued, based on his empirical research, that though differences exist, the clash of civilizations or cultural values between the East and West has been grossly exaggerated. He rejected Huntington's opinion on the transpiring of "a de-Westernization and indigenization of elites" in Asia by stating that "the interviews I carried out in the summer of 1994 suggest that opinion is considerably more variegated, even contradictory, among a cross-section of Asian elites."[13] He further showed that among the elites of culturally diverse Asian countries, there is no unanimity in the acceptance of the universal Asian civilization or "Asian way" advanced and extolled by the Singaporean school of thought. Indeed, the equating of the Singaporean philosophy and culture with the "Asian civilization" and the American philosophy and culture with the "Western civilization" is both misleading and wrong. As Masakazu Yammazaki bluntly said: "There has never been an Asian, let alone East Asian, sphere of civilization."[14]

Besides the internal conflicts and clashes of values among various social groups within each society, there are intraregional clashes of civilizations and values within the Asian and the Western worlds. At the same time, there are common values held and placed on human dignity and welfare of the people by different societies and cultures across the world.

Lack of unanimity among Asian elites and political leaders with respect to the relativity theory of Asian values and the view that democracy is a purely Western concept is most lucidity reflected in the statement made by Malaysia's deputy prime minister Datuk Seri Anwar Ibrahim:

Democracy is a basic necessity for responsible and ethical government. It is essential that power be vested in a democratically constituted authority rather than in the hands of the individual. Power personalized is power plundered from the people. Democracy is not a luxury that Asians cannot afford as some would want us believe. Democracy is not a Western concept. Asians can build on their past civilizational ideals and intellectual legacies to develop democracies based on ethical principles and moral uprightness. The Asian way is to reach consensus on national goals within a democratic framework, to take the middle path, to exercise tolerance and sensitivity towards others.[15]

Bilahari Kausikan, another Singaporean government official, holds that Asian historical experience "sees order and stability as preconditions for economic growth and growth as the necessary foundation for any political order that claims to advance human dignity."[16] Contrary to this claim, growth was never the top priority among the ideals of traditional Confucian and Neo-Confucian philosophy, which favors not pure economic growth but harmony and the "golden mean," which is embodied in the concept of *jen,* love and magnanimity, to attain and enhance human dignity. The same is true of traditional Buddhist philosophy of India and Burma, which prioritizes spiritual well-being, love, compassion, *myittah,* and the golden mean or the Middle Path, *Myitsima Padipadah,* over economic growth and desires and accumulation of material wealth, which are considered to be impermanent, *annica,* and the primary cause of sufferings, *dokka* (the Doctrine of Three Signatas and one of the Four Noble Truths in Buddhism).

The neo-Confucian Chinese philosopher Meng-tzu, or Mencius in Latin, asserted "that people are the most important element in a nation; the spirits of the land and grain come next; and the sovereign counts for the least."[17] He further argued that people had the right to revolt against rulers who did not tend to the welfare of the people. The Korean pro-democracy dissident leader Kim Dae Jung argued against Lee's contention of democracy as alien to Asian people (Chinese) by citing what Meng-tzu preached two millennia before John Locke:

The king is "the Son of Heaven" heaven bestowed on its son a mandate to provide good government, that is, to provide good for the people. If he did not govern righteously, the people had the right to rise up and overthrow his government in the name of heaven.[18]

Kausikan's contention of "order and stability" as Asian social character and preference applies not to cultural values or principles but to tactics of oppression used by ancient Asian despots and modern authoritarian rulers to safeguard their political power. Until recently, few peoples of many Asian countries have been able to express a choice about the type of government that should rule over them. The Singaporean civic and social culture that was labeled by Melanie Chew as *kaisu* is a cultural system commonly found among many Asian countries where acquiescence and strict conformity to the draconian orders and laws of authoritarian rulers pervade the souls of the people due to fear and helplessness.[19] To claim that this cultural experience demonstrates that Asians do not desire or value fundamental political and civil rights is cantankerous and illogical. At best, it is a rhetorical statement to justify authoritarian leaders' "natural right" to set their own human rights standards and govern without the consent of the people.

Crises of succession that so often follow the death of longtime dictators underscore the inherent instability of an authoritarian state in orderly transfer of power. Intense, anxious death watches of living dictators, such as Ne Win of Burma, Suharto of Indonesia, Castro of Cuba, and Hussein of Iran, with various speculation about the power struggles and political future of an authoritarian state upon the demise of these individual dictators, come from a lack of legal framework and alternative centers of power. The authority to govern in an authoritarian state is not born out of the voluntary social contract between the ruler and the ruled or the general will (Rousseau's *volonté general*) of the people. It traces to the individual will of a dictatorial ruler with access to, and use of, what John Kenneth Galbraith termed "condign and compensatory power" by punishing the foes and rewarding the loyal.[20]

ASIAN VALUES ON DEMOCRACY AND HUMAN RIGHTS: A BURMESE PERSPECTIVE

In the traditional philosophy and value systems of Burma and India, one can find emphasis on the wish and welfare of the people as the most important determinant of a good government. Traditional Burmese Buddhist moral codes of conduct mandate a king or a ruler to be just, benevolent, kind, patient, loving, charitable, peaceful, and caring for the welfare of his subjects or people. Buddhist texts of ancient India and Burma, *Razawwahda Sutra* and *Setkyawutti Sutra*, view that "kingship is essentially a contractual agreement between the People and the Ruler in which welfare of the country and its people is the sacred trust"[21] and prescribe 10 moral codes of conduct, one of which mandates a king not to oppose the wish of the people.[22]

The Burmese traditional political philosophy mandates that a good ruler or king, *razah* or *yahzah*, must give alms, *dahna*, speak with love and affection, *piya wahsah*, work and care for the welfare of the people, *a-hta sariyah*, and consider and treat the people as equals, *thamah na-tah*. The mandate for a good

Buddhist king not to oppose the wish of the people was told in one of the Great Stories of the 550 Buddhist Jatakas. The famous Bodhisattava (Buddha-to-be) King Waithandayah of Tilingana Kingdom was so pious and generous that he even gave away his own children as alms to the Brahman priests, *ponnars*, as a deed of merit. When he gave the sacred white elephant to the Brahman priests against the wish of his subjects, it resulted in drought and impoverishment of the people. Popular protest and wish demanded by the people led the king's father to dethrone Waithandayah and banish him from the kingdom to the forest of Wingabah mountain.[23]

It should be noted, however, that the story of King Waithandayah is only a legend. The chronicle of Burmese kings is replete with violations of the rights and wish of the people by malevolent kings to explain why Burmese have always considered a king or government as one of the five major enemies of life—water (*yay*), fire (*mee*), king (*min*), thief (*khothu*), and those who hate (*machit manitthet-thu*). The book of instructions, *Lawka Niti, A Guide to Good Living*, written by Satu Ringabala A-martkyee (Caturingabala), an ancient Burmese scholar and royal minister of the 14th Century Burmese kingdom of Pinya in Upper Burma, advised: "In this world one should shun fire, water, woman, fool, snake, and the royal family. They may harm and kill him instantly."[24]

With respect to the placement of family and social values by Asians over and above individual values and rights, the basic reason is not the fundamental difference between the Asian and Western cultural values or cultures but the differences in the stage of economic development and the consequence of industrialization. Using the extended family structure and system of preindustrial traditional societies of either China or India to generalize the family value orientation and cultural relativism of Asians is a misconception. The breakdown of family units and the erosion of family and community values are a phenomenon common to all industrialized modern societies. In each and every society and culture, one can find both individual and family values that often conflict with each other in the course of a country's development. To contend that, unlike the Westerners, Asians value family and society over and above individual rights and welfare is an excuse used by Asian authoritarian leaders to justify the right and power of an individual dictator and his entourage in the guise of state to intrude into the daily life of individuals and families.

In the Buddhist philosophy of Burma, the individual occupies the center of life. The Buddhist doctrine of karma, *kan* in Burmese, is based on the fundamental belief that no one but oneself or individual and individual action alone determines his or her present and future station or existence in society, *bathu ma-pyu meemee-mhu* in Burmese. According to the interpretation of learned Burmese Buddhist monks, "*karma*," *kri* in Pali, meaning action or work, conveys three basic things: performance of action, effect of the past action, and the present as the effect of the past action of an individual and individual alone.[25] The famed reverend U Thittila of Burma asserted: "Karma, though it activates the chain of cause and effect, is not determinism, nor is an excuse for fatalism.

Only the present moment exists, and the responsibility for using the present moment for good or ill lies with each individual."[26] Indeed, the fundamental opportunity and right of an individual in Buddhism are exemplified in the belief that anyone can become even a Buddha if he or she tries hard. This point was stressed by Daw Suu Kyi in a press conference given in July 1989 a few days before her house arrest when she said: "When I said that any human being can become an enlightened being, I mean any one can become Buddha. This is what every Buddhist knows. And we have a saying in Burmese, if you try hard enough, you can become a Buddha."

Daw Suu Kyi aptly evaluated the rejection of the quest of democracy by Burmese and the relativity theory of democracy and human rights advanced by Asian and Burmese authoritarian rulers:

Opponents of the movement for democracy in Burma have sought to undermine it by on the one hand casting aspersions on the competence of the people to judge what was best for the nation, and on the other condemning the basic tenets of democracy as un-Burmese. There is nothing new in the Third World governments seeking to justify and perpetuate authoritarianism by denouncing liberal democratic principles as alien.[27]

Developmental authoritarianism is a contradictory policy of giving limited economic freedom and denying other freedoms to the people for the benefit of the state. As Yaslt Ghai correctly assessed:

It is economic development, not economic rights, that they [Asian governments] emphasize. They are, however, content to seek economic rights of states, the so-called developing states (as in their advocacy of the right to develop). It is, of course, easy to understand why governments want economic development; it increases state resources, enables government to establish larger armies, enhances the status of their leaders, and secures the support of the populace."[28]

With respect to the negative impact of authoritarian rule on development, Jagdish Bhagwati argued: "Authoritarian governments are prone to extravagance and waste, inhibiting development, because there is no restraining hand among the citizenry to hold them back. The leaders of such governments often manage to delude themselves that the monuments they build for themselves are really gifts to posterity, equating personal indulgence with social glory."[29] For the likelihood of democracy to promote development, Mancur Olson argued that dictatorial regimes or "dictators, being self-regarding, are more likely to go overboard in the area of 'takings' from the subjects. The latter feeling less secure in their property, will have less incentives to produce, save, and invest. Indeed, the structure of democracy, by contrast, places restraints on 'takings.'"[30]

The so-called East Asian model or approach to development is not really new in the world history of the economic thought and practice. It is state capitalism or mercantilism of the pre-laissez-faire era cloaked under the garb of "a market-oriented economic system" and "an open-door market economy" designed to benefit the central power holders or "the strong state." The yardstick to measure a good government is not economic development per se but human or social development of the people, by the people, and for the people and their rights to life, liberty, and pursuit of happiness unfettered by fear and threat of an ominous state.

NOTES

1. Aung San Suu Kyi, "Empowerment for a Culture of Peace and Development," p. 5.

2. Jagdish Bhagwati, "The New Thinking on Development," *Journal of Democracy* (October 1995): 51.

3. Lee Kwan Yew, "Democracy and Human Rights," *Australia and World Affairs,* no. 16 (Autumn 1993): 10.

4. Ibid.

5. Ohn Gyaw, *Statement by His Excellency U Ohn Gyaw, Minister of Foreign Affairs and Chairman of the Delegation of the Union of Myanmar* (New York: Permanent Mission of the Union of Myanmar to the UN, September 17, 1996), pp. 4–5.

6. Amartya Sen, "Freedoms and Needs," *The New Republic* (January 10 & 17, 1994): 23.

7. "Economic Freedom: Of Liberty, and Prosperity," *The Economist* (January 13, 1996): 19–20.

8. Mahathir bin Mohamad, "Mahathir Hits Spendthrift West" excerpt from the speech delivered at the Europe/Asia Economic Forum, Tokyo, *Japan Times,* October 26, 1992, p. 17.

9. Kim Dae Jung, "Is Culture Destiny? The Myth of Asia's Anti-Democratic Values," *Foreign Affairs* 73, no. 6 (November/December, 1994): 191.

10. See Linda Lim, Pang Eng Fong, and Ronald Findlay, "Singapore," in Ronald Findlay and Stanislaw Wellisz, eds., *The Political Economy of Poverty, Equity, and Growth: Five Small Open Economies* (New York: Oxford University Press, 1993), Chap. 3.

11. See Alberto Alesina and Roberto Peroti, "The Political Economy of Growth: A Critical Survey of the Recent Literature," *The World Bank Economic* 8, no. 3 (September 1994): 355.

12. See Samuel P. Huntington, "The Clash of Civilizations?," *Foreign Affairs* 72, no. 3 (Summer, 1993): 25–27.

13. David I. Hitchcock, *Asian Values and the U.S.: How Much Conflict?,* Monograph (Washington, DC: Center for Strategic and International Studies, 1995), p. 6.

14. Masakazu Yammazaki, "Asia, a Civilization in the Making," *Foreign Affairs* 75, no. 4 (July/August 1996): 108.

15. Datuk Seri Anwar Ibrahim, "Asian Democracy," excerpt from the speech delivered at the Philippine's' Centennial Conference of 1896 Revolution, Manila, July 26, 1996, cited in Harn Yawnghwe, *Burma Alert,* vol.7, no. 9 (September, 1996): 6.

16. Bilahari Kausikan, "Asia's Different Standards," *Foreign Policy,* no. 92 (Fall 1993): 31.

17. *The Encyclopaedia Britannica,* London, 1980, p. 898.

18. Jung, "Is Culture Destiny?," 191.

19. Melanie Chew, "Human Rights in Singapore: Perceptions and Problems," *Asian Survey* 34, no. 11 (November 1994): 947.

20. See John Kenneth Galbraith, *The Anatomy of Power* (Boston: Houghton Mifflin, 1983), Chap. 2.

21. E. Sarkisyanz, *Buddhist Backgrounds of the Burmese Revolution* (The Hague: Martinus Nijhoff, 1965), p. 15.

22. *Mahnnun Yahzawintaw Gyi* (The Great Glass Palace History of Kings in Burmese) (Mandalay: Daw Hpwar Khin and U Hla Aung, 1957), p. 68.

23. See for details Dagon U Tun Myint, *Ten Great Stories* (in Burmese) (Rangoon: Baho Press, 1989), pp. 280–330.

24. *Loka Niti (A Guide to Good Living)* (Yangon: Ministry of Trade, January 1995), p. 103.

25. Bhikkhu Ananda Metteya, *The Religion of Burma* (Madras: Theosophical Publishing House, 1929), pp. 409–431.

26. U Thittila, "The Meaning of Buddhism," *The Atlantic Monthly* (Feb. 1958): 143.

27. Aung San Suu Kyi, "In Quest of Democracy," in Michael Aris, ed., *Freedom from Fear and Other Writings* (New York: Penguin Group, 1991), p. 167.

28. Yaslt Ghai, *Human Rights and Governance: The Asia Debate*, Asia Foundation's Center for Asian Pacific Affairs, Occasional Paper No. 4, November 1994, p. 12.

29. Bhagwati, "The New Thinking on Development," p. 57.

30. Ibid.

2

Stability and Discipline in Burma under Military Rule

From 1948 to 1962, the Union of Burma was a fledging democracy governed by a democratically elected civilian government of the late U Nu. There was freedom or democracy in the country, and the economy performed fairly well, although it experienced "political instability and lack of discipline" due to ethnic minority insurgency and the power struggle among civilian political leaders and political parties. In March 1962, General Ne Win and his commanders deposed U Nu and seized power and formed a military junta called the Revolutionary Council (RC). The RC imposed an iron rule over Burma and established "stability and discipline" by force, destroying all freedoms and democratic institutions. All civilian politicians and government leaders, including Premier U Nu, U Kyaw Nyein, and U Ba Swe, were arrested.

The Revolutionary Council government of General Ne Win declared all political parties and organizations illegal and abolished them under the Law to Protect National Unity and established a single party, the Burma Socialist Programme Party (BSPP), and military rule over Burma. On July 7, 1962, the military regime of Ne Win subdued political dissent by arresting and killing hundreds of Rangoon University student demonstrators and dynamiting the Rangoon University Students' Union Building, a citadel of political protests and nationalist movements against the British colonial rule. Freedom of expression was abolished by passing the 1962 Printers' and Publishers' Registration Law, nationalizing the private press, and jailing press owners and reporters. Since 1962, government has monopolized and controlled all news media and telecommunications. For more than three decades, the dominant daily newspaper in Burma has been the state-owned and operated *The Working People's Daily,* which was renamed *The New Light of Myanmar* in 1994.

In 1974, the Union of Burma was renamed the Socialist Republic of the Union of Burma. In the name of upholding the unity or stability of the state, hundreds of draconian laws were established to impose harsh discipline upon the people. Among these laws was the sedition law of British colonial legacy, the British Penal Code Section 124 A, which was renamed and passed in 1958 as the Union of Burma Penal Code, which specified various "Offenses against Public Tranquillity" in various sections of Chapter 8. In 1962, the provisions of this penal code were incorporated and passed as the Law for Law and Order and, in 1975, as the Law to Safeguard the State from the Danger of Destructive Elements. This generic law prohibits any act of sedition against the state, "offenses against the public tranquillity," and "assembly of five or more persons."

Another broadly worded sedition law was the 1950 Emergency Provisions Act, which contains provisions for the death penalty or life imprisonment or seven years' imprisonment for a broad range of activities including treason, sabotage, sedition and spreading of false news. Section 5 of this Act, known popularly in Burmese as *Poatma Ngar* (No. 5), was most frequently used to arrest any person suspected of opposing the government.[1] Since 1988, these two generic laws have been used indiscriminately to arrest, charge, and sentence any political activist with an arsenal of administrative security units made up of the ominous Military Intelligence (MI), the Special Bureau of Investigation (SBI), the five-man Security and Administrative Committee (SAC), later renamed the (seven-man) People's Council (PC), the People's Police Force, and the antistrike paramilitary unit *Lon Htein*.

THE STATE AND OTHER LAW AND ORDER RESTORATION COUNCILS (SLORC) AND (LORCS)

Following the military coup on September 18, 1988, with General Saw Maung as chairman, a 19-member military junta, the State Law and Order Restoration Council (SLORC), was created to govern Burma. The former administrative organization of the People's Council (PC) of socialist Burma was dismantled and replaced by the Law and Order Restoration Council (LORC). Hundreds of thousands of LORCs were formed on the state, district, township, and village level to maintain stability and enforce discipline on the people. The chairmen of all LORCs except the Village Law and Order Restoration Councils (VLORCs) are serving military commanders and officers. The rest of the members of the LORCs are civilians, most of whom are ex-military men and loyal supporters of SLORC, and government employees directly appointed by the General Administration Department (GAD) of the Ministry of Home and Religious Affairs.

As in the case of People's Councils of socialist Burma, the appointed civilian members of LORCs are ex-military men and those who are directly connected with the ruling military elite. The LORCs, together with the Burmese army, carry out the duties of general administration, implementation of development projects, inspection of publications, and enforcement of the national registration law. It should be noted that LORCs are the auxiliary administrative arms of the military government. With respect to the chain of authority, power, and control, the Burmese army and its commanders of seven states, seven divisions, and 314 district townships of Burma are the supreme administrative authorities and executioners of the orders and laws of the SLORC.[2] It has been reported that the LORCs have forced the people of villages and towns to provide donations and uncompensated labor for government development projects, including the provision of a certain quotas of supplies, soldier recruits, and porters for military offensives.

The LORCs of Myanmar in collaboration with the People's Police Force (PPF), the Special Bureau of Investigation (SBI), the Military Intelligence (MI), and the army enforce tight security across the country by monitoring and restricting the activities and movements of all Burmese citizens who are required to carry national registration certificates (NRCs) or identification cards (IDs) with personal photographs as passports to travel inside Burma. During the immediate years following the 1988 political uprising, the village and town LORC officials, accompanied by police or soldiers, closely monitored the movement of citizens and dissidents by forcefully entering and searching various households in various villages or sections of towns. For security purposes, the local LORC officials took census of households once or twice a week. In the 1990s, surprise security checks of travelers and households are made by the LORC officials and police in times of political unrest. Up to the present, the head of the household of towns and villages must report any visitor and give the identity of the visitor and duration of the visit. Failure to do so is subject to fine, interrogation, and detention at the LORC office or police station. As the Human Rights Watch/Asia reported:

Every person in Burma must carry at all times his or her identity card (ID card). The ID card must be produced in order to obtain a wide range of services and rights: to vote, to purchase tickets to travel internally, to stay in hostels or with friends and family outside their ward of residence, to receive health and educational services and so on. ID cards are also routinely demanded for checking by police and army personnel. Foreigners residing in Burma for more than three months have Foreign Registration Certificates which they must also carry at all times. The ID cards were changed in 1990/1991 to a new format, which includes not only the name, address and photo of the holder, but also his or her ethnic origin and religion. From this, anyone checking the card can know what class of citizen the holder is.[3]

DRACONIAN LAWS AND ORDERS

Within a year after the 1990 multiparty elections, the SLORC passed and enforced hundreds of draconian orders and martial laws, forcefully subduing NLD leaders, hundreds of elected NLD candidates, thousands of dissident students, Buddhist monks, and other dissidents by arresting them and passing out long-term jail sentences without due process. Some 11 sedition laws, some of which are the old sedition laws redressed and decreed as "orders" attached with numbers and years such as Order No. 1/88, Order No. 2/88, Order No. 1/89 and so on were deployed to suppress dissents and subdue political opposition to the military rule. The most generic and frequently used law to arrest and sentence dissidents up to the present is the 1950 Emergency Provisions Act. In general, the act empowered the government to convict any Burmese citizen for political activities and confer a death sentence or life imprisonment or imprisonment of up to seven years for either infringing "upon the integrity, health, conduct, and respect of State, military organizations, and government employees or spreading false news about the government."

Section 5 of the 1950 Emergency Provisions Act, known as *Poatma Ngar* in Burmese, has been the most indiscriminate law used to subdue and imprison dissidents. The three main subsections of Section 5 used to indict and jail dissidents are 5(A), 5(E), and 5(J), all of which carry a jail sentence of up to seven years or fine or both. Section 5(A) prohibits a person from influencing members of the armed forces or government servants to lose trust in the government, to mutiny or to commit treason or from committing an act that will affect the morale, loyalty, discipline, health, and training of members of the armed forces. Since 1988, Section 5(E) has been the most indiscriminate law to charge and jail a dissident for writing and distributing "incorrect news" and literature. Section 5(J) prohibits a person from committing an act with the aim to undermine the morality and alter the behavior of the people or a group of people in order to threaten the national security and the restoration of law and order. The most common laws with Burmese numbers and alphabets used to charge, arrest, and sentence political dissidents include; Poatma Ngar Nya or Section 5(J), Poatma or Section 17-1 and 17-2 for associating with, and being a member of, an unlawful organization, Poatma 19-Sa-Ngar or Section 19-F-5 for bearing arms, Potma 10-Kha or Section 10-B for engaging in any political activity, giving the authorities the right to detain, and Poatma or Section 122-1 for rebellion against the state. The penalty imposed under these laws ranges from 7 to 20 years in jail with fines or hard labor.

LAWS AGAINST FREEDOM OF ASSOCIATION AND EXPRESSION

In direct violation of Article 20 of the UN Universal Declaration of Human Rights which mandates freedom of assembly, the SLORC used the British Penal Code Section 124A of the 1908 or the 1957 Unlawful Association Act, renamed and decreed as Order No. 2/88 in 1988, to prohibit the assembly of more than five persons, subject to imprisonment of up to five years. Of all these laws, the 1975 State Protection Law renamed as the Law to Safeguard the State from the Danger of Destructive Elements in 1988, was used indiscriminately to detain or put under house arrest anyone for "a period not exceeding one year at a time up to a total of five years" without trial (the law by which Daw Suu Kyi was put under house arrest on July 20, 1989, and later extended year by year for five years).

Since 1962 to the present, the military governments of Burma have not allowed laborers to form any organization or trade union to protect their rights, and that legacy has been kept by the present military regime. The Report of the Committee on the Application of Standards of the Conventions of the International Labor Organization (ILO) reported:

The speaker stressed that the violations of human rights and of international labour standards in Myanmar were in direct proportion to the absence of trade unions there. Myanmar, which had no democratic regime, had resorted to forced labour as if it were a state policy. People built roads, railroads and bridges under the threat of bayonets, which was a sad repetition of history when the pyramids were constructed.[4]

As for suppressing freedom of expression and press, the SLORC in direct violation of Article 19 of the UN Universal Declaration of Human Rights enforced the 1962 Printers' and Publishers' Registration Law, by renaming and amending it as Order No. 8/88 in 1988, which banned any activity, literature, or speeches aimed "at dividing the Defense Forces." On June 18, 1989, the SLORC issued Martial Law 16/89, which increased the maximum sentences under the 1962 Printers' and Publishers' Registration Law to imprisonment of up to seven years and/or 30,000kyats (US$5,000 at official exchange rate) fines.[5] On June 27, 1989, Order No. 3/89 was issued to censor and regulate all publications of legal organizations, including handbills and posters, by mandating them to be submitted to the Ministry of Home and Religious Affairs for exemption from the 1962 Printers' and Publishers' Registration Law. The order further "specifies that, after obtaining the exemption, the organization can print and publish any material, provided the material does not contain anything which opposes SLORC, the regional law and order restoration councils at different levels, or the government; insults, slanders, or attempts to divide the Defense Forces; instigates action that affect law, order, peace and tranquillity; or contradicts the Orders that have been issued wherever necessary."[6]

The Press Security Board censors and controls every publication, domestic or foreign. Even after exemption from the Printers' and Publishers' Law and passing the censor of the Press Security Board, all publications must be resubmitted for final clearance by the board before distribution. It is not unusual to find pages of a book or journal ripped off or undesirable passages censored by black ink. In addition to strict censorship of domestic publications, the import and sale of foreign newspapers, journals, and books are strictly controlled, and any publication containing undesirable and politically sensitive articles is removed from sale by government authorities. In conjunction with this law, the military regime used other sedition laws to arrest writers, poets, musicians, and NLD members for expressing dissent against the state or the army as well as for using "decadent" Western cultural styles and values in their writings, songs, and performances.

Two additional laws repressing freedom of expression and opinion are the 1993 Myanmar Wireless Telegraphy Act (amended in October 1995) and the 1995 Video Law. Under the first law "whosoever possesses any wireless telegraphy apparatus without a license shall be punishable with imprisonment for a term which may extend to three years or a fine which may extend to 30,000 kyats, or both." James Leander Nichols, a close friend of Daw Suu Kyi and supporter of the NLD, was arrested in May 1996 and died in June while serving the prison term of three years under this law. Under the second law, "all videos must be submitted to the Video Censorship Board for security," and "those involved in the making, copying and distribution of videos have been threatened with prison terms of up to three years." In May 1996 U Win Htein, personal aide of Daw Suu Kyi, and two NLD members were arrested for videotaping the dry season paddy yield under this law and were sentenced to a seven-year prison term for spreading misinformation under the 1950 Emergency Provision Act.[7]

THE DENIAL OF FAIR PUBLIC TRIAL

The establishment of military tribunals to try political cases is a legacy of Ne Win's rule for 26 years from 1962 to 1988, during which arbitrary trials and sentencing of labor and student activists by military courts of the Burma Socialist Programme Party (BSPP) were regular rituals. This legacy was immediately revived soon after the 1988 political uprising. In July 1989 the SLORC issued martial laws Order No. 1/89 and Order No. 2/89, by which military tribunals were established. The military commanders of the tribunals were empowered to detain, arrest, and conduct "summary trials" of the civilians and sentence any dissident to death or life imprisonment or not less than three years' imprisonment with hard labor across the country. After the military tribunals were created, the subjugation of opposition that ensued resulted in the roundup of more than 6,000 NLD supporters, students, and activists, including the leaders of the opposition parties.[8]

The arbitrary nature of the proceedings of the military tribunals was assessed by the Lawyers Committee for Human Rights:

Trial proceedings before Burmese military tribunals are little more than the recitation of charges and the announcement of a guilty verdict. The basic notions of a fair trial has no meaning here. There is no "competent, independent and impartial tribunal established by law," as set out in the Covenant on Civil and Political Rights. Nor is the defendant permitted to defend himself in person or through legal assistance of his own choosing.[9]

Even after the dissolution of the military tribunals in 1991, the trials and persecution of prisoners charged under various draconian laws remain unfair and arbitrary due to the fact that the SLORC controls and represents the legislature, executive, and judiciary of Burma simultaneously. The US State Department describes the denial of fair public trial to the people of Burma as follows:

The judiciary is not independent of the executive. The SLORC names justices to the Supreme Court who, in turn, appoint lower court judges with the approval of the SLORC. Pervasive corruption further serves to undermine the impartiality of the justice system. Throughout the year, the Government continued to rule by decree and was not bound by any constitutional provisions guaranteeing fair public trial or any other rights.[10]

TORTURE AND ILL-TREATMENT

Since 1988, thousands of dissidents and opposition activists have been regularly arrested, detained, and tortured at hundreds of detention centers, including prisons, police stations, and military or Directorate of Defense Services Intelligence (DDSI) interrogation centers, 14 or more of which are located in Rangoon alone, across the country. Gruesome accounts of torture and ill-treatment at the interrogation centers and inside the prisons were also given by students whom this author interviewed.[11] Amnesty International reported the following types of torture:

Torture has a distinct vocabulary in Myanmar. Ordinary beatings may be followed by torture techniques such as the "helicopter"— being spun around while hanging from the ceiling, sometimes attached to a fan; "walking on the seashore"—being forced to crawl on broken glass or sharp gravel; "riding the motor-cycle"—being forced to crouch over an imaginary motorbike for long periods; the "iron road"—having an iron bar or a bamboo cane rolled up and down the shins often until the skin comes off; the "wet submarine"—near suffocation through drowning.[12]

Similarly, Asia Watch reported:

The Burmese government has imprisoned more than 10,000 for political offenses since the August 1988 [should be since March 1988] uprising. Estimates of the total number of political prisoners run as high as 30,000. Many have been tried by military tribunals without access to defense counsel. Others have been detained without charge by the Directorate of Defense Services Intelligence (DDSI). Torture, including electric shocks [often to the genitals], beatings, sleep deprivation, and cigarette burns, is widespread and has continued since the May [1990] elections.[13]

TORTURE AND ILL-TREATMENT AT INSEIN JAIL AND LABOR CAMPS

Since military rule was established over Burma in 1962, Insein Jail in the suburb of Rangoon has become what Alan Clements called the "darkest hell-hole in Burma." Since 1988 the average number of prisoners in this darkest hellhole of Burma has swollen to between 9,000 and 10,000, about 20 percent of whom are political prisoners. The following nightmare of a political prisoner aptly describes what goes on inside that infamous center of torture and ill-treatment:

I'm lying naked and cold, on a concrete floor. My back is a landscape of bruises. When I try to draw a deep breath, a piercing agony shoots through my chest, and I realize that my ribs are broken. Suddenly reality grips me by the throat. This is Insein Prison—the darkest hellhole in Burma. From a nearby room, I hear dull groans—followed by the snap of thick leather cracking across flesh. A scream pierces the darkness, and the whip cracks again and again.[14]

In confirmation of this prisoner's nightmare, Win Naing Oo, a dissident student of All Burma Students' Democratic Front (ABSDF) who was arrested in May 1990 and imprisoned for three years, gave the following description of six typical beatings given to political prisoners at Insein Jail: (1) the prisoner has to stand and embrace a post and is beaten while both hands are held firmly by another person, (2) the prisoner is beaten while lying on the ground, (3) the prisoner, both legs chained, is made to stand in standard no. 4 position (standing on tiptoes with knees bent at 45 degrees, a straight back, and hands clasped behind the head with the face raised up) and is beaten, (4) the prisoner is beaten while being forced to crawl along the ground, (5) the prisoner, shackled and with a long iron bar placed so that the legs are splayed, is forced to crawl along the floor and is beaten, and (6) the prisoner is forced to do squat-jumps (like in the game of leapfrog) and is beaten while doing so. The beatings are done by using a leather-coated pipe, a wooden stick, a stick made from three interlaced pieces of cane, a solid bamboo stick, or a hard plastic water pipe.[15]

He also told of the following torture and ill-treatment of a prisoner while in solitary confinement in Insein Jail, which can last at least one month and up to three months:

The worst type of solitary confinement is when a prisoner has to stand with both arms tied above the head. The prisoner has to defecate and urinate while standing. The authorities feed them no rice but give them only glue made from rice. Every day, the prisoner is taken out of the cell [the "dog cell," where well-trained military dogs used to be kept], forced to stand in no. 4 position and beaten.[16]

In an interview by the author, another dissident student, Maung Aung, who was arrested and sentenced to a seven year jail term in 1988 and released in 1994 after serving five years and seven months, gave the following account of the brutal punishment (a supplementary account of beating no. 5 given earlier) received by him or any defiant prisoner inside Insein Jail:

At any time a prisoner commits an offense, the jail officer would shout a canonical command, "Ponsan" (Example), forcing the prisoner to assume the position of squatting down immediately with straight back and head down and arms on the knees and hands stretched straight down to the ground. This, of course, is similar to the command of "Sit" given to a dog by his master. The prison guard then puts a hood over the prisoner's head and "shackles him with an iron rod across the ankles," *chai-gyin* and *daut khart*, and takes him to the military dog cell for solitary confinement. He would be beaten before putting him into the cell. The prisoner is taken out of the cell and beaten twice daily, once in the morning and once in the evening. The iron rod the prisoner has to wear across the shackled ankles varies in length depending upon the seriousness of the offense; 9 inches, 18 inches and 24 inches. The 24-inch rod is used primarily for punishing the criminals, such as drug traffickers, murderers, and robbers, while the other two rods are used in the case of political prisoners. For the punishment of major offenses, 9-inch rod and 24-inch rods are used, while an 18-inch rod is used for minor offenses. Depending on the types of offense, the duration of wearing the rod day and night varies from a minimum of two weeks for minor offense to a maximum of six months for major offense. After two months of wearing the rod, the prisoner upon release has to be taken to the prison hospital for treatment of the injuries. The pains and injuries to the ankles and legs suffered from wearing the rod, the 9-inch and 24-inch being the worst ones, for more than two months are so severe that a prisoner would lose the proper use of his legs and suffered from excruciating pains in walking. In wearing the rod for three months and beyond, the prisoner would be crippled for life.

Although the exact number of fatalities resulting from these gruesome tortures, beatings, and ill-treatment of detainees and prisoners is not available due to the government's absolute control of information and its restriction on access to prisoners, sporadic reports on the death of certain prisoners have surfaced in foreign news media and reports of various human rights groups since 1988. Amnesty International reported 10 deaths in custody.[17] According to Burma Information Group (BIG), some 200 opposition activists, including students and Buddhist monks, who were arrested and detained in the infamous Insein Jail of Rangoon on March 18, 1988, were beaten, tortured, and killed by the security squad, *lon htein*, inside the prison.[18] It also reported the names and detailed backgrounds of 24 political prisoners who died inside various jails: one leading Buddhist monk, U Zaw Tika; 15 older opposition leaders; and eight student activists who were arrested and imprisoned in 1988 and later years.

Perhaps one of the most compelling stories, not of pure physical torture as such but of excruciating mental torture inflicted upon a political prisoner at the military interrogation centers and Insein Jail, is the story of a young Burmese woman, Ma Yin Yin May, or Ma Nita for short, whom this author interviewed in 1994. She worked for the British Embassy in Rangoon as the information officer from 1987 to 1990. One night in September 1989 her home was raided and searched for the first time by some 15 Military Intelligence (MI) officers, including a policeman and a member of the local LORC. Her husband and she were blindfolded and taken away in separate cars. She was taken to Military Interrogation Center No. 6, located near the Rangoon Mingaladon Airport, where she was detained in a small room of four feet by six feet for 14 days, interrogated day and night, and deprived of regular meals and sleep.

During the last week of October 1990 she was arrested and taken away to the infamous military interrogation center of Yai Kyi Aying for one day and released and rearrested again the same day by the Special Branch. There she was questioned by military intelligence officers for three days and forced to confess and write down her communication with the opposition leaders. The next day she was taken away to the so-called civilian court at Mayarn Goan and was indicted under the Emergency Provisions Act, specifically under the Official Secret Act for spreading misinformation about the government. After the indictment, she was released and ultimately arrested on November 16, 1990, and taken away to Insein Jail. In December 1990 she was tried by the presiding military tribunal and sentenced to serve a prison term of three years with hard labor in Insein Jail. At the time of her arrest, she was two months' pregnant. The following is the account of the ordeal she went through in her own words:

On the night of Friday, November 16, 1990, a mob of twenty security officers with video cameras came in their cars and surrounded my house. They raided my home searching for documents and taking pictures. I was eventually taken to Insein Jail where I was taken to the women ward that housed about 500 inmates, criminals, and political prisoners, and I was put into a small cell of 6 feet by 9 feet which had a straw mat on the floor to sleep, a dirty pot for drinking water, and a commode. It was a very filthy room. The next day, I was put into the Lesson or Example Room, *Ponsan Kharn*, of 40 feet by 60 feet cramped into by 200 women, including common criminals and prostitutes for two days. The room was used by the prison authorities to give lesson or punish and demoralize a political dissident to the government. I could not bear the stink of body odor of the women with lice in their hair and soiled garments. I could not sleep sitting up in a space of no more than two feet wide cramped by several bodies all around me. This was the most tormenting and humiliating condition that I had ever faced in my life. After two days of excruciating sufferings and sleepless nights, I was taken upstairs where there were young dissident students and NLD members who were previously arrested and sentenced. These women political prisoners were called by the prison guards *Ngar Nya, mainma* or women who were indicted and sentenced under Law No. 5 (*Poatma Ngar* in Burmese). Food and water were scarce and very unsanitary. For bathing, women prisoners stood around the water tub and each of them was allowed to use two to three cups of water. Upon the shouting of the prison guard "dip, bath," we dipped our cups and bathed with not enough time and water to wash the body with soap. I also had to clean the floor and knit. The guards used foul languages whenever they slapped, kicked and beat the criminal inmates to intimidate and verbally abuse the political prisoners like me. I had never heard such filthy name-callings and the rape of ears with foul words in my life. The heat of the summer months of March, April and May was very intense inside and I could not sleep due to the trapped heat that emanated from the brick walls at night. With the baby inside my womb, my body heat was even higher and I needed to bathe to cool down the heat and humidity. But I could not do so and I could hardly breathe sometime due to the oppressive heat. My baby was due to be born in June. I was afraid of a possible mishap or death in labor unattended by a medical doctor. It was not easy to obtain permission to leave the prison to be taken to a hospital for medical care. I had seen many extremely sick prisoners die because of the delay in taking them to a hospital in time for treatment. So, I asked the visiting prison doctor to send me to the hospital one week before my final labor. But the request was ignored. On June 30, 1991, only after five hours had elapsed after I reported my contraction, I was taken from the prison in a truck guarded by a police woman to Insein Hospital for the delivery of the baby. My son was born on the same day. I spent two weeks at the hospital with my newborn. Holding my newborn in my arms, I thought to myself: "My son is an innocent human being and has not committed any crime or misdeed. Unfortunately for him, he was born into a world of repression with no fundamental human rights." According to regulation, the newborn baby must be taken back to the prison and then the mother must request for the baby's release to relatives. Luckily, my son was allowed to be released into the custody of my husband from the hospital. I was taken back to the prison and separated from my child for nine months. Finally in April, 1992, I was released from the prison to be reunited with him and able to hold him in my arms again.

Ma Nita was released from Insein Jail under the amnesty order of Senior General Than Shwe, who replaced Senior General Saw Maung as the new chairman of SLORC and head of the state of Myanmar in 1992, in an attempt to relieve international pressures on human rights violations and improve the image of the military regime. She eventually left Burma in 1993 and has lived and worked in London as a reporter in the Burmese Section of the British Broadcasting Corporation (BBC), United Kingdom. In 1997 she was awarded the Order of British Empire (OBE) by the British government.

The ultimate punishment—ill-treatment and torture often to death—occurs at various labor camps across Burma where gangs of prisoners in chains and shackles are forced to work under subhuman conditions. Political prisoners considered by the government as defiant and dangerous are sentenced to a prison term of seven or more years with hard labor to be performed at a labor camp. Typically, hard labor at a labor camp involves digging, pounding, and carrying crushed rocks that are used for government infrastructure development projects such as roads, railway stations, and airports to attract foreign tourists and investors. On March 18, 1996, two famous comedians and political satirists from Mandalay, Mustache Par Par Lay and Lu Saw, were sentenced to a prison term of seven years with hard labor at the labor camp of Kyein Karn Ka, located 25 miles from the capital of Kachin state, Myitkyina, in Upper Burma. Their crime was performing and poking fun at the military government at Daw Aung San Suu Kyi's residence in Rangoon, where Burma's independence day celebration was held on January 4, 1996. The following is an excerpt from the article "Drop-Dead Humor," which appeared in *The Nation/Focus* of Bangkok, August 4, 1996:

Prisoners are sent there when authorities want them to die from hard labor or ill-health. Two to three prisoners die every month from cholera, dysentery or other diseases, or in accidents when the hillside is dynamited to loosen rocks. Work begins at 6 a.m. Labor gangs must collect one truckload of stones every hour for the airport site. Prisoners have to pound and carry crushed rock every day. They can't take a rest. Their hands and feet are cut, bruised, and blistered from the work. Prisoners got weak and collapse when they're working, but they're not given medical treatment. All but two wear chains around their ankles. A routine camp practice is to make prisoners crawl over sharp stones. Anyone trying to protect himself by moving slowly is beaten by the head guard wielding a long bamboo rod two inches in diameter. Another common practice is to force prisoners to impersonate a motorbike or helicopter and respond to shouted directions such as "turn right" or "speed up." If the response is not quick enough, they are beaten. Par Par Lay and Lu Saw are forced to wear an iron rod [across the feet] which makes it extremely difficult for them to move around. Both comedians' heads have been shaved and Par Par Lay's famous mustache is gone. Both men are very thin and their health is deteriorating fast.[19]

THE SUBJUGATION AND PLIGHT OF OPPOSITION GROUPS

In the aftermath of the 1988 political uprising, more than 20,000 pro-democracy Burmese dissidents, including students, military officers, soldiers, and Buddhist monks, fled to the liberated areas along the Thai border controlled by the ethnic minority rebel groups of the Karen National Union (KNU) and the New Mon State Party (NMSP). Subsequently, they and the ethnic rebels formed the Democratic Alliance of Burma (DAB), a coalition of some 20 Burmese and ethnic minority opposition groups to the SLORC, with its headquarters at Manerplaw in the Kawthulay state of Karen. After the 1990 elections, NLD political headquarters in central Burma was virtually decimated, and a few NLD candidates who won seats in the election were forced to flee to the Karen state and formed the exiled government called the National Coalition Government of the Union of Burma (NCGUB) in association with the DAB. The NCGUB was headed by Dr. Sein Win, a cousin of Daw Suu Kyi, as the prime minister.

Between 1993 and 1994, two cabinet ministers of the NCGUB, the finance minister and the education minister, met mysterious deaths, one in Kunming, the capital of Yunan Province of China, and the other in Bangkok. In 1993, Sein Win, one of his cabinet ministers, and four other delegates of opposition groups toured the United States for support. They were forced out of their refuge from the headquarters of DAB at Manerplaw in the Karen state inside Burma by Thailand's refusal of their reentry visas. They have been stranded in Washington, DC, ever since, where the US branch of the headquarters of NCGUB, the prime minister's office, is now located. In 1995, Manerplaw was overrun by the Burmese army, and the headquarters of the NCGUB has been relocated to a new location in the Karen state near Mae Sot, Thailand.

Following the 1988 coup, Khin Nyunt reported on the radio that over 10,000 civil servants who were involved in the political uprising were removed from their jobs. Threats and directives of nonparticipation in politics were issued to all civil servants. All civil servants were forced to answer a two-page, 33-item questionnaire on their political views and attitudes toward dissident organizations, foreign media, and the army. In 1991, the SLORC and Burmese army also invaded the domain of the Buddhist clerical order in Mandalay and other cities, destroying several monasteries, arresting, disrobing, and jailing hundreds of dissident Buddhist monks. As for the elected NLD candidates who were not arrested, the ultimate act of intimidation by the SLORC was the issuance of 301 top-secret questions that were forced to be answered. The questions were designed historically to coerce the elected candidates to endorse the legitimacy of military rule over Burma since 1962 in protecting the unity and stability of Burma.

On December 15, 1991, the remaining NLD Central Executive Committee of central Burma, headed by Chairman Aung Shwe (ex-military commander) expelled Daw Aung San Suu Kyi from party membership, an abortive exercise made under duress and fear of the SLORC. From 1989 to 1994, the three leaders of the NLD, Daw Suu Kyi, U Tin Oo, and U Kyi Maung, were kept under arrest. In April 1995, U Tin Oo and U Kyi Maung were released. In June 1995, U Kyi Maung and five other dissidents were rearrested for one week and later released. Daw Suu Kyi was released from house arrest in July 1995. Since then SLORC has steadily increased its crackdown on Daw Suu Kyi party members and followers, hundreds of whom have been intimidated, detained, arrested, and sentenced to jail terms.

THE SUBJUGATION OF STUDENT OPPOSITION AND CONTROL OF TEACHERS

The main target of assault on the opposition to military rule has been the students who led the 1988 political uprising. More than 10,000 politically active students were forced to flee to the Thai border to join the DAB and set up camps and the headquarters of the All Burma Student's Democratic Front (ABSDF) at Down Gwin in the Karen state to continue their armed struggle against the SLORC. They set up some 20 camps in the liberated areas of the Kachin, Karen, Karenni, and Mon states in 1988. The majority of the student camps are located along the Thai border in the Karen and Mon states. Since then, the Burmese army in cooperation with Thai authorities along the border and inside Thailand has systematically chased, subdued, and repatriated thousands of beleaguered students.

The deportation of thousands of Burmese student refugees by the Thai immigration police began soon after the military coup staged by General Saw Maung in September 1988. In 1989, the SLORC government with the cooperation of Thai authorities launched a policy of ostensible amnesty for those students who returned voluntarily. It opened up 17 different reception camps along the Thai-Burmese border, the most famous being the Tak Center. The Thai government's trade-off for this cooperation was the securing of enormously profitable teak-logging and fishing concessions by Thai companies. The stories of many returnees' arrests and disappearances once they reached central Burma received the attention of the US State Department and other human rights groups. The initial estimate of the number of student refugees at some 30 camps in the Karen and Mon states along the Thai border after the September coup of 1988 was around 10,000. By 1991, the student population at these camps declined to between 3,000 and 4,000 due to death from disease, including malaria, starvation, voluntary return, capture, and deportation. In July 1993, the number of student rebels at some 28 camps was reported to have dwindled to 2,500.[20] In 1995, their headquarters at Down Gwin was overrun, at the same time Manerplaw, the headquarters of the Democratic Alliance of Burma (DAB) and the Karen National Union (KNU), was captured by the Burmese army. According to Naing Aung, the chairman of the ABSDF, the number of student rebels at the remaining 12 camps, 8 of which are located along the Thai border, had dwindled to less than 2,000 in 1997.

In central Burma during the three years following the 1988 political uprising, schools and colleges were shut down several times as the student protest against the SLORC continued. In the early 1990s, the military intelligence chief, Khin Nyunt, who had a two-year college education, assumed the chairmanship of the National Educational Committee and forced teachers to attend lectures and one-month refresher courses and training given by the military officers. The refresher or civil servant selection and training courses are the legacy of the past socialist state, which required all civil servants to undergo mixed paramilitary training and political indoctrination classes on the Burmese Way to Socialism at the Hpaung Gyi Village camps in Hlellgu district located between Rangoon and Pegu. This practice was revitalized in 1988 to coerce and indoctrinate all civil servants, including teachers, to accept the legitimacy of military rule and its benevolent development policies and programs of the SLORC.

These courses also gave instruction to teachers on how to monitor and discipline the students in the name of patriotism and safeguarding the unity and stability of the Union of Myanmar. The directives for policing student activities were issued to teachers, who themselves were closely watched by the military intelligence officers planted in classrooms and on campuses. Teachers, students, and parents were forced to sign papers under duress not to engage in any political activities or protests against the military regime. The penalty for parents in case of their children's misbehavior was arrest and loss of job or property.

The end of 1991 saw a brief revival of the failed democracy movement of 1988, with the eyes of the world focusing on Burma and pressuring the release of the 1991 Nobel peace laureate and transfer of power to the winners of the 1990 multiparty elections. On December 10, 1991, the day of the ceremony on which Daw Aung San Suu Kyi's Nobel Peace Prize was awarded in Oslo, college students of Rangoon University once again demonstrated on their campus, demanding democracy and release of Daw Suu Kyi from house arrest. It was the first major public protest by the students after more than three years of being silenced and subjugated by the military rulers. The demonstration continued on the next day, when soldiers moved in to subdue the students and seal the campus. They did not shoot them this time, although it was reported that hundreds were arrested. Colleges across Burma were shut down once again.

As the year 1992 began, the process of intimidation of students continued as Khin Nyunt warned them in his speech to the Rangoon University staff on January 7, 1992:

We know that a small group of youths and students and some public servants are still trying to undermine the work of SLORC. However, we repeatedly try to reform and educate them with *metta* [loving-kindness]. Despite this, some still have not learned their lesson [arrest and death]. There are those who do not have a clear view, those who are extreme in their personal attachment, those who look up to things foreign, and those who are greedy and immoral.[21]

In March 1993, students demonstrated against the national convention held by the SLORC to draw up the catch-22 constitution and celebrated the 31st anniversary of the July 7, 1962 destruction of the Rangoon University Students' Union, causing schools to be shut down briefly. The following speech given by Khin Nyunt on July 11, 1993, at the closing ceremony of Special Refresher Course No. 1 for junior and senior assistant teachers at the Institute of Public Service Training Hall in Hlegu township further highlights the unchanging mentality of the military rulers with respect to the demand for subservience of teachers to the ordinances of the state by invoking traditional culture, patriotism, and xenophobia:

The infiltration of alien culture among the young and thinking a great deal of material development of the people of that culture had eroded patriotism in them. It is now time for efforts to guide the young to know clearly of the designs of some neo-colonialist countries to enslave the country and to inculcate patriotism and to bear in mind never to yield to external influences and to prove the kind of spirit to uphold Myanma culture. Strive for the realization of educational policy objectives laid down by the State; not just to uphold our Three Main National Causes (the non-disintegration of the Union and national unity, the perpetuation of sovereignty, promotion and vitalization of national pride and the emergence of a prosperous, peaceful and modern Union of Myanmar) but also to organize the students to come to do so, with realization of the designs and attempts of the destructive elements to cause the disintegration of the State, to guide the students onto correct paths so that they will become good sons and daughters; and to play whatever role they are assigned by the State for the emergence of a lasting Constitution.[22]

The refresher or civil servant selection and training courses of the past socialist state were revitalized in 1988 to coerce and indoctrinate all civil servants to accept the legitimacy of military rule and its "benevolent" development policies and programs. These courses also gave instruction to teachers on how to monitor and discipline the students in the name of patriotism and safeguarding the unity and stability of the Union of Myanmar. The directives for policing student activities were issued to teachers, who themselves were closely watched by the military intelligence officers planted in classrooms and on the campuses.

Teachers, students, and parents were forced to sign papers under duress not to engage in any political activities or protests against the military regime. The penalty for parents in case of their children's misbehavior was arrest and loss of job or property. Table 2.1 indicates the continuing subjugation of university students by the government since 1991.

Table 2.1
Number of University Students Expelled and Imprisoned since 1991

Name of University	Number Expelled	Number Imprisoned
Medical Institute 1, Rangoon	4	30
Medical Institute 2, Rangoon		10
Institute of Medicine, Mandalay	2	15
Institute of Dental Medicine, Rangoon	5	10
Rangoon Institute of Technology	100-150	500
Government Technical Institute	30	300
Rangoon University (Main Campus)	200	500
Rangoon University (Hlaing Campus)	200-250	500
Rangoon University (Other Campuses)	200-250	500
Dagon University		50
Institute of Agriculture, Ye Zin	20	100
Mandalay University	30	200
Universities in Upper Burma (Myitkyina, Taunggyi, Lashio, Monywa, Magwe)	70	100
Moulmein University	20	100
Universities in Lower Burma (Pa-an, Tavoy, Pathein, Pegu)	30	150
Total	911–1,061	3,065

Source: All Burma Federation of Students' Unions (ABFSU), Information and Documentation Committee, *An Overview of the Current Education Situation in Burma,* privately published paper, December 1997: p. 12.

The political motivation of dispersing dissident students to prevent potential political unrest was also evident in the creation of a new Rangoon University in 1993 at the new satellite town, *Dagon Myothit* or New Rangoon, located far away from the center of Rangoon. In February 1995, some 50 dissident student mourners at the funeral of U Nu were arrested, and a few of them were sentenced to jail terms ranging from 7 to 20 years. The largest peaceful demonstration of major significance since 1988 took place in December 1996 on major college campuses in Rangoon, causing the government to shut down schools once more, and they have not been reopened. An underground dissident student organization called All Burma Federation of Students' Unions (ABFSU) reported the following strategy of the military regime to disperse and control university students:

While the condition of the students is reaching a hopeless dead-end, the military regime spends manpower and resources to control the entire student populace. They are pursuing a policy of separation and isolation of students according to their major subjects, so that they will not be able to contact each other. The SLORC is systematically taking such actions as building iron fences around Rangoon University campus, constructing big gates at Haling, Botataung, and Kyimyindaing campus to control the access, separating Rangoon University campus into arts and science branches, and dividing Institute of Economics into different estates.[23]

FORCED RELOCATION IN CENTRAL BURMA

Since 1988, the military junta has been violating Article 17 of the UN Universal Declaration of Human Rights, which mandates, "No one shall be arbitrarily deprived of his property." In launching the city beautification and development programs across Burma, the junta seized property and land and forcefully relocated hundreds of thousands of urban residents to new satellite towns. A number of satellite towns were created around major cities across the country, including the capital city of Rangoon and the famous ancient city of Mandalay in Upper Burma. Also, the villagers living at ancient tourist sites, such as Pagan and Amarapura in Upper Burma, were forcefully relocated for the purpose of renovating these sites for tourist attraction. Massive eviction similar to the style of Pol Pot or Khmer Rouge of Cambodia occurred in 1989, a year prior to the holding of the multiparty elections to disperse and disorient voters in major urban centers. The estimates of the number of forcefully relocated range from 1 million to 2 million in central Burma alone and 3 to 4 million in ethnic minority states, forcing them to take refuge across the borders into Bangladesh, India, Thailand, and China.

There are 10 satellite towns around Rangoon alone to which almost half a million people have been relocated. The government claimed that most of the evicted were squatters and fire victims who were not allowed to reacquire their old plots of land. However, the Burmese nationals reported that among the forcefully evicted were regular homeowners. The forcefully relocated homeowners also reported that the compensation paid for dismantling their homes was well below their market value. They were also asked to pay for the new plots of land in satellite towns. If they could not pay, they were moved farther away and forced to settle in shabbier satellite towns outside Rangoon division. The following are the satellite towns around Rangoon with the relocated population of close to half a million:

Satellite Towns around Rangoon

1. Aye Mya Thah-yah: Located 200 kilometers north of Rangoon, in Oak Hpo township, Bago/Pegu division. Population=9,433.

2. Aye Thu-kha: Located 160 kilometers north of Rangoon in Daik Oo township, Bago/Pegu division. Population=5,153.

3. Dagon Myothit (North and South): Located east of Rangoon, adjacent to, and east of, North and South Oakkalapas, North Dagon Myothit is rich, and South Dagon Myothit is poor. Combined population=116,846, plots=40,400 (40' x 60').

4. Hlaing Thah-yah: Established in September 1989. Located southwest of Rangoon across the bank of Hlaing River. Size=67.61 square kilometers Plots=80,182 (40' x 60') and 35 wards (*yart kwet*): Population in 1989=148,605; in 1994=160,000, in November 1995=159,381; in January 1995=163,303; and as of February 1995=164,040.

5. Htauk Kyant (extension): Located north of Padamyar Myothit. Population=6,019.

6. Mya Yadanah: Established in 1989. Located east of Shwepyi-thah: Population=3,824, plots=1,549 (30' x 50').

7. Padamyar Myothit: Established in 1989. Located east of Shwepyi-thah. Population=3,824; plots=1,352 (80' x 50').

8. Palell Myothit: Located east of Shwepyi-thah in Rangoon. Population=1,217.

9. Shwe Paukkan: Established in 1989 Population=6,071; plots=5,152 (40' x 60').

10. Shwepyi Thah: Established in July 1989. Located 30 kilometers northwest of Rangoon. Size=39.5 square km. Population=130,896; plots=7,429 (40' x 60').

Total population of 10 towns=447,323
Source: A non-governmental organization (NGO) allowed by the government to work in these satellite towns. The name of the group cannot be revealed.

Two types of relocation were made: forced and voluntary. Squatters and fire victims were forced to move to these satellite towns. Fire victims were not allowed to reacquire their old plots of land, and instead they were forced to move to new satellite towns. Both squatters and fire victims were asked to pay for the new plots of land, and if they could not pay, they were moved farther away and settled in shabbier satellite towns outside Rangoon division. Voluntary settlers are low-and medium-ranked government employees who were offered the chance to purchase plots of land and build homes through a program of a low-interest mortgage loans and purchase of construction materials at government-subsidized prices. Most of them settled in the best sections of, *Dagon Myothit,* mostly in North Dagon Myothit. On the other hand, high-ranking government officials such as deputy ministers, director generals, and managing directors secured plots of land and built luxurious homes with absentee ownership in the best quarters of *Shwe Pyithah, Shwe Paukkan, Ngwe Kyah Yan, Thuwana Myothit,* and *Palell.*

The following is an account given by a forcefully relocated person to the new satellite town of Shwe Pyi Tha:

I recently arrived in the Shwe Pyi Tha new town which is a new satellite village in the outskirts of Rangoon. Previously, the area was all paddy fields for rice production. The land was owned by farmers themselves. When the military took over state power, the junta confiscated the paddy fields without paying any compensations to the farmers. The poor people [from Rangoon] were forced to shift to Shwe Pyi Tha from their old houses because the military junta told them that their old area was needed to build roads, new buildings, offices and living quarters for the armed forces officers, or to build the new market etc. Even though the poor people's houses were destroyed by the junta, the people received no compensation, and still had to pay at least 3,000 kyats to 5,000 kyats to get a small piece of land in a new town.[24]

It should be noted that the Burmese people's lack of security with respect to the ownership of private property and land dates back to the days of Burmese kings whose ownership of water and land is proclaimed to be absolute. In Burmese, the king carries the title of *yai myay ashin*, which means "the lord over water and land." The consecutive governments of independent Burma, especially the military regime of Ne Win and the SLORC, destroyed that freedom by reviving and enforcing the legacy of Burmese kings by claiming, "The State is the ultimate owner of all natural resources, above and underground, above and under water, or in the atmosphere, as well as all land."[25]

Wanton confiscation of people's property and land without compensation and forced relocation of people to new satellite towns by the SLORC are direct evidence of the absence of economic freedom and property rights in Burma today. As *The Economist* pointed out:

Stripped to its essentials, economic freedom is concerned with property rights and choice. Individuals are economically free if property that they have legally acquired is protected from invasions or intrusions of others, and if they are free to use, exchange or give away their property so long as their actions do not violate other people's similar rights. That sounds abstract, but it comes to light as soon as you think how a government [such as the Burmese military regime] might restrict freedom. Failing to protect property rights would be one way. Others would be confiscation of property, to require individuals to give up time for military conscription [also forced labor in the Burmese case], or to lay down rules for what they may buy or sell and at what price.[26]

All of the preceding restrictions on economic freedom of the people of Burma have been imposed by the SLORC since 1988.

FORCED RELOCATION OF ETHNIC MINORITY POPULATION IN THE BORDERLANDS

Not only in central Burma but also especially in the borderlands or in the states of the ethnic minority population, the Burmese army has been reported to have committed atrocious human rights abuses, including killings, torture, rape, portering, forced labor, and "confiscation of property and forced relocation." According to the special rapporteur of the UN Commission on Human

Rights, Yozo Yokata, who testified at the 50th Session of the UN General Assembly on October 16, 1995:

There are still cases of torture, arbitrary killings, rapes, and confiscation of private property according to testimony and evidence acquired by me. They seem to be taking place most frequently by military soldiers in the course of military operations, forced relocations and development projects. Many of the victims of such atrocious acts belong to ethnic national populations, especially women, peasants, daily wage earners and other peaceful civilians who do not have enough money to avoid mistreatment by bribing.[27]

The plight of ethnic minorities is a by-product of the protracted civil war of over four decades between the ethnic rebel groups and the central Burmese government. Under the present military regime, the extensive use of "four cuts," or scorched earth tactics, by the Burmese army in its annual dry season campaigns against the ethnic minority rebel groups has resulted in massive forced relocations and desolation of villages, creating in its wake hundreds of thousands of refugees to cross over to Thailand. As the *Earth Rights International News* journal reported:

The long-running civil war between the ethnic groups and the central regime has provided the SLORC with the excuse of counter-insurgency to view all ethnic peoples— whose language they rarely understand—as insurgents. For example, SLORC's notorious "four cuts" strategy causes profound sufferings to civilians while masquerading as military security. The "four cuts" (the "new village" tactics developed by the British military in Malaysia) sever the links of food, monetary support, communication and recruits between ethnic villages and rebel armies, leaving many civilian areas devastated by scorched earth tactics as well. Ethnic peoples have also been particular targets of massive forced relocations and have recently seen their homelands suffer resource depletion as a result of unrestrained government timber and petroleum licensing.[28]

It has also been reported that "after relocation orders have been issued and people have been expelled from their homes, SLORC has declared expansive areas as 'free-fire zones'—any one who tries to remain in their homes can be shot on sight."[29]

Based on various sources, the number of forcefully relocated ethnic minority people, the Kachins, Karens, Karennis, Mons, Palaungs, Shans, and Tavoyans, under the "four cuts" policy and the so-called border area and infrastructure development programs of the SLORC since 1988 may be as high as 4 million. Most of the forcefully relocated ethnic minority population have been forced to take refuge inside Thailand subject to assault by the Burmese army crossing over the Thai border and deportation by the Thai authorities.

FORCED PORTERING AND FORCED LABOR

Article 4 of the UN Universal Declaration of Human Rights mandates, "No one shall be held in slavery or servitude." In violation of that article, the SLORC since 1989 has been using forced portering and forced labor, also forced donation of cash, in launching various infrastructure development projects to attract foreign investors and tourists. Human Rights Watch/Asia reported, "The Burmese army routinely uses civilians as unpaid porters to carry ammunition and food supplies to front lines positions or while on patrol in ethnic minority areas."[30]

At the June 1996 International Labor Conference of the ILO held in Geneva, the Workers' committee members pointed out that "the Government of Myanmar has had a long-standing reliance on forced labour with no improvements to date" and that "the economic crisis caused by the regime's policies had created a desperate need for hard currency which had led to a continued and massive use of forced labor."[31] Human Rights Watch/Asia also reported:

As with portering, forced labor is endemic in Burma. Since 1992, the military has forced at least two million people across the country to work without pay in the construction of roads, railways, and bridges. In recent years, the use of forced labor has increased, as the government tries to improve its infrastructure in order to attract foreign investment and tourism. Hundreds, if not thousands, have died from beatings, exhaustion, and a lack of medical care. Those forced to do such work include women, children and the aged.[32]

The practice of extracting forced labor in British colonial Burma was made under the Village Act of 1908 and Towns Act of 1907, which the ILO has been asking the present military government to repeal in compliance with the provisions of Convention No. 29 since 1992, to no avail. As the ILO reported:

Previously, the Government had claimed that the practice of forced labor, an inheritance of the colonial era, no longer existed and that the obsolete legislation would be repealed. Today, it affirmed that there was no longer forced labor and that it was the army which was carrying out the work in question. The Experts' report showed, however, that it was rather for the army, that this work was being carried out. The Government no longer said that the legislation would be modified nor that things would change in practice. On the other hand, it rejected proposals for technical assistance from the ILO.[33]

With respect to the ongoing use of forced labor or donations "that has been imposed upon the Burmese people in order to make the place 'respectable' for the tourists," Daw Suu Kyi in an interview with foreign journalists on November 17, 1995, said:

Telling them to donate their time, if they cannot give the time they have to donate money instead. Only last week, we were informed that in Hlaing Tharyar, which is one of the satellite townships of Rangoon, they were being asked to labor for a new road or perhaps for rebuilding an old road. And those families those households which cannot provide labor have to give 650 kyats each. That's a lot for people who don't have money, you know, who barely have enough to live on.[34]

The intelligence chief, Lieutenant General Khin Nyunt, labeled by dissidents as the "Prince of Darkness," admitted the conscription of uncompensated labor from the people and defended this feudal system of corvée as the voluntary "noble deed of merit" in Myanmar tradition performed by the Burmese people. On November 26, 1994, in the state-run *New Light of Myanmar*, he accused the "destructive elements" of Myanmar (foreign journalists, radios, neocolonialists, traitorous expatriates, and armed organizations under foreign influence) of spreading "concocted news" and "unfounded information" of forced labor, "despite full good will of local residents in their contribution of voluntary labor."[35] This justification replicates the one made by malevolent ancient Burmese kings to justify their acts of building gardens, roads, bridges, and pagodas for the atonement of their sins of torture and murder of their subjects.

The number of refugees along the Burmese-Thai border has been rising steadily ever since 1992. In 1992, the estimated number of Karen, Mon, and Karenni refugees forced to live in makeshift refugee camps along the Burmese-Thai border, most of which are located inside Thailand, was 65,000. The number climbed to 71,000 in 1993 and to 98,000 in 1996.[36] In 1997, due to the intensified offensive and forced relocation by the Burmese army, the number of refugees has increased prodigiously to nearly 112,5000. According to the Burma Border Consortium (BBC), a coalition group of nongovernmental refugee organizations that has been helping the refugees since 1988, the number of ethnic minority refugees at some 37 camps along the Burmese-Thai border in 1997 was 112,472, made up of 89,935 Karen, 11,544 Mon, and 10,933 Karenni refugees.[37]

MARGINALIZATION OF THE "LADY OF BURMA," DAW AUNG SAN SUU KYI, AND SUBJUGATION OF HER PARTY (NLD)

The focal point of Burma's democracy movement is the 1991 Nobel peace laureate Daw Aung San Suu Kyi, who was kept under house arrest for nearly six years. The junta's clever move to deflect whatever international pressure there was against its illegitimate rule was the staging of two meetings with her in late 1994 and her surprising release on July 10, 1995, along with the two ex-chairmen of NLD, U Tin Oo and U Kyi Maung. Releasing her removed international pressure against the regime. The outside world viewed her release as a "positive step" toward potential dialogue and reconciliation between the two adversaries for democratization of Burma. The ASEAN claimed her release as an achievement of its "constructive engagement policy" and welcomed with open arms Burma's accession to the 1976 Treaty of Amity and Cooperation as a first step toward becoming a full-blown member of the ASEAN. Japan, the largest historical creditor and aid donor of Burma under General Ne Win, has also shown eagerness to resume official aid to Myanmar based on this action. Following these positive international reactions, the defiant and confident SLORC stated bluntly that it saw no need to engage in any dialogue with Daw Suu Kyi for democratization and rejected the request of the NLD for the reinstatement of her old position of the general secretary of NLD to deny her political leadership.

On November 28, 1995, having no chance to negotiate with the Burmese generals for democratization, Suu Kyi initiated the anxiously awaited confrontation with the Burmese junta by calling the NLD delegates to boycott and walk out of the national convention held by the SLORC to draw up the catch-22 constitution that guarantees "the leading role for the army, *tatmadaw*," in the future government of Myanmar. The retaliation of the junta was to detain her briefly at a military interrogation center and issue stern warnings after she was stopped from attending the New Year's party of the Karen ethnic minority on December 24, 1995. On December 26, the powerful military intelligence chief Khin Nyunt indicted her and her party members as "the adopted sons and daughters of colonialists," traitors, and destructionists of the state who are "moving to cause disruption to the national convention for their party's interest." This xenophobic assault of opposition was aimed at Suu Kyi (who is married to an Englishman, Michael Aris).

On January 4, 1996, Daw Suu Kyi held the celebration of Burma's Independence Day at her residence attended by her followers and 13 artists. Following the celebration, these 13 artists were arrested, and 9 were released later. On March 17, 1996, using the reason of unsafe engine trouble of the train, military authorities stopped Daw Suu Kyi and her colleagues from traveling to Mandalay to attend the trial of four entertainers, including two prominent comedians, Par Par Lay and Lu Zaw. Subsequently, the two prominent comedians were tried and sentenced to seven years' imprisonment with hard labor. On March 28, the chairman of the NLD, U Aung Shwe, sent a letter addressed to the chairman of the SLORC, General Than Swe, protesting against the unlawful arrest, trial, and sentencing of three dissident students for attempting to remove barbed wire barricades in front of Suu Kyi's residence, and four entertainers for performing at Suu Kyi's residence and protesting against detention of political prisoners without due process. Meanwhile, intimidation, intensified crackdown, and arrest of her followers and NLD members continue to swell the number of languishing political prisoners at various jails in the nightmare state of Burma.

In May 1996, Suu Kyi called for the convening of the NLD congress in celebration of the sixth anniversary of the NLD's winning of the May 1990 election at her residence. In retaliation to prevent the holding of the congress, the government rounded up and detained over 250 NLD members, who were later released. However, the congress was successfully held between May 26 and May 28, during which a number of demands and resolutions were made, including the convening of the parliament, release of political prisoners, human rights and democracy restoration, unacceptability of the national convention, and dialogue between the government and the NLD. In the following months of June and July, some 14 elected NLD candidates in the May 1990 elections resigned from the party pressured by the SLORC.

On September 30, 1996, for the second time since May 1996, 109 delegates of the opposition party of Suu Kyi, the National League for Democracy (NLD), who came to attend the three-day congress called by their leader at her residence, were rounded up by the government security squads. As in the first case, the government claimed that the delegates were detained as "guests of the government" in order to question and brief them on the importance of the ongoing national convention to draw up the catch-22 constitution. For the first time since her release, she was prevented from giving her regular weekend speeches at her residence, which had been blockaded to stop the crowds, whose numbers have been reported to have dwindled.

By the second week of October, the number of people arrested was reported to have gone up to over 800. Meanwhile, Daw Suu Kyi was reportedly put under de facto house arrest, which was denied by the SLORC. After three weeks of limiting her freedom of movement, she was once again allowed to leave her residence, and she spoke to her followers near her residence and met with a Japanese diplomat and NLD leaders. On October 23, 1996, following the student sit-in demonstration surrounding the case of Rangoon Institute of Technology students' clash with a restaurant owner in the suburb of Rangoon, which resulted in the arrest and beating of students by security police, the colleague and vice-chairman of NLD, U Kyi Maung, was arrested. He was released a week later. Since then, intimidation, arrest, and arbitrary sentencing of NLD members and dissidents have become a daily ritual in Myanmar. In the closing months of 1996, the government news media began putting out warnings against Suu Kyi with the threat of potential arrest for committing the political crime of disturbing the tranquillity and unity of the state of Burma. She has also been accused of inciting political instability in collaboration with the Central Intelligence Agency (CIA) of the United States, which has also been accused of interfering in the internal affairs of Myanmar. The same accusation was made against her and dissidents during the 1988 political uprising.

On November 9, 1996, the intimidation of Daw Suu Kyi and her NLD party transpired into physical violence when her motorcade was attacked twice by a crowd pelting the vehicles with stones. Suu Kyi was unhurt, but her colleague and companion U Tin Oo suffered a wound on his temple in the attacks, which smashed her car's windshield. She later accused the government, specifically the members of the government political party, Union Solidarity and Development Association (USDA), of orchestrating the incident, which was denied by the government. The government, in turn, accused her and her party of instigating the incident to tarnish the international image of SLORC. But diplomats said that there is no doubt the government was involved to some extent in the incident. The United States and a number of countries expressed outrage over the attacks, demanding government action to punish the culprits and ensure Suu Kyi's safety. Japan, considered by Burma to be an ally and a potentially important source of financial support, also voiced regret over the incident and said it will urge the SLORC to show restraint in dealing with Suu Kyi.

In the first two weeks of December 1996, following the massive demonstration of students at various campuses, Suu Kyi's freedom of movement was once more restricted by barricading access to her residence in the name of her own safety, forcing her to stay inside her house. Since then she has been barred from holding the weekend meetings and delivering her speeches to the crowd from her residence. In the final analysis, the Burmese junta has been more or less getting away with its repression of opposition by using the Stalinist strategy of "one step forward and two steps back." This policy is reflected in the staging of two meetings with her in the late 1994 and her surprising release on July 10, 1995, along with the two ex-chairmen of NLD, U Tin Oo and U Kyi Maung to deflect whatever international pressure there was against its illegitimate rule.

The latest use of Stalinist strategy was to allow the holding of the Ninth Congressional Meeting of the NLD from September 27 to 29, 1997 at Suu Kyi's residence. The meeting, however, was held not completely without harassment and assault of the attendants by the authorities. During late October, the SLORC issued a statement saying that Suu Kyi's freedom of movement will not be restricted as long as she conducts her political activities within "the framework of the law." On October 26, 1997, she was allowed to make and complete a political campaign trip to the town of Thakayta. However, this seeming soft treatment of the opposition leader was short-lived and was ensued by a sudden crackdown of her political activities. On October 28, 1997, Suu Kyi and her party leaders ventured out to visit the town of Mayangon in the suburb of Rangoon and attempted to hold a political gathering or rally. The rally was crushed by the security squads, resulting in the confrontation, blockades of roads and arrest of eight NLD party members. Following this incident, in November the authorities cut off her access to the public and freedom of movement by erecting barricades around her residence once more. The cat-and-mouse game between the two adversaries and the political impasse with respect to democratization of Burma are going to continue for some time in the future.

An integral aspect of marginalizing the opposition leader is reflected in arresting and handing out harsh sentences to "dangerous" political dissidents who are close to, or related to, Suu Ky, followed by the soft treatment and the amnesty of nonthreatening political dissidents to appease public discontent and deflect international pressure. For example, the British husband of Suu Kyi, Michael Aris, and their two children were denied visitation rights for three years before they were allowed to visit in 1992. In April 1995, after three years of allowing them to visit her, once again the government denied the visitation rights of her husband by accusing him of instigating and influencing her political activities and defiance against the government.

In August 1993, Dr. Ma Thida, a dissident writer and medical doctor who had worked in the late 1980s as political campaign manager and personal aide to Suu Kyi, was arrested. On October 15, 1993, Ma Thida was given a 20-year sentence without due process, which she is currently serving in Insein Prison, known for its atrocious conditions, in solitary confinement. In June 1996, Suu Kyi's personal aide U Win Htein, along with five other NLD members, was arrested for videotaping the dry season paddy fields to show the plight of Burmese farmers who have been forced by the government to plant summer paddy crops and sell them at low prices to the government. In August 1996 all of them were tried without counsel and found guilty of spreading false news about the government and sentenced to a seven year imprisonment. In September 1996, Win Htein's sentence was extended to a 14-year term.

On April 1, 1996, a close friend of Suu Kyi and supporter of the NLD, James Lander (Leo) Nichols, an Anglo-Burmese businessman who served as an honorary consul to a number of Scandinavian countries and Switzerland, was arrested and sentenced to a three year jail term for possessing unauthorized facsimile machines and phone lines at his home. On the night of June 22, 1996, he suffered a stroke and cerebral hemorrhage while in custody at the infamous Insein Jail and died a few hours later in Rangoon General Hospital. In May 1996, a cousin of Suu Kyi, U Aye Win, the older brother of Sein Win, the prime minister of the exiled government NCGUB, was arrested under Section 10-B, which gives the government the right to detain any person indefinitely for engaging in unlawful activity.

In early June 1997, another cousin of Suu Kyi, U Cho Aung Than, his sister Nge Ma Ma Than, and her husband, Myint Swe, were arrested for allegedly smuggling Suu Kyi's videotapes out of Burma. On June 27, 1997, in his lengthy special news briefing intelligence chief Khin Nyunt charged Western powers (US Congress, CIA, and American pro-democracy human rights organizations in particular) with "aiding and abetting terrorism committed by certain organizations (Daw Suu Kyi and her party, the NLD, her cousin Dr. Sein Win and his exiled government NCGUB, the DAB, the ABSDF and a host of other opposition groups) operating under the guise of democracy and human rights by giving them assistance in both cash and kind."[38] At the same time, Khin Nyunt named and charged U Cho Aung Than, his sister Nge Ma Ma Than, and her husband, Myint Swe, with the same crimes. In August 1997, they were tried and sentenced to a jail term of seven years each.

ASSESSMENT OF THE POLITICAL OBJECTIVES OF THE SLORC

The four political objectives of the SLORC, printed in bold letters on the front page of the state-owned newspaper, *the New Light of Myanmar*, are:

1. Stability of the State, community peace and tranquillity, prevalence of law and order;

2.   National reconsolidation;

3.   Emergence of a new enduring constitution;

4.   Building of a new modern developed nation in accord with the new state constitution.

With respect to the first objective of the SLORC, it will be argued that there have not been "real stability and peace" in Burma since 1988, despite the claim of the SLORC. A series of student demonstrations and the mass demonstration by students against the government in December 1996, resulting in the closing of schools and colleges ever since; the violent physical assault of the motorcade of Daw Suu Kyi and her colleague U Tin Oo by government-backed USDA members in 1996; the unprecedented two explosions of terrorist bombs targeted to assassinate a high-ranking member of the SLORC in Rangoon (the first one was the explosion of two bombs at the Kabah Aye or Peace Pagoda that killed 5 people and wounded 17 on December 25, 1996, and the second one was sent by mail and exploded at the home of the secretary no. 2 of the SLORC, Lieutenant General Tin Oo, on April 6, 1997, resulting in the death of his eldest daughter); the protest by farmers in certain districts against the unfair quota delivery system of paddy to the government in 1996; and the religious unrest of Buddhist monks ransacking Muslim mosques, resulting in the imposing of curfew in Mandalay and other major cities in 1997—all point to real and potential sociopolitical instability and unrest in central Burma.

The highly publicized SLORC's claim of establishing "national peace and tranquillity" by entering bilateral cease-fire agreements with 15 ethnic minority rebel groups since 1993 has also been a facade, for it did not entail either the surrender of arms or the end of the protracted civil war of over four decades and the question of political autonomy and freedom of ethnic minority states. The unilateral breaking of the 1993 cease-fire agreement by the SLORC in 1995, the ongoing battles between the Karen National Union (KNU) and the Democratic Karen Buddhist Organization (DKBO) backed by the Burmese army, the breakdown of the bilateral cease-fire agreement in 1996 and the ensuing war between the Karenni rebels and the Burmese army, the meetings held in 1997 by the National Democratic Front (NDF),a coalition of seven ethnic minority rebel groups, and a group of ethnic rebels who entered a cease-fire agreement to discuss and resist against the increased pressure by the SLORC for surrender of arms—all testify to the fact that there are no real national peace and stability in Burma.

NATIONAL RECONSOLIDATION AND MILITARIZATION OF BURMESE POLICY

With respect to the second political objective of the SLORC, national reconsolidation, the actions of the SLORC since 1988 point to the systematic consolidation of military might and establish the stranglehold on political power rather than national reconciliation with the opposition groups. The immediate evidence of military fortification is the change in the size of armed forces from 180,000 men in 1988 to some 300,000 men in 1995, equipped with modern Chinese arms and with the projected goal of increasing the number to 500,000 men by the year 2000. In passing, it is noted that the size of 350,000-man Burmese armed forces is 70 percent of the size of the active 500,000-man US army.

To maintain the military stranglehold on power, General Saw reorganizing and expanded its two ruling bodies, the SLORC and the cabinet. By issuing Order No. 3/92 on January 29, 1992, the number of members in the SLORC was increased from 19 in 1989 to 22 by adding three new members, Major Generals Maung Hla (army secretary), Kyaw Min (northwest military commander), and Soe Myint (southeast military commander). On April 24, 1992, the SLORC issued Declaration No. 10/92, naming Lieutenant. General Than Shwe, who was a member and vice-chairman of the SLORC, as the new chairman of the SLORC, the prime minister, and the defense minister of Myanmar.[39] Thus, the total number of members in the SLORC was reduced from 22 to 21 with the retirement of Saw Maung. In 1989, the number of cabinet ministers was increased from 9 to 17, including the creation of two new ministries, the Ministry of Rail Transport and the Ministry of Communications, Posts, and Telecommunications, by splitting the Ministry of Transportation and Communication and the appointment of three regional commanders to new cabinet ministerial posts.[40]

The nomenclatural system of political patronage and promotion of commanders to higher ranks and cabinet posts that began in 1988 continues with full force to the present. On the auspicious Armed Forces Day of March 27, 1993, 11 major generals of the SLORC were suddenly promoted to lieutenant generals as their names appeared in the list of guests at the dinner party hosted by the chairman of the SLORC, General Than Shwe. Among them were Major General Khin Nyunt (the powerful military intelligence chief and secretary no.1 of the SLORC), Major General Tin Oo (the chief of staff of the army and secretary no. 2 of the SLORC), Major General Myo Nyunt (Rangoon commander), Major General Maung Aye (Eastern Command), and Major General Tun Kyi (ex-Central Command). As of 1995 the total number of lieutenant generals in the 21 member SLORC is 16, excluding the only senior general, Than Shwe, which is more than triple the original number of 5 lieutenant generals in 1988/89.

Khin Nyunt, who is acknowledged to be the most powerful and most feared person in Burma today, started out as a mere colonel in 1988 and skipped to the rank of major general in 1990 without ever becoming a brigadier general. In 1993, he was made a lieutenant general along with three other major generals. Among them was Maung Aye, a graduate of the Defense Services Academy (DSA), who was appointed army commander in Chief and vice chief of staff of the Defense Services. These two positions were left vacant by General Than Shwe when he replaced General Saw Maung as chairman of SLORC in 1992.

Maung Aye was also made the vice-chairman of the SLORC. The promotion of Maung Aye to these positions makes him second highest in command and a potential successor to General Than Shwe.

On September 23, 1992, the junta of General Than Shwe expanded the cabinet once more from 21 to 29 members by splitting the old ministries and creating new posts and ministries, including two deputy prime ministers, Vice Admiral Maung Maung Khin and Lieutenant General Aung Tin Tun, and four new ministers, Lieutenant General Tun Kyi as the minister of trade, Lieutenant General Maung Tint as the minister of border areas development, and Lieutenant General Kyaw Ba as the minister of hotels and tourism, and Lieutenant General Kyaw Min as the minister of mines. The four ministers of the four new ministries were regional commanders of central, northeast, northern, and northwest regions of Burma respectively, who were called back to Rangoon and rewarded with the ministerial positions. Knowledgeable Burmese believed that the main strategist of these moves is General Ne Win, who is behind all the major decisions and policies of the military regime.

On February 17, 1993, a new Ministry of Finance and Revenue was created by Declaration 2/93 with Brigadier General Win Tin as its minister, while Brigadier General Abel was appointed as the minister of national planning. Thus, the number of cabinet ministers/members of the military regime was increased from 29 to 30. The only member of the old cabinet who was not promoted to the rank of Lieutenant General and lost power and control of two key ministries, Trade and Finance, was Brigadier General Abel. He came to fame as the minister of a dual ministry, the Ministry of Trade and the Ministry of National Planning and Finance, when the so-called open-door market economy and the Burmese Way to Capitalism were adopted by the SLORC in 1989. In 1993, he also had to give up his powerful position as the chairman of the Foreign Investment Commission (FIC), which he occupied since 1989, to the newly appointed deputy prime minister, Vice Admiral Maung Maung Khin. The apparent reason for his decline in the power echelon of the military regime is that he is a Christian and a person with alien blood, as his very name, David Abel, suggests. By July 1995, through reshuffling, patronage and the creation of new positions, the number of ministers in the SLORC cabinet was increased to 36, including four newly positions attached to Prime Minister Office and one attached to Chairman of the SLORC Office. (Table 2.2)

Out of the 36 cabinet ministers, including 2 deputy prime ministers and other nomenclatural appointees, only 4 are civilians. Fourteen of the cabinet ministers are also members of the SLORC. In addition, there were 30 deputy ministers and officers attached to various ministries and offices, most of whom are serving and ex-military commanders. The total number of cabinet members stood at 66. On May 29, 1996, the SLORC cabinet was reshuffled once more by appointing new ministers to replace the old ones and adding more generals to the newly created offices. Five generals were appointed to the newly created Security Administration Committee (SAC).[41]

Table 2.2
The Cabinet of SLORC, July 1995

1	Prime Minister and Defense Minister	Senior General Than Shwe*
2	Deputy Prime Minister	Vice Admiral Maung Khin*
3	Deputy Prime Minister	Lt. General Tin Tun*
4	Prime Minister Office	Lt. General Myo Thant
5	Prime Minister Office	Brigadier General Lun Maung
6	Prime Minister Office	Colonel Pe Thein
7	Prime Minister Office	Colonel Than Shwe
8	Office of the Chairman of SLORC	Lt. General Min Thein*
9	Home	Lt. General Mya Thinn*
10	Agriculture	Lt. General Myint Aung*
11	Border Areas Development	Lt. General Maung Thint*
12	Cooperatives	Than Aung (civilian)
13	Construction	Major General Saw Tun
14	Culture Minister	Brigadier General Thaung Myint
15	Education	Lt. General Pan Aung
16	Energy	Lt. Colonel Khin Maung Thein
17	Finance	Brigadier Win Tin
18	Fisheries and Livestock	Brigadier Maung Maung
19	Foreign	U Ohn Gyaw (civilian)
20	Forestry	Lt. General Chit Swe*
21	Information	Brigadier Myo Thant
22	Immigration	Lt. General Maung Hla*
23	Industry 1	Lt.General Sein Aung*
24	Industry 2	Major General Kyaw Than
25	Health	Rear Admiral Than Nyunt
26	Hotels & Tourism	Lt. General Kyaw Ba*
27	Labor	Lt. General Aye Thaung*
28	Livestock	Brigadier General Maung Maung
29	Mines	Lt. General Kyaw Min
30	National Planning & Economic Development	Brigadier General David Abel
31	Posts and Telecommunications	Soe Tha (civilian)
32	Railway Transport	Colonel Win Sein
33	Religious Affairs	Lt. General Myo Nyunt*
34	Social Welfare, Relief & Resettlement	Major General Soe Myint
35	Trade	Lt. General Tun Kyi*
36	Transport	Lt. General Thein Win

* Members of SLORC

Source: Harn Yawnghwe, *Burma Alert* Vol. 6, No 7 (Quebec, Canada: July 1995).

THE CREATION OF NEW JUNTA: THE STATE PEACE AND DEVELOPMENT COUNCIL (SPDC)

On November 15, 1997, under Notification No. 1/97 the SLORC was dissolved by creating a nineteen-member junta with the new name of the State Peace and Development Council (SPDC). It was announced that the dissolution of the SLORC was made "with a view to ensure the emergence of an orderly and democratic system and to establish a peaceful and modern state." Out of the 21 members of the SLORC, only 4 (Senior General Than Shwe, Lieutenant Generals Maung Aye, Khin Nyunt, and Tin Oo) retained their membership and positions as chairman, vice-chairman, secretary no. 1 and secretary no. 2 in the newly created SPDC. A new position of secretary no. 3 of the SPDC was also created, which was assumed by Lieutenant General Win Myint who is a former Western regional commander and Adjutant General from the War Office. Seventeen members of the SLORC were removed and replaced by 15 new military commanders, including 2 commanders-in-chief of air and navy and 13 regional commanders. Under Notification No. 3/97, a fourteen-member Advisory Group or Council to SPDC was formed, made up of 14 out of the 17 ousted SLORC members. In effect, they have been pushed outside the center of the power echelon. In December, not even a month after its creation the Advisory Group was completely dissolved to indicate a permanent purge of its 14 members.

On the same day of creating the SPDC, under Notification No. 2/97 the junta's cabinet was reshuffled and enlarged from 36 ministers to 40 ministers. Most of the old ministers were replaced by newly appointed ministers, all of whom are military commanders. The objective of forming the new cabinet given by the newly formed SPDC was "to fulfill the goal of bringing forth a new developed and modern nation in the interest of the State and all the national peoples." Twelve old cabinet ministers, including foreign minister Ohn Gyaw, national planning and economic development minister Brigadier General David Abel, finance and revenue minister Win Tin, communication minister Soe Tha, co-operative minister Than Aung, and rail transportation minister Win Sein, retained their cabinet posts. Under Ordinance No. 1/97 signed by Lieutenant General Khin Nyunt, a new ministry of military affairs with Senior General Than Shwe as its minister was also created along with the ministry of electric power. On November 16, under the same Notification No. 2/97 signed by Lieutenant General Khin Nyunt, the appointment of 33 deputy ministers, most of whom were newly appointed, was also announced. Thus, the total number of cabinet ministers and deputy ministers of the ruling military junta has been increased from 66 in July 1995 to 73 in November 1997.

The reshuffling of SPDC's cabinet and removal or de facto purging of ministers from key ministries continued. On December 21, 1997, Brigadier General David Abel, the most articulate and internationally well-known spokesman for the SLORC, was removed from his cabinet post of national planning and economic development minister and was appointed the third minister of the SPDC chairman's office. His post was filled by former communications, posts, and telegraphs minister Soe Tha. Finance and revenue minister Brigadier General Win Tin was removed from his post and was appointed the new minister of communications, posts and telegraphs. Lieutenant Colonel Khin Maung Thein, former minister of energy, replaced Win Tin as the new minister of finance and revenue. Brigadier General Lun Maung of prime minister's office was named the new minister of energy. There were four other reshuffles, including the removal of Win Sein from his post of rail transportation minister and was appointed the new minister of culture, while Lieutenant General Pan Aung, former minister of education, was appointed as the new minister of rail transportation.

This latest development of creating the SPDC with a new portfolio of military commanders and reshuffling of cabinet is indicative of the typical process of permanent purge necessary to protect the political throne and power in a totalitarian state. In the Burmese case, it points to the continued legacy and the power and influence of the living dictator General Ne Win who has not simply faded away despite his alleged retirement from politics in July 1988. He resurfaced in the political arena when he visited Indonesia and Singapore in October, 1997, a month prior to the dissolution of the SLORC. His visit to Singapore for medical examination also coincided with the visit of trade delegation headed by his life-long disciple intelligence chief Khin Nyunt, not by trade minister Tun Kyi whose rise to power, fame, and fortune became the target of the purge. The dictator seems to continue to wield enormous power and control over the ruling Burmese generals in shaping the political destiny of Burma. During the 26 years of his iron rule, purging dangerous generals and reorganizing the inner circle of power-holders and power echelon among the Burmese generals was a regular ritual to secure the military grip on power whenever there were signs of power struggle, economic crisis, and sociopolitical unrest. Since the 1988 military coup and formation of the SLORC, reshuffling and enlargement of the SLORC cabinet as well as the promotion of powerful regional commanders to ministerial posts to halt their rise to power and sever their ties to regiments has been a regular ritual to indicate the persistence of General Ne Win's legacy and tactic.

The creation of SPDC is a political maneuver of removing the powerful, corrupt, and older SLORC members and cabinet ministers, the most rich and infamous among them were trade minister Tun Kyi, hotel and tourism minister Kyaw Ba, forestry minister Chit Swe, labor minister Aye Thaung, industry no. 1 minister Sein Aung, fishery minister Maung Maung and agricultural minister Myint Aung. It has also been reported that these ministers, their aides, and directors generals of various ministries were also questioned, and put under house arrest for corruption, along with the seizure of their properties and assets. It should also be pointed out that most of these ousted members of the SLORC and cabinet ministers are over 60 years old. Replacing them with less well-known and powerful but not necessarily less corrupt and younger military commanders is a calculated move to salvage the tarnished name, reputation, and a potential demise of military rule to distract the rising public dissatisfaction with the economic hardship brought on by the SLORC. In the final analysis, it indicates that the Burmese polity has been incrementally and totally militarized with a centralized feudalistic system of governance and distribution of power, privilege, and wealth among Burmese military commanders.

THE CREATION OF USDA TO RESURRECT A SINGLE-PARTY POLICY

Following the legacy of the Burmese Way to Socialism of General Ne Win, on September 15, 1993, the junta created a "social organization" named the Union Solidarity and Development Association (USDA), affiliated with the Home Affairs Ministry. The USDA has been formed systematically nationwide by forcing people to join, beginning with ward and village tracts in each township. The aims of this association are given as "non-disintegration of the Union and national unity, perpetuation of sovereignty, promotion and vitalization of national pride, and the emergence of a prosperous, peaceful and modern Union of Myanmar." A four-point oath and 11 duties are prescribed to would-be members. Among the duties of members are to render the army (Tatmadaw) all-around assistance, to preserve and protect national culture, to protect state and public property, to maintain law and order, to participate in antinarcotic law enforcement, and so on.[42] The top positions of the association are filled by five of the junta's cabinet ministers and the mayor of Rangoon. A nationwide campaign to recruit members by military commanders has been taking place since its inception.

All the aims and duties of USDA seem to point to the junta's real aim of securing its demand for a leading role in the future politics of Myanmar and solidifying the political base for the control of power. It is reminiscent of the nationwide drive to form a single party, the Burma Socialist Programme Party (BSPP), after the 1962 military coup of General Ne Win. Its organizational structure and operations emulate those of the Indonesian army-backed and controlled political party, Golkar, under Suharto. On January 15, 1994, three days prior to the resumption of the national convention, the junta staged a mass rally of the USDA in Rangoon. It was reportedly attended by some 100,000 people, mostly made up of government employees, students, and teachers of state schools and state-sponsored journalists and artists who did not dare to be absent. The rally was pictorially depicted on the front page of the state-run newspaper, *The New Light of Myanmar,* with the slogan printed in bold letters: "We firmly believe to fully support the one hundred and four State fundamental principles laid down by the National Convention," Similar rallies were staged in Mandalay and other cities across Burma. It was also reported that people were intimidated by local authorities and rounded up by soldiers to attend these rallies held across the country.

Since 1993, the formation and mobilization of the military-backed political party fashioned after the Indonesian Golkar party, the USDA, with Senior General Than Shwe, the chairman of the SLORC, as its patron, have been continuing across Myanmar. On August 29, 1994, Than Shwe delivered a speech at the closing ceremony of the USDA executive management course no. 3/94, stating that the goals of the SLORC are identical to the five aims and objectives of the USDA: "nondisintegration of the union; nondisintegration of national unity; perpetuation of national sovereignty; revitalization of patriotism with a view to enhancing national pride and prestige; and emergence of a modern and peaceful nation."[43] He emphasized that achievement of these goals hinged directly upon the attainment of economic strength and stability to establish a democratic system in the country. He contended that no political system, socialist or multiparty, could succeed without the fulfillment of the social needs of the people for food, clothing, and shelter.

On September 15, 1994, at its annual conference 400 members of the USDA voiced "unqualified support" of the 104 principles and various proposals made by the chairman of the Working Committee of the National Convention, U Aung Toe, for the eight groups of convention delegates. This USDA's action amounted to coercion of the convention delegates to endorse the principles and proposals laid down from above. At the time of the conference, the USDA claimed to have a membership of 830,322 and projected the membership to increase to over 1 million within the forthcoming year.[44] From the source of Burmese nationals, since its formation in 1993 forced recruitment of members has been continuing across Burma. It is assumed that in 1997 the membership of USDA had grown to several million.

THE EMERGENCE OF A NEW ENDURING CONSTITUTION

The third political objective (the main maneuver of the SLORC to prevent the transfer of power to the legitimate winners of the 1990 election and legitimate its rule) has been the emergence of the catch-22 constitution, which General Saw Maung spoke of in his July 5, 1989, statement that "until responsibility is transferred to a government according to the Constitution we [SLORC] are to continue to attend to our task."[45] The main goal and process of drawing up the mythical constitution by the SLORC are what Joseph Silverstein appropriately termed "Dictatorship in Constitutionalist Guise."[46] On April 24, 1992, the present head of the state of Myanmar, Senior General Than Shwe, announced the convening of the national convention to draw up the constitution within six months. The number of legal political parties that contested in the 1990 election was 93. By 1992, SLORC had deregistered these parties or declared most of these parties illegal by using a number of arbitrary rules. This left only 17 legal political parties recognized by the junta. Out of these 17 parties, 7 won seats in the 1990 election, although 27 parties won seats in the election. In selecting the delegates to attend the convention, the SLORC arbitrarily selected and formed the delegates into eight different groups, with the group of elected candidates as one of them. The delegates of the seven nonelected groups were picked by the SLORC to represent ethnic minorities, peasants, workers, intelligentsia, government employees, political parties, and independents. The group of elected candidates was made up of 99 members, 91 of whom were elected NLD candidates. Hence, the NLD delegates chosen by the SLORC to attend the convention accounted for only 14 percent of the total representatives (91 out of 702), although in the 1990 election the NLD candidates had won 85 percent of the votes.[47]

The convention was declared open by the SLORC on January 9, 1993. It took nearly three years after the election to hold the national convention to draw up the catch-22 constitution, which was labeled by Daw Suu Kyi as "an absolute farce."[48] At the very outset, the SLORC dictated that all the processes and procedures of the national convention and drafting of the new constitution are to be made in accordance with the six objectives, one of which is to endorse "a leading role for the *tatmadaw*, army," in the politics and governance of Myanmar.[49] Many dissident delegates who rejected this demand and objected to the undemocratic procedures of the convention and the military-dictated 104 principles of the constitution have been arrested by the SLORC since 1993. In August 1993, at the third convening of the convention, an NLD delegate, Dr. Aung Khin Sint, and one of his associates were arrested for distributing anti-government and anticonvention leaflets. Aung Khin Sint was sentenced to a 20-year jail term and was released in March 1994. When the convention was first convened in January 1993, the initial number of delegates was 702; this was reduced to some 643 delegates by April 1994. Including the two defected delegates, U Khin Maung Ko and Daniel Aung, to the liberated areas, the SLORC expelled 61 delegates out of the convention.[50] On September 2, 1994, after a long, five-month recess, the SLORC reconvened the convention for the sixth time in two years, with the number of delegates dwindling from 643 to 631. The number of NLD delegates attending the convention was further reduced from 91 to 86 due to defection and arrest. A majority of 71 delegates missing from the original total of 702 delegates in 1993 were either expelled or arrested by the junta for expressing their dissent against the undemocratic proceedings of the convention.

On September 3, 1994, the chairman of the National Convention Working Committee (NCWC), U Aung Toe, announced the committee's recommendations on self-administered areas (SAAs, both divisions and zones) and on the constituting of the legislative, executive, and judicial bodies of the future government of Myanmar Naing-gan. He stated that the legislative body of the future government of Myanmar was going to be bicameral. The leading role of the army, *tatmadaw*, in the government was also clarified by specifying the number of seats in the two houses of the Union Parliament to be occupied by military men who are appointed rather than elected: 110 out of the total of 410, including 300 elected members, in the lower house; and 56 out of the total of

224, including 168 elected members, in the upper house—12 from each of the 14 states and regions of Myanmar. The 14 regions and states will also have their own parliaments, consisting of two members elected from various townships plus members elected by the ethnic minority residents on the basis of one for each 44,000 persons. The military will occupy 25 percent of the seats in each of these parliaments.[51]

Previous meetings of the convention had already specified that the executive president of Myanmar shall be a military man. This time, it was stipulated further that "the President of the State is to obtain the nominated list of *tatmadaw* (army) members from the Commander-in-Chief of Defense Services in order that he may appoint ministers for Defense, Security/Home Affairs and Border Affairs."[52] The executive bodies of "regions, states, self-administered areas and districts" are also said to include *tatmadaw* members. As to the Judiciary, despite its ostensible claim of setting up civil courts and justices, the chief of justice and judges of the supreme court will be appointed by the president. In short, similar to the government of Indonesia, the government of Myanmar will be dominated by military men. The delegates from the opposition party of Daw Aung San Suu Kyi, the National League for Democracy, have been protesting these stipulations without success, and a few have been arrested.

The convention was recessed once more for six months and resumed on March 2, 1995, and took up the sensitive issue of the creation of self-administered areas (SAAs), which was proposed during the last convention held in September 1994. The SSAs are third administrative units distinct from the seven regions and the seven states established by the 1947 and 1974 constitutions of Burma. The recommendation put forth by the convention was the creation of SAAs for only 6 ethnic minorities out of some 127 minority people: the Nagas, Pa-os, Palaungs, Danus, Kokngs, and Was. The issue was not settled, and at the final session of the convention held on April 7, 1995, the chairman of the NCWC recommended the appointment of a special commission to deliberate the matter in future conventions. The convention was recessed once more for the summer months and scheduled to reconvene on October 24, 1996.[53]

During the month of October 1996, the NLD began to pick up its protest against the undemocratic procedures of the convention and announced that its delegates would withdraw from the convention. On November 23, 1996, a month after the scheduled date, the convention was resumed for the seventh time in three years. On November 28, 1996, Daw Suu Kyi asserted the undemocratic nature of the ongoing convention and the unconstitutionality of the constitution and that if the convention was to continue in its present form, the NLD has no alternative but to boycott the convention. In December, the NLD delegates boycotted the convention, and they were formally expelled from the convention by the SLORC. Thus, the total number of delegates left attending the convention was reduced from 631 to 545 with the departure or expulsion of

86 NLD delegates. The convention dragged on until January 19, 1997 when it was recessed once more. The convention has not been resumed up to December 1997. Thus, the third political objective of the SLORC regarding the emergence a new enduring constitution had not transpired and is not likely to occur in the foreseeable future.

With no specific timetable for finalizing the drawing up of the constitution, the SLORC has gained time in its efforts to dismantle the political structures and strength of opposition, especially the NLD. In more than seven years since the May 1990 election, "the Election Commission has stripped almost 25 percent of elected representatives of their elected seats, banned half of those from participating in future elections (which may never be held again), and deregistered more than 80 percent of the parties that participated in the 1990 elections." [54] Based on these facts, it is concluded that the national convention to draw up the catch-22 constitution is a calculated move of the SLORC to impede the democracy movement and establish military dictatorship over Burma.

NOTES

1. Lawyers Committee for Human Rights (LCHR), *Summary Injustice: Military Tribunals in Burma* (New York: LCHR, 1991), p. 35.

2. See SLORC, *Myanmar, the Nation-Building Activities; The Historical Chronicle of the Works of SLORC from 1988 to 1991* (in Burmese) (Rangoon: Ministry of Information, December 20, 1991), p. 194.

3. Human Rights Watch/Asia, *Burma: Children's Rights and the Rule of Law*, vol. 9, no. 1 (C), (January 1997): 11.

4. International Labor Organization (ILO), International Labor Conference, *Provisional Record, Eighty-Third Session, Report of the Committee on the Application of Standards*, no. 14, Geneva, June 20, 1996, p. 57.

5. Article 19, Country Report, *State of Fear: Censorship in Burma* (London: Article 19, December 10, 1991), p. 35.

6. International Human Rights Law Group (IHRLG), *Report on the Myanmar Election* (Washington, DC: IHRLG, May 19, 1990), p. 64.

7. Report of the Special Rapporteur, Rajsoomer Lallah, *Human Rights Questions: Human Rights Situations and Reports of Special Rapporteurs and Representatives* (New York: United Nations, General Assembly Fifty-First Session, October 8, 1996), p. 22.

8. Lawyers Committee for Human Rights, *Summary Injustice*, pp. 30–32.

9. Ibid., p. 46.

10. US Department of State: *Burma Report on Human Rights Practices* (Washington, DC: The Bureau of Democracy, Human Rights and Labor, January 30, 1997), p. 5.

11. See for detail Mya Maung, *Totalitarianism in Burma: Prospects for Economic Development*, (New York: Paragon House, 1992), Chap. 3.

12. Amnesty International, *Myanmar: Prisoner of Conscience, Torture, Extrajudicial Executions*, (New York: Amnesty International, August 1988), p. 11.

13. Asia Watch, *News from Asia Watch*, August 14, 1990, p. 3.

14. Alan Clements, *Burma: The Next Killing Fields?* (Berkeley, CA: Odonian Press, 1992), p. 10.

15. See Win Naing Oo, *Cries from Insein: A Report on Conditions for Political Prisoners in Burma's Infamous Insein Jail* (Bangkok: All Burma Students' Democratic Front (ABSDF), 1996), pp. 32–35.

16. Ibid., p. 32.

17. Amnesty International, *Myanmar, "No Law at All," Human Rights Violations under Military Rule* , October 1992, p 14.

18. Burma Information Group (BIG), *Heroes inside the Jails of SLORC* (Bangkok: BIG, November 1994), p. 7.

19. "Drop-dead Humor," *Nation/Focus,* August, 4, 1996.

20. Jesuit Refugee Service Asia/Pacific, *Burma Update* , August 10, 1993.

21. *The Working People's Daily,* January 7, 1992, p. 1.

22. *The New Light of Myanmar*, July 11, 1993, pp. 1–6.

23. All Burma Federation of Students' Unions (ABFS), Information and Documentation Committee, *An Overview of the Current Education Situation in Burma,* privately published paper, December 1997: p. 5.

24. Burma Underground Rights Movement for Action (BURMA), *Life in Burma's "New Towns,"* (Bangkok: BURMA, August, 1990), pp. 2–3.

25. Mya Saw Shin, trans., *The Constitution (The Fundamental Law) of The Socialist Republic of the Union of Burma* (Washington, DC: Library of Congress, Law Library, June, 1975), pp. 8–9).

26. "Economic Freedom: Of Liberty, and Prosperity," *The Economist* (January 13, 1996): 19.

27. United Nations, *Human Rights Situations and Reports of Special Rapporteurs and Representatives*, A/50/568, New York: October 16,1995, p. 9.

28. Earth Rights International, "The Current Political Players, The Ethnic Nationalities," *Earth Rights International News*, vol. 1, no. 2, April, 1996, p. 3.

29. The National Coalition Government of the Union of Burma (NCGUB), *Human Rights Year Book 1996: Burma* (Washington D.C.: NCGUB, July, 1997), p. 177.

30. Human Rights Watch/Asia, *Burma*, March 1, 1996, p. 5.

31. ILO, Provisional Record, p. 56.

32. Human Rights Watch/Asia, *Burma*.

33. Ibid., p. 57.

34. "Interview with Aung San Suu Kyi," *Burma Debate* (November/December 1995): p. 22.

35. *The New Light of Myanmar,* November 26, 1994, p. 1.

36. See Jesuit Refugee Service Asia/Pacific, *Burma Update*, Bangkok, June 22, 1992, August 10, 1993, April 1997.

37. "To Forcefully Relocate or Not: Thailand's Dilemma," *Burma Issues*, a special report, April 1997, p. 31.

38. See *Special News Briefing* (27/6/97)(1/6) given by the Secretary No. 1 of the State Law and Order Restoration Council, Lieutenant General Khin Nyunt in the Defense Services Assembly Hall, Yangon, June 27, 1997, p. 1.

39. Foreign Broadcasting Information Service (FBIS), *Burma* , April 24, 1992.

40. SLORC, *Notification No. 11/92*.

41. Harn Yawnghwe, *Burma Alert*, vol. 7, no. 6, June 1996, p. 7.

42. *The New Light of Myanmar*, September, 1993, p. 1.

43. *The New Light of Myanmar,* August 29, 1994, p. 1.

44. *The New Light of Myanmar*, September 15, 1994, p. 1.

45. *The Working People's Daily*, Yangon, July 5, 1989, p. 1.

46. Joseph Silverstein, "Burma's Uneven Struggle," *Journal of Democracy*, vol. 7, no. 4 (October, 1996): 94.

47. All Burma Student Democratic Front (ABSDF), Central Committee, *The Scrutiny of the National Convention* , Down Gwin, 1994, pp. 2–3.

48. Philip Shenon, "Law Maker Meets again with Burmese Dissident, *New York Times*, February 16, 1994.

49. See for detail Janelle M. Diller, *The National Convention in Burma (Myanmar): An Impediment to the Restoration of Democracy* (New York: International League for Human Rights, 1996), pp. 14–18.

50. ABSDF, *The Scrutiny*, p. 5.

51. *The New Light of Myanmar*, September 4, 1994.

52. Ibid.

53. See for detail Economist Intelligence Unit (EIU), *Country Report: Cambodia, Laos, Myanmar,* 2nd Quarter, *1995* (London: EIU, 1995), pp. 31–32.

54. Diller, *The National Convention*, p. 8.

3

Nature and Performance of the
Market-Oriented Economy

The four economic objectives of the SLORC:

1. Development of agriculture as the base and all-around development of other sectors of the economy;

2. Proper evolution of the market-oriented economic system;

3. Development of the economy inviting participation in terms of technical know-how and investments from sources inside the country and abroad;

4. The initiative to shape the national economy must be kept in the hands of the state and the national people.

In this chapter and subsequent chapters, the above four economic objectives of the SLORC printed in bold letters on the front page of *The New Light of Myanmar* since 1996, are scrutinized in light of various development programs, policies, and the performance of the Burmese economy under military management since 1988.

THE OPEN-DOOR, MARKET-ORIENTED ECONOMY OF MYANMAR

The first part of the fourth objective of the SLORC, "the initiative to shape the national economy must be kept in the hands of the state," rather than in the hands of the national peoples, can be deemed the prime objective and achievement of the military regime. The so-called open-door, market-oriented economy of Myanmar advanced and introduced by the SLORC is de facto state capitalism that retains state ownership and control of key natural resources, industries, and foreign exchange. One of the guiding principles forced upon the delegates who were chosen by the junta to attend the national convention and draw up the

Constitution of Myanmar Naing-gan asserts: that "the State economic system shall be a market economic system in which the state permits all economic forces such as the state itself, regional organizations, co-operative organizations, joint venture organizations, private concerns to take part in the economic activities for the development of the national economy," vowing to "prevent acts that harm public interests through monopolization and manipulation of prices."[1]

With respect to the second objective of "proper evolution of the market-oriented economic system," the SLORC has not initiated any program of dismantling hundreds of state agencies and 58 major state economic enterprises (SEEs), including seven state financial institutions, that operate about 1,800 factories and establishments. State enterprises with monopoly privileges continue to play a major role in the macroeconomic activity and performance, accounting for "22 percent of the GDP, 50 percent of the industrial value added, 50 percent of exports, 40 percent of imports, and contributes 40 percent of tax revenues through payments of commercial tax, custom duty and income tax."[2] Another indicator of the continued state control of the economy is the largeness of the size of SEEs relative to private enterprises in trade, industry, and finance. As the World Bank observed on the dominance of SEEs outside the agricultural sector: "While the private sector is made up of predominantly small establishments employing less than ten workers, SEEs account for over 95% of large establishments that employ more than 100 workers and about 80% of medium-sized establishments (between 51–100 workers)."[3] As of 1997, no large SEE has been privatized to indicate that the government's claim of establishing a market-oriented economic system and undertaking successful privatization measures is suspect. On the contrary, the state control of the key sectors of the economy has been amplified by establishing hundreds of state-owned and controlled joint ventures, including joint ventures with foreign investors in energy, hotel, and tourist industries.

Apart from the 58 SEEs owned and operated by various ministries, the Ministry of Defense owned 12 enterprises that are administered as part of the central government. The single clearest evidence of the military capitalism or state control of the rich natural resources and enterprises of Burma was the creation of a giant enterprise called the Union of Myanmar Economic Holdings Company Limited (UMEHC), totally owned and operated by defense services personnel, veterans, and military regimental organizations. It is reminiscent of the Defense Service Institute (DSI) and the Burma Economic Development Corporation (BEDC) associated with the name of Brigadier Generals Tin Pe and Aung Gyi in the 1950s and early 1960s. The military-owned and operated companies numbered more than 30 prior to the military coup of 1962. The UMEHC was created in 1990 with state funds or paid-in capital of Kt10 billion (almost 10 percent of 1990 GDP) to conduct businesses in various sectors of the economy at home and abroad. Forty percent of its shares designated as "Class A" is owned by the Directorate of Procurement of the Ministry of Defense, and the rest of the shares, designated as "Class B," are allocated to military personnel, armed forces cooperatives, regimental institutes, and veteran associations.[4] The management is totally run by the military commanders of the SLORC with Brigadier General Than Oo as the chairman of the Board of Directors and Brigadier General Win Hlaing as the managing director, along with other military cabinet ministers and commanders as members of the Board of Directors. Since its establishment, the UMEHC has entered several joint ventures with foreign companies to earn and amass foreign exchange in all sectors of the economy. This gigantic state enterprise reflects the basic objective of the military power-holders, whose economic base of power has been steadily enlarged to control the political power and future of Burma.

FOREIGN TRADE REGIME

On August 5, 1988, three days before the famous August 8, 1988 massacre of thousands of demonstrators by the Burmese army across Burma took place, the vice governor of Yunan Province, Zhu Kui, signed a border trade agreement with the Burmese military regime.[5] In December 1988, the SLORC formally legalized border trade with China and other neighboring countries. This shift to an "open-door economy" sought to attract direct foreign investments from the private corporate world. In particular, it sought Chinese trade and investment, economic, technical, and especially military aid. By 1990, the SLORC successfully struck an arms deal worth over $1.4 billion with China, which has become Burma's most powerful and biggest ally. A gigantic China-Burma cross-border trade conservatively estimated at $1 billion annually has been thriving ever since the formal legalization of border trade in 1988, which is presented in detail in a later chapter.

Except for opening the door of the economy to foreign investors to form joint ventures with 58 state enterprises in key industries, the Burmese economy remains primarily a centralized command economy. When the legalization of border trade was announced in December 1988, 16 commodities were banned from export across the border, including teak, rice, oil, and gems. On October 28, 1991, the SLORC increased the list of banned commodities to 23.[6] In July 1994, the list was increased further to 28. Among them were the four export products with the largest foreign exchange earning power, rice, teak, petroleum, and gems and jewelry, followed by gold, silver, jade, diamond, pearl, coal, zinc, lead, bronze, tin, wolfram, rubber, arms and ammunition, antiques, pulses and beans, corn, groundnut, cotton, coins, buffalo, cow, elephant and rare animals, fish, shrimp, animal horns, leathers, and so on.[7] Apart from this general list of contraband of the central government, district military commanders often impose their own ban on additional items of goods from cross-border trade. Despite these formal bans, the export of contraband across the border continues to flourish under the eyes of government officials, who permit it by taking bribes from the private traders.

The Ministry of Trade and the Myanmar Foreign Investment Commission (FIC) of the Ministry of National Planning and Development (MNPED) are the two most powerful state organs empowered with total control of foreign investment and trade. The FIC is made up of 16 ministers of SLORC's cabinet, with the minister of trade, finance, and planning, Brigadier General Abel, as the chairman up to 1993. In 1994, Abel was replaced by the deputy prime minister, Vice Admiral Maung Maung Khin, as the chairman of FIC. Abel became the minister of only one ministry, the MNPED, as two separate ministries, the Ministry of Trade and the Ministry of Finance and Revenue, were created with Lieutenant General Tun Kyi and Brigadier General Win Tin as their respective ministers.

On April 1, 1989, the Ministry of Trade was reorganized with six departments, which monitored and administered (1) trading activities, (2) finance, (3) export and import activities, (4) operation of companies, (5) promotion of foreign trade, and (6) trade inspection. The ministry with its 11 corporations established a trade regime by controlling and operating various commercial and trading activities. The direct control and participation of the Trade Ministry and its 11 corporations in the commercial activities were involved in the purchase and sale of agricultural output and general goods, automobiles and parts, printing, stationery, and film, medicine and medical equipment, and the operation of restaurants and beverage shops, department stores, hotels, and tourist agencies, export and import businesses, and inspection of goods and trade agents.[8]

The Ministry of Trade, the MNPED, and the FIC accept, approve, and monitor the formation and operations of all domestic and foreign companies and joint ventures. The Directorate of Trade of the Ministry of Trade controls export and import activities of foreign and domestic companies under strict rules by issuing permits/licenses on consignment on a yearly basis. Obtaining these permits by both foreign and domestic companies depends directly on personal connections, family ties, and bribery of the military commanders and corrupt officials. For example, the foreign oil companies that have invested heavily in Myanmar since 1990 must put up signature bonuses that run as high as $5 million to secure their exploration rights. The same is true for domestic companies, which must bribe various government officials in order to secure export and import permits.

On the export side, the Custom Department imposes tariffs that vary between 5 percent and 25 percent, payable in foreign exchange, depending on the commodities and shipments through the borders or the port of Rangoon. On the import side, the state monopolizes the import of arms and crude oil and imposes some 22 different tariff rates, which range from 5 percent to 500 percent on 210 tariff categories. An example of direct control imposed by the trade ministry on importers is the use of what is known as the "import first system" which links import and export together. Under this system, an importer is issued an import license on a consignment basis upon the condition that within a specified period of time, usually six months, it must export domestic products to earn foreign exchange. In order to pay for the import in foreign exchange, the importer must either establish a line of credit first with a foreign firm or pay for the import later after it earns foreign exchange from exports or purchase foreign exchange in the unofficial market to pay for the import.

With respect to state regulation and control of imports, US embassy reported that importers are continued "to be required to import GOB-designated 'priority' goods in amounts equivalent to one-fourth of their total imports. In FY 1994/1995, the GOB began to give import licensing preferences to firms that import at least 50% 'priority' goods. In July 1996, the GOB, facing a worsening public sector shortage of foreign exchange, began to ration private sector imports by licenses and openings of letters of credit."[9] These restrictions and regulations clearly indicate that the so-called open-door market economy of the SLORC was a sham and as in the past socialist state the Burmese economy primarily remains a command economy with state enterprises controlling all industries and directly monopolizing traditional export industries.

According to the Foreign Investment Law promulgated on November 30, 1988, and effective in May 1989, foreign companies may invest and form either wholly owned or joint venture firms with a minimum capital of 35 percent in various sectors of the economy. However, wholly owned foreign investment is allowed outside only the 12 areas that are reserved for the state under the State-Owned Economic Enterprises Law of March 31, 1989. The 12 areas reserved for the state enterprises by Article 6, Chapter 2 of this law include rice, teak, oil, and natural gas, fishery, pearls, jade and gems, transportation, postal and communication, banking and finance, metals and minerals, public utilities, and defense industries.[10]

By the end of September 1990, the state formed nine large so-called State-Private Joint-Venture Corporations, officially named the Union of Myanmar Public Joint-Venture Corporation (JVC) No. 1, No. 2, No. 3 and so on under the control of trade ministry. The nine JVCs with government's equity holding of between 40 percent and 55 percent were established in the areas of (1) general trading, (2) paddy, rice, and rice product trading (3) trading in papers and printed materials, (4) agricultural products other than rice and paddy trading, (5) construction works, production, and marketing of construction materials, (6) fish, shrimp, and other marine breeding and trading, (7) modern hospital, clinic, medicine, and medical equipment manufacturing, and trading, (8) general merchandise export and import and (9) the formation and supervision of companies and affiliates by the Union of Myanmar Economic Holdings Company Ltd. of the Directorate of Procurement of the Ministry of Defense. All these state restrictions and capitalist ventures of the SLORC represent an enlargement of the economic base of the military rulers to control political power. The JVC No. 2 is named Myanma Agricultural Produce Trading (MAPT) (formerly called the State Agricultural Marketing Board (SAMB) under the civilian government and Trade Corporation No. 1 under the socialist government) whose major line of business or operation is paddy, rice, and rice product trading with a monopoly on rice exports.[11]

Due to large-scale state controls of the economy and ostensible measures of liberalization, the Burmese economy seethes with corruption, bribery, and black marketeering. This was publicly acknowledged by the chief of intelligence, Major General Khin Nyunt, in his speech on the state of the Burmese economy delivered at a meeting held on May 21, 1991, at the Ministry of Trade: "Service organizations connected with trade matters, such as import and export work, services sector and collection of taxes, are taking bribes according to their ranks.[12] The terms used by Burmese for bribe money are "money for drinking tea or tea money," *la-phet yai boe*, and "money for eating cake or dessert," *mhoent boe*. The bribe is paid in cash or in kind by those who need favors or services from the military ministers, director generals, and other high-ranking government officials in charge of key government ministries and departments. For *mhoent boe*, the bribe is paid by using a large container of imported cookies or biscuits, *mhoent boans* in Burmese, stuffed with cash worth millions of kyats or gold or gems. The container is privately carried and delivered by the briber or the briber's agent as a gift to the wives or relatives of the officials at their private homes. It has been reported that sometimes the bribe takes the form of putting keys to one or more expensive modern automobiles into the cookie container as a gift at the wedding of the son or daughter of a military minister or a high-ranking government official. This practice cuts cross the entire spectrum of government administration.

FOREIGN EXCHANGE REGIME

The most widely noticed and criticized policy of SLORC by various analysts and foreign investors relates to the maintenance of a foreign exchange regime with a highly unrealistic official exchange rate (hovering around Kt6=US$1) that overvalues the Burmese currency, kyat, more than 20 times the free/black market exchange rate against the US dollar (Kt125=US$1) in 1996 and more than 30 times (Kt210=US$1) in 1997. Today, Burma is the only country in Southeast Asia that continues to relentlessly maintain such a rate and imposes strict foreign exchange controls by declaring the ownership and dealing in foreign exchange illegal. However, the government does not strictly enforce this law, as it permits the black market activities of buying and selling foreign exchange, especially the US dollar, at the going black market exchange rates in front of the Foreign Trading Bank, at the airport and bazaars, and in the streets of Rangoon and other major cities across the country. Consequently, the minister of national planning and development, Brigadier General Abel, and the finance minister Win Tin, expressed the view that the Burmese kyat is virtually devalued. This view is also held by the US Embassy: "In fact, however, the GOB (Government of Burma) has largely completed a gradual de facto devaluation of the kyat to market-determined exchange rate since the SLORC was formed in late 1988." [13]

The view of considering the government permission of parallel/black foreign exchange markets to exist and flourish as a de facto devaluation of the kyat is contrary to the accepted norm, meaning, and practice of devaluation in international finance. For one thing, the monetary authorities of Burma have not redefined or devalued the kyat in terms of the international standard money, the Special Drawing Right (SDR), or realigned its exchange rate with various foreign currencies of countries that are on a freely fluctuating exchange rate standard. For another, there is no free convertibility between foreign exchange and Burmese kyats at the official exchange rate for Burmese citizens. The primary reason that the Burmese government maintains an artificially fixed foreign exchange rate, which is overvalued more than 20 times the free market rate, has been to capture more foreign exchange from foreign investors and tourists. The main beneficiaries from the overvalued official exchange rate have been the state economic enterprises that form joint ventures with foreign investors, along with black market dealers and kingpins. The foreign investment capital in the joint ventures in key industries has to be paid in foreign exchange to the government at the overvalued official exchange rate. The net consequence of maintaining such a grossly overvalued official exchange rate was assessed by the International Monetary Fund (IMF): "Maintaining a grossly overvalued foreign exchange rate leads to inefficiencies in its use, adversely affects incentives to produce, reduces government revenue, and results in scarcities."[14]

In July 1996, the government practice of using the open or black market exchange rate instead of the official exchange rate in levying custom duties surfaced for the first time, causing the finance minister, Brigadier General Win Tin, to give a press conference on August 1, 1996, to deny the charge of this unfair practice by importers and defend the government's action. According to the minister: "Previously our custom tariffs were high, but in computing the assessed value of imported goods we applied the official exchange rate with the result that revenue collected was adversely affected." He went on to state: "On the other hand, the items are sold based on the unofficial rate. To be in accord with the policy of the market economy, custom duties were cut down to one-tenth (without specifying over 200 categories of custom tariffs imposed by the government) and arrangements are made to evaluate imported items on the open market rate." With respect to the impact of this action, a retired Burmese government's bank official with wide international experience observed:

Very recently, a rate of Kt100 to a dollar was used for custom duty and commercial tax calculations as well as for some official transactions. The inflationary impact of this change was mitigated to some extent by the lowering of tariffs. If this practice is extended to budgeting (no doubt accompanied by the raising of the budget deficits), it would represent a de facto devaluation of the Burmese kyat from 6 to 100 for a US dollar.

The obvious gainer from this action is the government in capturing more revenue, while the immediate losers are importers, and the ultimate losers are consumers of foreign products.

The reduction of custom duties by 10 percent represents only a minuscule fraction of the average open market exchange rate of Kt150 to US$1 in 1996, which is 25 times or 2,500 percent higher than the fixed official exchange rate of Kt6 to US$1. The net result has been a de facto increase in the custom duties rate by 22.5 times or 2,250 percent. This calculation is made by using the equation: (1-proposed percentage change in custom duties rate) times (the ratio of open market exchange rate to official exchange rate), which gives (1-.10)x25=22.5 or 2,250 percent. The intermediary importers or export-import companies are going to transfer this phenomenal increase in cost or tax burden of imports to the ultimate buyers or consumers of imported foreign goods by hiking the domestic prices to add more fuel to the already galloping inflation. It has been reported that in 1997 the official exchange rate of custom duty has been hiked to Kt180 to US$1 which would nearly double the effective custom duty rate presented above.

FOREIGN EXCHANGE CONTROLS

Strict foreign exchange controls are imposed by the two main state financial institutions of the Central Bank of Myanmar and the Myanma Foreign Trading Bank (MFTB) with respect to establishing the official exchange rate, foreign exchange transactions, and foreign exchange accounts of all foreign and Burmese nationals. The state control of foreign exchange is almost absolute despite the policy of allowing private citizens and companies to open foreign exchange accounts and use them under strict regulations of monetary authorities. Prior to 1996, all foreign exchange accounts are required to be kept at zero interest with the Myanma Foreign Trading Bank, the Myanma Economic Bank (MEB), the Myanma Investment and Commercial Bank (MICB), and other semi-state banks. In 1996, the government supposedly began allowing state and semi-state banks to pay interest on foreign exchange deposits and also a few private banks to deal in foreign exchange and pay interest on foreign exchange accounts. However, these unpublicized changes in the foreign exchange policy have not been fully enforced.

Since 1988, private citizens have no free access to, and use of, foreign exchange. For example, the maximum foreign exchange allowed to a Burmese national for ordinary and business travels abroad is limited to $15 and $65, respectively. Prior to 1993, the remittance of foreign exchange from abroad is controlled by allowing the recipient to withdraw on the spot 25 percent of the remittance in kyats translated at the official exchange rate of Kt6, compared with Kt120 to US $1, while the rest may be kept as a savings account at zero interest with the MFTB or can be redeemed at the official exchange rate. The use of the residual foreign exchange for purchase of foreign products is allowed with or without a license, depending on the type of import. Hence, most remittances from abroad are done through black market dealers at home and abroad.

The Central Bank of Myanmar, which sets the official exchange rate, and the MFTB, which is the main depository institution for all foreign exchange accounts of Burmese nationals and foreigners including the state economic enterprises, have total control over all foreign exchange flows into and out of Burma. The foreign exchange rate of the Burmese kyat against the US dollar was set at about Kt6.5 in 1990, which was more than 10 times overvalued relative to the black market rate of K70 or more per US dollar. The basic objective of this phenomenally unrealistic exchange rate was to capture a greater amount of foreign exchange by the state from service fees, taxes, and value of investments made by foreign firms. However, the main brunt of this irrational policy has been borne by native exporters in the phenomenal translation loss of their export proceeds in foreign exchange and inability to cover their costs of goods sold in kyats.

Apart from the MFTB, the second financial institution set up to control foreign exchange and trade is the Myanma Investment and Commercial Bank (MICB), which not only provides financial services for foreign exchange accounts but also makes local currency loans to both foreign and Burmese business enterprises. For example, if a local business firm acquires letters of credit from foreign business contacts for exports but lacks local funds to finance its operations, it can procure collaterized loans from that bank. The MICB would lend between 30 and 60 percent of the value of the collateral, depending on the type of collateral, such as gold or property. The credit lines are opened for these companies at an interest rate of between 12 and 25 percent. Not only private companies but also Burmese workers engaged by foreign firms who are paid in foreign exchange keep their accounts with this bank (a technician or doctor earns about between $500 and $1,000 a month, and a laborer $80–$100 a month). The formula applied for the use of their wages and salaries earned in foreign exchange is 25 percent in kyats immediately available, translated at the official exchange rate, and the rest may be used for purchase of foreign products sold in foreign exchange locally.

All exporters and importers are required to be registered at a fee, and a license must be applied for and approved by the Ministry of Trade. The registration fee is a minimum of Kt5,000 (roughly $769 at Kt6.5 per dollar) or more, depending on the product lines such as agricultural, animal, forest, and handicraft. Upon procuring a purchase order from a foreign buyer, a license must be secured at the cost of 5 to 30 percent of the value of export consignment, depending on the product. An additional service fee of a minimum Kt2,000 is imposed by the Inspection Agency Service (IAS) or Customs Department at the port of the shipment of goods. Every new consignment of export or import transaction must be applied for and approved by the Ministry of Trade and other state services, formerly called state corporations. Hence, all foreign exchange as well as trade inflows and outflows are under the direct surveillance and control of the Ministry of Trade and the Myanma Foreign Trading Bank.

BLACK/PARALLEL FOREIGN EXCHANGE MARKETS

The development of parallel markets for goods as well as foreign currencies is an aspect of the inefficiency of a centrally controlled dual economy. The black/parallel markets in Burma continue to persist due to trade and price controls, on one hand, and the foreign capital or foreign exchange controls imposed by the SLORC, along with the maintaining of artificially fixed foreign exchange rates, on the other.[15] The net consequence of the foreign exchange regime maintained by the government has been the development of black or parallel foreign exchange markets with phenomenal premia of free market foreign exchange rates over the artificially fixed official exchange rate.

In Burma today, there are three black markets for US dollars: (1) a personalized swap market for trading "black" US dollars or "greenbacks" as the Burmese traders call them (known as the *Hundi* system, which was used by Indian moneylenders in colonial Burma and throughout the Indian subcontinent, or the *Hawana*, or underground Chinese banking system, which is still being widely used throughout Asia), (2) a market for "white" dollars, and (3) a market for foreign exchange certificates (FEC), locally dubbed the "Burmese dollars." In the first market, the transfer of US dollars is made by an international network of *hundi* brokers/dealers serving as intermediaries for local buyers and sellers of dollars. The second market is made up of legal dollar deposits with state banks that entitle their owners to privately and legally transfer or sell their accounts to buyers of dollars at open or negotiated market rate of exchange. The third market developed due to the government introduction and declaration of foreign exchange certificates denominated in dollars as the second legal tender in 1993 that can be owned privately and used domestically.

DOLLARIZATION OF THE FINANCIAL SYSTEM

Dollarization signifies the displacement of a country's local currency by dollars in domestic pricing and trading of goods and services. This is happening in Burma today; everyone wants to spend or pass on "bad money," Burmese kyats, to someone else and receive and hold "good money," US dollars, as a store of value or wealth, indicating Gresham's law in operation. The US dollar has been used as a standard of value and a store of wealth in lieu of the kyat by the ruling elite as well as the public. Since 1988, the Burmese kyat has become bad money due to a lack of confidence, inept monetary policy of deficit financing by printing new banknotes, and the maintenance of an artificially fixed, unrealistic official exchange rate and strict foreign exchange controls by the government. The average black market exchange rate of the US dollar in the mid-1990s is over Kt120, compared with Kt6 to US$1 to indicate that the official exchange rate is 20 times overvalued.

The process of dollarization began in 1990, when foreign companies sold luxury consumer durable and household appliances at prices quoted and sold in dollars. Domestic private companies and even the state enterprises and state-owned shops began following the suit of foreign companies. The transactions conducted in dollars include the sale of new and reconditioned cars, gasoline, telephones, and foreign-manufactured consumer durables and the installation of phone connections at US$1,000 each and sale of cellular phones at $4,000 each by the Post and Telecommunication Department of the government. Buildings and apartments built by both state and private contractors are rented out in dollars to foreign companies and diplomats. The SLORC also passed a tax law requiring foreign firms and Burmese nationals who earned wages and salaries in dollars to pay their taxes in dollars.

FOREIGN EXCHANGE CERTIFICATES (THE BURMESE DOLLARS)

The dollarization of the Burmese economy was augmented further by the monetization of dollar-denominated foreign exchange certificates (FECs). On February 4, 1993, following the past Chinese example to capture foreign exchange from tourists, the Central Bank of Myanmar began issuing the 1, 5, and 10 US dollar-denominated FECs to boost foreign exchange earnings of the state and facilitate the exchange of hard currencies by tourists. These certificates were to be used only inside Burma and may be purchased with acceptable traveler's checks and Visa credit cards at Myanma Foreign Trading Bank, the airport's exchange counter, and other authorized agents. They were also decreed to be generally acceptable by any person in making them the second legal tender note, or "the Burmese dollar," as they are dubbed by the Burmese. They were to be freely convertible into other currencies at official exchange rates for use inside Burma. The Burmese citizens who came to own these certificates can hold them privately or deposit them in foreign exchange accounts with state banks. Under the old regulation, no one could hold foreign exchange without a license issued by the monetary authorities. The consequence has been the sale of foreign exchange acquired by Burmese citizens in the black market. The new regulation revoked this licensing requirement, supposedly giving freedom of foreign exchange ownership in the form of these certificates.[16] According to the government, this action was taken with the objective of eradicating the foreign exchange black marketeering; it also makes it easier for the government to monitor and control the private ownership of foreign exchange.

The new government regulation also required all foreign tourists to purchase a minimum of US$200 worth of certificates, which cannot be redeemed when leaving Burma. Any purchase above the minimum could be redeemed either in dollars or in pounds by presenting the proper receipts of the minimum US$200 certificates purchased. With the exception of local goods and services that are priced in dollars, the dollar cost of goods and services priced in kyats to a tourist remains high due to the possibility of obtaining kyats 20 times more than the official rate of exchange per dollar in the booming black market. Since the prevalent black market exchange rate is Kt120 to US$1, a tourist suffers an opportunity cost/translation loss of Kt113.75 per dollar exchanged or a total of Kt22,750 loss on the minimum $200 forced to exchange under the new law. For the military regime, it is a way of replenishing the dwindling foreign exchange reserves and monitoring the private ownership of foreign exchange. In March 1994, this minimum requirement was raised to Kt300 to capture more dollars from tourists. This requirement is a de facto forced conversion of US$300 into Burmese kyats at the official exchange rate of Kt6.25 for US$1. It also amounts to a tax or an entry fee imposed upon visiting Burma.

FECs received by a Burmese citizen can be deposited into the recipient foreign exchange account, or a recipient can open a new deposit account with a minimum of $100 worth of certificates at the state-owned MFTB or Myanma Investment and Commercial Bank (MICB) in accordance with the existing rules. In addition to not receiving any interest on the deposit, a holder of foreign exchange certificate accounts must pay a 10 percent service charge on the value of the deposit. The 25 percent of the remaining 90 percent of the deposit is no longer required to be exchanged into Burmese kyats as before. Prior to the issue of these certificates, a Burmese citizen could hold foreign exchange only with the foreign exchange acceptor/holder license issued by the Central Bank. Since any person is now allowed to hold FECs, the government has withdrawn the aforesaid licenses.

From these contrived rules and regulations, it can be seen that the single objective of the military junta is to generate foreign exchange earnings for the state in the form of collecting entry fees from foreign tourists and taxes imposed on Burmese depositors. Offsetting these fees and taxes is the advantage of owning and using these certificates over the use of rapidly depreciating Burmese kyats in buying goods, especially imported, foreign-manufactured goods that are being priced at the black market exchange rate for dollars.

A BLACK MARKET FOR FOREIGN EXCHANGE CERTIFICATES (BURMESE DOLLARS)

Since the dollar-denominated FECs have become the legal dollars that can be owned and used domestically in the purchase and sale of highly coveted foreign goods, they are demanded heavily relative to the black or illegal dollar (cash dollar) as a medium of exchange and store of value. Consequently, a black market for FECs has developed. In May 1993, the parallel exchange rate for one Burmese dollar is reported to be Kt108, compared with Kt117 for one illegal US dollar relative to the fixed official exchange rate of Kt6.265 for US$1. Initially, the reason for the higher rate of exchange for the illegal dollar was that it was more available and widely accepted in conducting foreign or border trade transactions. With time, the Burmese dollars have become more available, safer, and valuable to own and use as a legal tender inside Burma. Consequently, the gap between the two black market rates has narrowed, and during 1995 the black market rate for the Burmese dollar stood at Kt117, compared with Kt118 for an illegal dollar. During 1995, it has been reported that the free market price of FEC occasionally climbed above that of the black dollar to indicate the increased demand for FEC inside Burma.

The following table and chart indicate the phenomenal spreads between the average black market and official exchange rates for the period of 1988-1996, during which the black market premium of the US dollar jumped from 800 percent (40/5) to over 3,000 percent (184/6). It must be noted that the average black market exchange rate of the US dollar is an average rate of six different black markets or unofficial exchange rates; two different exchange rates of white and black dollars (green backs); two different FEC exchange rates (the official decreed exchange rate imposed by the authorities and enforced by military intelligence (MI) officers at the 10 licensed counters of Central FEC Exchange in Rangoon, satirically labeled by the Burmese as the MI rate, and the unofficial or illegal exchange rate offered by unlicensed dealers); and two privately negotiated rates of exchange used by exporters and importers in buying and selling goods. The following Table 3.1 and Figure 3.1 indicate the phenomenal spreads between the average black market and official exchange rates for the period 1988-1997.

Table 3.1
The Average Black Market and Official Exchange Rates of US Dollar

	1988	1989	1990	1991	1992	1993	1994	1995	1996	1997
US$1	Kt45	Kt60	Kt80	Kt122	Kt110	Kt117	Kt115	Kt120	Kt151	Kt210
Official	Kt5.00	Kt5.80	Kt6.62	Kt6.20	Kt6.30	Kt6.10	Kt6.10	Kt5.90	Kt5.90	Kt5.90

Sources: US Embassy, *Retail Prices of Selected Goods in Rangoon* (1988-1994); Burmese Magazines, *Dana* and *Myanma Dana;* the Economist Intelligence Unit (EIU), *Country Reports 2nd and 3rd Quarters, 1997* (London: EIU, 1997); and Private Information for 1996-1997.

The black market price of the US dollar has steadily climbed upward from Kt80 in 1990 to Kt120 in 1995, to Kt170 in November 1996 and all the way up to Kt300 in July 1997. The monthly fluctuations of the black market price of US dollar in 1994 and 1995 seemed to be somewhat stable and hovered around Kt120. The price of FEC followed the same trend as the dollar and both of them were reported to be around Kt168 in November 1996.[17] The average black market exchange rate of US dollar in the first half of 1996 was Kt136 to US$1 and the second half of 1996 was Kt165 to US$1 to give an average rate of Kt151 to US$1 for the year 1996, representing a 25 percent increase of black market exchange rate between 1995 and 1996.

Figure 3.1
Black Market Premium of US Dollar

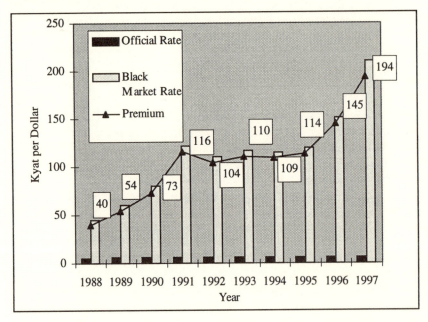

The phenomenal jump of the unofficial market price of the dollar and the FEC to Kt300 in July 1997 caused financial panic among traders and government officials. As in the past socialist era, the government blamed private foreign exchange dealers for the distress and raided FEC exchange counters and gold shops and arrested the heads of licensed FEC exchangers and dealers. In August, it was reported that the government imposed a quota of $10 FECs per person in the sale of FEC by money changers. Due to this action, the price of both the dollar and the FEC temporarily settled back down to below Kt300. However, in mid-December 1997, the unofficial price of both the dollar and the FEC began to climb above Kt300, reaching up to Kt380 at the end of December to indicate the ineffectiveness of the stop-gap measure of the authorities in stabilizing the value of Burmese kyat in the parallel foreign exchange market.

Based on monthly exchange rates, the average unofficial exchange rate of 1997 was Kt210 to US$1, representing a 39 percent increase from the previous year. The premium of the black market exchange rate over the official exchange rate of US dollar has increased from twenty times to thirty times in the post-1996 period. The prodigious jumps in the unofficial market price of both US dollar and FEC in 1996 and 1997 occurred in a climate of intensified sociopolitical unrest, the upsurge of renewed political protest, two terrorist bomb explosions, an increased crackdown of opposition groups, US new investment sanctions, the fear of potential devaluation and demonetization of kyat notes, and above all, the contagion effect of the regional financial crisis of Asia.

On the supply side, the inflows of both legal and illegal dollars seemed to have declined greatly due to a sharp decline in rice exports, a number of halts in cross-border trade between Burma and Thailand due to the closing of border outposts, withdrawal or divestment of a number of Western companies, and a drop in the number of tourists and a decline in the foreign exchange earnings of hotels and the tourist industry. On the demand side, the excess demand for dollar continued to increase as Burmese importers bought dollars to hedge against the foreign exchange risk, and foreign exchange speculators and dealers rushed to buy and accumulate dollars for arbitrage profit. This excess demand was augmented further by the government's inept monetary policy of introducing and putting into circulation a large quantity of FECs. At the same time, the Central Bank of Myanmar has been financing the mounting government deficit by printing and putting more and more worthless kyat notes with new denominations into circulation or into the hands of the public who, frenziedly buy and hoard dollars and foreign exchange certificates.

According to the International Monetary Fund (IMF): "Thus, as the Government's recourse to bank financing expanded significantly, monetary expansion accelerated sharply from 23 percent in 1993/1994 to 39 percent in 1994/1995." [18] From all indications, the monetary expansion continued into the ensuing years. Burmese citizens and economic magazines reported phenomenal jumps in the prices of rice, gasoline, and other basic necessities throughout 1996. Burma's inflation rate of 21.8 percent may be contrasted with inflation rates of its prosperous neighbors, Singapore's 1.2 percent, Malaysia's 3.8 percent, and Thailand's 5.6 percent in 1996.[19] The cause of the 25 percent increase of the Burmese black market exchange rate for US dollars from Kt120 in 1995 to Kt150 in 1996 can also be explained in terms of the purchasing power parity condition or theorem. Using the purchasing power parity equation (the percentage change of Burmese exchange rate=the Burmese inflation rate-the US inflation rate divided by 1+US inflation rate), the change of Burmese exchange rate is 18 percent. The Burmese inflation rate and the US inflation rate were 21.8 percent and 3 percent respectively, in 1995/1996. It should be noted that the 21.8 percent Burmese inflation rate reported by the government is grossly understated, and private estimates run as high as 60 percent.

The Burmese government also imposes ceilings of less than 17 percent on the lending rates of interest charged by private banks and lenders. Since the inflation rate estimated by outside observers and analysts is between 40 percent and 60 percent, Burma's legal real rate of interest is deeply negative, which should produce a decrease in the Burmese foreign exchange rate in light of the interest parity theorem. However, the illegal interest rates in Burma have been reported to be several times above the interest rate ceilings imposed by the government to make the Burmese nominal interest rates phenomenally higher than those of its neighbors and cause the persistent increase in the Burmese unofficial/black market foreign exchange rate. It has been reported that in the rural areas, private moneylenders charge an interest rate of 10 percent per month or 120 percent per annum for loans without collateral and 5 percent per month or 60 percent per annum for collateralized loans.[20]

Thus, the international Fisher effect or the combined purchasing power and interest parity conditions seemed to prevail in Burma between 1995 and 1996. That is, as a result of the government's inept monetary and fiscal policies, the inflation rate and nominal interest rate differentials between Burma and the United States and also its prosperous neighboring countries have widened greatly to cause the prodigious jump in the Burmese black market foreign exchange rate for the US dollar. However, in the absence of developed modern money and capital markets as well as the freedom of capital movement, the international Fisher effect is less important in the explanation of the rise in the Burmese foreign exchange rate. Basically, the accelerated rise in the Burmese inflation rate precipitated by the political instability and monetary expansion or the worsening of the purchasing power parity condition for Burma may be construed as the main explanation for the prodigious rise in the Burmese black market exchange rate for the US dollar since 1988.

In December 1995, the government opened up a central foreign exchange center with 10 counters in Rangoon to participate in the unofficial FEC black market by buying and selling FECs at the going black market rates. Since then, several FEC changers have been licensed to perform the same function. According to the government, the objective of this action was supposedly to eradicate the foreign exchange black market and stabilize the value of the kyat. Unlike the previous issuance of FECs to foreign tourists in exchange for dollars they brought into Burma, the government now seems to be printing and selling the FECs to money changers with no dollar backing or reserves of any kind. The consequence seems to be an increase in the money supply to add more fuel to the inflation and, in tandem, further depreciation of the kyat against the dollar and the FEC in the black market.

As long as the government continues to maintain a foreign exchange regime with no convertibility between kyats and dollars as well as the FECs at the official exchange rate of Kt6 to one dollar, excess demand conditions for dollars and FECs will prevail and continue to perpetuate black markets. Apparently, the Burmese government did not learn from its Chinese mentor's experience that using FECs to capture foreign exchange was an economic blunder to stabilize its currency. The value or strength of a nation's currency lies not in the power of the state to create new monetary notes and interfere with the functioning of a free and open market economy but in its ability to promote genuine economic growth and confidence of the people.

Further evidence of lack of trust or low value of Burmese currency can be found at the booming cross-border trade, where foreign exporters refuse to accept kyats for the payment of goods by Burmese importers. Consequently, most cross-border trade has been conducted on the basis of countertrade agreements or barter. The transactions involving currency or credit swaps require Burmese traders to deal in the unofficial foreign exchange centers/markets at the border. The value of the Burmese kyat at the border relative to currencies of neighboring countries further indicates phenomenal gaps between the official and unofficial rates of exchange. A detailed account of these gaps is presented in the later chapter on Burma-China cross-border trade.

ECONOMIC GROWTH: GROSS DOMESTIC PRODUCT, PER CAPITA INCOME, AND GROWTH RATES

Official reports tend to support the perception of foreign visitors to Rangoon and Mandalay that newly constructed hotels, high-rise buildings, and roads built with forced labor and foreign capital have propelled the Burmese economy into a rapid recovery and a near-boom in the 1990s. The military cabinet ministers and certain members of SLORC, David Abel and Khin Nyunt, for example, have been reporting in the news media, claiming the phenomenal performance of the "open-door market-oriented economy of Myanmar" under its management in the mid-1990s. The year 1992/1993 was proclaimed as "the Year of the Economy" with a 10.9 percent real GDP growth rate (later revised down to 9.8 percent), and 1993/1994 was the "Second Year of the Economy" with a projected real GDP growth rate of 8.5 percent (later revised down to 6 percent). The SLORC further proclaimed and envisioned the fiscal year 1994/1995 (April to March) to be "All-round Development Year" with a growth rate of 7 percent (later revised upward to 7.5 percent) and gave a targeted growth rate of 7.7 percent (later revised upward to 9.8 percent) for 1995/1996 with even more ambitious projects and objectives of economic growth.[21]

The most dramatic statement of spectacular economic growth and prosperity attained under the economic reforms of the military government was made by foreign minister Ohn Gyaw at the UN General Assembly meeting on September 27, 1996:

The Government (SLORC) has initiated economic reforms aimed at transforming the centrally-planned economy into a market-oriented one. The economic reforms are bearing fruit and has led to sustained growth. In the past 4 years the economy recorded an average growth rate of 8.2 percent resulting in increased employment opportunities and significantly rising living standards in the country, primarily in urban areas where private enterprises are flourishing, and in fertile rural areas where farmers have better incentives to grow and market their produce.[22]

It should be pointed out that his claim of 8.2 percent average growth rate for the period between 1992/1993 and 1995/1996 was made by revising the real GDP growth rates upward for the years 1993/1994 and 1994/1995 to 6 percent and 7.5 percent, respectively, and projecting a growth rate of 9.8 percent for 1995/1996.[23] The initial growth rates given in the 1995 official report for

1993/1994 and 1994/1995 were 5.9 percent and 6.8 percent.[24] Against his claim on increased employment opportunities and improved living standards in the urban areas, the Asian Development Bank assessed: "While data on a national basis are not available, partial surveys suggest that unemployment and underemployment are widespread on a seasonal basis and that underemployment in urban areas is pervasive."[25]

In July 1996 the US State Department and the US Embassy came out with reports on the economic conditions and performance of Burma that poked a deep hole into the stories of spectacular economic growth and prosperity attained for the people of Burma claimed by the SLORC. The report by the US Embassy assessed: "Governance in Burma is opaque and unaccountable. Declining real government wages exacerbate pervasive corruption," and "Burma's recent rates of real GDP growth may prove unsustainable in the medium and long terms" as "legal merchandise trade deficit (excluding military imports) grew from USD 412 million (in 1990/91) to USD 737 million (in 1994/95), gross legal investment declined from about 21 percent to 18 percent of legal GDP, foreign direct investments from 9.3 percent to 5 percent of legal GDP, the government's external arrears nearly doubled to USD 1.5 billion, and its stock of external debt (excluding debts for military imports) grew to USD 5.5 billion."[26]

Infuriated with the US critical reports, Burma's minister of national planning and economic development, Brigadier General David Abel, whose name came to fame with the so-called Burmese Way to Capitalism, in a press conference lashed out at the United States by denouncing the US reports as flimsy with an attempt "to cause mischief and to discredit the SLORC in its very successful economic endeavor and Nation-building programme." He also indicted the US reports as "fictitious political stories in trying to convince the public with inauthentic figures that have no statistical basis." Amidt these charges by the United States and counter charges by the SLORC on the reliability and transparency of macroeconomic data lies the truth that in Burma there is no true or transparent information except the information provided by what Orwell called the Ministry of Truth. Hence, there are two diametrically opposed reports on the economic performance and conditions of Burma: the good by the state and its lobbyists, on one hand, and the bad and the bleak by some foreign analysts and dissident Burmese nationals, on the other.

There are a number of problems in assessing the economic performance of Burma: (1) lack of accurate and reliable statistical data, (2) excruciating technical problems in translating the macroeconomic data of government expressed in Burmese kyats into equivalent US dollars due to phenomenal spreads between the official and unofficial/black market exchange rates, and (3) intentional manipulation of data for political purposes by the government. All these problems are the result of lack of transparency and freedom of information in the state of Myanmar. The following are the GDP data given by the government. Table 3.2 gives the GDP data given by the government.

In 1997, the MNPED came out with the new or revised GDPs at constant prices for the years 1994/1995 and 1995/1996 and the provisional figure for 1996/1997 which drastically changed the real GDP growth rates. Based upon the very data of the government, the average real GDP growth rate for the four-year period from 1992/1993 to 1995/1996 would be reduced from the exaggerated figure of 8.2 percent, which was reported by Foreign Minister Ohn Gyaw at the UN General Assembly September meeting in 1996 mentioned previously to 7.5 percent. Based on this new data of government, the average real GDP growth rate from 1990 to 1996 is 5.1 percent.

Table 3.2

GDP at Current and Constant 1985/86 Prices (Millions of kyats)

	1989/90	1990/91	1991/92	1992/93	1993/94	1994/95	1995/96	1996/97
Current prices	124,666	151,941	186,802	249,395	360,321	473,153	613,169	715,400
Constant Price (1985/86)	48,883	50,260	49,933	54,757	58,064	62,406	66,710	70,586
Real GDP Growth Rate*	3.7	2.8	-0.7	9.7	6.0	7.5	6.9	5.8

*The real GDPs and growth rates for 1995/96 and 1996/97 are provisional actual and provisional
Sources: Ministry of National Planning and Economic Development (MNPED), *The Union of Myan-mar, Review of the Financial, Economic and Social Conditions for 1996/1997* (Yangon: MNPED, 1997), pp. 23–25.

Based on these government data, the growth of current GDP from Kt124.666 billion in 1988/1989 to Kt613.169 billion in 1995/1996 represents a nominal growth rate of 30.4 percent, and the growth of real GDP from Kt48.883 billion in 1988/1989 to Kt68.528 in 1995/1996 represents an annual growth rate of 5.8 percent for the six-year period. In terms of Fisher's equation (real growth rate=nominal rate-inflation rate), the real GDP growth rate of 5.8 percent suggests an implicit assumption of 24.8 percent inflation rate.

These growth rates and the growth rate of 9.8 percent for the year 1995/1996 are grossly exaggerated by virtue of the fact that the deflator used by the government is based upon the grossly underestimated inflation rate assumption of less than 25 percent in contrast to the two privately estimated inflation rates of between 40 percent and 60 percent by some foreign analysts. For example, the Asian Development Bank (ADB) observed that the "unofficial inflation in some cases was two to three times that of the official figures."[27] Using the conservative estimate of 40 percent inflation rate, the real GDP growth rates reported by the government would be cut down to substantially lower rates of growth, averaging less than 3 percent a year since 1988/1989.

With respect to the underestimation of inflation rate by the Burmese government, the US Embassy in Rangoon observed:

The GOB (Government of Burma) generates three sets of published data describing aggregate price movements in Burma; A GDP deflator based on diverse sectoral producer price deflators; an index of consumer prices in Rangoon (Rangoon CPI); and household expenditure survey data for Rangoon and Mandalay. All these aggregate price indicators are flawed and understated the true magnitude of price inflation from FY 89/90 through FY 94/95.[28]

The main reason for this underestimation given by the World Bank and the IMF is that the government Rangoon CPI is based on a lower-income basket of basic necessities in FY 1985/1986, including no imported goods, which made up a large portion of an urban family's expenditures.[29]

The unreliability of government reports and shortage of empirical data on the true performance of the economy continue to persist in Burma today. For example, except for occasional confidential reports, the UN, the IMF, and the World Bank have not published Burma's annual macroeconomic statistical data for public use since 1988, with the exception of the World Bank Report *Myanmar Policies for Sustaining Economic Reform*, October 1995. Even the World Bank and the IMF reports relied heavily on the government statistical data and did not provide the dollar value of per capita GDP or national income to determine whether or not Burma has elevated from its 1987 least-developed country status. For 1994/1995, the government reported a real per capita income of Kt1,335 (at 1985/1986 constant producers' prices) or $222.5 at the official exchange rate of Kt6=$1.[30] This suggests that Burma is no longer a least-developed country since its per capita income has climbed above the United Nations' benchmark of $200. Using the average unofficial/black market exchange rate of Kt120=$1 in 1995, Burma's real per capita income was only $11.125, to unrealistically make Burma the poorest nation on earth.

Even if one accepts the opaque government macroeconomic data, there is an excruciating problem of the choice of "a correct exchange rate" in deriving the dollar value of Burma's macroeconomic performance to evaluate its least-developed country status. The exchange rate used by the UN and the UNDP in transforming the local currency values of GDP, GNP, and per capita income of various less-developed countries into dollars is the controversial purchasing power parity dollar (PPP$). Neither the World Bank nor the IMF has published the dollar values of Burma's GDP, GNP, and per capita income since 1988. The UNDP *1995 Human Development Report* gave Burma's real GDP per capita in 1992 and 1993 as PPP$751 and PPP$650.[31] Up until 1996, the exchange rate used by the United States in determining the GDP per capita of Burma seems to be the unrealistic official exchange rate, which gave a figure of around $900. However, in 1996 the US Embassy's *Foreign Economic Trend Report: Burma, 1995* gave more realistic figures of Burma's legal money GDP per capita in 1994/1995 as $113, illegal GDP per capita, including extralegal and uncompensated sectors, as between $200 and $300, and a GDP per capita figure of between PPP$600 and PPP$800.[32] All of these inconsistent figures show that nobody knows with absolute certainty what Burma's GDP per capita is since 1988 to assess its development status.

According to *The Asia Week* magazine, Burma's nominal per capita GDP in 1995 was PPP$676, which was well below the respective figures of most Asian countries. This figure may be contrasted with the per capita GDPs of the ASEAN countries: Singapore's PPP$20,470, Brunei's PPP$15,580, Malaysia's PPP$8,630, Thailand's PPP$6,390, Indonesia's PPP$3,140, and Philippines' PPP$2,660. It also indicates that Burma is poorer than the relatively poor countries of Southeast Asia, Laos, Cambodia, and Vietnam, whose per capita GDPs were given as PPP$2,071, PPP$1,266 and PPP$1,263.[33] The implied exchange rate used in translating the Burmese kyat into PPP $ is Kt14.7=PPP$1, since the nominal per capita GDP reported by the Burmese government in 1995 was Kt9,936 and its equivalent PPP dollar value given by *The Asia Week* was PPP$676. Using this exchange rate, the 1995 nominal per capita income of Kt9,626 reported by the Burmese government would result in PPP$654.8. However, using the same exchange rate, the 1995 real per capita income of Kt1,335 reported by the government is only PPP$90.8 (1,335/14.7) to indicate that Burma retains its least-developed country status with a real per capita income of below PPP$200.

Figure 3.2 on the dollar value of GDP at current prices shows how different assessments or claims can be made on the value and growth of GDP by using a more or less fixed official exchange rate at Kt6=$1 and steadily rising black market exchange rates.

As pointed out before, using the average official exchange rate of Kt6=$1, the growth of real GDP between 1989 and 1996 was 5.8 percent. However, using the black market exchange rates of Kt54=$1 in 1988/1989 and Kt120=$1 in1994/1995, the growth of current or nominal GDP from $1.466 billion in 1988/89 to $3.637 billion in 1994/1995 represents an average annual growth rate of 16 percent and a real GDP growth rate of negative 14 percent in terms of the Fisher equation and assuming 25 percent inflation rate of the government. Different growth rates of real GDP based on different inflation rates and exchange rate assumptions simply highlight the technical problem and the unreliability of government statistical data.

Although it is statistically quite insignificant, evidence of the manipulation of data by the Burmese government can be seen in the report of underestimated population growth rates to overstate the growth rates of per capita real GDP (Table 3.3).

Figure 3.2
Current GDP at Official and Black Market Exchange Rates

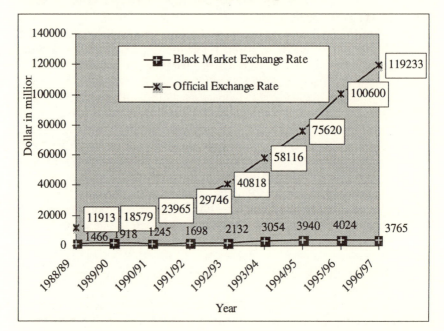

Source: Ministry of National Planning & Economic Development (MNPED), The Union of Myanmar,
Review of the Financial, Economic & Social Conditions for 96/97 (Yangon: MNPED, 97), p. 23.

Table 3.3
Government Data on Per Capita GDP, Population, and Growth Rates

	1988/89	1989/90	1990/91	1991/92	1992/93	1993/94	1994/95	1995/96
Nominal per capita GDP	1,940	3,114	3,725	4,496	5,891	8,357	10,764	13,490
Real per capita GDP	1,200	1,221	1,232	1202	1,293	1,347	1,421	1,491
Real per capita GDP Growth Rate		1.8	.9	-2.4	7.6	4.0	5	5
Population in mil.	39.29	40.03	40.79	41.55	42.33	43.12	43.92	44.74
Population Growth Rate		1.88	1.88	1.88	1.88	1.87	1.87	1.84

Source: Ministry of National Planning and Economic Development (MNPED), *The Union of Myanmar, Review of the Financial, Economic and Social Conditions for 1996/1997* (Yangon: MNPED, 1997), pp. 23-26.

There is no consistent and dependable figure of Burma's population to arrive at the true values of GDP per capita and its growth rates in the 1990s. The government report gave mid-year population figures of 43.92 million in 1995 and 44.74 million in 1996.[34] On the other hand, the UN *Demographic Year Book* and the World Bank's *World Development Report 1996* gave a 1994 mid year population estimate of 45.6 million, which is greater than the government figures for 1995 and 1996, and the US CIA *World Fact Book* gave an estimate of Burma's population in July 1995 of 45.103 million. However, the World Bank, the IMF, and the US Embassy used approximately the Burmese government data in reporting a population figure of between 43.5 million and 43.9 million in 1995.[35] It should also be noted that the last census taken by the government was back in 1983. Also, since 1988 the government has no complete control over what are called "gray" and "black areas" that are under the control of armed insurgents. These areas are the habitat of an ethnic minority population that is estimated to be one-third and even one half of Burma's total population. There are no exact or reliable statistics on the number of ethnic minority people in these areas as well as hundreds of thousands of refugees and migrant workers living and working in the borderlands and in the neighboring countries. In short, no one, including the Burmese government, knows exactly what Burma's population is in the 1990s.

According to the government data, the average growth rate of per capita real GDP between 1989 and 1995 was 2.72 percent (from Kt1,200 to Kt1,410). This is based on the government assumption of two constant population growth rates: 1.88 percent between 1989 and 1993 and 1.87 percent between 1994 and 1995.[36] These growth rates of less than 2 percent are contrary to the 2.2 percent growth rate for the 1960–1992 period and the projected rate of 2.1 percent for the rest of the 1990s reported by the United Nations Development Programme.[37] By keeping the population growth rate constant or declining and, at the same time, reporting phenomenal rates of growth of real GDP in the mid-1990s, the government can report higher per capita GDPs and growth rates or can proclaim the success of its economic reforms.

The indisputable evidence of Burma's continuation as an agricultural economy and its remaining one of the least-developed countries in the world can be seen in the unaltered distribution of sectoral contributions to GDP with the agricultural sector's contribution remaining dominant and constant at around 38 percent of GDP between 1988 and 1994, climbing to over 50 percent in 1995, while the contribution of the manufacturing sector remains stagnant at below 10 percent of the GDP since 1988—one of the benchmarks used by the United Nations in granting a least-developed country status. As of 1995, the sectoral contributions to GDP are 53.4 percent by agriculture, 23.4 percent by wholesale and retail, 7.3 percent by manufacturing and mining, 6.2 percent by livestock, fishery, and forestry, 2.7 percent by transportation and communication, 2 percent by construction and utilities, and .2 percent by banking and finance.[38]

NOTES

1. See *The New Light of Myanmar*, Yangon, September 17, 1993.

2. International Monetary Fund (IMF), *Myanmar, Recent Economic Developments* (Washington, DC: IMF, October 11, 1995), p. 10.

3. The World Bank, *Myanmar, Policies for Sustaining Economic Reform* (Washington, DC: October 1995), p. 53.

4. See the Government of the Union of Burma, *Notification No. 7/90* (Yangon: Ministry of Trade, February 19, 1990).

5. Joseph Silverstein, "Some Thoughts upon and Recommendations for a U.S. Policy toward Burma (Myanmar)," a paper prepared and presented for the US House of Representatives Committee on Foreign Affairs Hearing on US Policy toward Burma and Southeast Asia, Washington, DC, March 25, 1993, p. 8.

6. Foreign Broadcasting Information Service (FBIS), *Burma* (Washington, DC: October, 28, 1991, p. 28.

7. Government of the Union of Myanmar, *Myanmar Export/Import Rules and Regulations for Private Business Enterprises (1994)* (Yangon: Directorate of Trade, July 1994), p. 38.

8. SLORC, *Myanmar, the Nation-Building Activities; The Historical Chronicle of the Works of SLORC from 1988 to 1991* (in Burmese) (Rangoon: Ministry of Information, December 20, 1991), p. 225.

9. US Embassy, *Burma, Country Commercial Guide 1998* (Rangoon: US Embassy, 1998), p. 18.

10. *The Working People's Daily*, September 11, 1990, p. 1.

11. *The Working People's Daily*, September 1, 1990, p. 8.

12. *The Working People's Daily*, May 22, 1991.

13. US Embassy, *Foreign Economic Trend, Burma* (Rangoon: US Embassy, July 1, 1996), p. 55.

14. The World Bank's Country Report, *CEM Update Myanmar* (Washington, DC: The World Bank, privately published, September 13, 1990), p. iii.

15. See Pierre-Richard Agénor, "Parallel Currency Markets in Developing Countries: Theory, Evidence, and Policy Implications," *Essays in International Finance*, no. 188 (Princeton University, International Finance Section, November 1992) p. 2.

16. See *The Working People's Daily*, January 28, 1993.

17 *Dana* (Wealth in Burmese), vol. 7, no. 2 (November 1996).

18. IMF, *Myanmar*, p. 14.

19. *Asiaweek*, March 3, 1996, p. 60.

20. David Dapice, *Landlessness, Poverty, and the Environment in Myanmar: Can Grass Roots Initiatives Create Sustainable Progress?, A Report to the United Nations Development Programme* (Cambridge: Harvard Institute of International Development (HIID), February 10, 1995), p. 5.

21. The Ministry of National Planning and Economic Development (MNPED), *The Union of Myanmar, Review of the Financial, Economic and Social Conditions for 1994/1995 and 1995/1996* (Yangon: MNPED, 1995, 1996).

22. Ohn Gyaw, *Statement by His Excellency U Ohn Gyaw, Minister of Foreign Affairs and Chairman of the Delegation of the Union of Myanmar* (New York: Permanent Mission of the Union of Myanmar to the UN, September 17, 1996), p. 5.

23. MNPED, *Review 1995/96,* p. 32.

24. MNPED, *Review 1994/95* , pp. 23–24.

25. Asian Development Bank (ADB), *Asian Development Outlook, Myanmar* (Manila ADB, 1996), p. 147.

26. US Embassy, *Burma, Country Commercial Guide* (Rangoon: US Embassy, July 1996), p. 5.

27. ADB, *Asian Development Outlook,* p. 146.

28. US Embassy, *Foreign Economic Trend,* p. 60.

29. Ibid., p. 61.

30. MNPED, *Review 1994/1995,* p. 12.

31. United Nations Development Programme (UNDP), *Human Development Report 1995* and *1996* (New York: Oxford University Press, 1995, 1996), pp. 157, 145.

32. US Embassy, *Foreign Economic Trend,* p. 107.

33. *Asia Week,* March 3, 1995, p. 47.

34. MNPED, *Review 1994/95,* p. 24.

35. U.S. Embassy, *Foreign Economic Trend,* p. 107.

36. MNPED, *Review 1995/96,* p. 18.

37. UNDP, *Human Development Report 1995,* p. 187.

38. Economist Intelligence Unit (EIU), *Country Report, Myanmar (Burma)* 2nd Quarter 1997 (London: EIU, 1997), p. 5.

4

Inflation, Monetary, and Fiscal Policies

Like many underdeveloped countries of the Third World, Burma's financial system is in a state of infancy with respect to lack of modern financial intermediaries or institutions, financial instruments, and markets. It is structured on the basis of a centralized state banking system with a network of banks owned and controlled by the state operating in various sectors of the economy. The socialist legacy of centralized state banking and control of the financial system continues to persist, although a number of private commercial banks have been allowed to open and operate in 1993 under the military regime. Among the 10 duties, functions, and powers of the Central Bank of Myanmar stipulated in *The SLORC: The Central Bank of Myanmar Law* passed on July 2, 1990, the most prominent ones are the issuance of ban notes and coins to finance the expenditures of the SLORC, the government ministries, and state enterprises and the power to set the external value or the foreign exchange rate, the interest rate ceilings, and control of foreign exchange.[1] In short, the Central Bank of Myanmar and three other state-owned banks, the Myanma Foreign Trading Bank (MFTB), the Myanma Economic Bank (MEB), and the Myanma Investment and Commercial Bank (MICB), which is a subsidiary of MEB, along with the Myanma Agricultural and Rural Development Bank (MARDB), function jointly to control the entire banking and financial system of Burma, including foreign exchange and foreign capital movements.

Despite the changes in the names of state-owned banks, the banking system of Burma remains rigidly centralized, and the state-owned banks remain the major lenders in urban and rural communities. For example, the State Commercial Banks are renamed as Myanma Investment and Commercial Banks and Myanma Economic Banks to provide commercial, mortgage, and industrial loans to businesses and households in the urban communities, while the Myanma Agricultural and Rural Development Bank and the State Agricultural Banks of past socialist era are renamed as Myanma Agricultural Banks to provide credits and loans to farmers in the rural areas. The inefficiency and inability of this highly centralized state banking system to fulfill the demand for credit continue to persist, causing the government to repossess homes, land, and mortgages or to write off the arrears of unpaid loans. The credit need of the people that the private and government banks cannot fulfill in both rural and urban communities has been supplied by private moneylenders and pawnshops, which charge interest rates that are several times higher than the private and government bank lending rates.

In spite of the three banking laws, the Central Bank of Myanmar Law, the Financial Institutions Law, and the Myanmar Agricultural and Rural Development Law, passed in 1990 to promote various financial institutions, the development of a modern financial system with private financial institutions in Burma is in its infancy, lagging behind most of the neighboring countries. The majority of economic and financial transactions are expedited on a cash and personal basis throughout the country. Using checks and depositing funds with banks are exceptions rather than the rule, and there are no institutionalized money and capital markets for savings and investment outlets for the people. As in the past, the financial system of Myanmar is run by the state with thousands of government and semigovernment banks in both urban and rural areas. Apart from the four main government-owned banks, there are four semigovernment or state-private joint venture banks: the Myanma Citizen's Bank, the Co-operative Bank, the Myawaddy Bank, and the Yangon/Rangoon City Bank. The Myanma Citizen's Bank is backed by state-private joint venture corporations, the Co-operative Bank is backed by the state-sponsored cooperatives, the Myawaddy Bank is backed by the military, and the Yangon City Bank is backed by the Yangon/Rangoon City Development Committee or city government. Up until 1996, government banks and these four semigovernment banks were the only ones allowed to have foreign exchange accounts and deal in foreign exchange, although the government stated that "some private banks were allowed to engage in foreign exchange transactions."[2] In 1997, it was reported that the government allowed some seven private banks to deal in foreign exchange.

According to the government, there are some 17 domestic private banks, considering the four semistate banks as private, which were established since 1993. The 13 truly private domestic banks are the First Private, the National, the Yadanabon, the Yoma, the Myanma Mayflower, the Tun Foundation, the Kanbawza (at Taungyi), the Prime Commercial, the Myanmar Oriental, the Asia Wealth, the Myanmar Universal, the Myanma Eastern Division, and the Asian Yangon International Bank. The latest one is the USDA Bank, which is in the process of formation and was already preapproved by the state. It should also be noticed that almost all of these banks are housed in the city of Rangoon.

Among the semigovernment banks, the most famous is the Myawaddy Bank, privately labeled as the Military Bank, which is under the control of the Union of Myanmar Economic Holdings Company (UMEHC), whose formation and control by the Ministry of Defense were presented previously. Apart from the Myawaddy Bank, the military reportedly owned and controlled five or more private banks. Foreign banks were given license to open some 29 representative offices. Among them are six Thai, five Singaporean, four French, three Malaysian, one Indonesian, one Japanese, one Canadian, one Cambodian, one Hong Kong, one British, and one Bangladesh bank representatives.

The most glaring inept monetary policy of the Central Bank of Myanmar is in the regulation of interest rates in setting the maximum and minimum limits that a private bank can borrow and lend. In July 1992, the maximum interest rate payable on savings deposits/accounts was raised from 8 percent to 10 percent, and the rate on savings certificates was raised from 10.9 percent to 12 percent. Before 1995, an interest ceiling of 16.5 percent was imposed on the commercial bank lending rate. In January 1995, the Central Bank of Myanmar raised its discount rate from 11 percent to 12.5 percent and set the commercial bank lending rate at the minimum of not less than 3 percent and the maximum ceiling of 6 percent above the discount rate or the minimum 9.5 percent and the maximum lending rate of 18.5 percent. In addition, potential borrowers at that rate have to put up a collateral in fixed assets worth 200 percent of the loan, with the maximum maturity set at one year.

The following account of abnormally low profit made by private banks in 1994 is reported in the Burmese economic magazine *Dana*:

According to the Banking Regulation, 5 percent of the amount of savings deposits in a bank must be kept with the Central Bank of Myanmar. However, a bank cannot lend out the entire 95 percent of the amount of the savings deposit. Due to the need of minimum cash balance, only about 85 percent can be lent out at the annual interest rate of 16.5 percent. Thus, the interest spread (the net interest revenue) between borrowing and lending rates is around 4 percent. Deducting the operating costs of 3 percent on the advancement of the loan, the net interest revenue is around 1 percent.[3]

The net interest margin or the net interest spread on earning assets of private banks is not known, and it may be estimated at less than 1 percent, to conclude that private banking in Burma since 1993 has been highly unprofitable. If one accepts the government report of a 30 percent average inflation rate in the 1990s, the maximum ceilings of less than 17 percent imposed by the Central Bank of Myanmar on the lending rate of private banks would produce an incredible negative real rate of interest earned by banks to make private banking utterly unprofitable.

With respect to the deeply negative bank lending rates and a lack of real reforms in the financial sector, US embassy correctly assessed:

However, several recent highly publicized reforms in the financial sector have proved largely illusory. In 1995, the GOB raised nominal bank lending rates to levels that were briefly positive in real terms for a few months in late 1995 and early 1996; however, they quickly became steeply negative as price inflation accelerated. In late 1995, the GOB also announced its intention to permit joint ventures between local and foreign banks; however, the GOB has reneged on its initial assurances that these joint venture banks would be allowed to handle international foreign currency transactions, and no such joint ventures are yet operating, due to a lack of interest on the part of foreign banks.[4]

The question then is, how are these newly formed private banks surviving without going bankrupt? The answer to this puzzle lies in the fact that, like many government regulations, the banking regulations either are not strictly enforced by the monetary authorities or are successfully evaded by private banks through bribery, connection, and engagement in illicit or underground banking activities to earn abnormal profit. As in the case of the foreign exchange black market presented before, government restrictions and regulations of legal banking have led to the development, or rather, revival, of the traditional private moneylenders, such as the private pawnshops owned and operated by ethnic Chinese and Sino-Burmese and many businesswomen of middle and upper-income class. These lenders lend money at open market-oriented rates and flexible terms on a cash basis. The monthly interest rate charged by them has been reported to be as high as 10 percent. In short, the real banking system in Burma today is the highly efficient and personalized traditional underground or *hawana* banking system with a network of domestic and overseas *hundi* dealers and lenders, fulfilling most of the short-term and long-term capital needs of borrowers for personal and business loans.

INFLATION

Inflation is one of the most pervasive and persistent economic problems of our times— one which we may have to live with for a long time to come. It is an old problem which plagued mankind since money was invented. At the same time it is also a new problem because it can never be solved once and for all.[5]

Inflation has plagued mankind and all nations irrespective of their stages of economic development. Although from long historical experiences and economic analysis, inflation is easy to understand with respect to its causes and damaging effects on the economic life of the people, there has been no universal agreement as to how to contain and cure it. The reason for this is that inflation is the result of a combination of causes. However, among the various causes of inflation, the one that has been stressed the most is the inappropriate or inept monetary and fiscal policies of government in financing excessive fiscal deficits by printing and putting new banknotes into circulation. Based on the experiences of South American countries, Harberger observed: "Most of major inflations in the postwar period have had their roots in excessive fiscal deficits which the government could only finance by resort to the printing press."[6] This has been the case in Burma under the SLORC. Since 1988, the annual rate of growth of currency in circulation (coins plus banknotes) is between 30 percent and 40 percent (Table 4.1).

Table 4.1
Currency in Circulation (September)

Year	(In billions of kyats)	% Growth rate
1988	12.1176	
1989	18.8575	56
1990	27.5104	46
1991	37.0988	35
1992	52.1980	41
1993	65.8634	26
1994	81.2402	23
1995	110.8660	36
1996*	151.0610	36

* Provisional

Source: Ministry of National Planning and Economic Development, *The Union of Myanmar, Review of the Financial, Economic and Social Conditions for 1995/1996* (Yangon: MNPED, 1996), p. 227.

Beginning in 1992, the government began reporting a decline of currency in circulation to indicate a seeming correction of its inept monetary policy of deficit financing by new money. This downward trend in the growth of currency in circulation in the post-1992 period may suggest a contractionary policy pursued by the state. In reality, this contraction has been somewhat offset by the introduction of new kyat notes. On March 27, 1994, the Central Bank of Myanmar put into circulation the newly denominated banknotes of Kt500, Kt100, Kt50, Kt20, and Kt.5 (50¢) in addition to the existing legal tender notes of Kt1, Kt5, Kt10, Kt15, Kt45, Kt90, and Kt200. With the introduction of these new notes, there were 12 different kyat notes in circulation. Including the $3 dollar-denominated foreign exchange certificates introduced in 1993 and another $20-denominated FEC introduced in 1996, Burma now has altogether 16 different banknotes in circulation, including the oddly denominated Kt45 and Kt90 notes introduced by General Ne Win to counter bad omens in 1987. That is, the Burmese currency, the kyat, has the largest number of denominations or banknotes with different denominations in the world. According to the minister of finance and revenue, Brigadier General Win Tin, the new banknotes issued in 1994 were made "in accordance with the normal banking practices" and for the purpose of "easy handling in line with the market-oriented economic system."[7]

The issuance of dollar-denominated foreign exchange certificates as a parallel legal tender since 1993 has added an additional factor to the expansion of money supply. The amount of FECs issued in 1992/1993, 1993/1994, 1994/1995 and 1995/1996 are $.8 million, $15.1 million, $52 million, and $149.2 million, respectively while FECs in circulation are $.33 million,

Table 4.2
M1(Currency in Circulation plus Deposits) (September)

	(In billions of kyats)	% Growth rate
1988	15.67	
1989	21.31	40
1990	30.006	50
1991	40.882	36
1992	57.009	39
1993	72.221	27
1994	88.898	23
1995	122.139	37
1996*	168.074	38

* Provisional

Source: International Monetary Fund (IMF), *Myanmar: Recent Economic Developments* (Washington, DC: IMF, February 14, 1997), p. 94.

$2.5 million, $6.7 million,and $9.1 million respectively for the same years.[8] Table 4.2 shows the sustained growth of M1 from 1988 to 1996.

Currency in circulation accounts for more than 90 percent of M1, while the average currency deposit ratio in the 1990s is a little over 200 percent, to indicate that the Burmese economy has been functioning primarily on the basis of cash with little use of checks or modern banking facilities by the majority of people.

M2 (M1 plus quasimoney) has also been growing at slightly higher rates than those of M1. According to the International Monetary Fund, growth rates of M2 between 1988 and 1996 are 32.3 percent (1989), 38.2 percent (1990), 34.5 percent (1991), 34.8 percent (1992), 28.9 percent (1993), 25.8 percent (1994), and 43 percent (1995), and 39.4 percent (1996).[9] The percent of quasimoney in M2 has been relatively small, constituting only about 5 percent of M2 in the 1990s to further indicate the relatively undeveloped money market in the financial system of Burma. An unknown amount of illegal dollars permitted by the state to circulate that is not included in the official figures of M1 has also been causing the expansion of the money supply, while lack of confidence in the kyat has produced a high velocity of circulation (GDP/M1) that averaged around 3.5 in the mid-1990s.[10] Consequently, given Burma's relatively low growth rate of output, inflation continues to soar at an accelerated rate.

In December 1995, another inept monetary measure was introduced by the government in the name of eradicating the black market and stabilizing the value of the kyat. The state opened up a central foreign exchange center with 10 counters in Rangoon to participate in the unofficial FEC black market by buying and selling FECs at the going black market rates. Several FEC changers were also issued licenses to perform the same function. This action was taken with the supposed objective of eradicating the foreign exchange black market and stabilizing the kyat. Unlike the previous issuance of FECs to foreign tourists in exchange for dollars they brought into Burma, the government seems to be printing and selling the FECs to money changers with no dollar backing or reserves of any kind. If the new FECs are printed and put into circulation for direct exchange of the existing Burmese kyats in circulation, the amount of currency in circulation will remain unchanged. However, it seems that the government has been printing and injecting both additional kyat notes and FECs for purposes other than the simple swap between kyats and FECs. Hence, the money supply has increased to add more fuel to inflation and, in tandem, further depreciation of the kyat against the dollar and the FEC in the black market.

The majority of the new banknotes printed by the Central Bank of Myanmar have been used to finance the increment of armed forces from 180,000 men in 1989 to over 300,000 men in 1995, extravagant expenditures on state religious and cultural festivals, and increased salaries and rewards of 27 appointed military cabinet ministers out of the 31-member cabinet, 11 military commanders promoted to the rank of lieutenant generals, and loyal civilian government officials. Next to defense expenditures, the most extravagant state spending has gone toward staging various state-sponsored cultural and religious festivals for political distraction, involving billions of kyats. Among the festivals are the traditional arts, music, and sport competition, pilgrimage to famous pagodas, and giving homage and alms to revered Buddhist monks by the Burmese generals, including the highly publicized parading of the relic of Buddha's tooth loaned by China across the country for the people to pay homage and give donations in 1994 and 1995.

Normally, economic development tends to be associated with rising prices, and ideally, it should occur with a minimum rise in prices. In most newly industrializing countries (NICs) or Asian Tigers and developing economies of the ASEAN, the rate of inflation tends to be either equal to, or slightly higher than, the rate of economic growth. For example, in the 1990s the reported inflation rates (the CPIs) of Asian Tigers have been below 6 percent, and the inflation rates (CPIs) of the ASEAN countries have been below 10 percent. On the other hand, the average inflation rate of between 25 percent and 30 percent reported by the Burmese government has been the highest among the Southeast Asian counties with the exception of Laos in 1996.[11] This rate of inflation is indicative of the inefficiencies and abnormalities in the functioning of the Burmese economy.

Low productivity or growth of output relative to rising or excessive aggregate demand has been the major determinant of the escalating inflation rate in Burma since 1988. Professor Minoru Kiryu, in his report on the Burmese economy to the United Nations Development Programme (UNDP) in 1992, listed five major economic factors responsible for the abnormal price increases in Burma: supply shortage or stagnation of domestic production, increases in production costs, the increase in money supply, overvaluation of the Burmese currency, and the dual price structure. In addition to these bottlenecks, he gave the additional social factors of distrust in the stability of the Burmese currency due to past demonetization measures, and the lack of timely and accurate information was also noted.[12]

THE ILL EFFECTS OF INFLATION

The basic ill effect of governmentally induced inflation in Burma has been the distortion of financial costs and relative prices. It produces inefficiency in the allocation of resources, which, in turn, reduces the productivity of the economy. Since abnormal price increases and relative price distortions produce the market signal of making abnormal profit from short-run capital gains rather than long-run production, they cause excessive accumulation of inventory and a barrage of speculative investments in "luxury industries." As Professor Hagen aptly observed:

Inflation leads to emphasis on profiting from capital gains rather than production. It causes excessive inventory accumulation for this purpose. More important, the groups whom inflation benefits are likely to include not only high savers but also luxurious spenders. For this reason there will be increased demand for services of luxurious urban apartment houses, resort hotels, nightclubs, and the like. This demand increases the likelihood of capital gains from their construction. Resources tend to flow into such projects, which do little to further economic growth.[13]

His observation is also confirmed by Harberger, who stated:

Inflation undermines growth in two ways. First, it disturbs the most basic process whereby relative prices guide resources from lower-valued to higher-valued uses...The key to the process is clear signals about relative prices. Inflation, on the other hand—especially when it is unsteady and thus unanticipated—disturbs those signals by obscuring the between *relative* and *absolute* prices.[14]

As in these two observations, the ill effect of galloping inflation on the productivity and growth of the economy has been transpiring in Burma today, where industries that do little to further economic growth and elevate the living standard of the people at large—such as import and sale of foreign automobiles and construction of "luxurious" apartments, homes, hotels, restaurants and nightclubs to cater to military elite, foreign investors, and tourists—abound in the cities of Rangoon, Mandalay, and others. The main beneficiaries from this illusive boom of luxury industries have been the government, foreign investors, the state joint venture enterprises, and a few high savers and luxury spenders—black market kingpins, military elite and their families, and former political apparatchiks with capital, wealth, and political connections.

Meanwhile, many speculative investors in pursuit of abnormal profit from short-term capital gains in the congested luxury industries have been reported to go bankrupt with excessive inventory accumulation—large stocks of unsold automobiles, many luxurious and expensive apartments, homes, and restaurants that are beyond the means of ordinary people, and many empty and unprofitable hotels with no business or tourists in Rangoon and Mandalay and other major cities. In addition to lack of business and high costs of operation, the unfair taxes imposed upon the hotels by the government have been causing many hotels in the cities of tourist attraction to go bankrupt.[15]

With respect to perhaps the most damaging impact of inflation, especially when it is unanticipated and unindexed, it tends to "generate capricious transfers of wealth among economic sectors and groups. This breaks the link between earnings and efforts, and has been known to cause violent political upheavals sparked by the embittered losers."[16] Indeed, inflation and its consequence of inequality in income and wealth distribution which severs the link between earnings and efforts, were the catalyst for the violent 1988 political upheaval in Burma. The same thing seems to be occurring in Burma today, where the ill effect of inflation, especially the growing disparity of privilege, income, and wealth between the ruling military elite and its entourage and the embittered losers or the impoverished people, including fixed-income groups, students, and college graduates with no hope of gainful employment and forcefully subdued pro-democracy leaders, signals a potential violent political upheaval.

FISCAL POLICIES AND BUDGET DEFICIT

With respect to fiscal policy, the main function of the government budget has been the allocation of funds to various government agencies, departments, ministries, and enterprises with no monitoring and coordination between the monetary and fiscal policies. The three main divisions of the national budget are the budget of the central government or the state administrative organizations (the SLORC plus various government ministries, departments, and agencies), the budget of state economic enterprises, and the budget of the cantonment municipalities, which is made up of town and city development committees. The combined deficit of the three budgets increased from Kt7.7 billion in 1989/1990 to Kt29.6 billion in 1994/1995, while the deficit of the central government increased from Kt4.538 billion in 1989/1990 to Kt26.15 billion in 1994/1995.[17] On average, the annual government deficit is 6 percent of the GDP at current prices.

The combined deficit of the central government or state administrative organizations and state economic enterprises grew from Kt6.265 billion in 1988/1989 to Kt29.6 billion in 1994/1995. That is, for the six years between 1989 and 1995, the government deficit increased by almost 500 percent. Annual surplus of Kt4 million, Kt5 million, and Kt8 million were reported for the budget of town and city development committees for 1993, 1994, and 1995. This indirectly confirms the reports of Burmese nationals that the town and city governments or development committees have been imposing not only an additional number of fees and taxes but also higher rates. Among them are fees for cleaning roads, ditches, garbage collection, and business licenses and taxes on sales, advertisements, billboards, business profit, utility, telephones, automobiles, homes, business offices, and real estate. Since 1989, the city development committees have been imposing these fees and taxes as well as mandating the painting of homes and forced donation of free labor or money from the residents in launching the beautification and development programs of towns and cities by constructing new gardens, bridges, and roads to attract tourists and foreign investment.

DEFENSE EXPENDITURES AS THE MAIN CAUSE OF BUDGET DEFICIT

The main cause of the mounting government budget deficit, which increased from Kt7.7 billion in 1989/1990 to Kt29.6 billion in 1994/1995 has been a large apportionment to defense expenditures, which increased from Kt4.1billion in 1989/1990 to Kt14.1 billion in 1994/1995.

In the 1990s, the coefficient of correlation between defense expenditures and total government deficit was .841. The slope of the regression line between defense expenditures and the total government deficit is 1.7, indicating that an increase in defense expenditures by one kyat or Kt1 produces an increase of one kyat and 70 pyars (cents) or Kt1.7 in total government deficit. The cumulative government deficit for the five-year period from 1990 to 1995 was Kt89 billion, and the cumulative defense expenditures for the same period were Kt56.3 billion, which accounted for 63 percent of the cumulative deficit. For 1995/1996, the government projected a total deficit of Kt49.7 billion and defense expenditures of Kt21.9 billion, which will account for 44 percent of the projected deficit.[18] It should be noted that the majority of the defense expenditures are incurred in foreign exchange to pay for arms purchase from abroad, and the percentage of defense expenditures in the government's total deficit would jump prodigiously if the black market foreign exchange rate were used.

The major portion of Burma's defense expenditures has been on the purchase of arms and military equipment from China. For example, in 1989 Burma entered a $1.4 arms purchase deal, and in the 1990s, it struck several military cooperation and arms purchase agreements with its giant neighbor, including the upgrading of old naval bases, the construction of new naval bases and radar stations, the purchase of frigates, and the provision of technical assistance. The gigantic military regime's expenditures on defense are incurred in the procurement of arms from abroad and payments of salaries and supplies for the build up of an over 300,000-man armed forces (army, navy, air force, and paramilitary units) in 1995/1996 from a level of 180,000 men in 1988/1989.[19] It is interesting to point out that the size of the Burmese army alone is 250,000

Table 4.3
Total Government Deficit and Defense Expenditures (billions of kyats)

	1989/90	1990/91	1991/92	1992/93	1993/94	1994/95
Total Deficit	7.7	11.2	12.9	12.1	15.5	29.6
Defense Expend.	4.1	6.9	8.2	9.1	13.9	14.1

Sources: Ministry of National Planning and Economic Development, The Union of Myanmar, Review
of the Financial, Economic and Social Conditions for 1992/1993, 1994/1995, 1995/1996 (Yangon: MNPED, 1993, 1995, and 1996) and The SLORC State Budget Law published between
March 30 and April 1 of each year in various issues of the state-run newspaper, the Working
People's Daily whose name was changed to the New Light of Myanmar in 1994.

Figure 4.1
Total Deficit and Defense Expenditures

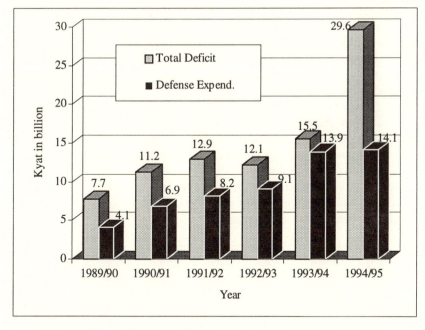

Sources: Ministry of National Planning and Economic Development, The Union of Myanmar, Review
of the Financial, Economic and Social Conditions for 1992/1993, 1994/1995, 1995/1996 (Yangon: MNPED, 1993, 1995, and 1996) and The SLORC State Budget Law published between
March 30 and April 1 of each year in various issues of the state-run newspaper, the Working
People's Daily whose name was changed to the New Light of Myanmar in 1994.

men which is one-half of the US army in 1995/1996. It has also been reported
that the goal of the SLORC is to increase the size of its armed forces to 500,000
men by the year 2000.

The bulk of the payment for defense expenditures on arms procurement
from foreign countries can be assumed to be made with foreign exchange, dollar, or barter agreements. According to the US Arms Control and Disarmament
Agency, the amount of dollars spent on arms procurement from abroad by the
military government was $20 million in 1988, $20 million in 1989, $110 mil-
lion in 1990, $390 million in 1991, $140 million in 1992, and $120 million in
1993. In 1994, it was reported that Burma's army chief of staff Lieutenant
General Tin Oo, visited China and struck an arms purchase agreement worth
$400 million.[20] If the black market exchange rate of Kt120 to $1, which is over
20 times higher than the official foreign exchange rate of Kt6 to $1 in the mid-
1990s, is used to translate the defense expenditures in dollars into kyats, the
percentage of defense expenditures in the government budget would jump prodigiously.

Defense expenditures account for roughly 40 percent of total expenditures
of the central government in the 1990s. It should also be noted that these published data on defense expenditures do not include hidden accounts and implicit income or privileges of military personnel, including payments in kind,
and access to goods distributed by the state at discounted prices, and expenditures on various internal security and military-related programs and projects by
state economic enterprises and cantonment municipalities. Including these undisclosed accounts, it is more than likely that defense expenditures can be as
high as 60 percent of the total government budget.

Apart from the gigantic defense expenditure of central government, other
causes of the mounting government deficit are politically motivated expenditures on extravagant, state-sponsored festivals for political distraction and sub-
sidies given to political supporters. With respect to the lack of fiscal discipline
on the part of the government reflected in the growth of the money supply exceeding the budget deficit in most of the years since 1988, a retired Burmese
government bank official observed:

Fiscal deficits have been the main cause of the increases in money supply. In addition, it
raised the question why the increase in money supply has exceeded the budget deficit in
most years, despite the deficits in the balance of payments current account. This has
raised doubt if there have been extra-budgetary financial flows from the Issue Department of the Central Bank to the Government, despite the Central Bank of Myanamr
Law of 1989 which expressly states that advances to the Government shall be limited to
20 percent of the previous year's deficit. Yet, it is obvious even from the published
budgetary figures that the budgetary deficit each year has far exceeded the 10 percent
margin of the preceding year's deficit.

Table 4.4

Government Expenditures on Defense versus Social Services (billions of kyats)

	1989/90	1990/91	1991/92	1992/93	1993/94	94/95
Defense (D)	4.1	6.9	8.2	9.1	13.9	14.1
Social Services (Ss)	5	7.1	7.9	8	8.6	9.2
D/Ss	.82	.97	1.04	1.14	1.62	1.53

Sources: Ministry of National Planning and Economic Development (MNPED), The Union of Myanmar, Review of the Financial, Economic and Social Conditions for 1992/1993, 1994/1995, 1995/1996 (Yangon: MNPED, 1993, 1995, and 1996) and The SLORC State Budget Law published between March 30 and April 1 of each year in various issues of the state-run newspaper, the Working People's Daily whose name was changed to the New Light of Myanmar in 1994. Notice that defense expenditures are given only in the current and supplementary budgets of the central government, whereas expenditures on social services are given in both current and capital budgets of central government, state economic enterprises, and cantonment municipalities.

Combined current and capital expenditures of government on defense relative to social services indicate a greater emphasis or priority given to military fortification relative to human development by a ratio of 1.5 to 1 in the 1990s (Table 4.4).

For 1995/1996, the projected expenditures on defense were Kt21.9 billion compared with Kt9.6 billion on social services. This gives a ratio of more than 2:1 between expenditures on defense and expenditures on social services to further indicate the government's commitment to resolve of military fortification for the rest of the 1990s.

Another equally important factor responsible for the incremental government deficit has been the inadequate base or lack of buoyancy in the tax system, which cannot generate sufficient revenues to offset the steadily rising expenditures of the central government and state economic enterprises. The inadequate tax base is reflected in the extremely low tax revenue of between 4 and 5 percent of GDP. One cause of the inadequate tax base may be the use of an unrealistically overvalued official foreign exchange rate, which resulted in the low tax yield or average effective tariff rate on imports. Another factor is the decline in contribution of the state economic enterprises (SEEs) to the tax revenue. The deficit of 59 SEEs has been rising steadily from Kt1.26 billion in 1989/1990 to Kt13.9 billion in 1994/1995, with a huge deficit of Kt23.49 billion projected for 1995/1996. Relative to the central government deficit, the rise in the deficit of SEEs has leveled off somewhat in the mid-1990s. The deficit and the declining contribution to revenue of SEEs have been largely due to inefficiency, corruption, and below capacity operations, along with increased costs of raw material imports over and above the revenues from domestic sales and exports.

Like all the laws passed by the SLORC, the tax laws are arbitrary and uncoordinated with monetary policy to promote growth and equity. For example, on November 10, 1994, in an apparent attempt to increase its revenue by gathering unpaid taxes from those who had earned "black money" (i.e., foreign exchange and money earned without paying taxes to the state), the SLORC offered partial tax amnesty to those who declared possession of black money. According to the government, the amnesty was given to the black money holders to participate more fully and freely in the private sector. Those who voluntarily declared the value of their holdings of either funds or assets worth Kt500,000 and above would be assessed a flat 20 percent tax rate.[21] This was the third time that the government has offered tax amnesty to those who had evaded tax payments to the state. The main beneficiaries of this action are the state, the military elite and their families, and the black market kingpins who have been amassing enormous amounts of foreign exchange and other forms of assets in the command economy of Burma.

Professor John Wong aptly summed up the linkage between chronic fiscal deficits and an excessive growth of the money supply as the underlying cause of inflation in Burma:

An important root cause of Myanmar's inflation is the chronic fiscal deficits. As typical of other transitional economies, Myanmar has not yet developed a viable revenue base while at the same time it has to subsidize the loss-making State Economic Enterprises. Unable to borrow from the domestic private sector or resort to external borrowing, Myanmar's government deficits had to be met by the central bank through printing more money, thereby resulting in an excessive growth of the money supply and hence the inflation.[22]

NOTES

1. *The Working People's Daily,* July 3, 1990, p. 1.

2. The Ministry of National Planning and Economic Development (MNPED), *The Union of Myanmar, Review of the Financial, Economic and Social Conditions for 1995/96* (Yangon: MNPED, 1996), p. 219.

3. U Wint Kyaw, "1994 Private Banking" (in Burmese), *Dana* (January 1995): 16–24.

4. US Embassy, *Burma, Country Commercial Guide 1998* (Rangoon: US Embassy, 1998), p. 17.

5. Chamber of Commerce of the United States, *The Mechanics of Inflation, an Analysis of Cost and Demand Pressures on the Price Level, Report of the Committee on Economic Policy*, Washington, DC, 1957, p. 3.

6. Arnold C. Harberger, *Economic Policy and Economic Growth* (San Francisco: Institute for Contemporary Studies, 1985), p. 9.

7. *The New Light of Myanmar*, January 15, 1994, p. 1.

8. International Monetary Fund (IMF), *Myamar, Recent Economic Developments* (Washington, DC: IMF, February 1997), p. 94.

9. Ibid.

10. Ibid.

11. *Asia Week*, March 3, 1996, p. 43.

12. Minoru Kiryu, *Immediate Measures for Price Stabilization and Achievement of Broad-Based, Consistent Growth Rate in Myanmar Naing-gan*, Report to the UNDP (New York: privately published, 1992), p. 2.

13. E. E. Hagen, *The Economics of Development*, 4th ed. (Homewood, IL: Irwin, 1986), p. 265.

14. Harberger, *Economic Policy*, p. 10.

15 See "Some Hotels in Mandalay Are Facing Shut-down before the Visit Myanmar Year Begins" (in Burmese), *Dana*, vol. 6, no. 10 (May 1996): 36.

16. Harberger, *Economic Policy*.

17. MNPED, *Review 1995/96*, p. 223.

18. Ibid., pp. 223–224.

19. Andrew Selth, "Burma's Arms Procurement Programme, Working Paper No. 289" (Camberra: Australian National University, 1995), p. 5.

20. Ibid., pp. 5–6.

21. *The New Light of Myanmar*, November 10, 1994, p. 1.

22. John Wong, "The Relevance of and Lessons of the Early Development Experience of Newly Industrializing Economies with Special Reference to Laos and Myanmar," a paper prepared for the United Nations by the director of Institute of East Asian Political Economy, Singapore, 1995, p. 1.

5

The Economic Plight of Urban and Rural Population

The consequence of ostentatious economic reforms undertaken by the SLORC has been the development, or rather perpetuation, of the nationwide parallel/black market economy that existed for 26 years under the military regime of General Ne Win. The following is a case study of the inefficiency as well as the inequity in the functioning of the parallel/black market economy of Burma to show the economic plight of ordinary Burmese people in urban communities based on a Burmese listener's report to the British Broadcasting Corporation (BBC) and reports of Burmese nationals.

GOVERNMENT EMPLOYEES' COOPERATIVE (GEC)

Soon after the military coup of 1988, to gain loyalty the SLORC set up welfare/discount shops for government employees to sell goods on a monthly quota basis at low official prices. For 26 years before the 1988 military coup, the same system of distributing goods through state cooperative shops was used by the military regime of Ne Win in running the command economy of the Socialist Republic of the Union of Burma. As in the past, the economy continues to be riddled with corruption, black marketeering, and evasions of state controls to generate phenomenal gaps between the official and unofficial prices that have taken an enormous toll on the economic life of government employees and ordinary folks.

In April 1993, the SLORC made an attempt to woo and appease economically distressed public servants by establishing government employees' cooperatives (GECs). A public servant who buys one share or more is entitled to the purchase of goods at GEC shops in various townships and districts. Shares in the GEC are sold at Kt1,000 per share, payable in total or in 10 installments. Any profit realized is to be distributed according to the number of shares owned. However, the right to buy goods at discount prices from the GEC is restricted to one share only.

When the GECs were introduced, it was rumored that they would eventually replace the existing government employees' welfare/discount shops. Worried government employees caught in the escalating inflation spiral were forced to join the GEC and began purchasing GEC shares. Their average monthly pay scale was raised by only 25 percent in March 1993, compared with the prices of goods, which have been rising at a rate of between 50 percent and 100 percent according to Burmese nationals in the unofficial/black markets since 1989. Most paid the first installment of Kt100. After one week, the government announced that goods would be distributed after the second installment of Kt100 was paid. Kt200 entitled the shareholder to purchase weekly on a quota basis of one share per person: four pyis (1py=4.68 lbs.) of rice, two bars of state-manufactured soap called Yellow Gold, 1/2 a vis (1vis=3.6 lbs.) of sugar, 1/2 viss of salt, two flashlight batteries, two bundles of candles, and one bottle of state-manufactured soda called Bali Yai. These "basic" goods are distributed on specified days set during the week according to government departments.

A public servant can make Kt110 profit from reselling his or her entire quota bought in the unofficial market. So many government departments exist that the distribution cannot be completed during the week. Shareholders need to transact on the weekend. For the goods allotted to any government department, distribution counters are set up according to types of goods at the GEC shop. These shops are typically housed in a central market, Theingyi Zay/Bazaar in Rangoon, for example. For a big government department, at least seven persons have to go to the GEC shop at 8 a.m. to buy goods. Since the distribution counter for rice is different from counters of other goods, buyers are required to stand in line at least two times. The process resembles queuing to buy the cheap Kt1 tickets that are sold at movie theaters. The crowd of buyers tends to be so large that money carried on one's person is often stolen by pickpockets, and jewelry worn by women is swiped by muggers. Delegated buyers or agents often do not get back to the department until 3:30 or 4 p.m. Other employees are asked to pay a commission fee of Kt3 per GEC booklet to the individual delegate who gets the goods for them at the GEC shops.

The basic goods are distributed once a week, albeit irregularly. Sporadically, two bottles of kerosene, two yards of diaper cloth, and office stationeries are distributed on some weekdays. These can be bought at discount prices by a public servant who visits the shop in person after showing the GEC booklet. Ordinary folks who are not government employees are permitted to buy nonbasic goods, watches, and other luxury goods sold by the GEC shops. The prices of nonbasic goods are either equal to, or exceed, prices in private shops. Because purchasers of basic goods from government departments overwhelmed the GEC shops, a new law was passed and enforced to control the distribution of limited goods. According to this new law, a delegated buyer/agent of a department is allowed to procure goods for no more than six GEC booklets at a time. Since neither departmental delegates nor ordinary government employees wish to go through the time consuming and irksome process of buying selected items from the GEC shops, private arrangements or markets developed spontaneously for trading goods to make arbitrage profit.

An example of this can be found in the case of procuring the two bottles of kerosene distributed by the GEC shops. Experienced and knowledgeable government employees still serve as intermediaries in this process. Agents would collect all the GEC booklets from all departmental personnel and sell these documents to private merchants via skilled brokers/dealers who have connections with corrupt officials at GEC shops. The brokers/dealers, in turn, strike deals with the ultimate buyers of these booklets or rights of purchase from the GEC shops—private merchants. Government employees who participate in this triangular linkage/arrangement are said to be "entering the line," *linewin* in Burmese. The cost of "entering the line" is Kt5—a commission fee charged by the broker/dealer.

Under this arrangement a government employee belonging to the GEC sells his booklet to purchase two bottles of kerosene to the merchant for Kt15 through the broker, who charges a Kt5 commission fee. Thus, the government employee receives Kt10. Like most officially distributed goods, the price of a bottle of kerosene sold by the merchants in the unofficial market is a large multiple of the official price. The size and volume of transactions in the unofficial kerosene market are so large that purchases and sales of kerosene are conducted not in bottles but in drums.

THE ECONOMIC PLIGHT OF GOVERNMENT EMPLOYEES

The single most important element in the living standard of Burmese families and the economic performance of their country has been rice, which they called the "golden fruit," *shwethee*. From the British colonial days throughout the independent period to the present, the politics of rice has dominated the history of Burma in terms of official slogans and development programs as well as the revolts of peasants and masses. The British colonization of Burma and the ensuing sociopolitical and economic changes were closely linked to the development of the rich Irrawaddy delta region of Lower Burma, known as the Rice Belt, and export of rice to the outside world. The Burmese nationalist revolt against British rule was instigated by the economic plight of the Burmese peasantry in the 1930s, while the 1988 mass revolt against the military rule was precipitated by the shortages and the escalating price of rice. For example, during the famous "Four Eight Affairs" (August 8, 1988, or 8/8/88), when thousands of demonstrators marched in the streets across Burma to protest against the military regime, they shouted this slogan to overthrow the 17-day president, General Sein Lwin: "*San tapyi setngar kyat Sein Lwin gongko phyat*," that is, "Since the price of one *pyi* of rice is 15 kyats, Sein Lwin's head must be cut."

Since 1988, with special attention given to the politics of rice, the SLORC has been distributing rice, and also other basic necessities to public servants through state-sponsored cooperative or welfare shops at discount prices. Initially, the official price for first-quality rice, *Pawsun Mhway*, sold to a public servant was Kt90 for 12 *pyis* of rice (Kt7.5 per *pyi*). In 1993, the price was hiked to Kt125 (Kt10.4 per *pyi*). More often than not, high-quality rice is not available, and instead the government employees' shops offer low-quality rice, *Nga Sein*. Since few public servants consume *Nga Sein*, these purchases are generally resold in the unofficial market. The proceeds from the sale are used to buy the high-quality rice in the unofficial market that costs as much as Kt60 per *pyi*. As in the past 26 years, the government has been distributing the first quality rice by blending it with a mixture of broken rice. Broken rice sells for Kt12 per *pyi* in the unofficial market. The GEC shops have been reportedly distributing rice with a 25 percent mixture of broken rice. However, 12 *pyis* of rice bought from these shops are found to contain a larger proportion of broken rice: 5 *pyis* of broken rice and only 7 *pyis* of *Pawsun Mhway* (a more than 40 percent mixture of broken rice). Table 5.1 shows the phenomenal gaps between official and unofficial/black market prices in Rangoon and reflect the economic plight of an urban family in Burma. (Table 5.1)

It should be noted that the average annual prices of selected commodities given in the Table are derived from mid-range monthly prices. These prices understate the wide magnitude of price fluctuations. The range of the price fluctuation of each commodity varies greatly from month to month. For example, during December 1997 the price of first quality rice, *Pawsun Hmway* or *Nga Kywe*, rose up to Kt145 per pyi, while the price of chicken rose up to Kt800 per *viss*, the price of snake head fish rose up to Kt500 per *viss*, and the price of the US dollar rose up to Kt385 per US dollar.

The economic hardship of an average government employee due to inaccessible basic necessities at discount official prices and the hidden tax of inflation has been compounded further by the government wage policy of keeping the monthly wage rates more or less fixed. On March 27, 1993, in honor of the auspicious 48th Armed Forces Day, the SLORC issued Notification No. 15/93 to increase the salary and wage scales of public service personnel to be effective on April 1, 1993, "to provide welfare to State service personnel." It was reportedly done to alleviate the economic hardship of rising costs of living due to inflation faced by government employees.

This was the second increment of pay scales made by the government since 1988, while the first increment was made in April 1989. The monthly pay scales of government employees were increased from the old minimum-maximum range of Kt450–Kt2,000 to a new range of Kt600–Kt2,500 (US$5-$20.80 at black market rate of exchange of 1 US dollar=Kt120) to be effective on April 1, 1993. This represents a 33 percent rise for the minimum wage earners and a 25 percent rise for the maximum wage earners or an average wage hike of 30 percent for all government employees over the four-year period

Table 5.1
The Gaps between the Official and Average Unofficial Prices of Selected Goods, US Dollar and FEC in Rangoon (1988–1997)

	Official Price, 1990*	1988	1989	1990	1991	1992	1993	1994	1995	1996	1997
Rice 1 *Pawsun Hmay*	Kt10.5 per *pyi***	Kt13.7.	Kt21.7	Kt18.4	Kt28	Kt42.6	Kt62.3	Kt66.3	Kt87.5	Kt115	Kt123
Rice 2-*Emata*	Kt6 per *pyi*	Kt10.9	Kt15.8	Kt10.6	Kt14.2	Kt27.5	Kt42.5	Kt43.8	Kt65	Kt95	Kt113
Fish-Snake Head	Kt90 per *viss****	Kt59.9	Kt60	Kt90	Kt120	Kt169.	Kt228.	Kt245	Kt300	Kt350	Kt450
Jumbo Shrimp	Kt200 per *viss*	Kt178.3	Kt215	Kt224	Kt300	Kt408	Kt955	Kt1,100	Kt1,500	Kt2,000	Kt3,000
Chicken	Kt120 per *viss*	Kt56.7	Kt76.4	Kt122	Kt180	Kt191	Kt252	Kt315	Kt325	Kt450	Kt565
Pork	Kt110 per *viss*	Kt48.9	Kt72.3	Kt158	Kt150	Kt156	Kt195	Kt280	Kt300	Kt350	Kt425
Ground-nut Oil	Kt34 per *viss*	Kt59.4	Kt60.1	Kt69.8	Kt160	Kt163	Kt145	Kt151	Kt225	Kt300	Kt415
Palm Oil	Kt18 per *viss*	n.a.	n.a.	n.a.	n.a.	Kt130	Kt112	Kt140	Kt150	Kt200	Kt325
Gasoline	Kt16 per gallon	Kt71.3	Kt80	Kt136	Kt190	Kt225	Kt204.	Kt198	Kt220	Kt270	Kt245
US$1	Kt6.25	Kt50	Kt60	Kt80	Kt122	Kt110	Kt117	Kt110	Kt115	Kt140	Kt210
FEC$1	Kt6.25						Kt115	Kt108	Kt114	Kt138	Kt208

* The official price is a discount price of goods distributed/sold by government welfare/co-operative shops on a quota basis to various state employees. In 1990, the official prices of rice and other goods were raised. Prior to 1990, official prices of rice 1(Ngakywe), Rice 2 (Emata), chicken and pork were set at Kt3.5 per *pyi*, Kt2.35 per *pyi*, Kt60 per *viss*, and Kt55 per *viss* respectively. Official price of gasoline was raised from Kt16 to Kt25 in 1994 and to Kt180 in 1997.

** 1 *pyi* of rice=4.6875 lbs.

*** 1 *viss*=3.6 lbs.

Source: US Embassy, *Retail Prices of Selected Commodities in Rangoon (1988-1996)*, EIU Country Reports, 3rd and 4th Quarters 1997, Burmese economic magazines, *Dana* and *Myanma Dana*, and private information.

from 1989 to 1993. The eight hour daily wage rate was also raised from Kt15 to Kt20. At the same time, the government kept the total monthly income tax frozen by not taxing the incremental pay. It also waived the 5 percent interest on home construction loans taken by the public servants since April 1990 and extended the repayment period from 10 years to 18 years.

According to official reports, the average annual increase of the consumer price index was 30 percent. Thus, the government pay hike of 30 percent seemed to have provided total relief from the cost-of-living increase in 1993. However, government figures on the consumer price index and the rate of inflation based on officially controlled prices are highly unreliable and grossly underestimated. According to private information, prices of rice and other basic necessities in the unofficial/black markets in Rangoon and other major cities across Burma have been rising at an average annual rate of over 100 percent since 1988. It must also be emphasized that the government wage hike was only a one time deal over the four-year period of 1989–1993. Accepting the understated annual increase in the consumer price index of 30 percent between 1989 and 1993 reported by the government, it would require more than a 30 percent wage increase every year or over 120 percent for the four-year period to keep the real wages constant. Hence, the 1993 government one time wage hike of 30 percent failed disastrously to solve the problem of the accelerated plunge in real wages that had been occurring since 1988.

A public primary school teacher earns a monthly income of Kt900 (around $7.50 at the average black market exchange rate of $1=Kt120 in 1995/1996), while a college assistant lecturer or assistant professor or a middle-ranked government official earns a monthly income of Kt1,500 ($12.50). In 1995/1996, the average price of even the lowest-quality rice, *Nga Sein,* in Rangoon was reported to have climbed to Kt70 per *pyi* (4.68 lbs.) and the price of the highest-quality rice, *Pawsun Mhway,* to Kt100. On average, a Burmese adult consumes around 6 *pyis* of rice per month. Even if we assume that a public high school teacher is forced to consume the lowest-quality rice, which is not usually the case, the monthly cost of rice consumption alone for the teacher would be Kt420 (Kt70 x 6 *pyis*), or 60 percent of his or her monthly income. For an assistant professor or a middle-ranked government official, who usually consumes the highest-quality rice, the monthly cost of rice consumption would be one-third of his or her monthly income. If the two are married with no children, and if we assume that they consume the highest-quality rice, the cost of rice consumption alone would be more than the monthly income of a public school teacher and 70 percent of the monthly income of a college assistant professor. The curious question is, How are these families surviving? The answer given by the Burmese nationals is that most government officials have been forced to take bribes, engage in black market activities by reselling rice and other goods that are secured at discount prices from government welfare shops in the unofficial market, and find jobs that pay in foreign exchange. As for ordinary people, they have been forced to consume the lowest-quality rice, broken rice, and even the boiled water of rice packaged and sold in bottles.

During the 1988 political uprising, the price of one *pyi* of rice was Kt15. In January 1996, the Burmese nationals and the private Burmese economic journals reported that the price of the best-quality rice had climbed to Kt135 per *pyi*. That is, between 1988 and 1996 the price of rice increased by 800 percent to indicate that the average annual increase in the price of rice during the eight-year period was 100 percent. In its February 1996 issue, the private Burmese economic journal *Dana*, reported that the price of top-quality rice, *Pawsun Mhway*, in Mandalay rose to Kt136 per *pyi*, and the price of lowest-quality rice, *Nga Sein*, climbed to 67.2 per *pyi* to indicate a worsening of living conditions for ordinary people.[1] In February 1996, the Rangoon price of *Pawsun Mhway* climbed to Kt140 per *pyi*. In October 1996, however, the respective prices of *Pawsun Mhwy* and *Nga Sein* settled back down to Kt110 per *pyi* and Kt54 per *pyi,* respectively.[2] In August 1997, the Burmese magazine, *Living Color*, reported that the prices of *Pawsun Mhwy* and *Nga Sein* in Rangoon climbed back up to Kt133 per *pyi* and Kt65 per *pyi*.[3]

Beginning in March 1996, in order to avoid public unrest due to skyrocketing rice prices, which had precipitated the 1988 political uprising, the government began dumping rice from government warehouses and distributing free rice to government employees at a rate of 14 *pyis* for a family man and 12 *pyis* for a single man in Rangoon to bring down the price. The government also advanced interest-free loans worth up to a 10-month salary of a government employee. In any event, in the long run such a stopgap measure is not going to alleviate the persistent shortages and halt the escalating prices of rice and other basic necessities. The evidence of this was reflected in the sustained escalation of rice prices throughout the last quarter of 1996 and continuing into 1997.

As in the past socialist state, ordinary people could not afford to buy not only the best-quality rice, *Pawsun Mhway*, but also the good-quality meat (fish, shrimp, pork, and chicken), cooking oil, and vegetables, whose prices had risen above their income. Those who could afford to buy them from the government welfare shops or from private shops in the unofficial market found these items to be not pure. For instance, the best-quality rice, *Pawsun Mhway*, would be mixed with lowest-quality rice, *Nga Sein*, and broken rice, while chicken, pork, fish, shrimp, and different meat would be injected with water to overweigh them in selling to the buyers. It has been reported that poor families can no longer afford to consume rice, and they have been forced to drink boiled rice water only, *htamin yay*, packaged and sold in bottles. The price per bottle of boiled rice water was also reported to have climbed from Kt5 per bottle to Kt10 per bottle during 1996.

It has also been reported that, like the first-quality rice, a delicacy crustacean like jumbo shrimp is either exorbitantly expensive or not available at all for consumption by ordinary people. The protein prices in Rangoon have also

Figure 5.1
Protein Prices in Rangoon

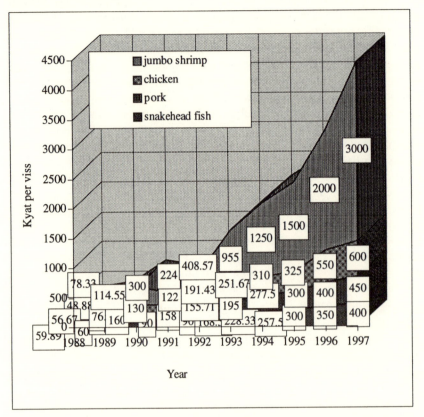

Sources: US Embassy, *Retail Prices of Selected Commodities in Rangoon*, Burmese Magazines,
    Dana, Myanma Dana, Living Color, and Private Information. It should be noticed that these
    prices are quoted per *viss*, the Burmese weight measure of roughly 3.6 lbs., for the best quality
    protein items.

been rising steadily since 1988 to indicate the rising cost of living for the urban
population (Figure 5.1).

In November 1996, it was reported that the price of top-quality jumbo
shrimp rose to Kt2,000 per vis, chicken to Kt500 per vis, pork to Kt350 per vis,
and snakehead fish to Kt350 per vis. In late 1997, the Burmese nationals in
Rangoon reported that the prices of these products had climbed to Kt3,000,
Kt600, Kt450, and Kt400 per vis respectively.

A shortage of energy persists in the major urban centers in Burma except
in ultramodern living quarters and villas of the military elite in exclusive sections of the city and new satellite towns around Rangoon. The supply of electricity would be shut down every eight hours or so and sometimes the blackout
would last four to five days. Meanwhile, the government hiked the price

charged on electricity used by Rangoon residents from Kt.50 (50 pyars or cents) per unit in 1993 to Kt2.50 per kilowatt in 1994. It has also been reported that instead of a bundle of wood, which normally contained about 10 sticks, the sellers are selling a bundle of 2 to 3 sticks of wood at a price of Kt50. Thus, the cost of 2 to 3 sticks of wood for cooking alone would exhaust 71 percent of the daily wage, since the minimum daily wage of a worker in Myanmar is set by the government at Kt70 (around US55 cents in 1994 and less than US40 cents in 1996 at black market exchange rates). The shortage of wood can be directly attributed to the rapid deforestation of the rich Burmese forests by some 47 Thai companies, which were granted logging concessions by the SLORC between 1989 and 1993. In 1994, the SLORC declared the rich forests in the Irrawaddy Delta region as "protected forests" in the name of environmental protection and conservation. The consequence has been a chronic shortage of wood and charcoal, whose prices have escalated. For example, the price of charcoal soared by 350 percent from Kt13 per vis (3.6lb) in 1993 to Kt45 per vis in 1994. Despite government cessation of logging rights granted to the Thai companies at the end of 1993, the ecological rape of Burma continues due to illegal felling of trees and smuggling of logs across Burma's border to fetch higher prices. The following Figure 5.2 shows the rising energy prices in Rangoon since 1988.

BLACK GASOLINE: THE SOURCE OF INCOME, PROFIT, AND WEALTH

The most glaring inefficiency and inequity in the functioning of the Burmese military command economy relate to the production and distribution of gasoline. Over the past three decades, the state has monopolized the production, import, and distribution of gasoline. Since 1988, the present military government has been distributing or selling gasoline on a quota basis of one to four gallons per week, according to different Burmese alphabets registered on the license plates such as *ka, kha, ga, nya,* and so on to differentiate new cars from old cars, to automobile owners at a discount price of Kt16 per gallon (3.8 liters). Like rice and other basic necessities sold by the state welfare and semistate cooperative shops at discount prices, there is a booming black market for gasoline, where the price was as high as Kt220 per gallon in 1994/1995 and climbed above Kt400 per gallon in late 1996. On August 4, 1994, the government hiked its distribution price of gasoline to Kt25 per gallon, representing a 56.25 percent increase.

Despite denial by the government, the shortage of energy has led to the signing of a contract to import 4 million barrels of crude oil from Mitsui of Japan for 1995/1996, the payment for which (estimated at $30 million) was reported to have been partially defaulted by the Burmese government. Consequently, Mitsui decided to halt its crude oil shipment to Burma. Following this incident, the unofficial/black market price of gasoline leaped to above kt400 per

Figure 5.2
Energy[*] Prices in Rangoon

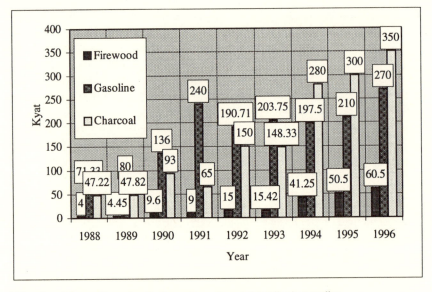

* The price of firewood is per bunch, charcoal is per bag, and gasoline is per gallon
Sources: US Embassy, *Retail Prices of Selected Commodities in Rangoon*, Burmese Magazines, *Dana*
    and *Myanma Dana*, and Private Information.

gallon before settling back down to Kt350 per gallon in September 1996. In November 1996, Daw Aung San Suu Kyi reported in a videotaped interview that the price of gasoline had climbed back up to Kt425 per gallon in Rangoon. In January 1997, it went back down to around Kt300 per gallon, which was still Kt100 more than the average price of 1996 to indicate a continued energy crisis for 1997.

In July 1997, the government once again hiked the gasoline price to an unprecedented level by 602 percent, from Kt25 to Kt180 per gallon, in an attempt to harmonize the official and black market price, and at the same time allowed the public to purchase an unlimited amount of gasoline on the day of the quota. The net impact of this action has been the passing of the increased cost of gasoline to the public by private taxies and buses in Rangoon. According to the Burmese nationals in Rangoon and other cities, transportation fares have gone up by five to six times, the same percentage increase as the official price of gasoline. Meanwhile, the black market price of gasoline remained the same as before, hovering around Kt300 per gallon. For how long the government will allow the purchase of an unlimited number of gallons of gasoline at the new price is uncertain. But it is certain that it cannot maintain this policy for a long time in light of the shortage of energy that Burma has been experiencing since 1988.

BLACK GASOLINE TO SUPPLEMENT FROZEN WAGES AND EARN ABNORMAL PROFIT

Only the privileged military elite, army, and high-ranking government officials have easy and free access to gasoline distributed by state-owned gasoline stations. In fact, Burmese satirically called gasoline *tartsi* instead of its real name, *dartsi,* by a play on words, which literally means that "army," *tart*, owns the "gasoline," *si* in Burmese. In an economy with a chronic shortage of energy, the state monopoly on production and distribution of gasoline represents the use of "compensatory power" or rewarding the ruling military elite and its followers for the control of political power. Free gasoline given to defense service personnel and top government officials exemplifies this process and the sale of gasoline at discount prices to government employees in general is a de facto subsidy given by the government for political support. For government employees, the reward of free gasoline and gasoline at discount prices distributed by the government is a source of extra income to supplement their more or less frozen wages and accumulate wealth depending on their ranks in the echelon of power and administration. For people in general, the scarce gasoline becomes an invaluable asset like gold or US dollars to own and trade for extra income or abnormal profit.

For those who are given free gasoline by the government, it is a process of commodity arbitrage to make abnormal profit from the phenomenal spread between the official and unofficial prices. For example, the government provides a top government official (the managing director, or (MD) of a state and a semistate bank or a state enterprise and the director general, or (DG) of government departments, most of whom are serving or ex-military commanders), four Japanese-made Mazda automobiles for use, two for official use and two for family use. They are also provided with 150 gallons of free gasoline per month for these cars. In the 1990s, the average black market or unofficial price of gasoline in Rangoon, Mandalay, and other cities is Kt200 per gallon. The main source of extra cash income for a MD or a DG is derived from the sale of unused gasoline in the black market. Assuming that the minimum amount of unused gasoline per month is 50 gallons, the cash income per month from the sale of the unused gasoline in the black market would be Kt10,000 (Kt200 x 50), which is four times higher than the monthly salary of Kt2,500 earned by a DG or a MD. Military officers and other high-ranking government officials earn similar implicit income by reselling in the black market free gasoline and other scarce goods purchased at discount prices from the government employees' cooperatives or welfare shops.

The General Manager of a state bank gets 2 cars for use: 1 green Mazda jeep and 1 T-2000 truck and 100 free gallons of gasoline per month. The maximum use of gasoline is 60 gallons a month. Therefore, the extra cash monthly income from the sale of 40 unused gallons of gasoline in the black market is Kt8,000 (40xKt200) which is four times greater than the Kt2,000 monthly salary of a General Manager.

In order not to mislead, it will be noted that although the largest benefactors from the resale of gasoline in the black market are top military and civilian government officials, some middle-ranked government officials, wealthy private automobile owners, and black marketeers also derive extra cash income from the sale of gasoline they obtain at discount prices based on the spread between the official and unofficial prices. A middle or low-ranked government official who owns a private car may not need to use the entire weekly ration of gasoline bought with his or her gasoline quota ticket, *dartsi letmart*, at discount prices from the government gasoline station. Each of them economizes on the use of gasoline by forming a car pool to commute to work. He or she can accumulate or store unused gasoline in cans, which have a ready market for sale to black market dealers in gasoline who pay regular visits to various clients in town to purchase them at a price slightly below the ongoing black market price. The major buyers of the black market gasoline include wealthy families and businessmen, hotels and travel agencies catering to foreign tourists, and private transportation companies that use large amounts of gasoline beyond the quotas allotted by the government. It has been reported that the Ministry of Trade itself is engaged in transportation business for profit, with hundreds of its buses and trucks supplied with free government gasoline.

THE ECONOMIC PLIGHT OF BURMESE PEASANTS

The Burmese economy was, and is, primarily an agrarian economy with a monocultural orientation to the production of paddy (unhusked rice) and export of rice. The contribution of the agricultural sector to the GDP is estimated to be over 50 percent, accounting for 76 percent of the total value of productive sectors and 50 percent of total exports and providing employment of two-thirds of the working population. Although the SLORC has introduced certain measures of liberalization with respect to price and cropping decisions of farmers, the major stumbling block in improving the economic lot of the farmers has been the state monopoly of rice export, on one hand, and the system of state procurement of paddy and rice at low prices from the farmers that amounts to net implicit taxation of farmers, on the other. In regard the negative impact of state interventions and control of the paddy and rice sector, the World Bank assessed: "These interventions, thus, reduce farm income by lowering the fragmented price of paddy. However, their medium-term effect is even greater because they are significant disincentives to farmers in making output and marketing decisions."[4]

For 26 years from 1962 to 1988, the military regime of General Ne Win managed the agricultural sector of the command economy of the Socialist Republic of the Union of Burma by institutionalizing "the advanced sale/purchase of paddy system" with state control on paddy output and price and monopoly on rice export. By advancing loans to farmers, the government established a system of quotas for farmers to sell their harvested paddy at predetermined prices to the state buying depots. In 1987/1988, the military regime decontrolled paddy and rice by allowing private traders to trade and export freely. At the same time, a new tax system was introduced that required farmers to pay land revenue and agricultural sales taxes in kind. The liberalization of the paddy and rice trade was short-lived, and by 1990, private export of rice was banned. The quota system of procuring paddy from farmers at low prices structured on the basis of repayment of government loans in kind by the state procurement agencies remains intact in Burma today.

Soon after the military coup of 1988, the military regime of General Saw Maung reinstituted the former state buying agency (State Corporation No. 1) as the Myanmar Agricultural Trading Produce (MATP). As in the past, farmers were supposed to meet their quotas of paddy sale to the state according to the credits or cash advances secured for their operation from the state agricultural banks. A farmer who could not meet the quota was subject to arrest and seizure of his farm by the authorities. The price of the sale of paddy to fulfill the quota at a predetermined procurement price was arbitrarily set by the state at a level several times below the average purchase or farm-gate prices. The MATP began to offer higher purchase or farm-gate prices for paddy left after the fulfillment of the quota to farmers. There are four competing buyers of paddy from the farmers: the state procurement agents of the MATP of the Ministry of Trade, the agents of the State Joint Venture No. 1 (a joint venture between the state and big private merchants), the co-operative agents of the Ministry of Co-operatives, and small, independent, private merchants. Each of them purchases paddy at different prices. The purchase prices offered by the first three state and quasi-state agencies are officially set at low levels relative to the high prices offered by the independent private merchants, most of whom deal in the unofficial/black market. The official purchase prices can be as low as 30 percent of the free market price of paddy and rice offered by private dealers and merchants.

In effect, this quota system of paddy procurement from the farmers was essentially the same "advanced purchase/sale of paddy system" practiced by the socialist government of Burma. It is based on the loan advanced to a farmer for paddy cultivation, which is to be repaid in kind after the harvest. The quota is set at 12 baskets per acre or 34 percent of the average yield per acre of high yield variety paddy (HYV paddy), which is between 30 and 40 baskets per acre. The required quota delivery of paddy to the government buying depots varies according to the size of the farm and the type of paddy planted (traditional versus HYV) by a farmer. For traditional paddy the quota is set at 5 baskets per acre. The average farm size in Burma is less than 10 acres under the anticapitalist and antilandlord policy of the socialist government. The amount of loan advanced by the state agricultural bank to a farmer is based on the amount of his quota on the basis of 12 baskets of paddy per acre valued at the predetermined government procurement price per basket. As the procurement price per basket of paddy (46 pounds or 20.86 kilos) set by the government in 1995 is Kt70, the government credit advanced per acre is Kt840. Assuming for simplicity that a farmer owns and cultivates 10 acres of paddy, he can borrow from the state agricultural bank a total loan of Kt8,400 (120 x Kt70 per basket). The farmer is required to pay back the loan in kind, that is, 120 baskets of paddy. In other words, all farmers who have to borrow from the government must make a compulsory sale or delivery of 12 baskets per acre to the government buying depots after the harvest. Any additional borrowing over and above the 12 baskets is also subject to the same system of quota delivery.

The private domestic market price in 1995 was Kt200 per basket, which was nearly three times the government procurement price. The difference of Kt130, per basket (Kt200 minus Kt70) between the private domestic market price and the government procurement price represents the price reduction or loss to a farmer in paying back the loan in kind. In monetary terms, the amount of interest on a Kt70 loan charged by the government is Kt130, which amounts to an effective interest rate of 185.7 percent (130/70). The time period of the loan is approximately six months, depending on the variety of paddy, that is, the period of cultivating, harvesting, and processing the paddy for delivery to the government buying depots. Hence, on an annual basis the effective compound interest rate charged by the government is 716.2 percent. The export parity price per basket of paddy in 1995 was Kt240.6 per basket. In 1995, the spread between the export parity price and the government procurement price of paddy or the amount of interest charged on Kt70 loan per basket was Kt170.6 (Kt240.6-Kt70). That is, the effective annual compound rate of interest on paddy loans or the implicit tax rate imposed on farmers by the government was 1,081.4 percent.[5]

LANDLESSNESS, INDEBTEDNESS, AND POVERTY

Based upon the survey conducted by the Burmese government's Ministry of Agriculture with technical assistance from UN agencies in early 1993, landlessness and poverty of farmers were found to be widespread. The survey found that about 12 million out of 28 million people or "more than 40 percent of the population supported chiefly by agriculture in 1993 had no land or livestock holdings at all—over and above 4.4 million people living in households with land holdings of less than 3 acres, generally too small for subsistence even for a small household."[6] It should be noted that Burma historically has no comparable landed aristocracy or latifundista of Latin America, which is responsible for the exploitation of rural proletariat and the creation of the problem of landlessness. Since its independence from the British rule in 1948 and particularly after the military coup of 1962, the underlying cause of such an incredible magnitude of landlessness of the Burmese agrarian population has been the government, which has been the de facto latifundista in exploiting the land and fruits of the labor of farmers. The inept and coercive policies of the military regime with respect to agricultural credit, paddy procurement, monopoly of rice exports, and land ownership have been the root cause of landlessnes in rural Burma.

There is a formal agricultural credit system in Burma with cash loans granted by the Myanma Agricultural Bank (MAB), formerly known as the State Agricultural Bank (SAB), that are "limited and too cheap: (while) other credit too costly."[7] It is limited because the cash loans advanced for certain crops given at 18 percent a year by the state village banks cover only about one-third to one-half of the cost of one bag of fertilizer. Hence, farmers have to rely heavily on private lenders to cover the cost of inputs. The private moneylenders charge an interest rate of 10 percent per month or 120 percent per annum for loans without collateral and 5 percent per month or 60 percent per annum for collateralized loans.[8] Thus, farmers in Burma have been taking a double beating by the government and the private creditors in borrowing loans at exorbitant rates of interest in addition to the implicit taxation of having to sell paddy at below market prices to the state and semistate buyers. The indebtedness problem of farmers due to the inefficient agricultural credit system and financial policy of the state dates back to the pre-1988 period. As Mya Than evaluated:

Although the MAB interest rate was very low, farmers had to turn to private money lenders as the gap widened between their requirement for credit and the credit received from the government. One possible reason for farmers resorting to private money lenders is that if they take more credit from the MAB, they are obliged to sell more paddy to the government. As for other crops, especially cash crops, this gap between credit-requirement and credit-receipt was even wider. Thus, about 50–60 percent of farmers were indebted.[9]

The fulfillment of the quota delivery of paddy is mandatory without any exception. Even if there were crop failures due to natural disasters of flood or drought, farmers would be forced to deliver the required quota. Farmers have to use the paddy saved for their own consumption, known in Burmese as *wunsah* (paddy or rice for the stomach), and seeds saved for next harvest, to fulfill the quota. In the event that these paddies saved were insufficient to meet the quota, they have to purchase the rest from private merchants at phenomenally high prices. It has been reported that farmers have been forced to sell their cattle, buffalo, farm equipment, and even homes to come up with the cash needed to buy the paddy to meet the quota. For those farmers with no assets to sell to meet the quota, they either have to borrow funds from private moneylenders at exorbitant interest rates or have been forced to donate labor for the construction of bridges and roads by the government. The net result has been landlessness and indebtedness, forcing many farmers to abandon their profession to migrate to towns.

The sale of paddy by farmers to the MATP procurement agents to meet the quota is subject to swindling by the head procurement agent. The agent may undercut a farmer's quota sold to the government by 10 percent to 12 percent or 10 to 12 baskets out of 100 baskets, as well as pay less than the government procurement price per basket of paddy sold. This is done by underweighing the paddy sold by farmers at the buying depots. Farmers dare not report this abuse to the military commanders who regularly visit village buying depots to inspect the paddy output in various regions. Farmers are under the threat of the head procurement agent, who intimidates them that if any farmer reports the theft to the military authorities, his next sale/delivery will be undercut further, 15 percent to 20 percent, or 15 to 20 baskets of paddy per 100 baskets, for example. The cooperative agent also collects a forced donation of 1 basket of paddy per acre for the army from each farmer.

Due to the low prices of paddy offered by the MATP and state-affiliated cooperative buying agencies, farmers are unable to recover their high costs of inputs and production. Consequently, they are forced to sell their paddy to independent private merchants who pay higher prices, facing the risk of not meeting the government quota. However, a farmer with a deficient quota of paddy can avoid this risk if he can come up with the amount of cash required to make up for his deficient quota of paddy with the state procurement agent. The amount of cash he needs is determined by the agent at the black market price per basket of paddy. Upon payment of the required amount of cash, the agent simply makes up the farmer's deficient baskets on his record book by using his stockpile of paddy that he undercut and stashed away at the buying depot from other farmers. By robbing the farmers' paddies and selling them in the black market to private merchants, the state procurement agents have reportedly become very wealthy.

A letter written in July 1997 by a farmer from Pathein (formerly Bassein) District in the Irrawaddy Delta underscores the plight of farmers and the injustice of forced procurement of paddy by the government:

Many peasants, who are victims of the flood, have suffered again due to the injustice. Last year, flood came three times and every time the water receded, they planted the paddy and their paddy failed every time. The authorities knew their situation but they still demanded the peasants sell their quotas of paddy, which is twelve baskets per acre (more than one-third of harvested paddy output per acre) to the government. They intimidated them and those who could not afford to buy the paddy from the merchants have to work as manual laborers for road construction and are detained many months. They told the peasants: "If you do not have the paddy to fulfill your quotas, sell your cattle, buffalo, pigs, chickens, carts, or even houses." So many of the peasants have to sell their cattle and other properties to purchase the paddy from the merchants or government paddy purchasing centers to fulfill their quotas. Peasants have to pay around 350 kyats per basket in buying the paddy from the government purchasing centers or the merchants, whereas the government buys the paddy paying only 85 kyats per basket. I have met many peasants who have to sell their cattle and some have no cattle left to plow this year. Many have to borrow money and some families have to abandon their lands and homes and migrate to towns. Many are in debt with some owing more than a lakh of kyats (100,000 kyats) that is too much to earn from farming.

This highly inefficient process of paddy procurement, which seethes with corruption and swindling of farmers by state officials at the village buying depots across the country, explains how and why there have been a widespread shortage of rice for domestic consumption and the escalating price of rice in major urban centers of Burma. It should also be pointed out that the export of rice is monopolized by the state to earn foreign exchange. Like other contraband, there is a thriving black market for the export of rice across Burma's borders. A majority of rice that flows to the black market came from independent merchants, state procurement agents, and state distribution shops. Like ordinary folks in urban communities, farmers have also reportedly been forced to buy rice and other basic necessities in the unofficial/black market. In Upper Burma or the dry zone of Burma, where paddy and rice output has always been low due to natural factors, it has been reported that people have to purchase and consume rice imported from China, which is cheaper than the imported rice from Lower Burma. This has caused resentment among Burmese consumers, whose country was once known as "the Rice Bowl of Asia" and the major exporter of rice to China and India.

Despite the liberalization of rice and other agricultural prices and increment of the government purchase price of paddy after 1988, the state continues to maintain the system of forced procurement of paddy from farmers at prices far below free market prices and its monopoly on exports. For example, the government procurement price of the quota has been kept constant at Kt350 per ton. Although since 1988/1989 the government and the state-sponsored cooperative purchase prices at the state buying depots or farm gates have gone up several times, they remained well below the free market price offered by private traders. For example, the government purchase price was Kt3,833 per ton, while the domestic free market price and export parity price per ton of paddy were Kt10,000 per ton and Kt12,030 per ton, respectively, in 1995. The private purchase price of paddy for the same year was Kt7,688 per ton, which was more than double the government purchase price.[10]

Figure 5.3 indicates the rising spread between the private and government purchase prices of paddy, which increased by almost 1,550 percent from Kt249 per ton (Kt2,546–Kt2,297) in 1991 to Kt3,835 per ton (Kt7,688–Kt3,833) in 1995. In 1991, the government purchase price of paddy was over 90 percent of the private purchase price, while in 1995 it was less than 50 percent of the price offered by private traders.

In 1994/1995, the spread between the export parity price of Kt12,030 per ton received by the government and the average farm gate price of Kt10,000 after procurement or delivery of the quota received by farmers was Kt2,030 per ton, to underscore the fleecing of farmers by the state for the purpose of export to earn foreign exchange. According to the World Bank's estimate, the total income loss of farmers due to implicit taxation and export ban by the government was over Kt14 billion for traditional paddy output, with loss due to the export ban accounting for over 70 percent of the total income loss in 1995.[11]

LAND OWNERSHIP AND TENANCY

Another inappropriate policy of the state that has been responsible for the stagnant agricultural productivity relates to the absence of the "security of property" in the Smithian sense of ability to own and enjoy one's fruits of work and accumulation of wealth under the just rule of law. In the case of farmers, the absence of security of property is reflected in the government policy with respect to their right to own and rent the land. In both ancient and modern Burma, the king or the state proclaims itself as the ultimate owner of land, water, and natural resources. The ancient Burmese king proclaimed himself as the ultimate owner and "lord of land and water," *yay myay thakin or ashin.* This tradition was kept by both the civilian and consecutive military governments of Burma after it gained independence from the British in 1948. On the eve of independence, with the primary objective of ending alien ownership of land and landlordism, the civilian government passed the Land Nationalization Act, and all alien-owned lands were nationalized, and many of them were distributed to native farmers. However, the ultimate ownership of these lands was retained by the state. This was explicitly stated in both the Land Nationalization Act and the 1948 constitution of the Union of Burma by asserting: "The State is the ultimate owner of all lands" with "rights to regulate, alter or abolish land tenures or resume possession of any land and distribute the same for collective or co-operative farming or to agricultural tenants."[12] However, the civilian government did not exercise these rights to significantly alter or completely abolish landlordism, private ownership of farmlands, and land tenures in the rural economy.

One year after the military coup of March 1962, the Revolutionary Council government of General Ne Win rigorously launched its programs of total nationalization of the economy and abolishment of all private enterprises and properties, including land, under the policy of the Burmese Way to Socialism. In 1963, the military government enacted the Law to Protect the Rights of Peasants and the Tenancy Act or Law, under which thousands of land committees, multipurpose cooperatives, and village banks were set up to "free the village economy from the manipulation and exploitation of the landlords and capitalists."[13] However, the 1963 Tenancy Act continued to allow the land tenure system to exist with the stipulation that "tenancy rent could be paid in money" in lieu of the old system of payment in kind. It also decreed that "the annual tenancy rent would be twice the value of the land revenues of land on which rice is planted," while it was set at three times for the land on which

Figure 5.3
Government versus Private Purchase Prices of Paddy

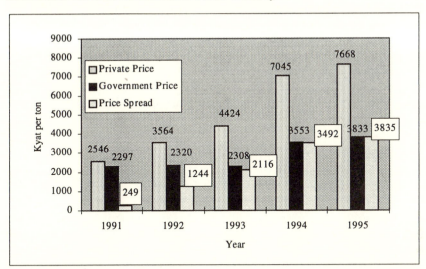

Source: The World Bank, *Myanmar, Policies for Sustaining Economic Reform* (Washington, DC: The World Bank, October, 1995), p. 36.

other cash crops were planted.[14] In 1965, this Tenancy Act was amended or revoked in passing the Law to Amend the Tenancy Act, by which the entire tenancy rent system was abolished and which established "the right only of tillers to till the land."

In 1974, the military government established the Socialist Republic of the Union of Burma, whereby the state's absolute right of ownership of all lands and natural resources was reaffirmed in Article 18 of the New Constitution of the Socialist Republic of the Union of Burma: "The State is the ultimate owner of all natural resources, above and underground, above and under water, or in the atmosphere, as well as all land; and in the interests of the working people of all national groups, is to develop, extract, exploit, and utilize these natural resources."[15] This proclamation, together with the 1965 Law to Amend the Tenancy Act (1963), made the state the sole owner and landlord of all Burmese farmers, who had no permanent right to own and rent out the land. The moment a farmer stops tilling the land, the land automatically reverts back to the state. However, it has been observed that, like all the laws and regulations passed by the military government, the private land ownership and tenure system continued to exist, riddled with loopholes and corruption in the rural economy of the socialist state of Burma.[16]

This highly inefficient system of land ownership and the tenure system remain intact under the present military regime's management of the agricultural sector since 1988. One of the guiding principles in drafting the constitution of the Union of Myanmar Naing-Gan by the delegates chosen by the SLORC asserts that "the State shall enact necessary laws to protect the rights of the peasantry, help equitable value for their agricultural produce, and implement a modern educational system that will promote all-round correct thoughts and good morals and contribute toward building of the nation."[17] In short, the economic insecurity of farmers persists in Burma today with respect to their right to own and rent their farmlands. This insecurity of property and the economic rents collected by the state in enforcing the quota system of paddy delivery at low prices and monopolizing the export of rice have been largely responsible for the disincentives of farmers and, in tandem, the decline in agricultural productivity.

THE PROBLEM OF RICE SHORTAGE

According to a government report, agricultural production increased substantially in 1992/1993 due to both good weather and successful development programs of the government. It reported that provisionally the total gross sown acres increased by 1.3 million acres or 5 percent between 1992 and 1993, from 25.4 million to 26.7 million. For 1993, the output of paddy was reported to be 14.9 million metric tons, a 12.8 percent increase from the previous year. However, the 1993 paddy output represents only a 4 percent increase above the paddy output of 1985/1986, the base year used by the government in reporting real economic growth data. Since population growth between 1985 and 1993 was 13.5 percent, the per capita growth rate of paddy output between 1985 and 1993 was a negative rate of over 9 percent. In 1995, the government reported:

Due to concerted effort, agricultural production has increased year by year. In 1994/95, the total sown acreage increased to 30.5 million acres, exceeding the previous year's figure by 2.33 million. Various means are taken to increase paddy production and consequently, the sown acreage cultivated amounted to 15.2 million acres including 1.2 million acres of summer paddy. Thus paddy acreage increased by 1.13 million acres and paddy production in 1994/95 was 901 million baskets exceeding substantially the previous year's production by 98.4 million baskets.[18]

Be that as it may, the curious question is, contrary to such government reports on the phenomenal growth of paddy and rice output, why have there been reports of persistent rice shortages for domestic consumption? There are basically two answers to this question: (1) official statistics on paddy and rice output are inaccurate and distorted, and (2) it is due to a highly inefficient system of procurement and distribution of paddy and rice and monopoly on export maintained by the state. Both seem to be occurring in Burma.

With respect to the first answer relating to the government reports of increased paddy and rice production and putting the blame for rice shortages and price increases on private traders' hoarding and smuggling of rice, a knowledgeable Burmese agricultural economist raised the question, of whither the rice surplus?:

We are of the opinion that, among other things, one of the main reasons for the decline in rice exports and price increases lies in a declining supply of rice which is not reflected in the ever-widening gap between government production figures and actual production. In other words, production figures provided by the government agencies are over-inflated.[19]

With respect to the second answer of declining agricultural productivity in Myanmar, another Burmese economist observed:

On the whole, in spite of some improvements in the year 1992/1993, agricultural production is considered as declining or to say the least stagnant. This condition could be partially explained by the fact that the quantity of important inputs such as fertilizers and other agricultural inputs made available to farmers has declined. The more fundamental problem is that Myanmar's agriculture, within the existing technology and available land, seems to have reached the production plateau.[20]

This was supported by an empirical study that showed the growth rate of agricultural net output and productivity of labor and land to be declining since 1982.[21] My own finding is that the real productivity of paddy per capita continues to decline after 1988 relative to 1985, despite the introduction of multiple cropping and launching of extensive irrigation projects in the arid areas of Upper Burma in the 1990s. The major causes of this decline are rising costs of inputs, disincentive on the part of farmers who have been forced to plant and supply paddy to the state buying depots, the continued maintenance of a highly inefficient quota system of procurement, and the unfair pricing policy of the state. Figure 5.4 testifies to this fact.

The real productivity index between 1985 and 1995 are arrived at by comparing the percentage change in yield to percentage change in population each year relative to 1985, based on the following equations:

1. p=a*y, where p=total paddy production, a=total sown acreage, and

   y=yield per acre=p ÷ a

2. %Δ in p=(%Δ in a) + (%Δ in y) + (%Δ in a) (%Δ in y).

   That is, (1+%Δ in p)=(1+%Δ in a) (1+%Δ in y)

   Hence, (1+%Δ in y)=(1+%Δ in p)÷(1+%Δ in a)

The real cause of the shortage of rice for domestic consumption relates to the second answer. The hallmark of the agricultural policy of the Burmese government since independence in 1948 has been the control of procurement of paddy and rice exports. The net consequence was the creation of a highly inefficient economic system that was riddled with corruption and smuggling of paddy and rice by farmers, government officials, and merchants to fetch higher prices in the unofficial/black market inside Burma and across the border. The

Figure 5.4
Paddy Productivity Index (1985=Base Year)

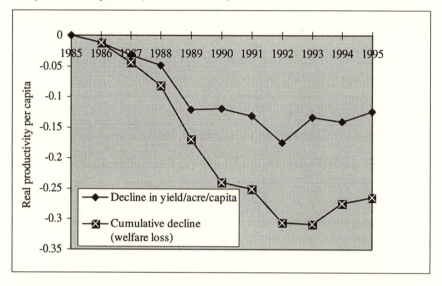

Source: Ministry of National Planning and Development (MNPED), *The Union of Myanmar, Review of the Financial, Economic and Social Conditions for 1991/1992* and *1994/1995* (Yangon: MNPED, 1992 and 1995).

same thing has been occurring in the so-called open-door, market-oriented economy of Myanmar today.

As in the past, the unknown amounts of rice hoarded to sell for higher profit in the fragmented domestic market and across the border by private traders as well as the amount procured and stashed away in government warehouses by the state for exports to earn foreign exchange may be deemed the key factors responsible for the problem of rice shortage for domestic consumption. In short, over the past three decades the single most important determinant of Burma's inability to exploit its relatively richer land resources compared to other Asian countries to increase paddy productivity has been the inappropriate policies of the consecutive military governments. As the World Bank assessed:

Myanmar's paddy yields are higher than in Thailand, Bangladesh, and India and not lower than in Sri Lanka and Vietnam. Its inability to exploit this agricultural potential since the 1960s reflects mainly inappropriate policies, in output pricing and marketing, input supply and land tenure.[22]

In addition to the unjust and inept policies of the military regime, the natural disaster of flood has magnified the problem of rice shortage and the plight of peasantry in Burma. There has been an unusual number of floods between 1996 and 1997, including the worst flooding in 30 years occurring during the months of August and September 1997 that destroyed thousands of paddy fields and homes in the Irrawaddy Delta and the Tenasserim region of Lower Burma. This rich and fertile region accounts for 80 percent of the paddy planted in the entire country and the majority of rice exports to the outside world. The ruling military junta which has a monopoly on information remained muted on the extent of the disaster with respect to the number of paddy fields, homes, and lives destroyed. From the limited reports by diplomats and journalists, nine of Burma's 14 states were affected by the flood, with a million acres of paddy fields destroyed along with the destruction agricultural infrastructure and some 100,000 people losing their homes and livestock.[23] There has also been some news of the Burmese government covertly asking for and receiving disaster aid from the UN and a number of countries, including Australia, China, Japan, and UK.

Burmese peasants, who make up two-thirds of Burma's population, are not going to be able to meet their quotas of paddy that they were forced to sell to the state buying depots at unfair prices. Knowing this situation well and playing the politics of rice, on November 11, 1997, at a ceremony held in Pegu the minister of agriculture Lieutenant General Myint Aung and the minister of trade Lieutenant General Tun Kyi jointly announced that beginning from 1997/1998 fiscal year paddy would not be purchased directly from the farmers as previously practiced. At the same time, Myanmar Agricultural Produce Trading (MAPT) of the trade ministry issued a notification putting into effect immediately the new system of purchasing paddy by a sealed tender bid process in lieu of the quota delivery system.

The two ministers were sacked and removed from their cabinet posts after their announcement of the new procurement system when on November 15, 1997, the SLORC was dissolved and replaced by the new junta, State Peace and Development Council (SPDC). According to the state-owned Burmese newspaper Mirror ((Kyay Mhon in Burmese), the abolishment of the quota delivery system of paddy and the new system of paddy procurement introduced by the MAPT have been maintained by the trade ministry of SPDC under its new minister Major General Kyaw Than. An additional change made under the new paddy procurement system is that government representatives from the trade ministry will visit various paddy-producing districts and purchase paddy at competitive or freely floating market prices from the farmers who are not obligated to sell.[24]

However, with respect to the state monopoly of rice exports, the US Department of Agriculture (USDA) reported that Myamar Export-Import Services of the trade ministry continues to handle and maintain its monopoly, soliciting bids from prospective foreign buyers and shipping limited amounts of rice exports. The USDA also reported that official sources said that the government will allow partial participation of the private sector in the rice export market.[25] Be that as it may, the problem of rice shortages for domestic consumption and exports facing Burma is far from over and cannot and will not be solved by the stop-gap measures of partial liberalization and privatization. The US Embassy in Rangoon gave the following likely economic consequences of the new paddy procurement system:

This liberalization measure is necessary but not sufficient to increase rice production and exports. If the GOB continues to monopolize rice exports, ending below market procurement would make the prices at which the GOB gets the rice it exports depend in part upon the quantity it exports. The GOB will be able to export at a profit only by keeping domestic rice prices [should be adjusted nominal prices at effective exchange rate] below world prices, and would maximize its rice export profits by restricting rice exports to a point at which domestic prices are well below world prices. Consequently, the returns to growing paddy might decrease relative to the returns to growing alternative crops, so farmers might seek to reduce their production of paddy, leaving the GOB with little exportable rice and meager rice export receipts in the absence of coercive measures to boost paddy production.[26]

It is obvious that the new procurement system is not going to cure the shortages of rice for domestic consumption and exports immediately due to the devastating flood. Even if one assumes a normal year of paddy and rice production, the new procurement system would entail the hiking of domestic rice prices adjusted for foreign exchange rate distortion to the level of world prices in order to boost paddy and rice production.

Although farmers and especially rice merchants would benefit somewhat by receiving higher prices, this measure alone without relinquishing the state monopoly of rice exports and the maintenance of foreign exchange regime with a dual exchange rate will perpetuate the problem of rice shortages and add more fuel to the galloping inflation. The reason is that since the purchase of paddy and rice at higher market prices by the government is paid in kyat, it has to be financed by printing more kyat notes. This will cause real prices or income received by farmers and rice traders from the sale of paddy and rice to the government to be well below world prices. This in turn will cause disincentives on the part of farmers to boost paddy and rice production for sale to the government. The net effect will be the continuation of black marketeeing in rice trade as well as the choice of planting crops other than paddy whose exports are not monoplized by the state. Hence, the new military regime, SPDC, which needs to monopolize rice exports and foreign exchange to maintain power, will retain the use of coercive measures other than the quota delivery of paddy, such as forced donation of paddy or rice to the army in lieu of forced labor and forced plantation of summer and multiple crops. It is also likely that the government will revert back to the use of quota delivery system or introduce another coercive paddy procurement system as it has done in the past.

The single most important determinant in the living standard of a Burmese family and the economic performance of Burma has been paddy or rice which the Burmese called the "golden fruit," *shwethee*. The politics of rice has dominated the history of Burma in terms of official slogans and development programs as well as the revolts of peasants and masses. The British colonization of

Burma and the ensuing sociopolitical and economic changes were closely linked to the development of the rich Irrawaddy Delta of Lower Burma. The Burmese nationalist revolt against the British rule was instigated by the agricultural indebtedness and economic plight of the Burmese peasantry in the 1930's, while the 1974 workers' strikes in socialist Burma was due to the devastating flood and the 1974 Rangoon University students' revolt in connection with the U Thant affair and the 1988 mass revolt against the military rule were all propelled by the shortages and the escalating price of rice.

Traditional Burmese believe that natural disasters of earthquakes, droughts, fires, thunder, storms, and floods are omens of an apocalypse of the kingdom of an unjust and ruthless Burmese king brought on by the guardian angels, *nat daiwahs*, of heaven. The belief in spirit, astrology, and numerology cuts across the entire spectrum of Burmese population, including the tradition-bound military rulers. The history of military rule over Burma over the past three decades is replete with the prophecies and omens of political misfortunes and performance of rituals to counter them by insecure Burmese military rulers. For example, dictator General Ne Win built a pagoda in Rangoon which was reportedly kept unfinished due to a bad omen of his downfall. In 1987, after consulting his personal astrologer, he performed a numerological ritual to counter the bad omen by introducing two oddly-denominated 9 and 45 (4+5=9) kyat notes, based upon the belief of number 9 as a numerologically lucky number. This eventually led to his resignation from the political throne in July 1988 and precipitated the mass political uprising of 1988.

The peasantry of Burma has been squeezed to destitution and death by the natural enemy of flood and the human enemy of an unjust military regime. The intolerable sufferings of the Burmese peasantry and ordinary people due to rice shortages caused by these two pincers of affliction signal another mass political uprising and violence in the Golden Land. It will be curious to see how the present tradition-bound military junta, the newly renamed State Peace and Development Council (SPDC), is going to counter the bad omen of the ominous flood and pending shortages of rice for domestic consumption that seems to signal the apocalypse of its unjust and illegitimate reign over Burma. One can only hope that the past history of mass slaughter of unarmed demonstrators does not repeat this time.

NOTES

1. "Rice Prices in Mandalay" (in Burmese), *Dana* (February, 1996): 16.

2. "Rice Prices" (in Burmese), *Myanma Dana* , no. 77 (November 1996): 12.

3 "Prices of Goods" (in Burmese), *Living Color Magazine* (September 1997): p.46.

4. The World Bank, *Myanmar Policies for Sustaining Economic Reform* (Washington, DC: October 1995), p. 38.

5. Ibid., p. 37.

6. US Embassy, *Burma, Country Commercial Guide 1998* (Rangoon: US Embassy, 1998), p. 14.

7. David Dapice, *Landlessness, Poverty, and the Environment in Myanmar: Can Grass Roots Initiatives Create Sustainable Progress?, A Report to the United Nations Development Programme* (Cambridge: Harvard Institute of International Development (HIID), February 10, 1995), p. 5.

8. Ibid.

9. Mya Than, "Growth Pattern of Burmese Agriculture: A Productivity Approach," Occasional Paper No. 81 (Singapore: Institute of Southeast Asian Studies, 1988), p. 6.

10. The World Bank, *Myanmar Policies,* p. 37.

11. Ibid., pp. 37–38.

12. *The Constitution of the Union of Burma* (Rangoon: Government Printing Press, 1948), p. 7.

13. The Burma Socialist Programme Party (BSPP), *Party Seminar 1965: Speeches of General Ne Win and Political Report of the General Secretary* (Rangoon: Sarpay Beikman Press, 1966), p. 80.

14. Ibid., pp. 75–76.

15. Mya Saw Shin, trans., *The Constitution (Fundamental Law) of the Socialist Republic of the Union of Burma* (Washington, DC: Library of Congress, Law Library, June 1975), pp. 8–9.

16. Than, "Growth Patterns."

17. *The New Light of Myanmar*, Yangon, September, 17, 1993.

18. MNPED, *Review, 1995/1996,* p. 3.

19. Mya Than, "Agriculture in Myanmar: What has Happened to Asia's Rice Bowl?, *Southeast Asian Affairs* (1990): 254.

20. Khin Maung Kyi, "Myanmar: Will Forever Flow the Ayeyarwady?", *Southeast Asian Affairs*, (1994): 216.

21. Than, "Growth Pattern," p. 18.

22. The World Bank, *Myanmar Policies,* p. 34.

23. Economist Intelligence Unit (EIU), *Country Report, Myanmar (Burma),* 4th Quarter, 1997 (London; EIU, 1997)), p. 28.

24. *Mirror* ((Kyay Mhon in Burmese), November 30, 1997, p. 6.

25. See United States Department of Agriculture (USDA), "Burma Rice Trade Report," Dow Jones, November 24, 1997.

26 US Embassy, *Burma, Country Commercial Guide 1988*, Ibid.

6

External Sector Performance: Foreign Trade and Investment

Historically, the Burmese economy is primarily an agricultural economy with a mono-cultural orientation to exports of primary products, especially rice, pulses and beans, timber, gems, and minerals. The single most important indicator of Burma's economic strength and performance has been rice exports. During the latter part of British colonial rule, Burma became a relatively developed export-oriented economy and came to be known as the "Rice Bowl of Asia." For example, the annual rice exports of British Burma (Lower Burma) averaged 811,106 tons between 1868 and 1874.[1] During the last two decades of British colonial rule, between 1920 and 1940, the average annual rice exports of Burma was between 2 and 3 million tons. This made colonial Burma the top rice-exporting country in the world in the first half of the twentieth century. The export industries of timber and teak, oil, and minerals likewise developed fairly well to impress many foreign observers in considering Burma a country with no sign of abject poverty and economic anxiety on the part of its population.

Even after it gained independence in 1948, Burma's status as the Rice Bowl of Asia was more or less retained until 1962, when the democratically elected civilian government of U Nu was deposed by General Ne Win and his Revolutionary Council government. The average annual rice exports of Burma under the civilian government from 1948 to 1962 was 1.5 million tons, although it was only two-thirds of the average annual rice exports of colonial Burma. (Table 6.1)

After the military coup of 1962, Burma's rice exports declined rapidly. By 1970, Burma's status as the "Rice Bowl of Asia" was completely lost. This is evidenced by the following dramatic decline of Burma's share of rice export in the world's total. (Table 6.2)

Table 6.1
Rice Exports in Millions of Metric Tons

1954	1955	1956	1957	1958	1959	1960
1.530	1.631	1.9310	2.005	1.4630	1.614	2.080

Sources: Government of the Union of Burma, *Economic Surveys of Burma*, 1956–1960 and *Quarterly Bulletin of Statistics*, 1956–1960.

Table 6.2
Rice Exports in Millions of Metric Tons

	1950	1960	1970	1976	1979
Burma	1.231	1.627	.5708	.4282	.6070
% of World	26.9	30.5	6.5	4.6	5.1
Thailand	1.294	1.255	1.372	1.685	2.723
% of World	28.2	23.5	15.0	17.9	22.9
World	4.584	5.338	8.794	9.400	11.887

Source: FAO, *Trade Yearbooks* from 1950 to 1980. Figures are in five-year average except 1979.

By 1974/1975, the year of the rice crisis due to unprecedented flooding and ensuing workers' strikes and political turmoil, Burma's rice exports dropped to 104, 000 tons. It was so alarming that Henry Kamm of *The New York Times* projected, "The world's one-time leading exporter will be importing the staple of its diet early in the next decade."[2] Between 1975 and 1988, the annual rice exports of the Socialist Republic of the Union of Burma averaged 500,000 tons,[3] which was only one-third of the average annual rice exports of Burma under civilian government, to highlight the poor external economic performance of Burma under military government.

As Mya Than observed, "It is remarkable that while Myanmar's population has grown by about 2.5 times since the 1930s, in 1987/1988, its rice exports fell more than ten times."[4] Burma's inability to recover not only its status of being the leading rice exporter in the world before the military coup of 1962 but also the average level of rice exports of socialist Burma seems to be continuing under the present military regime. The following table and chart show this as Burma's annual rice and broken rice exports between 1989 and 1997 averaged 275,677 tons, with an average annual earning of around Kt330 million or $55 million based upon the average unit price of $200 per ton.

In 1994/1995, the government attempted to achieve an ambitious target of exporting 1.7 million tons of rice, which was proven to be unrealized in light of the reports of the government's failure to fulfill its rice export contracts with Indonesia and China. This decision to increase rice exports in 1994/1995 to four times the level of the previous year was partly propelled by an increase in world rice price and partly by the decision to cut down the teak export. In an effort to fulfill this ambitious target, the government procurement agencies

Table 6.3

Rice and Broken Rice Exports in Millions of Metric Tons and Kyats

1988/89	1989/90	1990/91	1991/92	1992/93	1993/94	1994/95	95/96	96/97
.048mt	.169mt	.134mt	.183mt	.198mt	.261mt	1.041mt	.354mt	.0931mt
Kt54	Kt266	Kt172	Kt251	Kt249	Kt269	Kt1,166	Kt440	Kt125.7

Source: Ministry of National Planning and Economic Development (MNPED), *The Union of Myanmar, Review of the Financial, Economic and Social Conditions 1992/1993* and *1996/1997* (Yangon: MNPED, 1993 and 1997) and Central Statistical Organization (CSO), *Selected Monthly Economic Indicators* (Yangon: CSO, July-August, 1997).

Figure 6.1

Rice and Broken Rice Exports

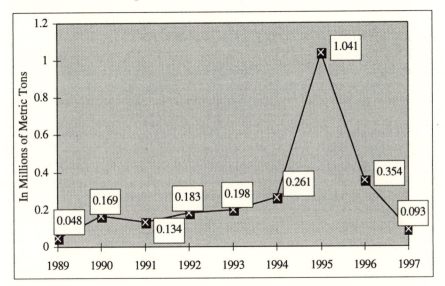

began to forcefully extract more supply from farmers and distribute less rice for domestic consumption, which resulted in phenomenal rises in domestic rice prices. The fear of another public unrest due to soaring rice prices and shortages like the one in 1988 led the government to play the politics of rice by distributing free rice to government employees and their families and order the Ministry of Trade to stop signing new rice exports contracts in February 1995 and ordered the Ministry of Agriculture to stop exporting rice in December 1994.[5] Consequently, the export target was not achieved.

There were also reports of bad, wet harvest and severe damages of rice stored for export in government warehouses due to insect infestation during 1996. According to the Central Statistical Organization of the government, during the fiscal year 1996/1997 rice exports fell by 73.7 percent in volume and

71.4 percent in value, from 354,000 metric tons to 93,100 metric tons and from Kt440 million to Kt125.7 million between 1996 and 1997.[6] In terms of dollar value, earnings from rice exports fell from $70.8 million in 1996 to $18.6 million in 1997 based on the unit price of $200 per ton. The plunge of rice exports continues into the fiscal year 1997/1998. According to the US Department of Agriculture, the "total recorded (legal) rice exports for the first half of the fiscal year 1997/1998, from April 1 through October 31, 1997, amounted to only 15,008 metric tons."[7] It is safe to assume that for the entire fiscal year 1997/1998, from April 1, 1997 to March 31, 1998, the volume of rice exports is more than likely to be less than 30,000 tons which is worth less than $6 million in light of the devastating flood of 1997 that destroyed thousands of paddy fields in the major paddy-producing regions of Irrawaddy Delta and Tenasserim. This would be the lowest level of rice ever exported by Burma since it gained independence from the British rule in 1948.

BALANCE OF TRADE AND PAYMENTS DEFICITS SINCE 1988

Since 1988, Burma has been suffering from a chronic trade deficit averaging over Kt2.5 billion (over $400 million at official exchange rate of $1=Kt6) a year. In 1995/1996, for the 19th year in succession, Burma recorded a trade deficit of Kt5.284 billion (about $881 million at the official exchange rate of Kt6=$1), which was the largest trade deficit ever recorded since 1977/1978. Exports fell by 7 percent to Kt5.017 billion, while imports rose by 24 percent to Kt1.03 billion from the previous year.[8] For 1996/1997 another larger trade deficit of Kt5.577 billion has been projected. The chronic trade deficit persists together with the deteriorating terms of trade and an outstanding foreign debt of over $6 billion. Using 1985/1986 as the base year, the terms of trade since 1988 also remains below 100, with a declining trend from 81 in 1989/1990 to 64.1 in 1995/1996 (Table 6.4).

The cumulative trade deficit from 1988/1989 to 1995/1996 stood at Kt24.0812 billion (about $4 billion at the official exchange rate of Kt6=$1) which has been the main source of drain in the foreign exchange reserves of the government (Figure 6.2).

As it was pointed out in Chapter 5, the main reason for the problem of rice shortages for domestic consumption and exports has been due to the inept and unjust paddy procurement policy and state monopoly of rice exports. Among the inept economic policies of the military government, the maintenance of a dual exchange rate system with the unofficial or black market foreign exchange rate climbing to a level of over 60 times (Kt380=US$1) higher than the official rate (Kt6 to US$1) in December 1997 has been most damaging to export expansion due to the reduction of incentives for domestic producers to engage in export industries. Conversely, it has expanded imports by encouraging importers with access to foreign exchange at official rate, most of whom are state

Table 6.4
Balance of Trade in Millions of Kyats

	1998/89	1989/90	1990/91	1991/92	1992/93	1993/94	1994/95	1995/96
Export	2193	2846.5	2961.9	2931.8	3655.4	4227.8	5405.2	5017.2
Import	3443	3395	5522.8	5336.7	5365.3	7923.3	8332.3	10301.6
Balance	-1250	-560.9	-2560.9	-2404.9	-1709.9	-3695.5	-2927.1	-5284.4

Sources: Ministry of National Planning and Economic Development (MNPED), *The Union of Myanmar, Review of the Financial, Economic and Social Conditions for 1996/1997* (Yangon: MNPED, 1996 and 1997), p. 177.

Figure 6.2
Cumulative Trade Deficit (1988–1996)

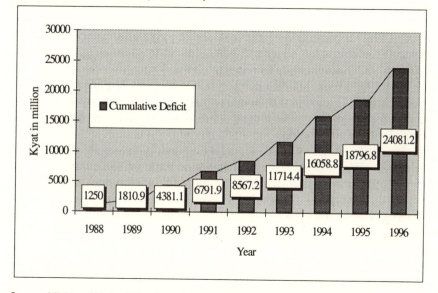

Sources: Ministry of National Planning and Economic Development (MNPED), *The Union of Myanmar, Review of the Financial, Economic and Social Conditions for 1996/1997* (Yangon: MNPED, 1996 and 1997), p. 177.

enterprises and private businesses with political connection, to import and reap abnormal profits. Apart from causing the chronic trade deficit, the highly inefficient dual foreign exchange rate system generates other negative consequences, such as the discouragement of reform or privatization of state enterprises, the proliferation of corruption, and the stimulation of rent-seeking activities.[9]

According to the World Bank, the current account deficits for the period from 1990 to 1995 are $77.5 million (1990), $526 million (1991), $344 million (1992), $275.4 million (1993), $292 million (1994), and $339 million projected for 1995.[10] The IMF gave the projected current account deficits, excluding official grants, of $303 million for 1995/1996 and $386 million for 1996/1997.[11] The financing of these persistent current account deficits has been made by the inflow of long-term foreign capital in terms of concessional loans and grants, mostly from Japan and former West Germany, and foreign direct investment from around the world. However, financing the current account deficits by these two sources has not been adequate to generate an equilibrium in the basic balance of payments due to the fact that since 1988 all bilateral aid from the West and multilateral grants and loans from international organizations, such as the IMF, the Asian Development, and the World Bank, have been halted. In other words, Burma faces a serious, long-term problem in meeting its external debt obligations and balancing its basic balance of payments. In the 1990s, long-term capital inflows in the form of foreign direct investments have dominated the capital account of the balance of payments as official financing of current account deficit has become less and less significant. The shortage of bilateral and multilateral loans has been partially made up by the disbursement of a number of new medium- and long-term concessional loans for railway, shipping, and fishery projects provided by China.

As for the external debt, it has grown steadily from $4.221 billion in 1990 to $5.518 billion in 1994/1995, with an annual average debt service ratio of 41 percent for the period.[12] The majority of Burma's medium- and long-term external debts are concessional loans, accounting for 90 percent of the total external debt, three-fourths of which are bilateral loans, with loans from Japan and the former Federal Republic of Germany accounting for 75 percent. As in the past socialist state of Burma, Japan and former West Germany continue to be the largest creditors of Burma. As of March 1993, the total outstanding and disbursed bilateral debt (including arrears on principal payments and excluding interest payments) was $3.290 billion, with $2.44 billion outstanding debt to Japan, $515 million to former West Germany, and $91.4 million to China. The outstanding stock of external debt service arrears, over 70 percent of which are owed to bilateral creditors, has also been rising. At the end of 1994/1995, it rose by some $137 million to almost $1.5 billion, 60 percent of which is owed to Japan.[13]

The external liquidity crisis of Burma due to insufficient long-term capital inflows continues to persist and is reflected in the overall balance of payments deficit (current account balance + net long-term capital movements + errors and omissions) since 1990, with the consecutive deficits of $370.9 million (1991), $232.4 million (1992), $279.4 million (1993), $248 million (1994), and $48 million (provisional deficit for 1995).[14] Hence, it can be inferred, as some private analysts suggested, that the major portion of financing the mounting licit/legal trade and current account deficits has been made by funds derived from the export of illicit/illegal drug or heroin from the Golden Triangle and other contraband to the outside world across the borders of China, India, and Thailand. To solve the external liquidity crisis, officials of the military government have been rigorously lobbying and asking for the resumption of loans, grants, and drawing rights, without success so far, from the two most important multinational lending organizations, the International Monetary Fund (IMF) and the World Bank.

The persistent trade deficit has been the major cause of the decline in foreign exchange reserves. Foreign exchange reserves reached a high of $454.4 million in 1989/1990 primarily due to the investment of more than a dozen foreign oil companies that entered onshore and offshore joint venture oil exploration contracts with the state-owned Myanmar Oil and Energy Enterprise (MOEG). It was followed by four consecutive years of decline, with $297.8 million in 1991, $283.3 million in 1992, $273.4 million in 1993, and $241 million in 1994. The projected foreign exchange reserves for 1995 was $327.6 million.[15] According to IMF, beginning in 1995/1996 external liquidity began showing signs of strain as exports started to stagnate, and foreign exchange reserves fell to $301 million. By August 1996, foreign exchange reserves plunged below $200 million when international news media reported that the government was running out of foreign exchange.[16] The decline in foreign exchange reserves is more than likely to continue in 1997/1998 and for the rest of the 1990s in light of stagnant exports relative to sustained rise in imports, new investment sanctions imposed by the United States, and EU's cancellation of Burma's general special privileges (GSP) status.

The major reason for the decline in foreign exchange reserves since 1989/1990 may be the military regime's rigorous procurement program and payments for arms and equipment purchased from the outside world, including the $1.4 billion deal struck with China in 1989, and deals with other countries (Yugoslavia, Poland, Portugal, North Korea, and Singapore). The exact payment in foreign exchange for arms purchases each year is not known and has not been revealed by the government. Based on the US Arms Control and Disarmament Agency's report, the average value of arms imported by Burma was almost $200 million a year between 1990 and 1993, which represented one-half of the average trade deficit of $400 million a year for the same period.[17] The most recent arms procurement from China was a package deal struck in November 1994 during the visit of the Burma army chief of staff and secretary no. 2 of the SLORC, Lieutenant General Tin Oo. It was reported to be worth $400 million, involving the procurement of helicopters, artillery pieces, armored vehicles, naval gunboats (including three naval frigates), military parachutes, and small arms.[18] There are also reports of recent arms procurement through arms brokers from a number of Western countries, including Belgium, Israel, Sweden, Switzerland, United Kingdom, and Russia.

The dependency of Burma on imports of foreign-manufactured consumer goods, raw materials, and capital goods has been continuing with no end in sight. The percentage share of consumer goods, in total imports has been greater than that of capital goods, to indicate Burma's inability to produce sufficient foodstuff and other consumer goods for domestic consumption. However, government reported the percentage share of capital goods in total imports to be consistently larger than that of the consumer goods since 1988, as indicated in Figure 6.3.

Contrary to the government report, the International Monetary Fund reported that there has been a shift away from the import of capital goods to the import of consumer goods since 1990. Figure 6.4 shows this shift.

The main explanation for the contradictory values of the ratio of consumer to capital goods imports given by the two is that the government data on imports of consumer goods exclude cross-border imports, especially large amounts of Chinese and Thai consumer goods, by classifying them under a separate category of "commodity unspecified" included in the IMF data. Despite their differences, since 1991 both reports showed a dramatic rise of foodstuff above other consumer goods imports to indicate Burma's growing problem of shortages in foodstuff. In other words, it seems to indicate that Burma has been unable to achieve import-substitution or self-sufficiency in domestic production of consumer goods.

Since the 1940s, the basic export structure of the economy remains unchanged, with rice and forest products changing back and forth in terms of value and volume, depending on the external market and domestic conditions and policy factors. Between 1981 and 1991 the share of agricultural products in total exports fell from 54.6 percent to 28.2 percent, while the share of forest products increased from 3 percent to 36.7 percent.[19] Most of the increase in the export of forest products was due to wholesale logging concessions granted to 47 Thai companies in 1989. The export of forest products fell in 1991/1992 and rose again after 1992/1993 with export of agricultural products climbing above the export of forest products in the post-1992 period.

Despite the intensified effort and claim of the government in increasing the acreage and production of paddy/rice, exports of teak and forest products have dominated over the exports of rice and broken rice since 1988. In 1993, the military regime canceled the teak and timber logging concessions granted to some 47 Thai companies in the name of environmental protection and conservation of forests. However, exports of teak and other wood continue to rise due to the illegal felling of teak and other trees by smugglers to sell them across Thai and Chinese borders, as well as the state-continued reliance on export of teak and other forest products to earn foreign exchange.

In terms of exports by country, Singapore has been the largest importer of Burmese goods with Kt819.8 million, followed by Thailand with Kt736.8 million, India with Kt634.7 million, Hong Kong with Kt453 million, People's Republic of China with Kt209.8 million, Japan with Kt187.6 million, and Korea with Kt35.1 million in 1993/1994. With respect to imports from country of origin, the majority of Burma's imports are from Japan, China, Thailand, Singapore, Korea, India, and Hong Kong in order of high to low ranking. In terms

Figure 6.3
Consumer versus Capital Goods Imports (Govt.)

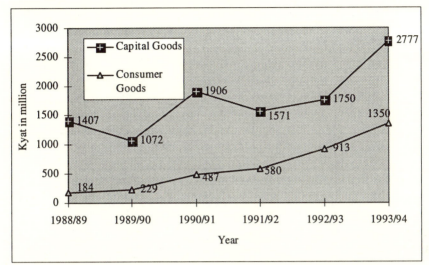

Source: Ministry of National Planning and Economic Development (MNPED), *The Union of Myanmar, Review of the Financial, Economic and Social Conditions for 1995/1996* (Yangon: MNPED, 1996), p. 173.

Figure 6.4
Consumer versus Capital Goods Imports (IMF)

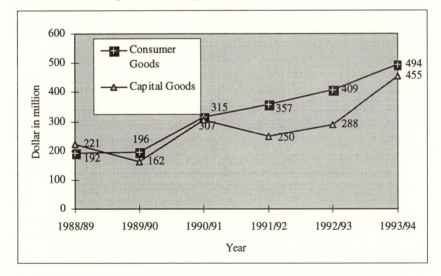

Source: The International Monetary Fund (IMF), *Myanmar: Recent Economic Developments* (Washington D.C.: IMF, October 11, 1995), p. 66.

Table 6.5
Exports by Type of Commodity (Millions of Kyats)

	1987/88	1988/89	1989/90	1990/91	1991/92	1992/93	1993/94	1994/95	95/96
Agricultural Products	454	128	432	942	1,011	1,299	1,358	2,478	2,321
Rice & Broken Rice	249	54	266	172	251	249	268	1,166	440
Pulses & Beans	131	53	123	515	429	667	724	799	1,358
Animal & Marine	76	67	137	169	161	261	373	622	622
Forest Products	754	702	1,014	1,131	943	1,120	1,357	1,205	1,275
Teak & Products	550	600	798	740	668	630	741	953	903
Minerals & Gems	225	173	208	173	111	155	365	222	213

Source: Ministry of National Planning and Economic Development (MNPED), *The Union of Myanmar, Review of the Financial, Economic and Social Conditions for 1992/1993 and 1996/1997* (Yangon: MNPED, 1993 and 1997).

of imports by country, imports from Japan have dominated all other countries with Kt2.2 billion, followed by China with Kt1.2 billion, Thailand with Kt865 million, Singapore with Kt820 million, Korea with Kt292.5 million, India with 281.4 million, and Hong Kong with Kt134.9 million in 1993/1994.[20]

With respect to total foreign trade (exports plus imports) by country, Burma's main trading partners are the Asian countries, with Japan as the largest trader with Burma, accounting for nearly 85 percent of Burma's total foreign trade: 81 percent of exports (Kt2.3232 billion out of Kt2.931 billion) and 86.6 percent of imports (Kt6.8655 billion out of Kt7.9233 billion) in 1993/1994. The percentage share of ASEAN countries and other Asian countries in Burma's total exports is almost equal, while the share of ASEAN was about 40 percent of Burma's imports in the same year. The share of the European Community countries accounted for more than 50 percent of Burma's trade with the rest of the world.

In terms of trade balance by country, Burma has the largest trade deficit with Japan followed by deficits with China, Malaysia, and Thailand, while it had trade surpluses with Singapore and India, between 1990 and 1994 which seemed to have reversed in 1994/1995. (Table 6.6)

Table 6.6
Trade Balance by Country (Millions of Kyats)

	1990/91	1991/92	1992/93	1993/94	1994/95
Japan	-679.9	-977.5	-1,385.7	-1,832.5	-1,700.7
China	-809.1	-456.7	-607.4	-1,051.6	-324.0
Malyasia	-342.6	-344.3	-269.5	-468.6	-679.9
Thailand	-389.9	-223.0	-95.3	-128.6	-287.5
Singapore	313.4	19.3	25.9	-0.4	-332.2
India	487	175.9	491.9	353.3	-31.1

Source: Ministry of National Planning and Economic Development (MNPED), *The Union of Myanmar, Review of the Financial, Economic and Social Conditions for 1994/1995 and 1996/1997*
(Yangon: MNPED, 1995 and 1997), pp. 172–174.

FOREIGN DIRECT INVESTMENT

Since 1988, no government has sanctioned Burma by imposing a total
trade and arms embargo. Despite verbal rebukes and resolutions passed against
the Burmese military regime's human rights abuses by the UN and the United
States, a multilateral arms embargo has yet to be imposed. In effect, the "constructive engagement" policy adopted and justified persistently by the ASEAN
has been based on the theory that isolation of Burma is counterproductive to
economic growth and democratization. The underlying motive of the ASEAN
as well as industrially developed Asian and Western countries with the Burmese military regime has been to establish new markets and exploit untapped
natural resources of Burma that the military regime has been putting up for sale
to capture scarce foreign exchange and sustain its control of power. The political motivation of "engagement" with Burma has been the concern over China's
increasing military influence over Burma, which represents a threat to regional
security.

By the end of April 1990, it was reported that the number of foreign companies that had applied for direct investments and had been accepted or approved by the Foreign Investment Commission (FIC) of the Burmese government was ten in oil and gas exploration, seven in manufacturing, four in the
hotel business, and two in mining. The estimated total value of the signature
bonuses paid by foreign oil companies ran as high as $55 million in 1989/1990
alone.[21] The total foreign direct investment at the end of 1990 was $655.29
million, accounting for 28.19 percent of Burma's total investment. It must be
noted that the approved dollar figures of foreign direct investment reported by
the FIC are nominal figures, whereas the realized or actual amount invested at
the inception of the investment project is only about one-third of the approved
figure in terms of paid-in-capital in foreign exchange.

By country of origin, Thailand topped the list with $160.97 million, followed by the United States with $125.19, Japan with $100 million, the Netherlands with $80 million, the United Kingdom with $72.695 million, Korea with $53.337 million, Australia with $25.2 million, Canada with $22 million, Hong Kong with $9.9 million, Singapore with $3.047 million, and Bangladesh with $2.96 million. By sector, direct foreign investment in the energy sector, mostly oil exploration, topped the list with $317.095 million, followed by mining with $105.95 million, hotels and tourism with $101.4 million, fisheries with $77.15 million, and beverage and food stuffs with $36.5 million.[22] The majority of investments in the energy sector were made by oil companies from the United States and other Western countries, such as the U.S. Amoco, Texaco and Unocal, the Petro-Canada, French Total, and the Premier Petroleum of United Kingdom. In 1993, a number of oil companies withdrew due to both the economic reason of no significant finds and international pressure for corporate withdrawal. However, American Texaco and Unocal, French Total, British Premier Petroleum, Thai Petroleum Authority, and Japanese Nippon Oil continue to operate their joint ventures signed with the Myanmar Oil and Gas Enterprise (MOEG) of SLORC, after their major finds of natural gas in the Gulf of Martaban and the Andaman Sea.

As of March 16, 1994, total approved foreign direct investments in Myanmar are reported to be $1.056 billion by some 91 foreign companies. By country of origin, Thailand remained the largest investor, followed by the United States, Japan, the Netherlands, the United Kingdom, the Republic of Korea, Australia, Canada, Hong Kong, Singapore, and Bangladesh. In terms of sectors, tourism replaced mining as the second most important sector of direct foreign investments in 1994. SLORC launched a rigorous campaign of promoting tourism with the slogan of "Visit Myanmar in 1996" to amass more foreign exchange. As of June 21, 1994, Abel stated that Singapore overtook Thailand as the top foreign investor, with its $500 million share out of the total foreign investments of $1.23 billion. Singapore's investments have dominated the hotel and tourist industry, which the SLORC has targeted as the largest foreign exchange earner under the rigorous international campaign of "Visit Myanmar in 1996." [23]

As 1995 began, there was a dramatic rise in approved foreign direct investment, which reportedly more than doubled, reaching a total of $2.4 billion in February 1995 with significant changes in the ranking of investment by country of origin and by sector. This dramatic rise was primarily accounted for by an additional investment of Total Oil of France, which owns a major interest in the joint venture project of offshore Yadana Natural Gas Well with the state-owned Myanmar Oil and Gas Enterprise (MOGE), for the construction of the proposed multimillion-dollar pipeline to ship natural gas to Thailand by 1997. France became the largest investor with its investment of $1.05 billion, accounting for 44 percent of the total direct foreign investments of $2.390 billion, to overtake Singapore ($265 million), followed by Thailand ($211 million) and the United States ($203 million). However, in March 1995 the United Kingdom replaced France as the largest investor in Burma with 24 percent, followed by France with 17.9 percent, Thailand with 16.1 percent, Singapore with 13 percent, the United States with 8.7 percent, and Japan with 3.8 percent. The combined investments of the U.K., France, and the United States alone accounted for more than 50 percent, while the total Western investment, including Australia, accounted for almost 60 percent of total foreign direct investment. The combined investment of three ASEAN member countries, Malaysia, Singapore, and Thailand, accounted for more than 30 percent of total foreign direct investment. Sectorally, foreign direct investment in oil and gas topped the list with 56.4 percent, followed by hotel and tourism with 21.9 percent, fisheries with 9.47 percent, mining with 7 percent, manufacturing with 6.7 percent, and the rest by less than 1 percent in agriculture and transport each.

As of November 30, 1996, the Myanma Investment Commission reported the approval of 226 foreign direct investment projects worth $5.271 billion, which was more than double the amount of the previous year. Singapore regained its top investor status of 1994 with $1.172 billion, followed by United Kingdom with $1.014 billion, Thailand with $960.15 million, France with $466.37 million, Malaysia with $446.27 million, the United States with $243.57 million, the Netherlands with 237.84 million, Indonesia with 208.95 million, Japan with 184.02 million, Austria with $71.5 million, Hong Kong with $64.44 million, Korea with $60.59 million, Australia with $39 million, Canada with $32.53 million, China with $27.95 million, and Germany with $15 million. Between 1995 and 1996, Singapore's investment in Burma increased by almost 250 percent, from $337.16 in 1995 to $1.172 billion in 1996 to claim its top investor status.

The share of Asian countries in total foreign direct investment in Burma stood at 59 percent, compared to about 40 percent share of the Western countries. The combined foreign direct investment of $2.788 billion by four ASEAN countries, Indonesia, Malaysia, Singapore, and Thailand, alone accounted for more than 52 percent of total foreign direct investment in Burma, to underscore their increasingly important role in the provision of external capital to Burma. The sectoral distribution of foreign direct investment in 1996 also changed despite the fact that energy or oil and gas remained the top sector ($1.498 billion), followed by manufacturing ($1.079) and real estate ($839.95 million), with hotel and tourism ($731.24 million) slipping down to the fourth place in ranking. It seemed to indicate that the official campaign of "Visit Myanmar in 1996" did not fare very well in attracting the projected number of tourists and new foreign investment projects.

As of February 1997, Myanmar Investment Commission reported the approval of 244 foreign direct investment projects worth $6.030 billion, representing nearly $1 billion increase from the previous year. This jump was largely due to the signing of more investment deals by US companies to beat the ban on new investment by President Clinton under the Cohen–Feinstein sanction bill, which was imposed in April 1997. Consequently, between November 1996 and February 1997 total foreign direct investment by US companies increased by 139 percent, from $243 million to $582 million, elevating the United States from the sixth to the fourth largest foreign investor in Burma, after the UK ($1.305 billion), Singapore ($1.215 billion), Thailand ($1.027 billion), France with ($470.4 million), Malaysia ($447.4 million), Indonesia ($208.95 million) and Japan ($192 million).The majority of US investments have been made by oil companies, Unocal, Texaco, and Arco. The sectoral distribution of foreign direct investment remained unchanged, with oil and gas ($2.13 billion) as the top sector followed by manufacturing ($1.096 billion), real estate ($875 million), and tourism ($763 million). It is safe to assume that investment by oil giants from France, United States and the United Kingdom augmented by the investment of oil companies from Japan and Thailand will continue to be the most important source of legal external capital and foreign exchange for the military regime for the rest of the 1990s.

OIL PRODUCTION AND INVESTMENT BY FOREIGN OIL COMPANIES IN BURMA

Burma was energy self-sufficient until the military seized power in 1962. Since 1962, the production of oil or petroleum has been the monopoly of the state. Oil production under the management of the state-owned Burma Oil Company began to dwindle rapidly, causing severe shortages of oil and gasoline for domestic consumption. To alleviate the shortage, between 1973 and 1977 the socialist government of General Ne Win invited a number of foreign oil companies to attempt offshore oil exploration, which resulted in no significant finds. Despite the financial and technical support of Japan in the 1980s, the oil output of Burma fell steadily from a level of 30,000 barrels a day in the late 1970s to around 12,000 barrels a day in 1991. In 1980, the oil production of the state-owned Burma Oil Company was 3,000 barrels a day, and in 1983 it dropped to 1,200 barrels a day. The need for domestic consumption was estimated to be between 30,000 and 40,000 barrels a day.

In 1989, the SLORC changed the name of Burma Oil Company to Myanma Oil and Gas Enterprise (MOGE), and it was put under the Ministry of Energy. The MOGE, together with Myanma Petrochemical Enterprise (MPE) and Myanma Petroleum Products Enterprise (MPPE), holds exclusive rights to explore, develop, and produce oil or petroleum and petroleum-related products. Since 1989, the crude oil production under the management of MOGE has been dismal and unable to meet domestic consumption due to depletion of fields, lack of modern techniques, and outdated equipment. In 1993, although the government was able to arrest the slide in oil production, the energy minister revealed that MOGE could produce only 16,000 barrels a day, which was less than one-half of the required output for domestic consumption of 35,000 barrels a day. The deficit oil production for domestic consumption has been made up by imports from abroad by the government, mainly from Australia and Japan.

Based on the government reports of crude oil production, the shortage of crude oil, also gasoline, for domestic consumption has not only persisted but also gotten worse in the 1990s. Since 1988, Burma's annual crude oil production has not been able to recover the 1980 production level of over 10.5 million barrels. In the 1990s, the annual production of crude oil has averaged less than 5.2 million barrels and has also been declining every year with the exception of one year between 1991 and 1992. In fact, the production in 1994/1995 was 1.3 million barrels below the 1989/1990 production to underscore the ongoing energy crisis confronting Burma that has impacted negatively on the living conditions and productivity of both private and state enterprises.

Table 6.7
Production of Crude Oil in Millions of US Barrels

1988/89	1989/90	1990/91	1991/92	1992/93	1993/94	1994/95
4.8	5.5	5.3	5.5	5.4	5.2	4.2

Source: Ministry of National Planning and Economic Development (MNPED), *The Union of Myanmar, Review of the Financial, Economic and Social Conditions for 1992/1993, 1994/1995* and *1995/1996* (Yangon: MNPED, 1993, 1995 and 1996).

In 1989, the SLORC invited and entered joint ventures with ten foreign oil companies: Amoco and Unocal of the United States, Royal Shell of United Kingdom/Netherlands, Croft Exploration, Clyde Petroleum and Kirkland Resources of the United Kingdom, Broken Hill Proprietary of Australia, Petro-Canada of Canada, Idemitsu of Japan, and Yukong of Korea. By 1992, nine more foreign oil companies joined the oil rush in search of great onshore and offshore finds. The new entries included Apache, Texaco, Trend, and Tyndall International of the United States, Premier Oil of the United Kingdom, Total and ELF of France, Nippon Oil Exploration of Japan, and Petronas of Malaysia. These oil companies acquired exploration rights or concessions by paying between $3 million and $8 million of signature bonuses to the Burmese military regime in bidding and securing the exploration right of certain blocks of land, such as Block A, Block B, Block C, and so on that, were auctioned off by the government. Most of the actual effort of exploration was undertaken by smaller multinational oil service and support firms farmed out by these oil giants.[24]

Toward the end of 1992 and during 1993, a massive exodus of these companies began to take place after spending between $450 million and $500 million for onshore search of oil and natural gas with no significant finds or losing the bid to a rival firm, as in the case of Shell, which lost out to Total of France, which won the bid by paying a signature bonus of $15 million. Total captured the production sharing contract of natural gas exploration in the Gulf of Martaban. The first to pull out of Burma was Australian Broken Hill Petroleum followed by Japanese Idemitsu, Petro-Canada, Amoco, and others. By the end of 1993, 13 out of 18 foreign oil companies had pulled out of Burma after no significant finds and paying a total of some $78 million signature bonuses to the military regime. Only 5 major oil companies, Texaco, Total, Unocal, British Premier, and Nippon Oil, which discovered significant offshore natural gas, have been left to continue their joint venture operations with MOGE in Burma today.

The exodus of the unsuccessful foreign oil companies was offset by the discovery of natural gas and condensate at the Yetagun Wildcat Well (*Sagarwah* in Brumes) by the U.K. Premier Consolidated Oilfields, which formed a joint venture with MOGE as British Premier Petroleum Myanmar Ltd., and Texaco's offshore natural gas find in the Isthmus of Kra located some 100 miles west of Mergui. The participating interests in the Yetagun Wildcat Well project are American Texaco, British Premier Petroleum Myanmar, and Japanese Nippon Oil Exploration Myanmar Ltd. The Yetagun field was discovered by the consortium of these three oil companies on October 25, 1992, in a block located some 420 kilometers south of Rangoon. On December 10, 1992, the government announced that the strike at Yetagun field #1 resulted in the natural gas flow of 75 million cubic feet per day (MMcfd) and an additional 1,800 barrels of crude oil. This strike halted the plunge of natural gas production by all existing gas wells in Burma to less than 70 MMcfd per day in 1990 and 1991. Indeed, "it can therefore be said that the 75 MMcfd of gas and condensate from the single test well [Yetagun] was more than Burma's entire national production at the time."[25]

The next most important and highly publicized offshore natural gas find was associated with the Yadana gas field in the Gulf of Martaban. In July 1992, French multinational firm MNC Total S.A. and Thai PTT Exploration and Production Public Co. Ltd. (PTTEP), a subsidiary of the Petroleum Authority of Thailand, signed an offshore natural gas exploration project of Yadana gas field with MOGE estimated to be worth over US$1.2 billion. The Yadana gas field is not a new gas field discovered suddenly in 1992. It was discovered back in 1982 by a joint venture exploration project between a Japanese oil company and the Burmese government that never transpired into a fully developed gas field for lack of funds on the part of the Burmese government. The participating interests in the 1992 Yadana gas field project are Total (52.5 percent), and PTTEP (up to 30 percent), the rest belonging to Unocal of United States with a 15 percent share option retained by the MOGE. The Yadana gas field concession covers an area of 26,140 square kilometers in the Gulf of Martaban, located some 250 kilometers southeast of Rangoon and 500 kilometers west of the Burmese border town of Three Pagodas Pass across Thailand. In 1994, the head of the state of Myanmar, Senior General Than Shwe, reported that the Yadana gas field has 6 trillion cubic feet of production potential instead of the initial estimate of some 2 to 3 trillion cubic feet of natural gas deposit. In 1994, Thailand signed an agreement to be the sole buyer of Burma's natural gas from the Yadana gas field by 1997 (later changed to mid-1998). In 1995, another American oil giant, Arco Richfield, signed two production-sharing agreements with MOGE to drill in Block M7 and explore natural gas in Block M9 in the Gulf of Martaban in the Bay of Bengal.

As of February 1996, the participating interests or ownership of the Yadana gas field joint venture stood at Total (36.75 percent), Unocal (33.25 percent), PTTEP (30 percent), with MOGE retaining the option to acquire up to 15 percent. If the MOGE exercised that option, the participating interests of these partners will change, and Total's share will drop to 31.2 percent accordingly. Total reported that the terms of contract struck with the SLORC gave Total full authority to take all necessary actions to ensure deliveries of natural gas to PTTEP, which will begin by July 1, 1998. There are reports of Total's engaging mercenaries to ensure safety against any terrorist assault on the project. The daily rate of delivery is projected to increase from the initial 65 million cubic feet per day (mncfd) to a plateau level of 525mncfd per day progressively over the next 14 months. Total's contract covered a 30-year span to produce and ship natural gas to Thailand by a 2,800-megawatt power plant managed by the Electricity Generating Authority of Thailand (EGAT). The projected output in the long run from the Yadana gas field is as high as 650 million cubic feet per day.[26]

In April 1996, Mitsui & Co. of Japan formed a consortium or a joint venture with Total of France and Unocal of United States by signing a Memorandum of Understanding (MoU) with the MOGE to become an additional joint venture partner of the Yadana gas field project. The newly formed consortium was granted exclusive negotiation rights with SLORC to carry out a project worth $700 million for the commercial and industrial use of the natural gas produced from the Yadana gas field. The project of the consortium, called Three in one, involved three schemes: building a 250-kilometer pipeline from Yadana gas field, connecting the pipeline to a proposed 200,000-kilowatt power plant, and building a urea fertilization production plant with a capacity of 570,000 metric tons a year. The consortium aimed to start the industrialized use of natural gas by July 1988, which would coincide with the projected time of full production and shipment of natural gas from Yadana gas field by the consortium of Total, Unocal, PTTEP and MOGE.

JOINT VENTURE AND PRODUCTION SHARING CONTRACT (PSC)

The contracts signed by foreign oil and gas companies with the MOGE of the SLORC are on "a production sharing basis" (PSC). According to the paper issued by the MOGE in February 1992, entitled *Prospects, Trends, Opportunities and Types of PSC (Production Sharing Contract) for Oil and Gas Exploration,* the concept of PSC is that the ownership of petroleum/natural gas in the ground is vested with Myanmar Oil and Gas Enterprise (MOGE) or the state of Myanmar such that it controls the management of the petroleum operation and operating foreign oil companies are contractors to the MOGE. The three main objectives of the PSC given by the SLORC are (1) to explore and develop the petroleum resources in the shortest possible time, (2) to provide the government with a fair share of income from the operation, and (3) to ensure that in case of unexpected favorable circumstances the government automatically earns a large share of profit. In other words, the SLORC's main objective in granting PSCs is to amass as much foreign exchange as possible from foreign investors. According to these contracts, if and when oil or natural gas is produced, the firm retains part of the production to recover its cost up to 40 percent. In addition, it obtains a certain share of the remaining production, which declines from 30 or 40 percent in the first stage to 10 percent in the last stage. The profit from the sale is also to be split between the foreign firm and the MOGE. The information on the percentage split of profit sharing between the two was not officially released in the news media. The firm secures a three-year tax holiday under the Foreign Investment Law. The firm incurs five main costs in securing the PSC, involving payments in cash and kind to the state: (1) bonuses in foreign exchange, (2) a minimum expenditure entirely in foreign exchange, (3) 10 percent of the oil produced upfront as royalty, (4) the sale of a certain percentage of production to domestic refineries, and (5) the payment of 70 to 90 percent of the government's share of production.

THE SIGNATURE BONUS

The signature bonus is the competitive bidding price by a foreign oil company for the right of oil and natural gas exploration in specific areas or blocks of Burma tendered by the SLORC. It is one of the three bonuses a foreign oil company must pay for securing the PSC from the government. The other two bonuses are for the approval of the firm's development plan for the block and for production beyond certain thresholds. The signature bonus is the same as the premium paid for the purchase of an option in finance. In Burmese, it is called *a-pyaut ngwe*, or "money that disappeared or was lost," which means up front money paid to a broker or dealer that cannot be retrieved by the customer. It is a common practice of real estate brokers or dealers who collect fees up front in securing the right to rent or buy an apartment or a house for a client in Rangoon. The signature bonus paid by a foreign oil company is tantamount to a flat fee paid to the state. These bonuses are to be paid in US dollars, which ranged from $3 million up to $15 million, as in the case of the French Total's exploration right that it secured in the Gulf of Martaban.

NATURAL GAS PIPELINE PROJECT AND THE "DEATH RAILWAY"

The two ongoing offshore oil and natural gas joint venture projects of Yetagun and Yadana gas fields are in the Gulf of Martaban. These two projects encompass the geopolitically strategic land areas along the Thai-Burmese border where the headquarters and population of the two strongest ethnic minority rebel groups, the Karen National Union (KNU) and the New Mon State Party (NMSP), are located. The control of these areas is a must for the SLORC for natural gas production and shipment from the gas fields. The main buyer of natural gas when it is successfully produced has been agreed to be Thailand. The surveying for the construction of a multimillion-dollar pipeline across the Burma-Thailand border was conducted by the Nortech Company of Canada. Initially, the pipeline was to be constructed linking the Burmese border outpost of Three Pagodas Pass and the Thai town of Rachanaburi across the border. Later, for both security and economic reasons the site or the pass was shifted to the town of Ban I Taung (Nat Ei Taung) village, which is located 50 kilometers south of Three Pagodas Pass at the narrowest section of the Tenasserim Peninsula with a shorter distance of 45 kilometers between the sea and Thai border to transport natural gas.

There have been reports of atrocious violations of human rights against the Karens, Mons, and the Tavoyans by the Burmese military's forcefully relocating villagers and using forced labor to build roads and the Ye-Tavoy Railway, labeled by the ethnic human rights activists as "the Death Railway." The *Multinational Monitor* reported:

The actions of the Burmese government to ensure the completion of the pipeline make the Thais look compassionate. Under the terms of the pipeline contract, the Burmese government provides security for the project. The junta has moved 17 battalions into Mon, Karen, and Tovoyan areas to secure control over the pipeline right of way. To supply those troops, the government is building a railroad and motor way between the cities of Ye and Tavoy. The railway is an extension of the old "Death Railway," which gained notoriety during World War II and was made famous by the movie the Bridge over the River Kwai. Although it was the use of westerners for slave labor that gained international notice, then, as now, it was local Mon and Karen villagers who wore the brunt of the demand for forced labor. Between 70,000 and 120,000 slave laborers are building the railway. Government troops round the laborers up into Conscription Control Center (CCC), a euphemism for concentration camps.[27]

TOURISM INDUSTRY

Next to the energy sector, foreign direct investment most sought after by the military government has been the tourism industry as a quick source of foreign exchange. After 1989 and especially during 1990, the year of the multiparty election, the SLORC forced a massive relocation of Burma's urban population to new satellite towns in the name of the Beautification and Development Program, *Sipin Thahyah Yay,* of cities. Forced relocation was part of the nationwide campaign of the SLORC to face-lift major cities to attract foreign tourists and investors. Besides Rangoon, Mandalay, and Pagan (the famed ancient city of architectural wonder and the main tourist attraction that housed thousands of Buddhist temples and pagodas built by Burmese kings), Amarapura, Mingun, Sagaing, Shwebo, and a host of other cities with ancient ruins, temples, and pagodas in Upper Burma were also targeted.

Like the energy sector, the state-owned enterprises have entered joint ventures with foreign investors for the development of infrastructure and construction of new hotels and refurbishment of old ones, such as the famous Strand Hotel and Inya Lake Hotel in Rangoon. Prior to 1992, the Ministry of Trade was in charge of tourism and the tourism industry. In 1992, the SLORC created the new Ministry of Hotels and Tourism (MHT) with Lieutenant General Kyaw Ba, a member of SLORC, as its minister. Since then, the MHT with its four Departments of Tourism Regulation, Myanmar Travel and Tours, Myama Hotels and Tourism Services, and Restaurants and Beverages Enterprises not only monitors and controls the tourist industry but also owns and operates a number of well-known hotels and resorts, some of which are joint ventures with foreign investors, in Rangoon, Mandalay, and other major cities of Burma.

As of 1993, according to official statistics, there were 46 state-owned hotels, including three foreign joint ventures with the state: the Strand, Inya Lake, and Thamada. State ownership and control of the tourism industry and related enterprises have been more or less absolute. A great many of the well-known hotels of international standard in Rangoon and provincial cities are either owned wholly or partly by the state or by the relatives of the past and present ruling military rulers. These include the Strand, Inya Lake, Thamada, Yangon City, Mya Yate Nyo Royal, owned by the Ministry of Defense, and Nawarat, built by Navarat Land of Singapore and nicknamed Sanda Win Hotel in reference to the daughter of General Ne Win, and three *Mya Yate Nyo Hotels* in Rangoon owned by the Ministry of Defense and the Ministry of Industry in Rangoon. The Yangon or Rangoon City Hotel is owned and operated by the Yangon City Development Corporation, headed by the powerful mayor of Rangoon, ex-military commander U Ko Lay. Other hotels either owned wholly or jointly by the government are the Mandalay, Maymyo, and Mya Mandalar Hotels in Mandalay, the Taung Gyi Hotel in the Shan state, and the Ngapali Beach and Sandoway Hotels in the Arankan state.

As 1994 began, the minister of hotels and tourism, Lieutenant General Kyaw Ba, embarked upon a number of projects to attract foreign tourists by opening new tourist resorts with the help of foreign companies. In order to capture foreign exchange from visitors to Burma, the government relaxed visa restrictions and took steps to extend the visiting visa permit from two weeks to a month. Not only foreign visitors but also Burmese overseas were targeted in promoting tourism. Even those Burmese who became foreign citizens were coaxed into returning for a visit to their native land. Attracting and increasing the number of foreign visitors to Burma, both for visiting cultural sites and for recreational purposes, were the goal of the government during the year 1994/1995. The main target of the government was to be able to attract a number of tourists comparable to that of its neighbors, Thailand and Singapore, in about five year's time. Until 1994, Burma received a maximum of 42,000 visitors a year—a fraction of what its two neighboring countries receive annually.

The majority of foreign companies engaged in the hotel and tourism industry of Burma are from Hong Kong, Japan, Malaysia, Singapore, and Thailand. However, firms from Singapore have become the most active and dominant investors in the construction of new hotels and establishment of tourist service agencies and airlines. In January 1994, Singapore's Nawarat Land Company opened its 80-room Nawarat International Hotel in Insein near Rangoon. In December 1994, System Bilt Co. opened its 250-room Park View Hotel in Rangoon. In April 1994, Liang Court Hotel opened via Regional Hotels group in Rangoon. In 1996, the Shangri-la Group opened its two Shangri-la Hotels in Rangoon, while Straits Steamship Land of Singapore opened the Straits Greenfield Hotel in Rangoon and the New Mandalay Hotel in Mandalay. In 1996, the Greenfield Development Limited of Singapore began the construction of a 12-floor and 450-room Sidona Hotel in Rangoon with an estimated total investment of $80 million.

On August 24, 1994, *Striat Times* reported that Singapore had proposed to help Burma in expanding its air link with other countries to promote and facilitate tourism. On October 6, 1994, the state-owned Myanmar Airways signed a joint venture contract with Air Mandalay Holding Pte. Ltd. of Singapore to operate scheduled and chartered airline services in Myanmar. This joint venture airline, Air Mandalay, began its operation in November 1995 and serviced four flights per week between Rangoon and Mandalay and Pagan in Upper Burma and Heho in the Shan state. Another joint venture airline formed between state-owned Myanmar Airways International and Singapore's High Sonic Enterprise services international routes between Burma and Singapore, Hong Kong, and Kuala Lumpur.

THE POSITIVE OR NEGATIVE IMPACT OF TOURISM ON ECONOMIC GROWTH?

The Burmese military regime's ability to sustain political power has been made possible, in part, by the outside world's willingness to invest, trade, and establish economic ties. Despite the verbal resolutions and rebukes of blatant human rights violations of the Burmese military regime by the UN, the United States and other countries in the West, there has been a trend of convergence between the foreign policies of the ASEAN and the West toward Burma. Both of them presume that trade and investment promote economic growth, and in tandem, encourage the military regime to undertake political reforms or democratization. The corollary premise of this presumption is that economic sanctions are counterproductive to democratization or isolation of a dictatorial regime such as the SLORC can only hurt the people at large.

Since 1993, a number of visitors to Burma began reporting impressive changes and attractiveness of Myanmar for foreign visitors. In 1994, Philip

Shenon wrote in his lengthy article "On the Road to Mandalay" in *The New York Times*:

For travelers, much has changed in Myanmar, the long-isolated nation still better known to the outside world as Burma: Tourist visas, once good for only one week, are now good for one month; foreign visitors are no longer being coerced into changing money at a ludicrous, larcenous official exchange rate that one time had made Mandalay as expensive as Manhattan. There are several international standard hotels and many more on the way; with a new international airline, Myanmar Airways International, flying to Myanmar need no longer be a death-defying act.[28]

Shenon failed to observe that even though foreign visitors are no longer coerced into changing money—$200 at a ludicrous and larcenous official exchange rate prior to 1994—they are now required to change $300 into foreign exchange certificates (FECs), locally dubbed "the Burmese dollar," a parallel legal tender introduced in 1993. That is, tourists are still coerced into changing $300 into FECs, which cannot be redeemed upon departure from Burma, or the government still collects foreign exchange from the tourists at the port of entry. Travel by automobiles and trains still remains arduous, expensive, and hazardous with a number of accidents on poor roads, highways, and railways that are in dire need of improvements.

Another American reporter, Barbara Bradley, whose audience with finance minister Win Tin appeared on the front page of *The New Light of Myanmar,* wrote in *The Christian Science Monitor:* "Many travelers probably associate Burma with political repression, narcotics from the Golden Triangle and 5 1/2 year house arrest of Nobel laureate Aung San Suu Kyi. But much is changing even on that score."[29] On the incredible boom of Burma under the tourist campaign of "Visit Myanmar" and the "open-door policy" of welcoming foreign investors by the SLORC, Paul Strachan wrote:

By the end of 1996, Rangoon will reportedly have more than twenty internationally owned top-end hotels. Some of these, like the Straits Steamship Co. Hotel, will have nearly 500 rooms. By conservative estimate, there will be something like 8,000 to 10,000 top-end beds available in Rangoon on any give night. This calculation does not include the 200 privately registered local hotels that have sprung up.[30]

He went on further to praise the economic boom of Myanmar under the management of SLORC:

"In fifteen years of acquaintance with the country, I have never known Burma so prosperous as it is now. Last time Burma boomed it was under the Raj, now she booms again under a different kind of colonialism—'the foreign investors.' It is sad to see the splendid old buildings go, but heartening to find healthier, happier Burma. A buzz has replaced the stagnation of pre-'90s Rangoon—people are busy doing things."[31]

Understandably, Stratchan has a vested interest in his appraisal of Burma's economic boom. In January 1995, he turned into a tourist businessman as the owner of the Irrawaddy Flottila Company & Kiscadale Publications. By joining and gaining favor from SLORC in the promotion of "Visit Myanmar Year 1996," his newly formed Irrawaddy Flotilla Company has been conducting a luxury cruise on the famed Irrawaddy River between Mandalay and the tourist sites of Sagaing and Pagan. The price he asked for the luxury river cruise under the advertisement of the "Reconnaissance Voyage with Irrawaddy Princess" was £1,600 British pounds or roughly US$2,500 per person.

In direct contrast to these accolades of positive changes in Myanmar as an attractive place for foreign tourists and a happy, healthy, and prosperous country for the Burmese people, Spencer Ifsley wrote:

Lying in the pink floral Chinese bedspread in 106-degrees heat watching the ceiling bulb flicker while the walls rumble from the *karaoke* show upstairs is wonderfully conducive to reflecting upon the future of *Myanmar*, this "New Burma" of quasi-marketdom. The brand new Hitachi refrigerator still sitting in its packing crate base, motor off, is somehow symbolic. There's a lovely view of a dozen different construction sites outside, only the windows are painted shut and the air conditioner isn't working either. Even the shower installed in an unventilated closet with exposed pipes is not the afterthought it seems. These lodgings that cry out for refurbishment are scarcely two months old, a new private venture of the Myanma Mineral Prospecting Enterprise just unveiled this February in Mandalay. She (the floor maid) apologizes, but cannot say whether the generator output for the entire building is being siphoned off to the rooftop stage spectacle. Apparently, "up-country" entrepreneurs and military officers' kids with thousands of *kyats* to spend on coloured lights, Tiger Beer, and mini-skirted Shan girls perch higher on the scale than Western tourists paying in Foreign Exchange Certificates. But then, looking down on the streets below, half the city of Mandalay is blacked out, each neighborhood sharing a rotating minimum of electricity maybe three nights a week.[32]

He went on to explain the cost of a room in such a mediocre hotel: "The room charge is not quite laughable $18 for foreigners, but an impossible 600 *kyats* for locals. Just under $5 by black market rates, or an absurd $100 if anyone actually took the official K6-to-$1 rate seriously, in *kyats*, however, one overnight costs almost three weeks' wages for the typical public servant."[33] Indeed, the overnight cost of a room in a five-star hotel like the Strand in Rangoon runs as high as $300, which is 36,000 kyats at the black market exchange rate of Kt120 to $1 in 1995/1996 and Kt51,000 at the black market rate of Kt170 to $1 in 1996/1997. This overnight cost of a room is well above the annual salary of Kt30,000 earned by a highest-ranking government official or a military commander.

The following evaluation made by a Western-educated Burmese economistwith extensive international experience who chose to remain anonymous underscores the unpleasant reality of the illusive economic boom in Rangoon that seems to have impressed many casual foreign visitors:

Visit any modern air-conditioned department store in Yangon [new name of Rangoon] with escalators and sales girls in smart uniforms. One sees racks of designer clothes, bucketsful of brand name perfumes and toilet articles, imported foods of all kinds from potato chips to Swiss chocolates, shelves of expensive foreign liquors, wines, and spirits, and fancy goods of all kinds—you name it we have it. One would think that he is in Singapore or in Bangkok and not in Yangon. These things are very impressive to a casual foreign visitor. I remember taking a visiting foreign friend to the Bogyoke Market. His reaction: "This place is booming." To this, I can only respond with a painful smile because Shakespeare would describe the situation as "a goodly apple rotten at the heart." What we have to realize is that for everything that comes into the country, something has to go out. Given the porous border and the general unreliability of foreign trade statistics, what has gone out to bring in these fabulous things into the country is sometimes too frightful to think. At the more fundamental level, Myanmar is a least developed country with a per capita income of US$285, according to the latest UNDP Human Development Report. It is not in the character of the Burmese people to say unkind things about itself [themselves or their country] but we have to face the unpleasant reality that Myanmar is a third rate economy. A third rate economy cannot support high government spending on festivals and monuments that do not contribute directly to production, nor can it sustain a lifestyle of a consumer society more appropriate for a $10,000 per capita income country. That is, no deep economic analysis or imagination is really required to find out why inflation has been raging at double digit rates or why the FEC rate [the unofficial foreign exchange certificate rate of exchange] has been exploding. It is simply that the economy cannot support the spending habits of the government and the lifestyle of a wealthy urban consumer society.

THE MANDALAY MODEL FOR PROMOTING TOURISM

The case of forced relocation and the ensuing economic plight of forcefully relocated urban population of Mandalay may be used as an example of the overall social and economic cost of tourism to Burma's urban population in general. After 1989 and especially during 1990, the SLORC forced a massive relocation of Burmese Mandalaynians to new satellite towns. In the 1990s, after the forced relocation and subjugation of dissidents and Buddhist monks of Mandalay were accomplished, a different process of population relocation and restructuring of Mandalay took place. By 1993, new satellite towns built by the SLORC on the outskirts of Mandalay, such as *Pellhpyu Goan, Kanthah-yah, Myaye Nandah, Myaye Kan-thah,* and *Mya-mahlah,* have become the centers of Burmese culture where the relatively poor ethnic Burmese of Mandalay have congregated. In contrast, the central quarters of Mandalay has been transformed into a thriving business center of Chinese culture with modern homes, hotels, shops and high-rise buildings teeming with wealthy foreign and local Chinese businessmen (called *lawpans*), ethnic Chinese drug warlords (Kokangs), and other Asian merchants. Only a handful of native-owned business establishments, such as printing houses, shoe shops, and cheroot factories, are left, dwarfed by the towering buildings and offices of foreign enterprises.

According to the official census of 1993, the population of Mandalay is over 653,000, with over 2,670 aliens. Unofficially, the total population of Mandalay may be as high as 1 million, due to a large number of unregistered illegal aliens.[34] The majority of the alien population consists of foreign-born Chinese who reportedly have become Burmese nationals overnight by acquiring the national registration cards (NRCs) in the black market. It has also been reported that many Chinese families from the Yunan Province have crossed over the border to establish and settle in a number of villages inside northern Burma. The native Burmese residents of Mandalay have gradually moved away from the center to settle in the peripheral areas of Mandalay.

THE ECONOMIC PLIGHT OF FORCEFULLY RELOCATED MANDALAY RESIDENTS

The economic plight of the majority of the native residents of Mandalay stems from the fact that most of them earn their livelihood as artisans in traditional cottage industries: making furniture, artwork, antiques, cheroots, gold leaf, tapestry, carpentering, masonry, precious stone polishing, embroidery, weaving, tailoring, and so on. Low wages in these professions relative to the skyrocketing prices of domestic and imported consumer goods have been pushing their standard of living below subsistence. Since 1989, the price of the main staple food, rice, in Mandalay has been steadily increasing with no end in sight. In 1989, the price per *pyi* (4.7 lbs.) of first-quality rice, *Pawsan Mhway*, was Kt12 which has been rising steadily upward to Kt50 in 1992, to Kt75 in 1993, and to Kt136 in 1996, an increase of over 1,000 percent in seven years.

The cost of everything has been rising so much that a Mandalay resident satirically said, "It is not only very expensive to live but also to die in Mandalay." On January 5, 1990, the military regime ordered all local cemeteries closed in Mandalay proper for the purpose of face-lifting the city. The new burial ground was established at the village of *Kyahni Kan* some 15 miles away. The total funeral costs, including Kt1,500 to transport the corpse by car to the village, are Kt4,000 to K5,000 ($33 to $41 at the 1993 black market exchange rate of Kt120=US$1), which is well above the maximum monthly pay of Kt2,500 earned by a government worker in 1993. Hence, it was said that "most native residents of Mandalay can no longer afford to die nowadays."[35] With respect to forced relocation of not only the living but also the dead in Mandalay to make room for hotel construction to attract tourists, an American traveler to Myanmar in 1996 wrote: "Even the dead must make way for the hotel boom. The new Novotel Hotel, a very concrete high-rise expression of French faith in Myanmar, sits on what was the military cemetery near the foot of the Mandalay Hill. As soon as the deal was signed, the deceased soldiery were summarily evicted to open the country and reportedly, though I was not able to confirm this, burned and discarded."[36] Although he may not have been able to confirm the story of burning and discarding the dead, it is a common knowledge among Burmese that beginning in 1990 the military regime ordered all local cemeteries closed and moved them from their central locations to the outskirts of the cities in Rangoon, Mandalay, and other major cities across Burma to face-lift the cities for tourist attraction.

FORCED LABOR OR DONATION IN MANDALAY

In 1994, in preparation for the "Visit Myanmar Year 1996" the central commander of the Mandalay division, Than Tun, ordered Mandalay residents to dismantle their homes, which happened to be on the 26 B Road, which runs east to west along the moat of the ancient palace of the last Burmese kingdom, the Konbaung dynasty. The houses were to be dismantled by the people themselves within one week. It was warned further that if a family failed to do so, the army would forcefully dismantle the house. No cash would be paid to compensate for the house. But a plot of land at the new location would be given free, and building materials for the construction of a new home would be sold to the families at subsidized prices on a quota basis. No cash would be given for the costs of carpenters and construction of new homes.

A host of foreign news media and reporters began reporting the human rights abuse with documentary pictures of some 2,000 forced laborers, including old men, women, children, and prisoners, working to clean up the moat. The *New York Times* reported: "In April 1994 orders were given to clean up Mandalay Palace, including a project to dredge the moat. Alongside shackled prisoners, two thousand ordinary farmers and city folks were used to work on this giant project."[37]

An anonymous Burmese dissident gave the following gruesome account of forced labor used in refurbishing the Mandalay's moat:

In Mandalay, you will know that the moat is being reconstructed and reinforced by new banks made of big stones. Thousands of city folks are driven into it. Each family has to contribute one laborer at a required time, which comes often, or contribute 150 to 200 kyats each time. Citizens are seen working in mud and water, like Israelite slaves building Pyramids for the Pharaohs. Finding insufficient time and labor, SLORC summoned more forced laborers from other districts around Mandalay. When citizen-workers could not finish their daily assignments, they pay bribes to the sentry-soldiers and went home. Bribery was followed by corruption and the works remained unfinished. Unequal distribution of bribes among the military caused fights and bites. The people had to work under a ruthless sun in a very hot climate, and naturally felt thirsty quite often. But no drinking water was provided anywhere near the work-site. So people had to ask for water from homes nearby. There are no latrines or water supply. Sanitation around the moat is so bad that one is unable to breathe or walk around. Labor units coming from townships far from Mandalay cannot go home every evening after work, since transport is rare and cost of gas is enormous. So after the work, they got to rest and sleep in *zayats* [shelters for pilgrims] on Mandalay Hill. This human congestion leads to bad sanitation and the sacred Hill is fouled with bad smell. The worst is yet to come. Although the ruling authorities (most of them are military) ignored the working units' welfare, they were being busy with filling their pockets—stealing away construction materials to black markets. For example, the cement bags go to the black market—so much that the moat banks, constructed without cement but only with sand and mud, crumbled under a light rain in no time.

THE FAILED "VISIT MYANMAR YEAR 1996" CAMPAIGN

In 1995, the government embarked upon a rigorous campaign of "Visit Myanmar Year 1996" with an ambitious target of attracting up to 500,000 tourists, watered down to 300,000. The target of half a million tourists represents an overly ambitious dream of increasing the number of tourists by 16 times the 31,000 average number of tourists who visited Burma annually between 1990 and 1995. As the year 1996 began, the junta's campaign of "Visit Myanmar Year 1996" began to suffer setbacks as political unrest, an intensified crackdown of opposition, and confrontation between Daw Suu Kyi and SLORC transpired, along with a number of tourist groups', lodging protests against the military regime's restrictions on the freedom of mobility and harassment by soldiers and intelligence officers as well as the denial of their request to visit and meet with Daw Suu Kyi. Consequently, the starting date of "Visit Myanmar Year 1996" had to be postponed to October 1996.

According to official statistics, the provisional number of tourists in 1996 was 105,863. Other estimates cited 150,000 tourists. Even assuming this figure was realized, it would represent the fulfillment of a 30 percent of the 500,000 target or 50 percent of the revised target of 300,000 to indicate the failed campaign of "Visit Myanmar Year 1996."[38] The clearest evidence of Burma's inability to promote tourism as an impetus for economic growth can be seen in the relatively small number of tourists it received in 1995/1996 compared with those of other neighboring countries of Southeast Asia: Malaysia with 7.9 million, Singapore with 6.6 million, Thailand with 6.5 million, and Indonesia with 4.6 million.

Table 6.8 on the number of tourists and foreign exchange received from tourism further highlight the failed "Visit Myanmar Year 1996" campaign. Throughout the 1990s, the growth rate in the number of tourists visiting Burma has been several times greater than the growth rate in foreign exchange received from tourism. The US Embassy reported that the number of legal foreign visitors, excluding (low-spending) arrivals by land on tourist visas, rose "at an average annual rate of 84.7% from FY 91/92 to FY 94/95" compared to receipts from the legal travel service exports, which rose "at an average annual rate of 62.4%" for the same period.[39] It also reported a continuous decline of the American share in total legal foreign tourists in the 1990s. It is a reflection of the continued strained relationship between America and Burma and some success of the boycott campaign of tourism to Burma by dissident groups.

Table 6.8
Number of Tourists and Foreign Exchange Received from Tourism

	1990	1991	1992	1993	1994	1995	1996
Number of Tourists	8,968	8,061	13,523	26,607	62,547	91,859	105,86
Foreign Exch	$9.4mn	$13.7mn	$19.5mn	$20.8mn	$22.2mn	$34.3mn	$33.9mn
Per Capita Foreign Exch. Received*	$1,048	$1,699	$1,442	$782	$355	$373	$320

Source: Ministry of National Planning and Economic Development (MNPED), *The Union of Myan-mar, Review of The Financial, Economic and Social Conditions 1994/1995* and *1995/1996* (Yangon: MNPED, 1995 and 1996), p. 178 and p. 181.
*The average official foreign exchange rate of Kt6=$1 is used in translating the kyat figures given by the government.

Like most statistical data reported by the government, the inverse relation-ship between the growth in the number of tourists and the per capita foreign exchange received from tourism may have been due to the exuberance of the government to claim its success of promoting tourism by overstating the num-ber of tourists. The drastic drop in the rate of per capita foreign exchange re-ceived from tourism from 1993 onward suggests that each tourist has been spending less and less despite the fact that the length of the stay in Burma was extended to a one-month visa instead of one week by the government in 1994. One possible explanation for this is that the government has not been able to record all the foreign exchange expenditures of tourists or foreign exchange received from tourism due to corruption and underinvoicing of foreign ex-change receipts by various government agencies and businesses in the tourism industry. It is very likely the foreign exchange received from tourism found its way into the pockets of corrupt government officials or into the black market.

A more plausible explanation for the low correlation between the rising number of tourists and foreign exchange received from tourism lies in "the cli-entele effect," or composition and types of tourists. Contrary to the government report, due to both geographic proximity and the booming cross-border trade, it can be assumed that more tourists, legal and illegal, from neighboring Asian countries, especially from China and Thailand, than tourists from the West entered Burma via the border gateways by land and sea. A majority of them are short-term visitors, often overnight, and low-spenders, which can account for the decline in per capita foreign exchange received from tourism. In addition, most of them have been able to exchange their own currencies rather than dol-lars into Burmese kyats in the booming foreign exchange black market at vari-ous border outposts.

Figure 6.5
Number of Tourists per Year

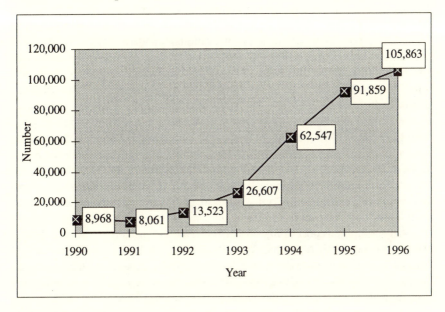

Figure 6.6
Per Capita Foreign Exchange Received from Tourism

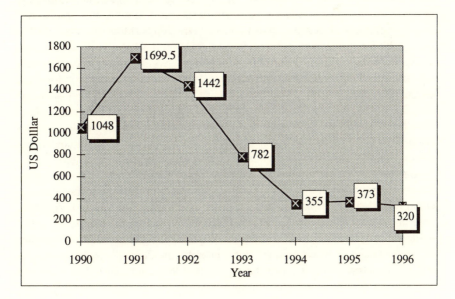

The US Embassy report raised an interesting issue: "Why investors have continued to build hotels, despite widespread expectations of a short-run glut, is not clear."[40] To begin with, the glut of hotels with empty rooms and suboptimal occupancy is not a widespread expectation but an actual event that has already occurred in Burma. According to the Burmese magazine *Myanma Dana*, in 1996, there were some 40 hotels of international standard (three-star and five-star hotels) with about 8,000 top-end beds or rooms available for tourists to Myanmar. In addition, there were 11,000 beds or rooms available at some 500 small and medium-sized local inns and hotels to give a total of 19,000 rooms available for tourists to Myanmar.[41] The average number of rooms at the 35 top-end hotels of around 230 is in line with the data provided by Henrich Dahn, who gave the following numbers of top-end beds available at some 23 selected hotels in 1996; two hotels with between 700 and 500 rooms (Shangri-La and Emerald Rose Garden), five hotels with between 300 and 200 rooms (Beach Resort Sofitel, Golden Triangle Paradise Resort, Inya Lake, Kandawgyi, and Summit Park View), and the rest with between 200 and 50 rooms, most of them with fewer than 100 rooms.[42]

Accepting the report of *Myanma Dana* , the number of 106,000 tourists at the end of the "Visit Myanmar Year 1996" was a little over 120,000, or 329 tourists arrived in Burma daily (120,000/365 days).[43] Assuming that each tourist stayed two weeks on average instead of one month or on a visa issued by the government, there were 4,606 tourists (329x14 days) looking for a room at a hotel on any given day. That is, the occupancy rate of 19,000 rooms available at all the hotels of Burma is 24 percent (4,606/19,000), which is 40 percent of the 60 percent occupancy rate required to break even for a hotel industry in an advanced economy and 60 percent of the 40 percent occupancy rate required to break even for a hotel industry in a less-developed economy such as Burma. Based on these data, Burma needs to attract over 200,000 tourists a year just to break even for its tourism industry. Indeed, 500,000 tourists a year, which is the target of "Visit Myanmar Year 1996," will be needed in order to make Burma's tourism industry highly profitable and dynamic to serve as the engine for rapid economic growth.

The answer to why local investors have stampeded into hotel and tourist businesses is clear. It has been propelled by the market missignals and relative price distortions generated by an escalating inflation and the state controls of prices, wages, and foreign exchange. Jobs and enterprises with foreign exchange earning power are sought after the most by the Burmese. For example, it has been reported that college graduates and other professionals have become either tourist guides or taxi drivers for hotels and tourist agencies to earn wages paid in dollars. The obvious reason for this is that wages or income earned in dollars are worth more than 20 times the wages or income earned in local kyats in the unofficial or black market. Unfortunately, the demand for jobs that paid in foreign exchange outstripped the supply by a thousand fold to benefit only a few who are connected with the ruling military elite.

The answer to the question of why foreign investors continue to build hotels despite the glut of hotels and seeming losses is a bit unclear and more complex. One likely explanation is that since most high-spending tourists and rich foreign businessmen stay at the five-star hotels built by foreign investors, it can be assumed that the occupancy rate is high at these hotels, or they are not operating at a below break-even point of profit. Even if the occupancy rate is below the break-even point, other factors, such as tax holidays, cheap labor, relatively low leasing cost of land, and auxiliary income derived from various hotel-related services, have been making them profitable. Another explanation may be that even if some of these hotels are operating at a loss, foreign investors have a long-run hegemonistic interest in the market share of trade, investment, and exploitation of Burma's rich and untapped natural resources. The residual explanation may be due to their ulterior wish and need to maintain historical, political, economic, and financial ties, as in the cases of Japan, which has been historically the largest creditor of Burma, and Singapore and Thailand, which have been the most vital and indispensable trading outposts and financial conduits of Burma under the past and present military regimes.

OBSTACLES TO THE GROWTH OF TOURISM INDUSTRY

Undoubtedly, Burma has a great potential for growth of the tourism industry. It is a fascinating land that remains more or less untouched or destroyed by the ill effects of modernization and industrialization. It has a wealth of historical sites, ranging from the famous Shwe Dagon and Sule Pagodas in Rangoon, to the breathtaking sites of over 2,000 temples and pagodas built by ancient Burmese kings at the historically famous Pagan or Bagan, and ancient ruins and pagodas in the famous City of Gems (Mandalay), Amarupura, Mingun, Sagaing, and Pyay (Prome) in Upper Burma. It also has a great potential for the development of beaches and resorts along its some 1,200-mile serene western and southern coastlines which stretches along the Bay of Bengal and the Andamen Sea to the southernmost tip of Victoria Point on the northern entrance of the Strait of Malacca. However, as Henrich Dahn correctly assessed: "But to become a prime tourist destination, a country needs more than breathtaking scenery and historical monuments. It needs the human comforts and diversions demanded by the modern vacationers."[44] Moreover, Burma's potential to become a prime tourist country has been hampered by the image problem caused by the ruling military junta itself, which has been ostracized by the UN, United States, and international human rights organizations as one of the most repressive regimes in the world.

The main economic obstacle to the growth of the tourism industry in Burma has been the poor infrastructure and lack of modern facilities, on the one hand, and the government's regulations with respect to freedom of travel and mobility, on the other. The domestic transportation system is antiquated, with poor roads, highways, and railways that are being renovated by the government by using forced labor. Despite the official claims of improvements in the transportation infrastructure, foreign investors and travelers have noted that it is still woefully inadequate. The clearest example is that most of the 446-mile Rangoon-Mandalay highway is a bumpy, single-lane road with the additional problem of delays in travel due to several military checkpoints posted along the road. Consequently, it takes more than 12 hours to travel between the two cities. In the upcountry areas the roads are maintained by villagers who are forced to clean and sweep the roads.

Most of the new roads, bridges, and railways have been built with poor materials by using untrained, conscript labor. As a result of the inadequate materials, energy supply, machinery, technicians, and capable managers that are needed for maintenance, there has been a rapid deterioration of the so-called new infrastructure built by SLORC. As Susan Berfield wrote:

Yet another economic drawback is infrastructure: there is no efficient transport, constant power supply or reliable telecommunication. How bad is the situation? A local distributor of Rothmans cigarettes in the central town of Taungyi told her managing director that she preferred to transport her shipments to her hometown by air rather than by land; the 400-km journey takes a good truck driver five days.[45]

The fuel rationing system also makes traveling expensive, as private citizens and transport business owners are allowed no more than 8 gallons a month at Kt25 per gallon compared with 80 gallons a month allotted to high-ranking government officials and unlimited amounts to the army and government ministries. Thus, most of the gasoline needed for personal use and to operate tourist businesses has been supplied in the black market by the army and government officials at a phenomenal price of Kt200 per gallon in 1995, which has gone up to Kt400 per gallon in 1996 and 1997.[46]

THE MORAL AND CULTURAL COST OF TOURISM

According to Burmese nationals and outside observers, the Asia Watch, for example, Burma has been experiencing a rapid development of sex trade and industry inside the country and across the Thai border under the open-door tourist policy and the lack of real economic development for the people. Even Lieutenant General Khin Nyunt, the powerful director of intelligence responsible for the campaign of "Visit Myanmar 1996," has expressed his concern for the cultural erosions under the impact of tourism that the military regime has been promoting. On August, 28, 1993, in his address in the state media he stated that the new boom in tourism would bring a flood of people of "diverse races, habits, and character," including those "who want to meddle in Myanmar's political and economic affairs, to peddle narcotics, or to have an excessive indulgence in [sexual] pleasures." He warned that "the entire people of the country should therefore beware of such tourist types and see that they do not do anything that might harm the dignity of the nation."[47]

With respect to this cultural cost of booming sex industry as a consequence of tourism promoted by the government, a Burmese dissident wrote:

Apart from illegal and heroin businesses, Chinese have discovered another lucrative enterprise in "Hotel Business," where Karaoke is a "must" and everyone knows that Karaoke is a veneer of the sex-trade. More and more hotels are rising up in preparation for the "Visit Myanmar Year 1996." Poor Burmese girls are lured into the business of prostitution to entertain rich foreign clients. People are complaining that the SLORC is now utilizing its last inexhaustible resource for its own benefit—Burmese girls and women. In doing this, the SLORC is destroying the moral and social fiber of the country by spreading AIDS to the citizens.

The well-known Burmese comedian and political satirist Zargana (meaning tweezers, in reference to the fact that he is a dentist; his real name is Dr. Thura), who was arrested and tortured three times since 1988, made a very subtle joke against SLORC's "Visit Myanmar 1996" during the shooting of a video in 1995. In Rangoon, in front of a state propaganda billboard of promoting "Visit Myanmar Year 1996," Zargana displayed some traditional Burmese boxes woven out of bamboo. The word for these boxes in Burmese is *hpah,* which also happens to be the word for "prostitute." He had arranged the boxes in front of him, in the manner of a street-side hawker with price tags on each of the different boxes, ranging from 2,000 kyats to 5,000 kyats. The prices did not match the prevalent market prices of woven bamboo boxes, which are less than 500 kyats, but match the prevalent prices of prostitutes in Rangoon. Under the billboard he raised a big banner that read, *Myanmar hpah myar, kabah go hlwan sei ya myee* (Burmese *hpahs* or prostitutes have to be made famous all over the world). This is a satirical parody of SLORC's propaganda slogan *Myanmar arrgazar, kabah go hlwan sei ya myee* (Burmese sports have to be made famous all over the world).

In 1993, the face-lifted city of Mandalay has began to take on the less savory characteristics of Bangkok, known as the tourist capital of night life and prostitution in Southeast Asia. Expensive hotels, bars, nightclubs, restaurants, and massage parlors have proliferated for young Burmese girls. The streets in the business centers of Mandalay are filled with the sound of Chinese music pouring out of thriving Chinese shops. In the evening, at the OK Karaoke Lounge of the most fashionable and busiest hotel, the Silver Cloud, built by a local Chinese businessman named U Kyaw Than in 1992, daughters of business and military elite and young ladies entertain and sing along to the latest songs from laser discs made in Hong Kong.[48] The Karaoke style of business operations sets popular standards for all other hotels and restaurants to emulate by opening lounges and hiring waitresses not only to cater but also to sing, entertain, and massage rich clients. The hourly wage of a masseuse is as high as Kt300, which is one-third of the average monthly salary, Kt900, earned by a public school teacher.

Another sign of cultural and moral decay in Mandalay, Rangoon, and other major cities is reflected in the rising tide of liquor consumption (especially Chinese Tiger beer) among the Burmese Buddhists, an act considered a sin according to one of the Five Commandments of Burmese Buddhism. In the past, drinking and the sale of liquor were done privately. Today, they are done openly everywhere in Mandalay. Although Chinese beers are illegal import products, they have been flowing freely into Burma. Chinese beer consumption has risen greatly relative to that of the famous domestic Mandalay Beer, manufactured and sold by the state enterprise at Kt9 per bottle to a privileged few at state shops and at Kt100 per bottle in the black market. Even though the retail price per bottle of Chinese beer is about the same as that of the black market price of the Mandalay Beer, its consumption has increased greatly. A longtime resident in the northern Shan state said, "The number of beer bottles entering Burma from China is so large, one wonders whether or not forty million Burmese are becoming beer drunkards."[49]

The erosion of the traditional Burmese Buddhist cultural life in Mandalay under the massive Chinese onslaught has been causing resentment and apprehension not only among the laymen but also among the Buddhist clergymen, *thangahs*, of Mandalay. The distinguished Buddhist monk Ashin Myittah Nanda deplored the potential demise of Buddhist culture in Mandalay under the cultural onslaught of non-Buddhist Chinese and alien population. He attributes a drastic decline in the number of Buddhist monks in central Mandalay to monks facing difficulties in receiving rice, alms, and robes from non-Buddhist residents as well as from impoverished worshipers in distant satellite towns. Foreign observers might be tempted to dismiss a Buddhist monk's partisan concerns about cultural decline in Mandalay. But many Burmese dissidents of the SLORC are similarly disturbed by what is happening to the sacred City of Gems and to Burma as a whole.[50]

DISPARITY OF BENEFITS FROM TOURISM

Benefits from tourism industry have been accruing mostly to foreign investors, government ministries, military elites and their families, and black market kingpins, including drug traffickers. The reason is that most hotels of international standard, which were built mostly in Rangoon and Mandalay by investors from Singapore, Hong Kong, and Thailand, are joint ventures formed under the memorandum of understanding with the Ministry of the Hotels and Tourism (MHT) and its departments and the giant military enterprise the Myanmar Economic Holding Company (MEHC). Moreover, the Ministry of Trade, the MHT, and the MEHC engage in the transportation and restaurant businesses catering to foreign tourists to earn foreign exchange. Most important of all, a large portion of foreign exchange received from tourism industry accrues directly to the government in the form of profit sharing, rent collected from leasing the land, and income and utility taxes collected in foreign exchange. It should be noted that one of the major sources of foreign exchange for the government comes from leasing the land and buildings to foreign diplomats, businessmen, and investors. In Burma, the state is "the ultimate owner of all land," while foreigners or foreign investors cannot purchase or own land to construct homes, hotels, or business offices. Even the owners and employees of domestically owned small and medium-sized inns and hotels have to pay their land, utility, profit, and income taxes in foreign exchange to the government.

There has also been alleged drug money laundering by former and present drug traffickers in the tourism industry of Burma. Local drug kingpins have been implicated in the laundering of their illicit profit from drug trafficking through their front companies to participate in a number of hotel projects undertaken by foreign investors. The most recent allegations of money laundering relate to the business operations of two infamous drug warlords of the Golden Triangle of Burma, Khun Sa and Lo Hsing Han. Khun Sa surrendered to the Burmese government in 1995, who was indicted by the United States in 1990, and its request for extradition after his surrender was denied by the Burmese government. It has been reported that Khun Sa, with his new Burmese name of "Htet Maung," has been allowed to live freely without prosecution and safe from extradition to engage in gems business and that he has successfully diversified his business operations into hotels, resorts, and transportation.

Lo Hsing Han and his son Steven Law, the chairman and the managing director of the Asia World Company, have been charged with drug money laundering in connection with the two hotel projects in Rangoon, the Traders Rangoon and Shangri-La Yangon Hotels. Steven Law (Law is the Anglicized version of Lo) was denied visa to the United States in 1996 for his alleged drug links. The two projects are undertaken by Steven Law's partners, the Singapore-based Sino-Malaysian tycoon Robert Kuok, the owner of Kuok Oil Company, which deals in cooking palm oil, and a Singapore construction company, Syntech, which is building the two hotels.[51] It is interesting to note that there is even a five-star hotel with the name of Golden Triangle Paradise Resort in the famous poppy land of the Golden Triangle of Burma. The land for the hotel was leased by the Burmese government to a Thai developer, Vitavas International, in the early 1990s. In Rangoon and elsewhere, the military government's ownership or participating interest by families with the military connection in a number of newly built five-star hotels is a well-known fact among the Burmese.

Private owners of small and medium-sized hotels have been reported to be suffering from losses and economic pains. Speculative investment in hotels in anticipation of a tourism boom under "Visit Maynmar Year 1996" has been causing a glut of inns and hotels with no business or tourists in Rangoon, Mandalay, and other major cities. In addition to lack of business and high costs of operation, the unfair taxes and regulations imposed upon the hotels by the government have been causing many local hotels in the cities of tourist attraction to go bankrupt. With respect to this condition in Mandalay, the Burmese economic magazine *Dana* reported;

Anticipating positive changes and growth in the economic system, many Burmese nationals have invested in the hotel business. But before 18, 11, 1996 [November 18, 1996] that began the "Visit Myanmar Year," hotel owners said that some are facing bankruptcy and shut-down. One of the major reasons for this condition is besides the need to pay the license fee or tax to the Ministry of Hotel and Tourism (MHT), hotels must pay additional license fee or tax to the Mandalay City Development Committee (MCDC). Hotels have to pay license fee once every two years, ranging from Kt7,000 to Kt20,000 depending upon the size or number of rooms of the hotel, to the MHT. In addition, they have to pay tax once a year, ranging from Kt1,000 to Kt3,000 per room of the hotel, to the MCDC. The annual cost of a hotel in license fees or taxes alone ranges from Kt30,000 to Kt250,000.[52]

Apart from these taxes, the Mandalay City Development Committee (MCDC) has also been reported to have imposed taxes on the advertisement logos of the hotels according to size. It has also been reported that the MCDC plans to impose on all motels, inns, and hotels, that conduct business in foreign exchange or receive foreign guests, a water tax in foreign exchange at a rate of one dollar per unit (cubic meter) of water usage or half a dollar a day of stay by a foreign tourist.[53]

In July 1997, *Dana* reported that a drastic decline in the number of foreign tourists visiting the city of Mandalay has forced small local inns and hotels to cut their room rates in order to stay in business. At the railway station and long-distance bus gates, hotel agents aggressively competed for a small number of foreign tourists, grabbing their hands and telling them that they can stay at the hotel for two dollars or three dollars per night. On June 12, 1997, at a meeting with hotel owners the government's Council of Monitoring Hotel Business decreed that "no inns or hotels shall charge or accept less than five-dollar room rate." The reason given was that the rate below five dollars would not cover the costs of operation and payment of taxes to the government.[54] Of course, forcing the hotel owners to abide by this rule cannot deter many hotels from going out of business due to excess supply of hotels and shortage of demand or clients. This exemplifies the inept government intervention in the functioning of the so-called market-oriented economic system of Myanmar.

STATE GEM ENTERPRISES AND EMPORIUMS FOR FOREIGN EXCHANGE

Next to promoting the tourism industry to earn foreign exchange, the SLORC has relied heavily on the sale of Burmese gems to foreign companies from around the world by holding annual gem emporiums. Among the most famous gems of Burma are the Burmese ruby, jade, and sapphire. Like all natural resources with foreign exchange earning power, the state ownership of gem mines is absolute, and export of gems has been the monopoly of the state. Annual gem emporiums, also called gem and pearl emporiums prior to 1988, have been held every year since 1964, with the exception of 1988, by the military regimes of Ne Win and SLORC. General Ne Win's own personal interest in, and the wealth amassed from, the private sale of the most valuable gems, including pearls, abroad through his sale representatives (e.g. his personal aide, the military intelligence officer Lay Maung and Aye Zaw Win, the husband of his daughter, Sanda Win, who was the director of Pearl and Fishery Enterprise) are common knowledge among Burmese during his reign over Burma. Prior to 1988, since all industries and trade were nationalized, the government was the sole owner, producer, and seller of gems to foreign buyers. Private mining and sale of gems were done illegally inside Burma and across the border of Thailand.

Since 1988, the Ministry of Mines, headed by minister Lieutenant General Kyaw Min, who is also a member of SLORC, with Mining Enterprises nos. 1, 2, 3, as well as Myanma Gems Enterprise (MGE), Myama Pearl Enterprise (MPE), and Myanma Salt and Marine Chemical Enterprise (MSMCE), has more or less a total control of the gem industry with a monopoly on gem exports. In December 1989, under the directive of SLORC, the main Department of the Ministry of Mines, Geological Survey and Mineral Exploration Department (GSMED), began the highly publicized state gem exploration project named "the Land of Nine Gems," *Nawrart Yadana Myay* in Burmese, at Pyinlon in the Namkhan township (formerly the Namtu township) of northwestern Shan state. On April 4, 1990, SLORC issued Announcement no. 6/90 to declare Pyinlon as the "Land of Nine Gems" belonging to the state, which has the sole right to explore and mine gems. On April 24, the SLORC announced the discovery of a high-quality raw ruby weighing 9.7 carats, which was estimated to produce a 5.25 carat gem after polishing, at Pyinlon. The ruby was proudly named the *Nawarart Tharapu* and proclaimed as the exemplary state-owned ruby. Another raw ruby weighing an incredible 469.5 carats was discovered at the famous gem mine of Mogok, a historically famous city for its Burmese pigeon-blood rubies and ultramarine sapphires in Upper Burma. The ruby was reportedly discovered or illegally mined by an individual miner, Naypyidaw Than Tun, who smuggled it across the Thai border and sold it to black market dealers. Upon his return, he was arrested and imprisoned for this illegal act by the authorities. Eventually, the ruby was recaptured by the SLORC in 1990 and was proclaimed the property of the state. Hence, it was appropriately named the Na Wa Ta or SLORC ruby, whose picture was shown in the state-owned newspaper, *The Working People's Daily*, across Burma.[55]

Between 1989 and 1991, an extensive state exploration of gems under the "Land of Nine Gems Project" was launched at various sites that stretched from Namkan township of the Shan state and Namsah township of the Kachin state across the Kokang and the Wa lands in northern Burma to the townships of Kyaington, Mhineyan, Mhinekaht, Tachilek, Mhineton, and Mhinesat of the

Shan state in southeastern Burma. Apart from the two rubies mentioned before, the government also reported the discovery of two raw sapphires, one weighing 979 carats, and the other weighing 1,383 carats. As of February 1991, the government reported the sale of 1,015 carats of polished gems, 841 carats of gems from Pyinlon and Namsah mines, to foreign buyers at the 28th Annual State Gem Emporium valued at $20.430 million.[56]

Beginning in March 1990, the government permitted private domestic and foreign gem enterprises to form joint ventures with the Ministry of Mines. Over 50 joint ventures were formed and began operating various gem mines, most of which are located in Upper Burma. Only in September 1995, the government passed the Myanmar Gem Enterprise Law to permit pure private gold and gem mining and trading enterprises. Individuals and cooperatives have been allowed to enter the gem industry. However, the government continues to maintain tight controls on private gem mining by requiring all private miners to secure mining permits or rights. The cost of securing a mining right, which is determined on a competitive bidding basis, runs up to Kt500,000 (more than $83,000 at the official exchange rate) per acre of the virgin gem mine. After the successful exploration and find, the miner must declare or register the find with the Ministry of Mines and pay tax according the assessed value of the find. Additional sales tax must be paid upon the sale of the gems to buyers. Main buyers of the gems are wealthy ethnic Chinese and Sino-Burmese business tycoons called *lawpans,* who also finance the majority of gem prospectors or miners.[57]

Beginning in 1993, the government allowed private local gem sellers or jewelry shops to sell gems and jewelry to tourists in dollar and dollar-denominated foreign exchange certificates or Burmese dollars. Consequently, in 1994 some 38 jewelry shops were reported to spring up at major markets or bazaars in Rangoon, Thenigyi Zay, and Bogyoke Zay, for example. These shops must obtain sale permits or certificates from the Ministry of Mines for a fee and pay a sales tax of 15 percent to be paid in foreign exchange on the value of gems sold to tourists.[58]

The majority of foreign exchange proceeds from gem sales accrues to the state. Like all citizens and private enterprises of Burma, the gem miners and sellers cannot keep or use foreign exchange personally, since the ownership of foreign exchange remains illegal. As mentioned previously, all foreign exchange must be kept at the state, semistate, and other eligible banks. Before 1993, the government's regulation allowed private exporters of Burmese goods, including the gem sellers, to use part of the foreign exchange proceeds from the sale of gems to import foreign goods, and the rest of the proceeds were paid to them in kyats translated at the official exchange rate. In 1993, this rule was abandoned, and with the introduction of dollar-denominated foreign exchange certificates as the parallel legal tender, private sellers of gems can receive and keep their proceeds from the sale of gems in these certificates.

Since 1993, private gem sellers have been nominally allowed to participate in the state-run annual and midyear gem emporiums. Those who want to sell gems at these emporiums are required to pay fees for participation and taxes according to the values of their gems assessed by the government's appraisers. Private sellers are not allowed to negotiate their sales or prices of gems directly and freely with foreign buyers at the emporium. They simply submit their gems and the price they wish to receive to government agents. In other words, all sales of gems, including the private gems allowed to be put up for sale at the gem emporium, are carried out by the government officials from Myanma Gem Enterprise of the Ministry of Mines. The exact percentage distribution of the values of government and private gems sold at these emporiums is not known, although the latter's share can be concluded as relatively small. It should also be noted that, like any enterprise with foreign exchange earning power, most of the lucrative private gem enterprises are owned and operated by those who have connection with the past and present ruling military elite. Hence, a majority of the private sales of gems at these emporiums have been made by these enterprises.

With the exception of 1988, the SLORC has held gem emporiums annually between 1981 and 1996. Beginning in 1992, midyear emporiums were added for increased sale of gems to capture more foreign exchange. Hence, between 1992 and 1996 the number of gem emporiums held doubled to 10 instead of 5. The average annual proceeds from the sale of gems at the gem emporiums held between 1981 and 1991 were $8.74 million, compared with $18.51 million between 1992 and 1995.[59] More than doubling of the dollar revenue from the gem emporiums held in the post-1992 period has been due simply to the holding of two emporiums instead of one each year. In any event, all the foreign exchange proceeds from the annual and midyear gem emporiums accrue to the government by virtue of its maintenance of foreign exchange regime. As in the past, the net consequence of the government's monopoly on gem exports and controls imposed on private gem enterprises has been the perpetuation of smuggling to sell gems across the Chinese and Thai borders, presented in detail in the following chapter.

THE IMPACT OF ENGAGEMENT POLICY AND FOREIGN DIRECT INVESTMENT: POSITIVE OR NEGATIVE?
US POLICY FROM ENGAGEMENT TO DISENGAGEMENT

Since the massive crackdown on the democracy movement and the military coup of September 18, 1988 staged by the Burmese military, the US government has imposed four basic sanctions on Burma: the cancellation of the general system of preference (GPS) status, the stoppage of aid, the arms embargo, and the banning of the issuance of visas to Burmese military rulers and their families in 1996. In October 1996, the "Foreign Operations, Export Financing and Related Appropriations Act (H.R.3540) was enacted with the amendment by Senators Cohen and Feinstein to impose "potential sanctions on new investment by US companies in Burma." On April 21, 1997, President Clinton invoked the standing Cohen-Feinstein bill banning new investments of American firms in Burma.

The United States also has not appointed or sent an ambassador to Burma since 1988, although numerous diplomatic exchanges and visits have been made by a host of US legislators and diplomats, including the former US ambassador to the UN Madeleine Albright, who visited the pro-democracy leader Daw Aung San Suu Kyi in 1995. The US State Department has also been very critical of SLORC's human rights abuses by putting out annual human rights violations report in Burma since 1989. However, up to the present the US government has yet to take the definitive step of imposing comprehensive arms, trade, and investment sanctions against Burma. Such a comprehensive sanctions bill was proposed back in 1989 by Senator Patrick Moynihan, which was passed by both houses but never became law.

The US policy of not imposing total economic sanctions against Burma is greatly influenced by its concern over the steadily increasing export of heroin of some 200 tons a year to the outside world, most of which has been reported to find its way to the United States from the Golden Triangle of Burma. The United States government and a number of legislators initially believed and hoped that Burma's heroin export would be halted by engaging the Burmese military regime and giving technical assistance to its highly publicized programs of eradicating poppy growing and drug trafficking—a hope that has been proven to be utterly wrong. Apart from an economic interest, the reason why the US and the West, along with Asian countries pursue the policy of engagement instead of disengagement with the Burmese military regime with one of the worst human rights violation records in the world is that there is an intense "China Watch," as China has gained steadily economic and military influence over Burma. Particularly, China's access to the Indian Ocean and the Andaman Sea via Burmese land and waters for the expansion of naval power threatens the national and regional security of Asia. This reason for engagement with the Burmese military regime has also proven to be wrong in light of the fact that China's military and economic influence over Burma has not only waned but steadily increased to make Burma a vitual satellite of China.

In 1995, Senator Mitch McConnell's bill of economic sanctions against Burma was proposed as an Amendment no. 2744 (Burma Freedom and Democracy Act) to the Foreign Operations, Export Financing and Related Appropriations Act (H.R.3540) and was temporarily approved by the US Senate on September 21, 1995. But it immediately ran into trouble as the main opponent to the bill, Senator John McCain (R-Arizona), protested for a lack of debate and considerations of its impact on the most-favored nation status of China, Thailand, and other ASEAN countries. The familiar US foreign policy of not imposing sanctions against a ruthless regime unless there is international support triumphed as McConnell's bill was thrown out by the senators and the spokesmen of the Clinton Administration.

In July 1996, McConnell's bill, which was co-sponsored by Senators D'Amato, Moynihan, and Leahy, calling for US unilateral economic sanctions of Burma, was resubmitted. It was defeated and a different amendment to H.R.3540 was proposed and submitted by Senators Cohen and Feinstein. The new Appropriations Act, including the Cohen-Feinstein amendment, was approved by both Senate and House conferees on September 2. On October 4, 1996, it became law upon its signing by President Clinton with the provision of "a potential US sanction to be imposed upon 'new investment' by American companies if and when the Burmese military regime harms or arrests Suu Kyi or mounts a massive repression against the dissidents."

Coinciding with the passing of this law, the Burmese military regime began to slander Suu Kyi as a traitor and collaborator with the United States to destroy the unity and stability of Burma and threatened to rearrest her, along with an increased crackdown on her party members and dissidents. In reaction to this repression in Burma, President Clinton issued a proclamation banning the issuance of visas to Burmese military rulers and their families which was retaliated by the Burmese junta by banning the issuance of visas to US officials and their families. On October 29, the European Union followed the suit of the United States.

On November 9, 1996, the intimidation of Daw Suu Kyi and her NLD party transpired into physical violence when her motorcade was attacked twice by a crowd pelting the vehicles with stones. Suu Kyi was unhurt, but her colleague and companion U Tin Oo, the vice-chairman of the NLD, suffered a wound on his temple in the attacks, which smashed her car's windshield. During the first two weeks of December, following the massive demonstration of students at various campuses near her residence and at central places in Rangoon, Suu Kyi's freedom of movement was restricted by barricading access to her residence in the name of her own safety, forcing her to stay inside her house. Since then she has been virtually kept under house arrest by not allowing her to give weekend speeches and prohibiting thousands of her supporters who come to hear her at her residence.

Meanwhile, there has been an increasing call for economic sanctions against Burma in the United States. Students from a number of US colleges and universities joined the Free Burma Coalition and Corporate Withdrawal Movement to boycott products of American companies, Pepsi-Cola, Unocal, Texaco, and Taco Bell, for example, doing business in Burma. The cities of Ann Arbor, Berkeley, Cambridge, Chicago, Madison, New York, Oakland, San Francisco, Santa Monica, and Seattle have adopted resolutions on the condemnation of human rights violations and passed selective purchasing legislation of banning the products of American firms investing and conducting business in Burma, condemning the SLORC's human rights abuses, and calling for the imposition of unilateral US economic sanctions on Burma. On June 25, 1996, Massachusetts became the first state to pass the "selective purchasing bill" (H2833), sponsored by Massachusetts Representative Byron Rushing, calling

for sanctions against American firms that are investing in Burma, which was
signed by Governor William Weld to become the law of the commonwealth.

Under the impact of the Free Burma Coalition and Corporate Withdrawal
from Burma campaigns to boycott products of US firms investing and conducting business in Burma and the Massachusetts sanctions bill, many US
companies began pulling out of Burma in 1996. Among them were Apple
Computer, Kodak, Motorola, Phillips Electronics, and Hewlett-Packard. In February 1997, Pepsi-Cola, which was heavily targeted by college students and
dissidents, completely withdrew its investment from Burma. Long before them,
four American clothing companies withdrew their business operations in
Burma based on their concern over the human rights violations of the SLORC;
Levi Strauss was the first to withdraw in 1992, followed by Liz Claiborne in
1994, Spiegel's Eddie Bauer in 1995, and Columbia Sportswear and Macy's
Federated Department Store in 1996.

DAW SUU KYI'S CALL AND ARGUMENTS FOR SANCTIONS ON FOREIGN INVESTMENT

Although Daw Suu Kyi did not definitively call for sanctions against foreign investment in Burma prior to 1996, she stated her view on foreign investment back in February 1994, when the US congressman William Richardson,
the present US ambassador to the United Nations, was allowed by the Burmese
government to visit and meet with her while she was under house arrest: "Too
many nations use economic carrots, and not sticks to encourage improvements
in Myanmar's human rights records and the fundamental question is whether
the outside world's investments and trade with Myanmar is really helping the
people of Myanmar or is it simply helping the Government to dig in its
heels?"[60]

In 1996, in an interview by John Pilger, a London-based freelance reporter,
at her residence in Rangoon, Daw Suu Kyi gave her definitive answer to the
question of whether or not foreigners should invest in Burma:

"I do not think they should come yet—and I am speaking for them as well as for the
people of Burma. From the point of view of the people of Burma, there is hardly any
investment coming in now that will provide employment and better standards of living
for those who really need help. From the point of view of the investors, the basic structures necessary for sustained economic growth do not yet exist in Burma. Investing now
may go against economic growth because it may make the authorities think that the half-
measures they have taken are sufficient. But they are not and this will lead to social and
economic problems which will work against the interests of the investors themselves."[61]

In a message to the UN Human Rights Commission, she further argued
that "those who are simply looking at the economic benefits that they hope to
reap from Burma today are working against their own long-term interests and
the long-term interests of the international community in general." Against the

background of increased crackdown on dissidents and widespread repression of
the democracy movement in Burma since her release from house arrest in July
1995, Daw Aung San Suu Kyi called for US sanctions against foreign investment in Burma under the Cohen-Feinstein amendment bill. She also produced
a list of some 105 people who were arrested by the authorities since December
1996 and reported the order to kill her issued by the minister of railways, Win
Sein, to substantiate her call for US sanctions.

On April 21, 1997, to the surprise of many Burma watchers, President
Clinton invoked the standing the Cohen-Feinstein bill banning new investments of American firms in Burma. It should be noted, however, that US action
of invoking the Cohen-Feinstein bill is not a blanket economic sanction against
Burma, since it does not call for a complete withdrawal of all American companies, especially the oil companies, which have invested the most in Burma
prior to April 1997. In fact, after the sanction was announced, the value of
American investments in Burma jumped upward, elevating the rank of America
from the fourth to second largest investor in Burma. This was due primarily to
the new contracts of oil exploration rights signed by Unocal just a few weeks
before the sanction was imposed. Hence, the question of whether or not the US
administration will allow what level of investment to meet outstanding com-
mitments in Burma remains unanswered. In a sense, there is no complete sev-
ering of American business ties or US disengagement from Burma.

THE EUROPEAN UNION AND THE ASEAN POLICY

On March 24, 1997, the European Council of Ministers approved the recommendation of the European Commission to cancel the general special privileges (GSP) granted on agricultural exports of Burma based on the finding of
the use of forced labor by the Burmese government. A similar decision of canceling GSP status of Burma was made with respect to industrial exports in December 1996. However, the European Union and Japan, which has been historically the largest creditor of the Burmese military regime, lodged a protest
against the Massachusetts selective purchasing law as illegal with the US State
Department. Both of them have threatened to take their complaints to the
World Trade Organization (WTO) should the United States fail to respond to
the protest.

The ASEAN remains firm in its commitment to pursue the constructive
engagement policy in dealing with Burma. Following the US imposition of
sanctions on new investment in Burma in April, the Malaysian prime minister,
Mahathir bin Mohamad, began to emerge as the leading spokesman for the
ASEAN to accept Burma as its member, stating openly in a press interview in
Kuala Lumpur that the unusual circumstance under which Burma's entry into
ASEAN will be denied is "if five million people were slaughtered" by the
SLORC. On July 23, 1997, Burma was inducted into the ASEAN despite the

disapproval, protest, and charges of blatant human rights violations by the US and other Western countries.

On July 28, 1997, at the of Postministerial Conference, the Nine-plus-Ten Session of the ASEAN Regional Forum with Western powers, human rights violations in the region and Burma's admission into the association and political crisis flared into a heated debate. The ASEAN, spearheaded by the Malaysian prime minister and foreign minister, Abdulluah Badawi, defended its decision of admitting Burma and Laos by reasserting the familiar argument of constructive engagement that trade and investment promote economic growth and democratization as well as the fundamental differences between the Asian and Western values and standards of human rights.

However, the onslaught of Asian regional financial debacle and economic crisis in the late 1997 and the increased pressure from the US and European Union on Burma's human rights violations seemed to have soften the ASEAN's constructive engagement policy toward Burma. It has led to the adoption of a new policy of "constructive interference" in the internal affairs of its new members, Burma and Laos, to improve human rights conditions and encourage democratization. The European strong stance of rejecting Burma's attendance at the next summer's Asia-Europe summit meeting has apparently led to Malaysian Prime Minister Mahathir's concessionary statement of not extending the new members of the ASEAN, Burma and Laos, to attend the meeting which is to be held in London. The apparent motivation for this concession is not to alienate the Europeans and hinder the flow of capital and investment for the alleviation of ASEAN's financial debacle. This, of course, indicates that when it comes to a trade-off between national and regional interest or survival, the individual members of the ASEAN are going to choose their own national interest and economic security.

The West, headed by the US secretary of state, Madeleine Albright, called for greater improvements of human rights conditions in the region. She specifically singled out Burma and criticized its slow pace of democratic reforms, human rights abuses and refusal of the government to have dialogue with the opposition leader, Daw Suu Kyi. Albright called Burma "an anomaly" of human rights abuses and charged it with drug trafficking and money-laundering by stating: "The primary source of these drugs (cheap heroin and mehaphetamines) is Burma, which is itself experiencing an alarming rise in drug abuses and AIDS infection. Indeed, it is hard to imagine a lasting solution to this region's narcotics problem without a lasting solution to Burma's political crisis.[62] This is why President Clinton has barred future US investment in the country." Countering to these charges and criticisms, the defiant Mahthir and other Asian ministers responded by saying that the nearly 50-year old UN Universal Declaration of Human Rights and other documents are archaic and proposed to review and rewrite them in accordance with Asian standards, [63] incorporating perhaps the limit of human rights violation or standard set by Mahathir of "killing five million people by an Asian government," as in the case of Burma.

PRO-INVESTMENT AND NON-ISOLATION ARGUMENTS

The view that isolation and sanctions of a repressive state like Burma are counterproductive to helping the people and democratization is exemplified in the statement made by Roger C. Beach, the chairman and chief executive officer of Unocal Corporation of California in defense of the Yadana natural gasfield project to dispute *The New York Times'* negative editorial on "Doing Business in Myanmar," December 16, 1996, and those who call for economic sanctions of Burma:

If history has shown us anything, it has shown exactly the opposite: economic isolation generally causes chaos, suffering and hardship for the very people it was intended to help. It rarely does anything to advance democracy or improve human rights. In the case of Myanmar, 30-years of self-imposed isolation brought only poverty and misery to the nation's people. It is only thorough economic development that a strong framework for lasting social change can be established. The Times asserted that Unocal "cannot claim it is bringing change to this blighted nation." But Yadana project is doing just that. Our project has already provided significant benefits to the 35,000 people who live near the pipeline area—an extremely poor and undeveloped region of Myanmar.

In a different twist, Thomas Vallely of the Harvard Institute of International Development (HIID) argued that "further unilateral isolation of Burma by the United States would have little effect on SLORC, since other countries would fill the investment gap. But sanctions could affect long-term economic prospects for Burma." Labeling the economic policies of Daw Suu Kyi and her party, NLD, as "enlightened socialism" and charging that the economic policies of both SLORC and NLD are naive and misguided, he argued that investment sanctions "would further reduce contact between the United States and China at a time when Burma is heavily influenced by China, and when the drug trade in Burma is flourishing."[64]

ARGUMENTS AGAINST ENGAGEMENT AND NONSANCTIONS

Unocal's chairman Beach conveniently ignores the fact that Burma was under a ruthless military dictatorship during those nearly 30 years of self-imposed isolation. Burma is still under military dictatorship today, and the poverty and suffering of its people not only continue but worsen under the so-called open-door market economic system adopted by the SLORC. In his eagerness to defend and justify his company's investment project, he deliberately misreads Burmese history by conceiving isolation, not military dictatorship, as the progenitor of the chaos, suffering, and hardship of the Burmese people. The 35,000 people whom the Yadana project has supposedly helped may be contrasted with the plight of over 250,000 displaced political and economic refugees along and across the Thai border as a consequence of the oil exploration and natural gas field projects of foreign oil giants, including Total of France,

Arco, Texaco, and Unocal of the United States, and PTTEP of the Petroleum Authority of Thailand, in joint venture with the state-owned Myanmar Oil and Gas Enterprise (MOGE).

Above all, the emphasis of Beach on the need for economic development at any cost to bring about lasting social or political change, which is based on the maxim of the Singaporean school of thought, misconstrues what world history has shown us with respect to trading, investing, and engaging with ruthless dictatorial regimes. The long history of military dictatorship or authoritarian regimes in various countries has shown that foreign investment, trade, and aid promote neither real economic development for the people nor democratization. On the contrary, in most cases they tend to enrich and empower the ruling elite to commit further human rights violations. Burma under SLORC is an exemplary case in point.

The argument given by Vallely and a number of US legislators with respect to the ineffectiveness of US unilateral sanctions is misguided and fails to see that the United States as the leader of democratic nations of the world ought to spearhead and set an example to other nations in its commitment to the fundamental principles and ideals of democracy, rather than follow the actions of other nations in condoning atrocious human rights violations in favor of economic interests. The second part of Vallely's argument is equally misguided in that, since 1988, the continued diplomatic visits, engagement, and cooperation of the United States with SLORC have neither stopped Burma from becoming a virtual economic and political satellite of China nor hampered the increased flow of heroin to the outside world from the Golden Triangle of Burma. On the contrary, US engagement and investment by American companies have been providing scarce foreign exchange, which SLORC needs badly to buy arms and strengthen its symbiotic relationship with China for military fortification and subjugation of the democracy movement in Burma. Burma's estimated potential heroin production, which accounts for 60 percent of the world production, has also gone up from 180 tons in 1989 to 250 tons in 1996.

The argument that in the context of an extremely poor country such as Burma, foreign investment will improve long-term prospects for economic growth has also proven to be wrong. Studies on recent economic developments in Burma by the US Embassy, the IMF, the World Bank, and the Asian Development Bank have all shown that "half-measures" of reforms undertaken by the SLORC have rendered medium-and long-term prospects for Burma's economic growth bleak. In economic terms, "in some countries, FDI [foreign direct investment] may augment capital formation, while in others it may represent a substitute capital flow or crowd out domestically financed investment."[65] Neither seems to be occurring in the Burmese case, where the gross capital formation since 1990 as a percentage of GDP has shown a brief rise from 13.4 percent in 1990/1991 to 15.3 percent in 1991/1992, while it has shown a declining trend to an estimated level of 11.9 percent in 1995/1996.[66] The apparent reason for the negative correlation between FDI inflow and capital formation and, in tandem, no positive impact on growth rate of real GDP in the Burmese case has been largely due to the fact that FDI has been used by the government as the main source of amassing wealth by corrupt ministers and external financing of extravagant state expenditures that contribute very little to production and real economic growth. In fact, according to Asian Development Bank, Burma's investment as a percentage of GDP averaged 12.4 percent between 1993 and 1995, which was the lowest among 18 selected Asia and Pacific developing countries: including Bangladesh with 14.1 percent, Cambodia with 18.4 percent, Pakistan with 19.8 percent, Nepal with 20.6 percent, Thailand with 40.5 percent, and the People's Republic of china with the highest 41 percent.[67]

With respect to the negative impact of engagement or FDI on human rights conditions, Neier correctly assessed: "They [proponents of engagement policy] assume that trade will modify behavior of governments [like China and Burma]. There is scant evidence that trade does modify behavior, and that Clinton's 1994 decision to end the link between Most Favored Nation (MFN) trade status and China's human rights puts a major burden on those who would argue that increased trade does improve human rights."[68] In the first week of February 1997, in his public television appearance to explain the US State Department's Human Rights Report on 109 countries, the assistant secretary of state (human rights), John Shattuck, openly admitted that the US administration's engagement policy with China by delinking MFN trade status and human rights has not only improved but actually made them worse in China. The same has been true of Burma.

On the surface, the continuous inflow of foreign capital and investments may seem highly conducive to the economic growth of the country and welfare of the people of Burma. In reality, due to the maintenance of trade and foreign exchange regimes by the state, the impact of foreign direct investment has been more negative than positive on the economic welfare of the people. The clearest indicator of this negative impact of foreign investment is to be found in the energy sector of the Burmese economy. Despite being the top sector of foreign direct investment made by Western and Japanese oil companies, the energy sector of the Burmese economy has not grown to produce enough gasoline, oil and natural gas for domestic consumption. The main beneficiaries from over $1 billion of foreign investment in the newly discovered natural gas fields, Yetagun and Yadana in the Gulf of Martaban, are going to be Thailand as the main buyer of the natural gas at bargain prices, foreign oil companies, and the Myanma Oil and Gas Enterprise (MOGE) of the government. The projected profit share of MOGE from the sale of natural gas to Thailand by the year 1998 is between $300 million and $400 million. As M. J. Fry observed: "in the presence of financial and trade distortions, FDI can remove from the host country more than it contributes. In other words, it can be immerserizing"[69] and generate suboptimal welfare conditions and even reduce the general welfare of the people of Burma, as this study has shown.

NOTES

1. C.J.F. Smith-Forbes, *British Burma and Its People: Native Manners, Customs, and Religion* (London: Spottswood & Co., 1878), p. 5.

2. Henry Kamm, "Socialist Burma: Pervasive Poverty, Indifferent Military Rule," *The New York Times*, June 25, 1975.

3. See Mya Than, *Myanmar's External Trade: An Overview in the Southeast Asian Context* (Singapore: Institute of Southeast Asian Studies, 1992), p. 27.

4. Mya Than, "Agriculture in Myanmar: What has Happened to Asia's Rice Bowl?", *Southeast Asian Affairs* (1990): 240.

5. US Embassy, *Burma, Country Commercial Guide* (Rangoon: US Embassy, July 1996), p. 23.

6. Central Statistical Organization (CSO), *Selected Monthly Economic Indicators* (Yangon: CSO, July–August, 1997), p. 6.

7. See The United States Department of Agriculture (USDA), "Burma Rice Trade Report," *Dow Jones*, November 24, 1997.

8. Ministry of National Planning and Economic Development, Central Statistical Organization (CSO), *Selected Monthly Economic Indicators* (Yangon: CSO, March and April 1997), pp. 1–2.

9. See Government of Australia, Department of Foreign Affairs and Trade, *Burma, (Myanmar)*, May 1997, Canberra, 1997, p. 20.

10. The World Bank, *Myanmar, Policies for Sustaining Economic Reform, Report No. 14062-BA.* (Washington, DC: The World Bank, October, 1995), p. 112.

11. IMF, Myanmar: *Recent Economic Developments* (Washington, DC: IMF, February 14, 1997), p. 99.

12. The World Bank, *Myanmar: Policies.*

13. IMF, *Myanmar: Recent Economic Developments* (Washington, DC: IMF, October 1, 1995), pp. 18–19.

14. The World Bank, *Myanmar: Policies*, p. 105.

15. Ibid., p. 110.

16. IMF, *Myanmar* 1995, p. 29.

17. Andrew Selth, "Burma's Arms Procurement Programme," Working Paper No. 289 (Camberra: Australian National University, 1995), p. 5.

18. Ibid., p. 6.

19. Mya Than, *Myanmar's External Trade*, pp. 22–23.

20. Ministry of National Planning and Economic Development (MNPED), *The Union of Myanmar, Review of the Financial, Economic and Social Conditions for 1994/95* (Yangon: MNPED, 1995), pp. 170-174.

21. The World Bank, *Myanmar, CEM Update* (Washington, DC: The World Bank, privately published, September 13, 1990), p. iv.

22. Ibid.

23. *The New Light of Myanmar*, June, 21,1994, p. 1.

24. See for detail "Burma Big Oil Fuels Oppression," *Multinational Monitor* (October 1992): 9–10.

25. "Mya Yadana Report: Deadly Energy," *Green*, no. 32 (December 1993): 4.

26. See All Burma Student Democratic Front (ABSDF), *The Dawn Star* (February 2, 1996).

27. "Blood in the Pipeline: Multinationals and Human Rights," *Multinational Monitor* (January/February, 1995): 24.

28. Philip Shenon, "On the Road to Mandalay," *The New York Times*, Sunday, April 14, 1994, p. xx.

29. Barbara Bradley, "Under Burmese Junta Tourist Dollars Rule," *The Christian Science Monitor*, December 29, 1994.

30. Paul Strachan, "Burma: To Go or Not to Go?" *Burma Debate*, vol. 2, no. 5, (November/December, 1995): 15.

31. Ibid., p. 17.

32. Spencer Ifsley, "Let's Not Visit Myanmar Year '94," *Dawn News Bulletin* (May/June 1994): 31.

33. Ibid.

34. Kyaw Yin Myint, "The 1993 Model Mandalay," (in Burmese) *Dana* (January 1993): 53.

35. Ibid.

36. Andrew Cockburn, "Dilemma on the Irrawaddy," *Condé Nast Traveler* (June 1995): 166.

37. *The New York Times*, September 17, 1994.

38. Ministry of National Planning and Economic Development (MNPED*), The Union of Myanmar, Review of the Financial, Economic and Social Conditions for 1995/1996* (Yangon: MNPED, 1996), p. 181.

39. US Embassy, *Foreign Economic Trend, Burma* (Rangoon: US Embassy, 1996), p. 12.

40. Ibid., p. 13.

41. Maung Thet Pyin, "Where to Go in 1997" (in Burmese), *Myanma Dana* (January 1997): 68–69.

42. Henrich Dahn, "The Hotel and Tourism Industry in Myanmar," *The Standard Charter Indochina Monitor* (June 1995): 15.

43. Maung Thet Pyin, "Where to Go," p. 72.

44. Dahn, "The Hotel," p. 14.

45. Susan Berfield, "Myanmar Takes a Circuitous, Rocky Route Toward Prosperity," *Asiaweek* (January, 5, 1996): 3.

46. See Economist Intelligence Unit (EIU), *Country Report, Myanmar* (Burma), 3rd Quarter 1994 (London: EIU, 1994), p. 41.

47. *The New Light of Myanmar*, August 28, 1993, p. 1.

48. Angus MacSwan, "Some Get Rich On the Road to Mandalay," *Burma Monitor* (March 1993): 7.

49. Zin Thant, "Myanmah Pyi's or Burma's Northeastern Gateway" (in Burmese), *Dana* (June 1991): 53.

50. See for detail Mya Maung, "On the Road to Mandalay: A Case Study of the Sinonization of Upper Burma," *Asian Survey*, vol.34, no. 5 (May 1994).

51. Gordon Fairciough, "Good Connections: Firms Linked to Junta Draw Lion's Share of Business," *Far Eastern Economic Review* (August 15, 1996): 67.

52. "Some Hotels in Mandalay Are Facing Shut-Down before the Dawning of the Visit Myanmar Year" (in Burmese), *Dana* , vol. 6, no. 10 (1996): 36.

53. "Water Must be Used Like Dollar, Golden Mandalay" (in Burmese), *Dana* (May 1996): 72.

54. "Hotel Rate Must Not be Cut" (in Burmese), *Dana*, vol. 7, no. 10 (July 1997): 14.

55. SLORC, *Myanmar, the Nation-Building Activities; The Historical Chronicle of the Works of SLORC from 1988 to 1991* (in Burmese) (Rangoon: Ministry of Information, December 20, 1991), pp. 329–341.

56. Ibid., p. 330.

57. Kachin Land Thant Zaung, "To the Tamah Khan Land Jade Joint Ventures" (in Burmese), *Myanma Dana* , no. 70 (April, 1996): 85–86.

58. Zaw Tun Myint, "'94 Gold and Gem Market" (in Burmese), *Dana*, vol. 5, no. 6 (January, 1995): 84.

59. MNPED, *Review 1995/1996*, p. 180.

60. Phillip Shenon, "Lawmaker Meets Again with Burmese Dissident," *The New York Times*, February 16, 1994.

61. "Icon of Hope," *News International*, London (June 1996): 21.

62. Madeline Albright, "The Burma Daze," *The New Republic* (December, 4, 1996):1.

63. See Kulachada Chaipipat, "ASEAN Stuns West with Plan to Review Rights," *The Nation*, July 30, 1997.

64. Investor Responsibility Research Center (IRRC), *Corporate Social Issues Reporter* (April–May, 1996): 10.

65. Maxwell J. Fry, *Foreign Direct Investment in Southeast Asia* (Singapore: Institute of Southeast Asian Studies, 1993), p. 43.

66. IMF, *Recent Economic Developments* 1997, p. 63.

67. Asian Development Bank (ADB), *Annual Report 1995* (Manila: ADB, 1995), p. 205.

68. IRRC, *Corporate.*

69. Fry, *Foreign*, p. 61.

7

Burma-China Border Trade

In fifty years, still more in a hundred years, there will be a very different China across the border, and it may have a very different effect on the Shan domains. They may be changed beyond recognition: their mineral secrets discovered, their jungles cleared, malaria conquered, new roads built, Arcadia invaded.[1]

The geographic proximity between Burma and China has historically played a vital role in the economic and political relations between the two countries. Burma's northern and northeastern border with China is about 1,350 miles long: 112 miles between Tibet and the Kachin state and 1,238 miles between Yunan and the Shan state. The famous Burma Road connects Yunan with the Shan state, while the Leodo Road of General Stiwell traverses the city of Myitkyina, the capital of the Kachin state, to connect with Yunan, and the old "Ambassador Road" connects the city of Bahmo in the Kachin state with Yunan. In short, Burma-China border trade is primarily trade between the Shan and Kachin states of Upper Burma and the Yunan Province of China.

Burma-China border trade is as old as Burma itself and dates back at least to the eleventh century Pagan dynasty of Burmese kings. Many centuries before the arrival of Western traders, and travelers, Burmese and Chinese royal diplomats, traders and laborers traveled and traded across the northeastern border of Burma. For hundreds of years, the rich Bawdwin silver mine at Namtu in the Shan state was worked by the Chinese after they came across the border and settled in the valley. In the middle of the nineteenth century they left due to disturbances in Yunan. In the beginning of the twentieth century, the British came and worked on the mine to take out 30 million tones of ore in 30 years' time. During nearly 100 years of British colonial rule over Burma, Chinese, most of whom were Yunanese, traders, pawnbrokers, carpenters, and laborers found their way to Burmese towns in Upper Burma.[2]

During the 26 years of General Ne Win's rule from 1962 to 1988, when the economy was nationalized, and all private external trade was banned, the illegal border trade of Burma with China along with Thailand, Bangladesh, and India flourished. Hong Kong, Singapore, and Malaysia also traded illegally with Burma. It became the largest market for contraband in Southeast Asia. This legacy of illegal cross-border trade with China and other neighbors persists under the present military regime, which seized power in 1988. During the political uprising of 1988 and soon after the coup, the SLORC quickly established a symbiotic relationship of "relatives born together," *swemyo pauk hpaw* in Burmese, with its giant neighbor.

AN OVERVIEW OF CHINA INROADS TO BURMA

In December 1988, the SLORC formally legalized border trade with China and other neighboring countries. This shift to an open-door economy sought to attract direct foreign investments from the private corporate world, particularly Chinese trade, investment, and economic and especially military aid. Since then, not only Chinese goods of all kinds but also Chinese settlers, merchants, diplomats, technicians, and weapons have been flooding the Burmese land and sea. By 1989, the SLORC had successfully struck an arms deal worth over $1.4 billion with China, which has become Burma's most powerful and biggest ally. The cessation of Western and multinational aid to Burma after the 1988 political uprising has been more than made up by Chinese official loans and aid to make Burma a virtual satellite of China. In October 1989, the army commander in chief, Lieutenant General Than Shwe, the present head of state of Myanmar, called upon China prime minister Li Peng to establish and strengthen friendly relations between the two countries. Li Peng promised to cooperate in military, economic and trade matters to usher in the era of what the Burmese called *swemyo pauk hpaw,* or "relatives born together," in setting the stage for Sinonization of Burma.

Since the legalization of border trade, China began to gain access to Burmese land by renovating old roads and building new roads and bridges in northern Burma to ship goods and arms. The main route of Burma-China border trade has been the old Burma Road, which connects the famous Burmese city of Mandalay via Lashio and Musé with the ultimate border outpost of China, Wantin. On the Burmese side, the ultimate border outpost is a small Shan town of Kyukok located across the Wantin rivulet. The construction of a new Wantin-Kyukok Bridge to facilitate the booming Burma-China border trade and shipment of Chinese arms began in 1992. On May 30, 1993, the opening of the bridge for use was inaugurated by high-ranking officials of the SLORC and the vice governor of Yunan Province, applauding the mutual cooperation and friendly relations between the two countries.

To facilitate the booming cross-border trade, the Burmese junta with the help of Chinese engineers and aid has been building bridges and new roads and renovating old trading routes in the northern states of Kachin, Chin, and Shan. Among the old roads renovated and reopened for use are the famous Burma Road, the Old Silk Road, and the Ledo Road of US general Joseph Stilwell, which came to fame in the latter stage of World War II. The three districts of Yunan Province that are adjacent to the Burmese border for travel and cross-border trade are Yingchiang/Yingjiang, Lungchuan, and Tengchung. The main route of Burma-China border trade has been the old Burma Road, which connects Mandalay via the Shan cities of Lashio and Musé with the two Chinese cities of Wanding (Wantin in Burmese) and Riuli (Shwelei in Burmese) of Dehong Dai Jingo Prefecture in the Yunan Province. Burma's border outposts are the two cities of Namkham, Musé, and a small Shan town or village of Kyukok located adjacent to Wanding across the Wanding rivulet of Ruili River.

In May 1991, Burmese foreign minister Ohn Gyaw signed an agreement with his counterpart, M. Qi Muai Yuan, to build two bridges across the border over the Shweli River linking Musé, Wantin (Wanding), and Ruili. The first bridge was completed and opened for use in October 1992. In January 1993, a series of arms shipments across this bridge, dubbed locally as the "Gun Bridge," by the Chinese was reported. The deliveries included light infantry weapons, rocket launchers, mortars, recoilless rifles, and armored personnel carriers.[3] The construction of the second bridge linking Wantin and Kyukok also began in 1992. On May 30, 1993, the opening of the newly completed Wantin-Kyukok Bridge for use was inaugurated by high-ranking officials of the SLORC and the vice governor of Yunan Province, affirming mutual cooperation and friendly relations between the two countries.[4] Between 1990 and 1992, it was reported that using the renovated old roads and new ones, China shipped to Burma 16 war planes (F6), about 100 amphibious tanks (T69 II and T63, the Chinese version of Soviet PT 76), 160 armored vehicles, 25 antiaircraft guns, 6 Heinan-type cruisers, several hundred trucks, and thousands of tons of light weapons and ammunition.[5]

On January 1, 1993, a 35-mile road from Yinchaing to the Burmese towns of Taihone, Moe Mauk, and Bahmo began, and it has been opened for use. On April 7, 1993, the authority of the Lung Chuan district completed the construction and opened for use a 56-mile road from Lianghe to the Burmese city of Bahmo. On May 15, 1993, the SLORC held an inauguration ceremony for opening the Myitkyina-Sadon-Sailaw-Mangmin Road. Construction for this new road as a link to the Burma Road began in 1992 under an agreement between Burma and China. The 21-mile road connects the capital of Kachin state, Myitkyina, with the Tengchung district.[6] On April 7, 1993, the authority of Lonchung district completed the construction and opened for use a 56-mile road to Bahmo. On May 30, the Chinese news agency, Xinhua, announced the opening of another Sino-Burmese boundary highway connecting Zhanfeng, a port of entry of Yunan Province, and Bhamo, a thoroughfare in northern Burma.

On February 1, 1993, the foreign minister of China, Qian Qichen, arrived in Rangoon to reaffirm the symbiotic Sino-Burmese relationship that has been maintained during the past four years. According to official reports, the talks and agreements were established on the promotion of border trade and economic cooperation at all levels and on the cooperation of the two governments with the international organizations' attempts to eradicate opium growing and drug trafficking along the Sino-Burmese border. Unofficially, Burma watchers and Asian diplomats believed that during his visit the Chinese foreign minister promised increased military and economic aid to the Burmese military regime in exchange for access to the Indian Ocean through the naval bases in the Burmese waters. The belief was based on China's recent efforts to become a two-ocean naval superpower, which was denied by China as a fabrication. However, it is confirmed that China has helped the SLORC build a naval base on Haing-gyi Island at the mouth of the Bassein River in the Irrawaddy Delta and refurbish the naval facilities on the Coco Island in the Andaman Sea.[7]

On May 27–28, 1993, members of the SLORC met with officials from China, Thailand, and Laos to construct a modern highway system called the "Golden Square Highway Network" linking the four countries with vested interests in drug trade. Overlooked by China, Thailand and Laos and Burma border each other to form the famous Golden Triangle, which accounts for roughly 60 percent of the world's opium/heroin supply. The first section of the network (a Thailand-Burma-China highway) will connect the Thai city of Chaing Rai with the Burmese or Shan cities of Tachilek and Kengtung (the center of drug and contraband traffic) and ultimately with the Chinese city of Ta Lua. Thailand plans to lend Burma 300 million baht ($12 million) at 3 percent interest for 10 years with a 5 year grace period. The second section of the network (a Thailand-Laos-China highway) will connect the Thai city of Chiang Khong with the Laotian cities of Luang Namtha, Bo Tan, and Huey Sai and ultimately with the Chinese city of Jinghong. This superhighway system is a part of the recent plan undertaken by China, Burma, Laos, and Thailand to develop "the Golden Quadrangle," a trade zone at the confluence of four countries. The four countries plan to jointly approach the Asian Development Bank, the World Bank, and the UN Development Programme for loans and assistance.[8]

On July 9, 1993, Burma and China signed six new agreements involving trade, transportation, and infrastructure. The visiting Chinese delegation was led by Pu Chaozhu, special adviser to the government of the Yunan Province in signing these agreements with the SLORC. Under these agreements, Burma will sell timber cut in the Kachin state to China across the border, while the Chinese will help construct hotels in Rangoon and a hydroelectric plant at Chin Shwe Haw near the Chinese border. Burma will also purchase 30,000 tons of rail, locomotives, and spare parts and $2 million worth of motor vehicles and spare parts from China.[9] This agreement to cut timber in the Kachin state for sale to China replaced the junta's announcement of the cessation of 47 logging concessions granted to Thai companies to cut timber in the Karen state by the end of 1993.

On July 30, 1993, Burma and China signed an agreement on economic and technical cooperation. Representing the two respective countries, the agreement was signed by Burma's minister of national planning and economic development, Brigadier General Abel, and People's Republic of China State Council deputy secretary, General Li Shizhong. The Chinese envoy emphasized the symbiotic relations between the two countries and the provision of a Rmb50 million interest-free loan (roughly US$8.6 million at official exchange rate of $1=Rmb5.8) "as a symbol of the amity and cordiality of Chinese Government and people towards the Myanmar Government and people and for further promotion of Sino-Myanmar relations and economic and technical cooperation."[10] He intimated further that a number of new projects were mapped out for bilateral co-operation on the eve of the opening of the recently completed Rangoon-Thanlyin Bridge. The new projects included provision of parts for Mawlamyine (formerly Moulmein) Electrical Power Plant construction, for the establishment of a satellite ground station, and for the survey of a satellite television retransmission station.

Before 1989, Burma purchased most of the railway locomotives and coaches from Japan, France, Germany, and Korea. After 1989, it purchased them mostly from China under a series of contracts, including concessionary loans. On December 4, 1993, the Ministry of Rail Transportation of the Union of Myanmar and Yunan Machinery and Equipment Export Import Corporation (YMEC) of the People's Republic of China signed a contract for purchasing locomotives, coaches and machinery equipment. Under the contract Burma is to purchase six 2,000-locomotives, ordinary class coaches, and heavy machinery and equipment. On September 25, 1993, it was reported that the first consignment of six diesel locomotives, two upper-class coaches, and two ordinary class coaches purchased by Myanmar Railways from China arrived and was commissioned into service. They were purchased under a contract signed in April 1992 between China and the Myanmar Railways of the Ministry of Transportation. The purchase was made with a $20 million loan granted by the YMEC and Huaxia Company of China.[11]

The year 1994 saw an accelerated establishment of a symbiotic relationship between Burma and China with several diplomatic, trade, and military ties and agreements signed between the two countries. The diplomatic exchanges during that year included the visit of a Chinese military delegation led by General Li Jiulong, commander of China's Chengdu military region, in August to Myanmar and the visit of a Burmese military delegation led by the intelligence chief and secretary 1 of SLORC, Lieutenant General Khin Nyunt, on September 7, 1994, to China. The Burmese news media reported that during Khin Nyunt's seven-day visit the two parties discussed such issues as expanding bilateral trade, enhancing mutually beneficial cooperation, upgrading Myanmar-China border trade, and inauguration of a direct airlink between Rangoon and Kunming of Yunan Province. Khin Nyunt's visit was followed by the visits of secretary 2 of SLORC and army chief of staff, General Tin Oo, in November and the construction minister, Lieutenant General Thein Win, in December. In November four Chinese economic delegations visited Burma followed by the visit of the Chinese premier Lin Peng in December.

The symbiotic Sino-Burmese relationship reached its apex when the highest-ranking Chinese official, Premier Li Peng, paid a three-day official visit to Rangoon from December 26 to 28, 1994. Li Peng is the most senior official and the fourth Asian head of state to visit Burma since 1988. At the end of his visit, he held an hour-long press conference and answered reporters' questions, denying international accusations and regional concerns over China's hegemonistic activities and its growing economic and military influence over Burma as an access to the Indian Ocean for the expansion of its naval power. Chinese premier Li Peng met with Khin Nyunt and said that China's policy was to consolidate and promote friendly and good-neighbor relations with Burma, which is beneficial not only to the two countries but also to peace and stability in the region.

However, Burma's neighbors, India and Thailand, have been apprehensive of the increasing commercial and military influence of China over Burma, in particular, China's access to Burmese waters for the expansion of its naval power into the Indian and Andaman Seas. China has been reported to have helped in the upgrading of the Burmese navy by providing cruisers and technical aid in the construction of new Burmese naval bases at Heingyi Island in the Bay of Bengal, the upgrading of naval facilities at Ramree Island south of Akyab, Mergui, and Burma's Coco Island in the Indian Ocean, and the latest news of Chinese access to the Zedetkyi Kyun or St. Mathew's Island off the southernmost tip of Tenasserim Peninsula. The Chinese access to the Burmese island of Zedetkyi Kyun is the most worrisome since it is located at Victoria Point which is close to the northern entrance of the Strait of Malacca.[12] In September 1994, Burma purchased three Chinese frigates capable of being fitted with ground-to-ground missiles to modernize its navy. In mid-August 1994, India's worry over China's presence in the Indian Ocean was confirmed as three cargo tonkins flying the Burmese flag and carrying 55 Chinese seamen were seized by the Indian coast guard near the Negro Islands located 60 kilometers north of the Indian Coco Island in Indian waters. It was reported that there were no cargoes on these vessels.[13]

These exchanges between the two countries resulted in Burma's purchase of ships, locomotives, building materials for bridges, and military equipment from China financed by interest-free or concessionary loans from Chinese state corporations. The Chinese interest in supporting Burma's projects of upgrading the transport system is directly linked to sustaining the giant Burma-China border trade, which has greatly benefited China with its steadily increasing exports of both consumer and capital goods to Burma in exchange for cheap

Burmese agricultural, forest, fishery, and mineral products. The years 1995 and 1996 saw further economic agreements and greater military cooperation between the two countries. In May 1995, Burma's Ministry of Transport's Myanmar Five Star Line agreed to purchase two coastal cargo ships from the Yunan Industrial Import and Export Corporation with the delivery of the first ship due in November 1996 and the second in August 1997.[14]

The symbiotic relationship between Burma and China continued to develop with the visit of the chairman of SLORC, Senior General Tha Shwe, in January 1995, during which three agreements were signed: economic and technical cooperation, cultural cooperation, and the provision of concessionaire credits to purchase Chinese goods and arms. In February 1995, Burma signed an agreement to buy $50 million worth of locomotives and signaling equipment from China National Complete Plant Import Export Group, and in April 1995, another agreement of buying $40 million worth of railway equipment from the same group was announced. In October 1996, the vice chairman of SLORC, the army commander in chief and vice chief of staff of the Defense Services, General Maung Aye, paid a visit to China and struck several trade and military agreements. During his visit the Chinese premier told General Maung Aye that more military exchanges between the two countries will help promote all-around friendship and cooperation. In the first week of January 1997, Senior General Than Shwe paid another visit to China, during which the two countries agreed to expand the symbiotic relationships and explore new ways and areas of economic relations. Given this historical background of multiple diplomatic exchanges and agreements signed between the two countries, Burma-China border trade should be viewed as an aspect of the multidimensional relationship, which involves more than simple trading of goods and services.

CONTRABAND OPIUM/HEROIN TRADE

For the past three decades, the two most important and lucrative cross-border trades of contraband that are of vital interest to Burmese and Chinese authorities are opium/heroin and jade trades. Despite the highly publicized SLORC's eradication of opium growing and antidrug production programs funded by the UN Drug Control Programme (UNDCP) and technically assisted by the Drug Enforcement Administration (DEA) of the United States, opium production and heroin export from the Burma side of the Golden Triangle (estimated at around 2,000 tons of opium or roughly 200 tons of heroin annually in the 1990s by the ethnic Chinese called Kokang, Wa, and other Chinese and Sino-Shan drug warlords) have not decreased. On the contrary, the growing of opium and heroin exports are reported to have more than doubled since the SLORC came to power in 1988. This has been due largely to the freedom of movement and unrestricted commercial activities given to the two largest opium growers and heroin traffickers, the Kokang and Wa armies, by the

SLORC when they mutinied against the Burma Communist Party (BCP) in 1989.

Before 1992, the majority of heroin exported from Burma's Golden Triangle to the outside world (estimated at 60 percent of the world supply) was made by southern routes to Thailand. Since then, it has been reported that the drug warlords of Burma (the most internationally known among them is the Sino-Shan drug kingpin Khun Sa) have diverted their drug trafficking eastward to Indochina. Laos, whose border with Burma and Thailand makes up the area of the Golden Triangle, has become the main conduit for the shipment of heroin that is refined inside Burma. More than 50 percent of the shipment of Burma's heroin is now reportedly transported via China and Laos to the Cambodian port of Koh Kong. The reason for this diverted traffic has been the increased crackdown by the Thai authorities and lack of drug enforcement by Laotian and Cambodian military authorities with vested interest in drug trade.[15]

The increasing role played by China in the export of heroin from the Golden Triangle of Burma is an integral part of the symbiotic relationship established by the SLORC to seek economic and military aid from its giant neighbor. The legalization of border trade by the SLORC in 1988 with China, or rather with Yunan Province, that resulted in the construction of new roads and refurbishment of the old ones with Chinese economic and technical help has facilitated the rerouting of the shipment of heroin away from Thailand. Yunan Province and its frontier town of Ruili emerged as the most important corridor of heroin export from Burma. Keith B. Richburg labeled this corridor "the Wild West" of China under the grip of heroin, crime, disease, and prostitution. As he narrated:

Yunan Province has emerged as the most important corridor for the heroin coming from Burma, which is the source of the vast majority of the heroin making its way from Southeast Asia's Golden Triangle onto the streets of America's cities. From laboratories in Burma's Kokang region—where opium is refined into heroin—the drugs leave Burma by trucks or mule caravan across the thousand miles of mountains that separates China from Burma. Once inside China (Yunan), the drugs are sent to the provincial capital, Kuming, for repackaging. The traffickers then have several options for moving the dope to markets in the West. Some of the heroin is moved overland to China's coastal provinces of Guandong and Fugian, where it is loaded onto ships: sometimes it is sent to Hong Kong by air freight, for later movement onto the United States. A favored new route is over the newly opened border with Vietnam, giving access to ports at Haiphong, Danang and Ho Chi Minh City, as well as several airports.[16]

The two major traffickers of heroin from the Golden Triangle of Burma to the West, mostly to the United States, are the ethnic Chinese and Nigerians. According to the testimony of the DEA administrator, Thomas Constantine, to the US Congress Subcommittee on National Security on September 19, 1996:

Heroin produced in Southeast Asia (80 percent of which is from Burma) is shipped to the United States by two methods (two goups). The ethnic Chinese utilize commercial cargo to transship heroin in 50 and 100 kilogram quantities, frequently through Canada to the United States. Organizations controlled by Nigerians are also responsible for smuggling significant amount of Southeast Asia heroin and selling it in the streets of the United States. Many Nigerian organizations are based in, and controlled from, Lagos, Nigeria, and these groups are formed on tribal lines. Nigerian traffickers maintain a large stable of couriers who either body-carry, ingest, or use luggage with concealed compartments to smuggle multi-kilogram quantities of heroin from Thailand to the US mainland."[17]

DRUG TRAFFICKING BY WAS AND KOKANGS

Until 1988, the basic goals of US policymakers were anticommunism and drug suppression, which presume that drug trafficking originates with certain ethnic minority groups. Having no noncommunist alternative to working with the central Burmese government, the US government wound up aiding and abetting one of the world's most antidemocratic and repressive regimes.[18] The United States provided antinarcotic aid in the form of helicopters, herbicides, and funds, which were used by the Burmese government not to eradicate opium growing and drug trade but to decimate the ethnic minority insurgent groups. It was also discovered that the Burmese government itself became heavily involved in drug trade, sometimes in cooperation with the BCP and sometimes in alliance with the drug warlords of the Golden Triangle, especially with the most famous kingpins like Khun Sa and Lo Hsing Han, to subdue ethnic minority insurgents.

Since it seized power in 1988, the SLORC has been using its ostensible drug eradication programs orchestrated with the highly publicized arrest, seizure, and ceremonious burning of narcotics as a political weapon to extract financial aid from the UN drug control agencies and technical and political support from the United States. Like the national convention to draw up the mythical constitution, Foreign Minister Ohn Gyaw and a number of representatives to the United Nations have lobbied and used the success of SLORC's drug control programs to legitimate its government and halt any potential international sanctions. Following the military coup of 1988, the United States halted all military aid to Burma, including narcotics assistance and liaison activities of the Drug Enforcement Administration (DEA). However, for some unexplained reason, the DEA resumed its liaison activities in the early 1990s, and at the same time, the State Department nominally continued to rank human rights, not counternarcotic, as the top priority of U.S. foreign policy toward Burma.

The SLORC with the help and vested interests of China and Thailand has been able to uproot the ethnic minority insurgents' control of their respective natural resources and border trade with a number of bilateral cease-fire agreements struck between the ethnic rebels and the SLORC beginning in 1993. However, the politics of heroin production and trade remains the main source of power and foreign exchange for the SLORC's success in averting international sanctions. It was accomplished by striking bilateral cease-fire agreements with the Burma Communist Party (BCP) and with the two most important opium-growing and drug-trafficking ethnic minority insurgent groups, the Kokang and the Wa, which mutinied against the BCP in 1989. The ceasefire agreements struck with the SLORC under the leadership of the powerful chief of intelligence, Khin Nyunt, gave the Kokangs and Was the right to keep their pocket armies and the right to continue their traditional enterprise of opium growing and drug trafficking. The Burmese satirically referred to the freedom and privilege of operation given to these two groups by Khin Nyunt as their owning Khin Nyunt *letmart,* or "ticket" to engage in drug trade. Although the complicity and the exact amount of drug money involved and laundered by the Burmese military commanders are unknown, most Burmese know that the main source of funds for the Kokangs, Was, and military elite to purchase and live in the wealthy estates came from the drug trade.

Following the ceasefire agreements with these two groups in 1989, Burma's opium and heroin production as well as heroin exports immediately leaped upward by threefold. For example, the US State Department's *International Narcotics Control Strategy Report, 1991,* reported an increase in Burma's opium cultivation from 103,200 hectares in 1988 to 161,012 hectares in 1991, with annual production of heroin skyrocketing from 68 tons to 185 tons for the same period, of which 181.5 tons were meant for export. The National Institute on Drug Abuse reported an increase in the number of heroin users from 1.9 million to 2.9 million for the same period in the United States.

Increased opium cultivation and heroin output in the Golden Triangle areas of Burma have taken place despite the highly publicized program of eradicating opium cultivation in the name of Border Area Development Program (BADP) launched by the SLORC since 1989 under the chairmanship of intelligence Lieutenant General Khin Nyunt. The BADP, or the "BAD" program, as dissidents labeled it, was launched with the financial and technical assistance of seven separate UN agencies, including the UN Development Programme (UNDP), the UN Drug Control Programme (UNDCP), the UN Capital Development Fund (UNCDF), and the Food and Agricultural Organization (FAO). In 1994, the UNDCP provided $4.54 million to SLORC for drug eradication purposes. Indeed, as D. J. Porter remarked, "there is no question that SLORC squeezes the U.N. commitment to the Border Area for every ounce of legitimacy it can gain," and as "the successful negotiation of 'project' by the ministry officials is a key in political patronage."[19]

Bertil Lintner charged UN agencies' "preventive crop substitution" programs launched after 1988 in collaboration with the SLORC as counterproductive based on a "dramatic narcotic boom" as "the area under poppy cultivation rose from 103,200 hectares in 1988 to 161,102 in 1991."[20] He also revealed the manipulation of US administration by the DEA country attaché to Burma, Angelo Saldino, who sent a memorandum to Khin Nyunt in 1991, advising in detail how to deceive the US government on narcotic control programs. Saldino was recalled and replaced by Richard Horn, who became an apologist for the SLORC's antinarcotic programs.[21]

THE WAR AGAINST DRUG WARLORD, KHUN SA

The legacy of the central Burmese government's involvement in drug trade continues in the post-1988 period with the new twist of waging war against Burma's most infamous Sino-Shan drug warlord, Chang Chifu, better known as Khun Sa, and giving freedom of operation in drug trade to former communist drug warlords and opium-growing ethnic minority groups such as the Kokangs, Was, and Pa-os in the Shan state. Although the US State Department has emphatically charged Burma with ineffective efforts of drug eradication and high-level official complicity in drug trade, the DEA has cooperated with the SLORC and applauded the success of the Burmese government's antinarcotic programs. Different views and disagreement between the Clinton administration and the DEA continued into 1994, when the disgruntled DEA country attaché, Richard Horn, filed a civil suit against the US chargé d'affaires, Franklin P. Huddle, Jr., for harassment and the US government for transferring him out of Burma on the ground that his effectiveness in getting SLORC to cooperate in war on drugs ran counter to US government policy and effort of discrediting the junta. Horn also alleged that the Burmese junta was making substantial progress in halting opium production and heroin trade and that the US State Department and the CIA had "a political and personal agenda to thwart" antidrug missions in Burma.

The SLORC continues to use its antinarcotic and BAD programs as a political ploy to lure the United States for the resumption of antinarcotic aid, including specifically the supply of American-made weapons to wipe out the bases and operations of Khun Sa and his Mong Tai army. In March 1990, the US attorney general, Richard Thornburgh, indicted Khun Sa in absentia for exporting 1.6 tons of heroin, valued at $350 million. Using US interest in the capture of Khun Sa and the stoppage of his drug trafficking, the Burmese commander in charge of the antinarcotic program stated that American-made weapons were needed since the Chinese-made weapons were ineffective in wiping out the Mong Tai army of Khun Sa. However, without the supply of American weapons, Khun Sa's headquarters at Ho Mong was overrun by the Burmese army in late 1994. Khun Sa and his Mong Tai army were on the run and relocated their headquarters along the Laotian border, although in March 1995 it was reported that Khun Sa soldiers fought the Burmese troops and raided Kentung. In April 1995, Khuna Sa also raided Tachilek, the border trading post and the capital of drug trafficking located near the Thai border in southern Shan state.

After the fall of the KNU headquarters at Manerplaw and other camps in early 1995, Khun Sa and his drug empire became the final target of the Burmese army to decimate and claim its suzerainty over the entire borderland of Burma. In June 1995, like other ethnic minority rebel groups, Khun Sa's Mon Tai army began to break up by the mutiny of the Shan State National Army (SSNA), led by a young Shan nationalist, Sai Kan. At the same time, the Mon Tai army suffered serious losses at the onslaught of both the Burmese army and its major rival opium trafficker, the Wa army. At the beginning of January 1996, more than 1,000 Burmese troops marched uncontested and captured Khun Sa's headquarters of Ho Mong with the help of the Mon Tai army leaders, who surrendered the camp with no resistance. On January 7, 1996, after entering a cease-fire agreement earlier, Khun Sa staged the first mass surrender followed by a second mass surrender on January 18. Although a large segment of the Mon Tai army (MTA) has surrendered, and a majority of Khun Sa camps and heroin refineries are under the control of the Burmese army, many defectors vowed to take up arms and continue to fight the Burmese government by joining with the Shan State SSNA, led by Sai Karnyord.

Meanwhile, the US government put a $2 million bounty on the capture and delivery of Khun Sa and asked the Burmese government for his extradition, to no avail. Thailand also refused the US request for help in its extradition attempt. The SLORC adamantly refused the US request by claiming that Burma and the United States have no extradition treaty and that Khun Sa would be tried according to Burmese laws. Khun Sa reportedly struck secret deals with the SLORC, involving the payment of $5 million to a certain general for his safety and leniency in surrendering. It should be noted that Khun Sa was captured and jailed for drug trafficking before and was set free by the military regime of Ne Win in the 1980s. He was also reported to have suffered a heart attack at his camp, although in February he was taken to Rangoon. He appeared on the Burmese media with the honorary Burmese title of "U" Khun Sa and was also reported to have been given freedom to reside in a luxurious home and set up legal business enterprises by the government in Rangoon. These enterprises were those he had set up and operated at his headquarters to launder his drug money in ruby, jade, and jewelry design, gem cutting, and import of Chinese goods. Apart from these, it has also been reported that Khun Sa has successfully diversified his business operations into hotels, resorts, and transportation.

Amist all the conquests and ceasefire agreements of the Burmese army with various armed ethnic rebel groups, including Khun Sa and his Mon Tai army, the reality of Burmese politics for more than three decades under military rule has been what Alfred W. McCoy labeled the "politics of heroin." The Shan state of Burma is "a natural outlaw zone" of political intrigues of cooperation and power struggle among the Burmese generals and a host of ethnics, the Wa and the Kokang, and Chinese drug warlords besides Khun Sa to control and extract wealth from the most lucrative trade in the world—heroin. The real issue in formulating a correct US policy to curb the increasing flow of heroin from Burma's Golden Triangle is not to single-mindedly focus on the capture of Khun Sa but to heed the following observation made by Chao-Tzang Yawnghwe:

As events have it, since 1989–1990, the SLORC regime has consolidated its position in the opium-heroin complex of investment, trade, and profit by becoming a patron to various Kokang-Shan and Chinese ex-communist warlords in Shan State, such as Phung Ja-sin, Phung Ja-fu, Liu Go-shi, Hong Lau-san (born in Yunan), Zhang Zhi-min (U Kyi Myint) and Lin Ming-xian, a.k.a., U Sai Lin (both born in China and former Mao's Cultural Revolution Redguards). Nonetheless, the SLORC regime would very much like to carry on with the police-military "war on drugs" policy of the 1970s and the 1980s, and obtain, in the bargain, monetary assistance from the U.N. [also financial and military aid from the US] for "Border Areas Development."[22]

Concurring with this observation, the US State Department made the following observation:

The State Law and Order Restoration Council's (SLORC) cease-fire agreements with these drug-trafficking armies (Kokang and Wa) have prevented the implementation of any meaningful drug enforcement operations in areas under the control of ethnic armies. As a result, these regions have become drug trafficking havens where heroin is produced and trafficked without risk. Leaders of these drug-trafficking armies have benefited immensely from their good relationship with the Rangoon regime: their businesses—legitimate and illegitimate—have prospered. The top traffickers of these ethnic groups are: U Sai Lin a.k.a. Lin Ming-shin of the Eastern Shan State Army (ESSA); Yan Mao-liang, Peng Chi-sheng, and Liu Go-shi of the Myanmar National Democratic Alliance Army (MNDA0-Kokang Chinese); Pao Yu-chiang, Li Tzu-ju and Wei Hsueh-kang of the United Wa State Army (UWSA); and U Mahtu Naw of the Kachin Defense Army (KDA). The Burmese government continues to look to United Nations International Drug Control Program (UNDCP) and the United Nations Development Program (UNDP) assistance to bolster its own development program in ethnic Wa, Kokang, and Shan areas of the Shan State. Nevertheless, Burmese Government cooperation in implementing UNDCP projects declined in 1995.[23]

Indeed, despite the surrender of Khun Sa to the Burmese government in 1995, the production and export of heroin from Burma have not declined, to indicate that there are many more heroin traffickers than Khun Sa, who is now living free from persecution by the Burmese government and extradition by the United States. Specifically, the ostensible subjugation of Khun Sa and his Shan United Army (SUA) produced a small dent into the overall opium cultivation and heroin output, 80 percent of which is reported to be controlled by the 15,000-man United Wa State Army (UWSA). As pointed out earlier, USWA's freedom to engage in drug trafficking was accommodated by the Burmese government.[24] As the US Drug Enforcement Administration acknowledged: "Most of the heroin in Southeast Asia was produced along the Burma-Thailand and Burma-China borders, in areas controlled by the United Wa State Army

(UWSA), the Kokang Chinese, or the Shan United Army(SUA). Most analysts believe that the UWSA eclipsed the SUA in terms of total heroin production."[25]

The following data on the production of opium and heroin in the Golden Triangle of Burma confirm the failure of effort by the United States and UN drug agencies in cooperation with the SLORC to halt Burma's opium and heroin production since 1988:

Table 7.1

Estimates of Burma's Opium and Heroin Production (in metric tons)*

	1987/88	1988/89	1989/90	1990/91	1991/92	1992/93	93/94	94/95
Opium	816	2,450	2,250	2,350	2,280	2,575	2,030	2,340
Heroin	68	204	186	196	190	215	169	195

Source: The US Department of Justice, the Drug Enforcement Administration (DEA), the National
        Narcotics Intelligence Consumer Committee, *The NICC Reports 1991 and 1995* (Washington
        DC: DEA, 1991 and 1996).
*The conversion ratio of opium to heroin is roughly 10 to 1, and the ratio in this table is 12 to 1.

The value of Burma's average annual heroin production of roughly 195 tons since 1989 may be estimated at $1.95 billion ($10,000x195,000 kilograms). This figure is arrived at by transforming the wholesale price of heroin sold in unit of 700 grams into wholesale price per kilogram (1,000 grams). The estimated average wholesale price per unit of pure heroin or "China White" at the refinery inside Burma in the mid-1990s was around $7,000 per unit or $10,000 per kilogram. That is, the value of Burma's heroin production in 1995 was 54 percent of Burma's $3.6 billion legal GDP at the black market exchange rate. The wholesale price of Southeast Asian or Burmese pure heroin in New York is between $80,000 and $90,000 per unit or $114,000 and $128,600 per kilogram. The DEA's estimate of the price of heroin in the United States ranged up to $260,000 per kilogram in 1995.[26]

It should be reemphasized that more than the doubling of heroin production between 1989 and 1990 occurred after the military regime struck ceasefire agreements with the two major opium growers and heroin traffickers, the Was and the Kokangs. Also, according to DEA, the sudden drop of opium and heroin production between 1993 and 1994 was due mainly to bad weather conditions rather than to the Burmese government's successful effort in the eradication of opium cultivation and heroin production.[27] The US State Department's annual survey gave an estimate of Burma's potential opium production for 1996 as 2,560 tons or roughly 212 tons of heroin, 9 percent increase from the previous year, to indicate that the flow of drugs from the Golden Triangle of Burma to the outside world is not likely to subside for the rest of the 1990s.[28] Indeed, Robert S. Gelbard, the US assistant secretary of state for International Narcotics and Law Enforcement Affairs, openly indicted the Burmese government: "From a hard-headed, drug-control point of view, I have to conclude that SLORC has been part of the problem, not the solution."[29]

CHINESE UNDERGROUND BANKING OR INDIAN *HAWALA* SYSTEM OF DRUG MONEY MOVEMENT

As in the case of many South American and other authoritarian regimes around the world, the ability of the Burmese military junta to stay in power is directly linked to its ability to derive hard currency from drug trade and money laundering in order to fortify its military might. Although exactly how much hard currency is involved and collected by the military rulers and commanders from heroin traffickers is not known, most analysts agree that it amounts to millions of dollars and plays a major role in the narcopolitics of Burma and the rest of Southeast Asia. The Chinese connection in drug trade and money laundering by ethnic Chinese, Sino-Shan, and ethnic minority drug warlords of Burma is to be found in the highly efficient system of money movement called the Chinese Underground Banking System (CUBS), which is identical to the Indian *Hawala* System. It is a system of "parallel banking" by which large sums of money are transferred or remitted with a minimum of paperwork by bypassing regular banking or legal procedures.

The CUBS and the *Hawala* System share the common characteristics of trust, confidentiality, and efficiency. The word *hawala* (*hawwalla, havala, or havalah*) means "reference" in Hindi, "money transfer" in Arabic, and the word *hundi* means "trust" in Urdu. Irrespective of differences in names, the basic foundation of this ancient method of cash or money transfer used by people in general in the Indian subcontinent and throughout Southeast Asia is trust or confidentiality based on personal relationship. Even after the Western colonization of India and other Asian countries and the ensuing development of international commerce and industries, the system continues to persist and function efficiently in various colonies. This ancient practice remains prevalent up to the present in Burma and other Southeast Asian countries used extensively by native domestic and foreign traders, tourists, businessmen, black market brokers and dealers in foreign exchange, smugglers, and drug traffickers.

In recent times, however, the Chinese and ethnic Chinese have emerged as the major movers of funds in developing a worldwide network of the Chinese version of the Hawaii System, which is called *Hi Kuan* in Manadrin Chinese or *Phoei Kwan* in Teo Chew Chinese, that stretches from one end of the world to the other or from Bangkok, Hong Kong, Singapore, and Taiwan to New York and Vancouver. The most extensive users of the system have been drug traffickers and money launderers from Southeast Asia. Although "profits (ranging from $100,000 to $1 million) from the sale of Southeast Asian heroin in the United States generally are smuggled to Hong Kong in courier-carried luggage, within Asia, heroin traffickers and suppliers—among whom ethnic Chinese are preeminent—use the well-established unofficial Chinese banking system to move both their operating funds and illicit profits."[30]

Millions in hard currency are transferred quickly and efficiently within hours through a network of ethnic Chinese brokers and dealers with family ties who are internationally linked via telephones, faxes, and telegrams. There is no physical transfer of funds, and transactions are made in bookkeeping entry forms by brokers and dealers who set up and operate front companies in various countries. Brokers and dealers issue certificates or receipts to money transferors as evidence of remittance. Foreigners call this practice the "chop system" or the "chiti system," referring to the ivory or wooden name stamp or a simple "chit" as a receipt of evidence that money has been transmitted.[31] This system of transferring funds without involving the physical use of cash in executing business transactions by traders is called the *hundi* method in India and Burma. The Burmese call it "striking hundi," *hundi yite,* with a hundi broker who issues a certificate or receipt that is used by a trader and presented to another hundi broker in a different location or city as evidence of remittance of cash or transfer of funds.

As to the techniques of moving heroin-trafficking proceeds and accumulating them as assets by heroin traffickers, the DEA observed:

Ethnic Chinese or Sino-Thais use simple but effective money moving techniques. Profits from their heroin trade are smuggled from the United States in luggage with bulk amounts up to $1,000,000 on the person of a courier. To facilitate handling, proceeds may be converted to cashier's checks or money orders that are carried overseas. However, these monetary instruments often are mailed overseas either by parcel post or by one of the private delivery services, such as Federal Express or DHL. In addition, bank transfers under the $10,000 reporting threshold are used, with Asian traffickers frequently opening accounts under the names of relatives or spouses in the United States and in the receiving country to facilitate the wire transfers. These traffickers' assets usually are stored in bank accounts in Hong Kong, or used to purchase real estate and businesses in transit or home countries, such as China, Hong Kong, Taiwan, or Thailand.[32]

In addition to these financial methods, the drug traffickers often use precious gems, such as diamonds, rubies, and emeralds, to launder their illicit proceeds by buying them in the United States or elsewhere and reselling them for profit in Asian cities or countries, such as Hong Kong, where there is no requirement for reporting on the import of diamonds or other precious gems.

With respect to the emerging trends or outlook of Burma's heroin trafficking and money laundering through the underground Chinese banking system, the DEA in 1994 observed:

1. China and Taiwan will remain significant transshipment points for heroin moved to the United States. Hong Kong will be a major transit point for heroin smuggled across China;

2. South Korea, Vietnam and other nations in the region will be used increasingly;

3. Nigerians will move bulk quantities of heroin by commercial air and sea cargo, initially to staging locations in Nigeria.[33]

THE BURMESE DRUG MONEY MOVEMENT AND LAUNDERING

Drug traffickers, also other smugglers of contraband in the Burmese case, use four basic methods of money transfer: bulk smuggling, invoice manipulation, forged letters of credit, and front companies.[34] The weak enforcement of the law regulating the amount of currency that can be brought into an Asian country allows bulk smuggling, while bribery and corruption of government officials make invoice manipulation a means for smugglers not only to avoid high duties and taxes but also to launder illicit profits made in hard currency. The use of forged letters of credit and front companies to transfer funds and launder drug money is made possible because of the lack of legislation and the inability or, rather, unwillingness of the government to regulate existing institutions combined with widespread corruption among government officials who are lured into the process of highly lucrative drug trade and money laundering

The following account given by the DEA shows how a tourist company was used to move US dollars into Burma through the Chinese underground banking system involving money exchangers and corrupt Burmese security officials:

In one recently discovered scheme, a tour company, established by Taiwanese businessmen to provide tours to Burma, served as vehicle for moving money. Burmese money exchangers contacted their Taiwan counterparts and arranged the recruitment of tourists to participate in the money laundering plan. The tourists were told by tour organizers the amount of U.S. currency to declare when entering Burma, even though they were not carrying the currency. Bribed airport security personnel were provided with tourists' names and the amount of U.S. currency to give each of them. When the tourists arrived, they collected the currency from the security personnel and completed the currency declaration form. As the tourists left the airport, they were met by a Burmese money exchanger, who took possession of the currency and declaration form.[35]

According to Burmese law, the declared amount of US currency can be used to buy expensive, imported, foreign-manufactured goods, such as automobiles, televisions, videos, and appliances, that are priced and sold in US dollars. Thus, the Burmese money exchangers would use the declaration forms to purchase them and resell them at highly inflated prices in kyats at the black market foreign exchange rate to make abnormal arbitrage profit. The US dollars used in this case were reported to have been obtained at the Indian border in exchange for gold, which needs not be the case. The same can be done at the Chinese and Thai border cities, where gold and gems are regularly smuggled and traded for millions of dollars.

CHARGES OF THE SLORC'S INVOLVEMENT IN DRUG MONEY LAUNDERING

The Burmese military regime has been charged by the US State Department and independent reporters as the blatant exploiter of drug trade and participant in drug money laundering by allowing drug traffickers to launder their illicit profits through official banking institutions and front companies. One of the reasons for these charges has been the carrying of news by the Burmese government's news media on various social and economic activities of former and present drug traffickers blessed and honored by the high-ranking members of the ruling junta. For example, on August 3, 1996, the government-owned newspaper *The New Light of Myanmar* openly carried news with pictures of Pao Yu-Chaing, the head of the United Wa State Army, which is the largest heroin-trafficking organization in Burma and East Asia, shaking hands with the famous mayor of Rangoon, U Ko Lay, who is an ex-military commander and the director of Yangon (Rangoon) City Bank, in the purchase of part of a new Rangoon tower.

The political patronage of a major drug trafficker by members of SLORC was shown in the same newspaper with pictures of the minister of hotel and tourism Lieutenant General Kyaw Ba, as the guest of honor, along with three other members of SLORC and ethnic drug warlords attending the lavish spring 1996 wedding celebration of a highly successful international businessman, Stephen Law, the son of Burma's legendary drug warlord Lo Hsing Han. Law is considered by various international drug enforcement authorities as one of the major drug traffickers and money launderers in Southeast Asia. The same newspaper has carried the pictures of two of the most infamous "former drug warlords," Lo Hsing Han and Khun Sa, who have been allowed to roam freely and conduct their "legal businesses" in Rangoon as patrons of the government.

Two American investigative reporters, Bernstein and Kean, charged Minister Kyaw Ba and Lieutenant General Maung Aye, the present vice chairman of SLORC and vice commander in chief of Defense Services, with amassing enormous wealth from bribes funneled from bottom up by gem smugglers and drug traffickers, including Khun Sa, while the two were divisional commanders before 1994. Between 1988 and 1992, Brigadier General Kyaw Ba was the commander of Northern Command and chairman of the Law and Order Restoration Council of Kachin state or division with control over the rich jade mines, while Brigadier General Maung Aye was the commander of Eastern Command and chairman of the Law and Order Restoration Council of the Shan state with control over drug trade and traffickers in the southern Shan state or division.[36]

They cited the testimony heard by the Australian Parliament Committee on Foreign Affairs, Defense, and Trade: "Burma's narcotics trade was protected at the highest level of Government and that the SLORC's involvement occurs on an individual basis for personal profit, covering areas of responsibility for transport, protection, and patronage; and as a matter of policy, either explicit or covert, in order to raise government revenue."[37] They also reported that a memo from the Thai government's Office of Narcotics Control's Lieutenant General Khin Nyunt, the powerful intelligence chief and secretary 1 of SLORC, in allowing the Kokang drug warlord Lo Hsing Han to smuggle heroin from the Kokang group to Tachilek, the drug capital in the southern Shan State of Burma, across the Thai border.[38] The Burmese satirically nicknamed the intelligence chief "Pho" or "Four" Khin Nyunt, in reference to "no. 4" pure "China White" heroin, as well as "Bain" or "Opium" Khin Nyunt, for his links to drugs, drug warlords, and traffickers, Konkangs and Was.

Another study the two reporters and others cited for the allegation of money laundering activities by the SLORC was a four-year investigation conducted by François Casanier, a drug intelligence analyst of Geopolitical Drugwatch in Paris, in his report that the Digpresie published in November 1996. The report implicated SLORC with drug money laundering through its Myanmar Oil and Gas Enterprise (MOGE). It involved $15 million signature bonus paid by the French multinational oil company Total to MOGE for the natural gas exploration rights at Yadana gas field in 1992. The money was reportedly paid into MOGE's bank account at Singapore Overseas Union Bank (SOUB). At the same time, SLORC entered a contract to purchase some 24 second-hand military helicopters and training for pilots, which was worth four times the value of the signature bonus. The payment for the contract was made from MOGE's Singapore bank account. The question raised was where the money for such a large sum of payment for the contract came from in light of the fact that MOGE has no other source of foreign exchange income other than the limited amount of signature bonuses paid by foreign oil companies. Between 1993 and 1994, military officers reportedly funneled huge sums of hard currency received as bribes or profit sharing from drug traffickers through SOUB's branch banks in Thailand into MOGE's Singapore bank account. Hence, it was alleged that most of the money deposited in the MOGE's Singapore bank account was illicit drug money laundered by the SLORC.[39]

Although there is no hard evidence of direct involvement of Burmese generals in drug trade and money laundering, from these observations it seems apparent that the ability of SLORC to fortify its military might and hang on to power has been closely tied to its complicity in drug trade and money laundering conducted with impunity by the drug warlords of Burma's Golden Triangle. Thus, Robert S. Gelbard, the US assistant secretary of state for international narcotics and law enforcement affairs, aptly assessed and concluded:

SLORC has brazenly exploited drug-trafficking money to finance projects that do little to improve the lot of the Burmese. Drug traffickers and their families are among the leading backers of high-profile infrastructure projects in Burma. They launder their money with impunity in banks controlled by the military. Burma has few legal exports and its trade imbalance last year (1995) was 15% of GDP, yet its cities have been flooded by luxury imports—paid for in hard currency that could only be generated by the drug trade. Meanwhile, in the opium-producing Shan state, trafficking continues largely unhindered. Several groups are branching out into other drug activities, including production of methamphetamines that find a ready market in the region.[40]

"SINGAPORE SLING" OR CONNECTION IN BURMA'S DRUG MONEY LAUNDERING

Singapore's political and economic linkage with Burma is one of the most vital factors for the survival of both the past military regime of General Ne Win and the present military regime. For 26 years from 1962 to 1988 under the rule of General Ne Win, next to Thailand, Singapore was the most important contraband trading outpost of the reclusive socialist state of Burma. It served as the major center for Burmese military rulers and their families as well as government officials and black marketeers to conduct legal and illegal businesses and gain access to modern goods and facilities such as automobiles and medical services. This has not changed since 1988 as former and present military rulers, including the retired General Ne Win, and their families continue to own and conduct businesses and visit freely and obtain modern goods and services in Singapore, which has been recognized as the most modern and prosperous island republic of Southeast Asia. Singapore, in turn, with a vested interest in the rich resources of Burma has not only accommodated these facilities but also openly supported the rule of SLORC and provided capital with trade and investment to become the top foreign investor in Burma in 1994 and 1996.

One of the most intriguing developments in drug trafficking and money laundering by so-called retired drug warlords of the Golden Triangle of Burma was the implication of the Singapore government's connection with the business operations of Lo Hsing Han, a historically well known ethnic Chinese Kokang drug warlord of the Golden Triangle. His connection with the drug trade and control of the poppy fields and heroin production of the Shan state date back to the days of General Ne Win in the 1960s and 1970s. In the 1960s, both Lo Hsing Han and Khun Sa were appointed as commanders to aid and cooperate with the Ne Win government when it launched a military campaign called KKY (Kar Kwe Yay) against the Shan rebels and communists in the Shan state. Khun Sa became the informal head of KKY.

In 1970, however, with the detention of Khun Sa, Lo Hsing Han became the unofficial leader of all KKY forces. In 1973, Thai police snatched him from inside Shan state and lured him onboard a helicopter to Bangkok, where he was arrested and extradited to Rangoon. In 1974, in fear of Lo's growing drug empire and heroin trafficking, which came under international scrutiny and pressure, the Burmese government tried him and imprisoned him for seven years. However, he served only five years in jail without receiving the death penalty and was released in 1981. Upon his release, "he was placed in charge of a Kokang settlement near Lashio, believed to be involved in the distillery business and other trading activities."[41] Since then he set up his Kokang Import Export business and resides in wealthy residences in Rangoon and Lashio in good relationship with the Burmese government.

Although overshadowed by Khun Sa since SLORC took hold of power in 1998, Lo Hsing Han, who had allegedly retired from drug trafficking, continues to play a major role in the drug trade and money laundering by setting up front companies owned and managed by his son, Steven Law, who was denied a visa to the United States in 1996 upon suspicion of his drug trafficking links. He and his son reportedly own and operate a number of businesses based in Singapore. On October 12, 1996, the Australian government's Special Broadcasting Service (SBS) broadcast "Singapore Sling" in its television program *The Date Line*, with allegations of the connection of the Singapore Government Investment Corporation (GIC) with the businesses of Lo Hsing Han and his family. Specifically, the Myanmar Investment Fund (MIF), whose core shareholder is GIC, was charged in connection with money laundering by Lo Hsing Han and his son, Steven Law. The MIF was set up by Robert Kuok Group of Singapore and Malaysia and Ho family of Thailand in 1994. The MIF has a 25 percent interest in the Asia World Industries Company, which is a subsidiary of the Asia World Company. The chairman and the managing director of the Asia World Company are Lo Hsing Han and Steven Law.

The Asia World Company was formed by Steven Law in 1992 as a trading company in bean and pulse and later diversified into construction, manufacturing, and retailing. Law is the local partner of Chinese-Malaysian tycoon Robert Kuok and his Kuok Oil, which deals in the Malaysian cooking palm oil imported heavily by Burma. He is also a participant in Kuok Oil's operations in the manufacturing of ready-mix cement and polypropylene bags and two hotel projects in joint venture with the Burmese government in Rangoon, the Traders' Rangoon and Shangri-La Yangon Hotels. The Asia World Company of Law also formed a joint venture with a Singapore construction company, Syntech, which is building the two hotels with a 10 percent participation option in each project.[42]

The seriousness of the charges made by "Singapore Sling" of the Singapore connection with money laundering by Lo Hsing Han and his son Steven Law led to a joint statement made by Chee Soon Juan, the chief of Singapore's opposition political party, Singapore Democratic Party (SDP), and the Singapore Malay National Organization (MNO), asking the Singapore government to answer the truth about the charges. Chee said that if the charges were true, they have cast a "terrible slur on Singapore's integrity and the scandalous and serious aspersions must be refuted rigorously."[43] The Singapore High Commission in Canberra, Australia, reportedly filed a protest with the Australian Special Broadcasting Service (SBS), which was responsible for broadcasting "Singapore Sling." However, in November 1997 these charges led to the announcement of liquidating the Singapore Government Investment Corporation (GIC) share in the Myanmar Investment Fund (MIF) by the Singapore Embassy in Washington DC. Amidst the charges and denial of Singapore's connection with drug trade and money laundering by Burmese drug warlords and military rulers lies the truth that for more than three decades Singapore has been one of the most vital contraband trading outposts for Burmese traders and a welcomed place for the military rulers and their families to visit and acquire modern goods and services, as well as to conduct businesses and amass foreign exchange and wealth.

CONTRABAND JADE TRADE

Next to the illegal border trade of opium and heroin, the largest and the most lucrative trade for native smugglers, the Kachins and Burmese of Upper Burma, has been jade. Most of the rich jade mines are located in the Kachin state of northern Burma, the most famous one being Mogaung, which is a town west of the capital city, Myitkyina, and the center of a jade-mining district. It has been reported that "the rich soil of this region was well known to the Chinese as long ago as 2000 B.C." The jade stone was "a mirror of virtues worthy of an emperor. So this "Imperial jade" was imported to China from Mogaung."[44] To Chinese, jade is "a symbol of protection, health and strength, something fortunate to own and felicitous to give" that has been "carved into ritual objects and ornaments for close to 7,000 years."[45] The historical Chinese interest in the Burmese jade, more correctly jadeite, dates back to the seventeenth century, when the emperors of the Qing dynasty extended their dominion into the Yunan Province and over the border into the Kachin territory in northern Burma.[46] The link between the Yunanese merchants and the Kachin and Burmese jade traders has never been severed throughout the history of Burma.

Mandalay has been the main trading center and conduit for smuggling jade and other gems out of Burma. During the 26 years of General Ne Win's rule, when all domestic and foreign trade was nationalized, illegal trading of gems was made by hundreds of traders gathered together at certain sites located at 34th, 35th, and 38th Streets in Mandalay. They were called *kyauk wines,* or "gem circles," which were often raided by the authorities. The biggest one was called the *Hmaw Gyi Wine,* located on 34th Street. The main foreign buyers of Burmese jade were agents of Hong Kong merchants. In the post-1988 period, Mandalay has truly become what foreign visitors to ancient Burma called the "Gem City," teeming with businesses, hotels, and gem shops owned and operated by ethnic Chinese. Foreign buyers of jade and gems have been flocking to the city, with Chinese from Hong Kong continuing to be the main customers. The city has also been virtually Sinonized economically and culturally, to the resentment of Burmese natives.

The transformation of Mandalay into a booming, modern metropolis of foreign businesses and gem trading centers occurred under the auspices of the present minister of trade, Lieutenant General Tun Kyi, when he was the powerful commander of Northwest Command and chairman of the Law and Order Restoration Council of Mandalay Division before 1992. The Burmese nicknamed him "Yandanabon" or "Bundle of Gems" Tun Kyi as well as "Sein" or "Diamond" Tun Kyi in association with the enormous power he wielded and the phenomenal wealth he amassed from his control over gem trade and enterprises in the Mandalay Division. This nickname is also associated with his attempt to establish a new satellite town called "Yadanabon" as a playground or resort for the rich and famous located some 21 miles east of Mandalay on the road to Maymyo, the former summer residence town of the British governor, renamed by SLORC as Pin Oo Hlaing. The illegal "gem circles" in Mandalay are no longer raided by the authorities, and the sale of jade and gems has been done out in the open. As in the past, the major buyers of Burmese jade remain Chinese from Hong Kong, followed by Taiwanese and mainland Chinese.

During the 26 years of General Ne Win's rule from 1962 to 1988, when the Sino-Burmese border was closed, and cross-border trade was illegal, the main route of jade smuggling from the rich mines of the Kachin state controlled by the Kachin rebels, the Kachin Independence Organization (KIO), was to Chiang Mai in Thailand and ultimately to Hong Kong. However, with the opening of the Sino-Burmese border in 1989 after the legalization of border trade, the illegal trading of jade has been diverted to routes eastward to China similar to the new routes of drug trafficking. The traditional Chinese interest in Burmese jade, some sold illegally by the Kachin insurgents and Burmese smugglers for profit and some sold by the ruling Burmese military junta in exchange for Chinese arms, has not waned, and it has been one of the main determinants of the symbiotic Sino-Burmese relationships.

As in the past, the government's continued control and banning of jade and gems from cross-border trade put Burmese cross-border traders at a disadvantage. The disadvantage or weakness of bargaining power on the part of the Burmese traders in negotiating the terms of trade for the sale of jade across the border has been the asymmetric government regulations on border trade imposed by foreign and Burmese governments. A Burmese trader lamented:

On our side of the border certain goods are banned from cross-border trade making them extremely scarce, while on other sides of the border (China and Thailand) they are legal products (gems, jade, teak, rice, beans and pulses etc.). If we make them legal, they will make them illegal as in the case of cross-border trade of transit cars in 1994. The goods that are banned by the SLORC from cross-border trade are not banned in China and Thailand. There are large number of government-subsidized and private companies for the purchase of Burmese contraband—jade, gems, teak, and others—at the border outpost cities in China and Thailand. In the Chinese border cities of Shweli and Wantin, the streets are jammed with government-subsidized and private gem and jade shops worth hundreds of millions of kyats. The Chinese government subsidized these shops with low interest loans. Especially, the Burmese jade are purchased by them. In Shweli, there is a long section of gem shops. The same is true at the Thai border cities of Chiang Mai and Mae Sot where there are many big gem-manufacturing factories and companies with investment capital worth hundreds of millions of bahts. We supply raw jade and gems for their lucrative business. A piece of raw jade smuggled out of Burma and sold by Burmese traders to these shops weighs as much as 100 to 150 viss (360 to 540 lbs.). The amount of the lowest-quality Burmese jade sold to them may fetch up to a million kyats.[47]

He further complained that in selling the raw jade and gems to the Chinese and Thai buyers, he has to wear "a small face," meaning he is forced to take whatever prices they offer since he is dealing in contraband under the Burmese government's regulation. As he stated: "The Chinese buyer would stand with his hands straddled around his waist in arrogance and would ask how much the Burmese seller wishes to sell the raw jade for. If he comes to Burma to buy them, he cannot behave like this. But the way things are, the Burmese sellers have to sell the gems wearing 'small faces' on the other side of the border."[48] In other words, the cross-border jade market is a monopsony of foreign buyers.

BORDER OUTPOSTS AND TRADING ROUTES

Burma's two main border outposts are the towns of Musé and Namkham in the Shan state at the northeastern border. The main border outposts of China are the cities of Wantin and Riuli (Shwelei in Burmese) in Dehong Dai Jingo Prefecture of the Yunan Province. Historically, Burma's main border trading outpost with China has been the Shan town of Musé located at the foot of Burma's northeastern mountain range, Shan Yoma. The city of Riuli is the major border outpost of China's trade with Burma. After the legalization of border trade in 1988 by the SLORC, the town of Musé, located close to the Selkaung Bridge, reemerged as the hub of booming Burma-China border trade, replacing Namkham. Namkham is no longer a prosperous town. All legal and illegal goods have been shipped from Musé to Riuli across the Selkaung Bridge via Wantin across the 50-foot-long Wantin Bridge. However, most shipments of goods are now made to Wanding rather than to Riuli. Although Wantin is located in Yunan Province, it became the ultimate border outpost of China administered directly by the central Chinese authorities. It is a booming town with modern houses, high-rise buildings, hotels, shops, and offices in contrast to the small Shan town of Kyukoke or Pansine with its traditional shabby houses and buildings across the bridge on the side of the Burmese border.

The two most important districts or prefectures of China's border trade with Burma are Dehong and Xishuangbanna Prefectures in Yunan Province. Dehong Prefecture has been the fastest growing prefecture in Yunan Province since 1982. With opening of the Burma-China border and legalization of cross-border trade, by the SLORC, it has become the main thoroughfare of cross-border trade with 10 roads connecting the four counties of Yunan with Burma. According to an empirical research, "most of the border trade was handled by Riuli (about half) and Wanding city; 65 percent of exports came from beyond

Yunan; about 70 percent of exports were then shipped to destinations in north-east Burma and another 20 percent to Lower Burma and Rangoon."[49]

THE COMPOSITION OF BURMA'S EXPORTS AND IMPORTS

Burma's exports across the border to China are mostly made up of agricultural and forest products, while its imports from China are manufactured products of all kinds. Burma's exports across the northeastern border include not only domestic Burmese goods but also reexport goods from other industrialized countries, American, German, Japanese, and Korean automobiles, for example. Among the exports of agricultural, animal, and forest products banned by the Burmese authorities are rice, teak, rubber, pulses and beans, corn, cotton, fish, shrimp, rare animals, animal horns, leathers, and plants used for vegetable oil. As in the past, however, there is a thriving black market for these contraband at the border. The estimates of illegal rice and teak exports by the private smugglers run as high as 50 percent of the official exports by state enterprises. With the exception of teak, all other kinds of wood are allowed for export. Exporters on the average pay a custom duty of Kt300 per ton of wood. In the northern Shan state's District no. 21, which includes Chauk Township, the custom duty for the export of Burmese rosewood, *pyingadoe*, is as high as Kt4,000 per ton.

Other Burmese forest export products are cane, flower root, *mahlah-ouo*, and dried orchid, *thitkwa chauk*, which are used by Chinese for medicinal herbs. The Burmese fruits exported are apples, mangoes, oranges, pineapples, and water melons. Although sometimes there are losses, exporting oranges usually yields a profit of one to 1,000–2,000 kyats after each trip of sale made across the border. The price of a big, juicy watermelon found in Rangoon has gone up to Kt140 in the city of Lashio, reflecting its scarcity domestically because of its booming export to China. Fruits are exported according to their seasons. For example, *Aung Din* and *San Ya* mangoes, which are sold for Kt1.5 in Mandalay, can fetch up to Kt5 and Kt6 in Riuli. However, the Chinese reexports of these mangoes sugared cans are sold at a value-added price of five to six times above the original export price. The same is true of other canned fruits that are reexported to Burma, indicating Burma's worsening terms of trade with China. This has also been one of the factors for Burma's continuous trade deficit and decline in the economic performance of the manufacturing sector of the Burmese economy since 1989.

IMPORTS FROM CHINA

Different types of Chinese products, mostly manufactured consumer goods, enter Burma at different times. The history of Burma's border trade with China under the military rule from 1962 to the present began with the *Pagan* (Plate)

Era, when Chinese household plates entered in massive quantities. It was followed by a period of massive importation of textiles and clothing, *A-wut A-htel Era*. Today, it can be called the *Beer Era*. Beers are illegal import products, and, as usual, importing them generates huge profits. The cost of a bottle of Chinese beer purchased from the factories inside China is Kt18. In Musé, the retail sale price per bottle is Kt35, and in Mandalay, it is between Kt60 and Kt70. As a Burmese remarked: "The number of beer bottles entering Burma is so large, one wonders whether or not forty million Burmese are becoming beer drinkers."[50]

Trucks carrying beer arrive at Lashio around 10 a.m. Dealers collect it and send it to merchants in Mandalay. Some of the trucks go directly to Mandalay without entering Lashio. Like beer, matches, soap, toothpaste, and detergent powder are collected by dealers in Lashio and sent to merchants in Mandalay. Toothpaste comes in big and small tubes, called *Saypyar Gyis* and *Saypyar Lays* by Burmese. Like beer, some of these products are also sent directly to Mandalay and are redistributed back to Lashio. Hence, these products are sold for higher prices in Lashio than in Mandalay.

So many varieties of goods are imported from China that it is not easy to list them. Whatever one wishes, one can get. It is said that apart from parents, anything can be obtained at a price from China. A resident of Lashio said, "Even if you want to obtain the tusk of *Sadarn Sin Min* (the Buddhist elephant king of mythical India), you can get it from China," satirically suggesting that the sacred elephant has wandered into China after losing its way from India.[51] Chinese goods imported into Burma include virtually everything: basic necessities, household products, electric appliances, cosmetics, building materials, marble and glass wares, plastic products, medical products and instruments, textiles, watches, shoes, and so on. Besides arms and black opium, other products that are banned from import are gunpowder, white opium, liquor, and beer. However, these illegal products find their own way into Burma.

Apart from Chinese products, products from other countries enter into Burma via China. For example, goods from Hong Kong are transported into Burma through China by land. This is shorter in time and distance and costs less than the alternative of transport by sea. Cheap parts and used batteries for watches are bought from Japan and reassembled with Chinese-made casings and bands. Many Chinese watches have been entering Burma. These watches are cheap and sell for Kt40, Kt50, Kt60, or Kt100. Burmese consumers, who cannot afford to buy highly expensive foreign watches, are buying and wearing these cheap Chinese watches called, "Paw Chaung Kongs."

Even though the Chinese do not wear the *pasoes*, sarongs or lower garments, that the Burmese do, they produce and export them for use inside Burma. Although the quality of material and design of Chinese *pasoes* are good, their color tends to fade more rapidly than the domestic *pasoes*. However, in recent times domestic *pasoes* are sold at prices above Kt100, while Chinese *pasoes* are sold at prices under Kt100. Consequently, the Chinese *pasoes* are bought and worn by Burmese in Rangoon and other cities. In medicines and medical products, the prices of Chinese products compared to domestic, Thai, and Western products are phenomenally low. For example, the domestic medical tablet called C-Vit (vitamin C tablet) sells for Kt2.50 per tablet, whereas the Chinese counterpart can be bought at 15 pyars (Kt.15) in Lashio and 25 pyars (Kt.25) in Rangoon. All medical supplies for hospitals are bought from China at the border. Apart from them, medical instruments, such as stethoscopes, intravenous needles and tubes for glucose injection, blood pressure cuffs, sphygmomanometers, thermometers, and syringes are imported from China. The scarcity of cement inside Burma led to a massive import of Chinese building materials including cement, concrete posts, wires, and nails. Moreover, a new product for building houses is also imported from China in the form of rolls of tar, which are thick papers pasted with tar. They are used for the roofs and walls of houses constructed with timber. Although they are not as fireproof as tin roofs, they are safer than the traditional thatch roofs used by the Burmese. They are 3–75 feet in length. In roofing, these rolls of tar are simply pasted over the base layer of bamboo.

BURMA'S BORDER TRADE AND BRIBERY

The most important aspect of the so-called open-door market economy of Myanmar is that all foreign trade and investment transactions are conducted through personal contact and connection with the ruling military elite and their families, cabinet ministers, and directors of various government ministries and departments. The door of Myanmar's economy is open to those who can contact and provide scarce foreign exchange or fringe benefits to corrupt government officials who are empowered to grant the right to conduct business. From the smallest to largest joint venture operations, personal contact, connection, and bribery are needed. Bribery is not the exception but the rule of conduct in the economic life of Burma today. The following scenario given by a Burmese border trader depicts how Burmese traders conduct border trade by bribing corrupt government officials.

IMPORT TRANSACTIONS AND BRIBERY

Import of foreign goods into Burma is done through a network of brokers, dealers, couriers, and corrupt government officials to avoid heavy import duties imposed by the government. The main objective of an importer is to minimize costs. The amount of government duties a Burmese importer must pay varies depending on the types of products. The duty on products like gold bars and automobiles can be as high as 500 percent of the value of import. For example, assuming a 40 percent duty levied on the import of a hypothetical Thai-manufactured product worth Kt500,000 through regular/legal official channels, the total cost to an importer would be Kt200,000 in duties. On the other hand, the cost of importing through illegal channels, by engaging a broker/dealer who takes the responsibility of shipping the good to the ultimate destination, can be as low as Kt70,000. While most export-import merchants are Chinese and Sino-Burmans, the majority of brokers are Indian descendants, called *Kalars* in Burmese.

The broker serves as an intermediary and assumes the responsibility of bribing the officials involved in transporting the goods. Goods are shipped in packages or bags. In our example, let us assume that the goods are divided into 10 bags. The broker charges a fee of Kt2,000 per bag (a total of Kt20,000 in our example). Bags of goods are transported by car through the Thai border gate, which charges a fee of 50 baht per bag or $2 at the official exchange rate $1=25 Baht. The total cost of the fee is 500 baht or $20, whose kyat equivalent is Kt2,000 at the black market exchange rate of baht1=Kt4 at the Thai border (official Burmese exchange rate is baht1=Kt.24. Once these bags of goods arrive at the Burmese side of the border, carriers are hired to transport the bags to the airport at Tachilek. The carrier charges Kt50 per bag (a total of Kt500). The broker must pay the Burmese border police Kt50 per bag (a total of Kt500), the Burma Engineering (BE) soldiers assigned to check weapons Kt200 per bag (a total of Kt2,000), the custom officer Kt500 per bag (a total of Kt5,000), and the air security officer Kt1,000 per bag (a total of Kt10,000). Total costs of these payments to transport the bags to Tachilek airport amount to Kt40,000. An additional bribe of Kt30,000 is incurred to pay the Military Intelligence (MI) officer, the Bureau of Special Investigation (BSI) officer, the airline pilot, and the airline hostess. Payment is made according to the number of bags, which are divided among these officials. In our example, the MI officer claims the largest number of bags, 5 bags or Kt15,00 (50 percent of Kt30,000), the BSI officer claims the second largest share of the bags, 3 bags or Kt9,000 (30 percent of Kt30,000), and the rest is claimed by the airline pilot and hostess, 2 bags or Kt6,000. After receipt of appropriate bribes, they will mark the bags as their property carried on the plane. Upon the arrival of the plane at Rangoon, these bags with government officials' markings are cleared through customs without a hitch. Goods are then smoothly delivered to the importer's home or office. By conducting these illegal transactions by bribing corrupt government officials, the importer saves Kt130,000 in costs—the difference between Kt200,000 duties he would have to pay to import the goods legally and the cost of only Kt70,000 he incurs in importing the goods illegally by bribing corrupt government officials.

Squabbling among governmental officials to divide up the bags or shares of bribe money often occurs. On one occasion, the plane broke down at the Tachilek airport. A mechanic had to be sent from Rangoon. The mechanic wanted his share of the loot and told the dealer that he wanted a bag or bribe money for a bag. If there are many bags, he may demand more than one bag. If his demand is not met, he will not sign the paper authorizing that the plane is safe to fly. He could ground the plane for five days, causing delays and losses to the importer. The dealer and the merchants involved had to plead with the MI and SBI officers and other officials to chip in and share the bags with the mechanic. The important point to notice in this economic saga of corruption and bribery is that government employees are forced into taking bribes mostly because they cannot support their families with the more or less frozen legal income they earn as government employees due to skyrocketing prices of basic necessities.

STATE FEES, DUTIES, AND TAXES

In the export sector, the export items allowed to the private sector are relatively minor compared to the export products reserved for the state in terms of foreign exchange earning capacity. All exporters and importers are required to be registered at a fee, and a license must be applied for and approved by the Ministry of Trade. The registration fee is a minimum of Kt5,000 (roughly $769 at Kt6.5 per dollar) or more depending upon the product lines such as agricultural, animal, forest, and handicraft. Upon procuring a purchase order form, a foreign buyer must secure a license at a cost of 5 to 30 percent of the value of export consignment, depending on the product. An additional service fee of minimum Kt2,000 is imposed by the Inspection Agency Service (IAS) or Customs Department at the port of the shipment of goods. Every new consignment of export or import transaction must be applied for and approved by the Ministry of Trade and other state services, formerly called state corporations. Hence, all foreign exchange as well as trade inflows and outflows are under the direct surveillance and control of the Ministry of Trade and Myanma Foreign Trading Bank. Apart from the license fees, service charges, and custom duties imposed on exporters in central Burma, the military regime also collects taxes from traders along the Thai and Chinese borders by opening up more than a dozen check points or tax collection centers. The majority of this trade is conducted on a barter basis or countertrade of Burmese agricultural and forest products for Thai-and-Chinese manufactured products.

FOREIGN EXCHANGE BLACK MARKET AND RATES AT THE BORDER

Due to trade and foreign exchange controls, the gaps between the official exchange rates and the black market rates for foreign currencies in Burma have been phenomenal. For example, in the mid-1990s the official exchange rate of Burmese kyats for US dollars has been set at between Kt6 and Kt6.26, and the average black market rate of exchange for US dollars, has been between Kt120 and Kt130 or, on average, 20 times higher than the official exchange rate. The same is true of the Thai baht, whose Burmese official exchange rate is set at 1 baht=Kt.25, based on the official exchange rates of US $1=Kt6 and US $1=25 bahts. In the black market, as in the case of US dollars the exchange rate for 1 baht is Kt5 or 20 times higher than the official exchange rate.

In 1991, the official exchange rate for 1 Chinese yuan is approximately Kt1.30, or one Burmese kyat and 30 pyars. The official name of Chinese currency is renminbi (Rmb) instead of yuan, as the border traders call it. This official exchange rate of Y1=Kt1.30 is derived from the average official exchange rates of 1US$=5Rmb and 1 US$=Kt6.5 for 1991. In 1992, the average official exchange rate was changed from 1 Rmb=Kt1.30 to 1Rmb=Kt1.13 based on the data of US$1=5.521Rmb and US$1=Kt6.265.[52] This drop in the official exchange rate for Chinese renminbi is meaningless since the monetary authorities of Burma, the Myanma Central Bank, and the Myanma Foreign Trading Bank have a monopoly on all foreign exchange. For both Burmese and foreigners, most of the foreign exchanges needed to travel or conduct businesses have to be secured from the unofficial sources.

At the border due to foreign exchange controls imposed by both Burma and China, the exchanges between the Burmese and Chinese currencies are made at unofficial rates by dealers in front of various shops. The black market exchange rate at the border has shown an accelerated depreciation of Burmese currency. In 1992, the black market exchange of two currencies was made at the rate of Y1=Kt12.5, which is almost 12 times the nominal official exchange rate of Y1=Kt1.08. It corresponds directly to the average black market exchange rates for US dollar in the two countries: US$1=Kt120 and US$1=Y10 in the mid-1990s. It reflects the true values of the two currencies in terms of their purchasing power parities in the unofficial markets. Between 1988 and 1996, the Chinese yuan appreciated against the Burmese kyat by some 172 percent: the average black market exchange rate in 1988 was Y1=K6.25 compared with Y1=Kt12.5 in 1992, Y1=Kt15.625 in 1993, Y1=Kt16.6 in 1994, Y1=Kt15 in 1995, and Y1=Kt17 in 1996. (Table 7.2)

Since 1995, the value of Burmese kyat has been plunging downward against the US dollar, Thai baht and Chinese yuen. According to the Burmese magazine, *Living Color*, on August 23, 1997 the black market Burmese foreign exchange rates for these three currencies stood at US$1=Kt185, Thai Baht1=Kt7 and Chinese Yuen or Renminbi1=Kt19.[53]

In theory, under the assumptions and conditions of free trade, the Burmese exports would expand as the Burmese foreign exchange rate depreciates. The Burmese exporters' income or profit in local currency should either increase or remain unaffected, since they can sell their exports at constant prices in kyats. Conversely, the Chinese imports of Burmese products should increase, since the Chinese importers pay less for their imports in yuan. Thus, Burma should develop a surplus in trade balance with China. In reality, the inefficiency of the Burmese military command economy and the import inelasticity of Burma with respect to Chinese-manufactured goods together with the import elasticity of China with respect to Burmese agricultural and forest products have produced a trade deficit for Burma. From 1990, Burma has been suffering from a continued

Table 7.2

Exchange Rates Used in Cross-Border Trade (1995)

	Burmese Kyat (Kt)	Thai Baht (B)	Chinese Yuan (Y)	US Dollar ($)
Kyat (Kt)				
Official	----------	4.013	0.9237	0.1596
Black Market		0.20	0.067	0.00833
Baht (Baht)				
Official	0.25	--------	0.231	0.04
Black Market	5.00		0.32	----------
Yuan (Y)				
Official	1.083	4.344	--------	0.1728
Black Market	15	3.125		0.1042
US Dollar ($)				
Official	6.265	25.14	5.787	----------
Black Market	120.00	----------	9.60	

Source: *Far Eastern Economic Reviews*, Hong Kong, 1996; private information.

trade deficit with China annually at an average of Kt734 million ($122 million at official exchange rate) that is about one-third of Burma's total annual average trade deficit with the rest of the world (Table 7.3 and Figure 7.1).

Table 7.3

Burma's Trade Balance with China (Millions of kyats)

1988/89	1989/90	1990/91	1991/92	1992/93	1993/94	1994/95
Kt13.4	Kt283	-Kt808.7	-Kt456.7	-Kt607.4	-Kt1151.6	-Kt741.9

Source: Ministry of National Planning and Economic Development (MNPED), *The Union of Myanmar, Review of The Financial, Economic and Social Conditions for 1993/1994* and *1996/1997*
(Yangon: MNPED, 1994 and 1997), pp. 174–176.

The Burmese exporters have been forced to hike their export prices in kyats, partly because of higher procurement costs and partly because of higher export taxes and fees imposed by the government. Thus, the inflationary pressure is accentuated in the domestic sector of the Burmese economy. Hiking the prices of exports to China by the Burmese exporters does not automatically lead to an increase in exports or profits in yuan, since the Chinese demand for Burmese exports is elastic. The major reason for this is that with the exception of jade, teak, and opium, Burma's exports of raw materials and other extractive products to China are in direct competition with those of other less-developed Southeast Asian countries: Cambodia, Laos, Indonesia, Malaysia, and Vietnam.

Figure 7.1
Burma Trade Balance with China (Kyats in million)

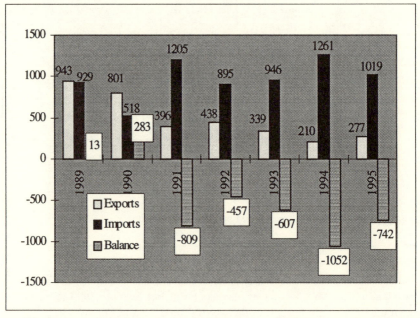

The Burmese population in general has been suffering due to the increased value of the yuan and high prices of imported products. Importers hike local sale prices to avert their losses. For example, in the past era of Kt100 = 16 yuans, the cost of buying a Chinese product priced at Y1 was Kt6.25. The product was resold for Kt7, and the seller's profit was Kt.75. After 1990, the price of 1 yuan has gone up to Kt12.5, forcing the seller to resell the imported Chinese product at Kt14 to compensate for the translation loss, making Kt1.5.[54] This is possible because of the persistent shortage of basic necessities and manufactured products for more than three decades in the Burmese command economy that makes the import elasticity of Burma for Chinese manufactured products highly inelastic.

As in the past era when an importer with an investment of Kt6.25 made Kt75 profit, an importer with an investment of Kt12.5 makes Kt1.5 profit to show that border traders are unaffected or, in fact, better off, as the value of yuan slides upward against the kyat. The same is true for the profit and business of Burmese exporters. Since domestic prices of export products remain unchanged or increased, the exporters' proceeds in local currency do not change downward due to the depreciation of Burmese kyat relatives to yuan. The Burmese exporters do not suffer, although the Chinese importers of Burmese products pay less in yuan and benefit. In general, the increased cost of the imported Chinese-manufactured products in terms of Burmese kyats is passed on to the consumers in the form of higher prices. The net effect is higher prices for all imported Chinese products.

THE BORDER MARKET STRUCTURE

Generally, there are six types of border traders or merchants who have been enjoying prosperity. The first three groups may be labeled as the super-merchant group. The first supermerchant group is made up of former black market traders and dealers who are now given legal rights to fell timber and other commercial rights to develop the frontier areas. The second supermerchant group is made up of the recipients of the state medals of honor for their services to the state who are now rewarded with special commercial rights and trading privileges at the border. The third supermerchant group is made up of members from the former security administrative organizations known as the People's Councils. Most of them are ex-military officers and ex-party bosses who are now rewarded with trading privileges for serving the socialist state of Burma.

The fourth group is made up of private companies with legal export and import permits issued by the Ministry of Trade, while the fifth group is made up of those who trade freely without the legal permits. The sixth group is made up of small independent merchants from the past era of illegal border trade. During that era, they were the major traders who successfully made their living with a capital of about 3,000 kyats. They are now being replaced by the groups of supermerchants and other companies whose capital ranges from 1 million to 100 million kyats. They found themselves unable to compete with these giant enterprises. However, they continue to operate and survive by leveraging their operations. The capital of their businesses is small, part of which is their own, and the rest is borrowed. Usually, half of the goods they bought are paid in cash, and the rest on credit with interest.

Most of these small traders are exporters rather than importers of Chinese products due to lack of funds, connections, and privileges given by the state. Additionally, the majority of them are young women 20–30 years old. The role of women in the Burmese economy as traders and entrepreneurs is a histori-cally recognized cultural fact. Young businesswomen engage in both legal and illegal border trade. The reason for trading the products illegally is that they cannot sell their products to the Chinese buyers across the border at the same prices sold by the supermerchants. Due to their small size and high operating costs, they are unable to compete with the large exporters and suffer losses. Hence, instead of themselves exporting directly to the Chinese buyers, they are forced to buy and sell agricultural products that are legally permitted for export to the supermerchants internally. The latter, in turn, after buying the legal products wholesale from the small traders and others, export them to the buyers in China.

COMPETITION BETWEEN CHINA AND THAILAND IN BURMA'S BORDER TRADE

Ever since the military coup of 1962 up to 1989, Thailand dominated the illegal border trade of Burma. Since 1989, it faces the fearful economic rival of China, whose goods came to dominate various urban centers of Burma. Although Thai products are better in quality, they are more expensive than the Chinese products. Selling its products at cheaper prices, China has been able to outcompete and take over Thailand's dominant market share at the border and inside Burma. The following patterns of relative percentage share of China and Thailand in Burma's total imports attest to this fact (Table 7.4 and Figure 7.2).

Table 7.4
Percentage Share of China and Thailand in Burma's Total Imports

	1988/89	1989/90	1990/91	1991/92	1992/93	1993/94	94/95
China	27	15	22	17	18	16	12
Thailand	4	16	17	10	13	11	10

Source: Ministry of National Planning and Economic Development (MNPED), *The Union of Myanmar, Review of the Financial, Economic and Social Conditions for 1993/94* and *1996/97* (Yangon: MNPED, 1994 and 1997).

Figure 7.2
Share of China and Thailand in Burma's Trade

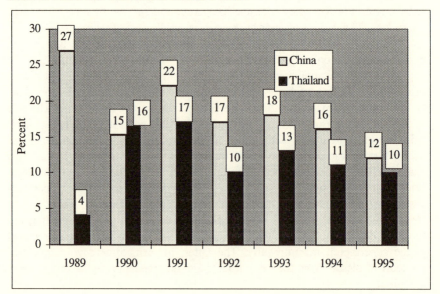

However, since Thailand has been a longtime trading partner of Burma, it has been forced to maintain its trade relationships with Burma in the name of "constructive engagement policy." It has been reaping its comparative advantage over China by securing the majority of teak-logging concessions and fishing rights from the SLORC. However, Burma's relationship with Thailand has been straining due to a series of events in the 1990s that resulted in the Burmese junta's announcement of canceling the logging concessions and fishing rights granted to Thai companies at the end of 1993. China's dominance over Burma points to a decline in the market and trade shares of Thailand that has led to a frenzy of diplomatic negotiations and visits to Burma during 1993 by high-ranking Thai officials, including its foreign minister, Squadron Leader Prasong Soonsiri, to improve the relationship between the two countries. It has also led to the Thai prime minister's lobbying for Burma's entry into the Association of Southeast Asian Nations (ASEAN).

DISPARITY OF ECONOMIC GROWTH AND BENEFIT FROM BURMA-CHINA BORDER TRADE

The most penetrating analyses and evaluations of economic growth and benefit from Burma-China border trade are given by a group of Burmese cross-border traders and merchants in the Burmese economic magazine *Dana* in an article "Walk to the East and Look Back to the West: 1993 Border Trade," cited before. The article begins with the observation and questions on disparity of development between Burmese and adjacent foreign border outposts:

The moment we cross over the border, we land immediately at big modern cities. On our side, the border outposts are traditional villages. Looking across the border from our side, we can see modern high rises lit with bright lights. Looking from the other side back to our side, everything is dark. Why is there such a difference between them and us in development, despite the fact that both sides have been trading equally? Their roads and infrastructure are well developed and their living standard is also markedly higher than ours. Whatever pair of border cities you look at, you find the foreign border cities more developed and richer than the Burmese counterparts. They have become rich at our expense. Shouldn't we also developed like them? What is happening in trading across the border? We should look for the answer.[55]

The question on the disparity of development between Burmese and foreign border towns was raised, and the answer was given by a retired army commander, ex-brigadier/Bogyi Thein Naing, director of Thit Min Hotel and Company at Musé:

Why has every foreign border town that trades with Myanmar visibly changed and developed into prosperous towns, while border towns on our side have been left behind? Is it because, our race is inferior? No that cannot be, since we are smart. If so, why are we left behind? What conditions cause this situation? We have too many restrictions and regulations on our side in cross-border trading. We need to reform and change our economic and business system. We present the changes we should make to the authorities. But they are not accepted and the decisions are postponed. We are very slow to wake up. The border trade will continue even though our money is not accepted by foreign buyers at the border. All the manufactured goods, electric appliances and the machinery for our factories we need from them will be paid for in kind with our agricultural, forest, fish, and mineral products they need on a barter or counter-trade basis.[56]

Another observation on the changes needed in determining the export of Burmese products in terms of the elasticity of demand of Chinese consumers and development of export industries and requisite manufacturing facilities was given by a Burmese border trader:

We do not think of the goods that can be exported regularly. We export to China only seasonal goods. If the Chinese want mangoes we export them and if they do not want them we have to stop. In exporting, we must know what the Chinese buyers want the most. If they want polished jade, we must manufacture and export it. Yunan Province is located inside China far away from the sea. It has no supply of seafood and must be imported from us. Chinese love fishes and shrimps. Burmese traders [government] do not take advantage of this market. We must develop our fishing industry, refrigeration facilities and transportation by cars equipped with iced boxes. Crabs are allowed to be exported, but we do not develop facilities to export them. Burmese traders engage in seasonally popular export items and not the ones that have a solid and regular market.[57]

Changes in economic policy adopted by China have generated adverse effects on the Burmese border traders. In early 1993, China adopted a tight monetary policy by reducing loans to banks and businesses. Consequently, Chinese companies could not advance liberal trade credits to Burmese merchants. The prices of Chinese goods also started to climb steadily. For example, in June 1991 the price of a box of Chinese soap powder was 36 yuan, in June 1992 it was 44 yuan, and in June 1993 it climbed to 50 yuan. The reason given by Chinese sellers for this and price increases in general was the high cost of electricity and transportation.

The real reason for high costs of Chinese goods is due to the deteriorating conditions of roads or poor infrastructure inside Burma and the inept Burmese government policy. According to a Burmese cross-border trader:

The government considered that damages to roads were caused by automobiles. To correct the situation, instead of repairing the roads it imposed ceilings on the weight of the load carried by trucks. That is, the foot was cut off to fit the shoe. Big and heavy trucks could no longer be used and only small trucks had to be used in order to meet the new weight restriction. Beginning on October 16, 1993, the government mandated that the weight of the trucks leaving Lashio could not exceed 13 tons. The result was the increase of transportation cost from between Kt7 to Kt8 per viss (3.6 lbs.) to between Kt10 and Kt12 per viss. We need to build new and sturdy roads to travel without restrictions on the weight of trucks imposed.[58]

In direct contrast to the criticisms of the inappropriate government's border-trade regulations and policies given by a majority of cross-border traders, a merchant with military connections blamed the Burmese traders and merchants for their wrong mentality and lack of unity. He asserted: "Burmese merchants need to change their mentality of selling goods at whatever prices they can obtain. Foreign merchants are united, while the Burmese merchants are not. Burmese merchants do not wait to sell goods until the prices are well established. Instead, they compete and destroy each other in selling to damage the market."[59] This view was shared and reinforced by Commander Sein Win, the secretary of the District Law and Order Restoration Council (DLORC):

The primary change needed is that Burmese merchants must be united. Who should be responsible to bring about this change? They are the border authorities, the Customs Department, the Myanma Export Import Service (MEIS) and the Big Border Merchant Association (BBMA). The most important organization is the BBMA. It must control export and import prices. The leading members of BBMA must be qualified persons; they must love the country, they must be far-sighted and unselfish. The merchants must not be solely preoccupied and satisfied with the operations of their own companies. They must see to it that merchants do not sell to make lower profits.[60]

This statement typifies the Burmese government's official view on the cause of various problems of Myanmar since 1988. As in the past socialist state of Burma, the present government continues to blame traders and merchants instead of its own inappropriate regulations and policies for the economic maladies of the country. Based on the facts presented in this chapter, the real culprit for the disparity of economic development and benefits from the booming cross-border trade between Burma and China has been government's maintenance of trade and foreign exchange regimes that resulted in the comparative disadvantage of Burmese traders with respect to terms of trade and bargaining power.

The following observations and recommendations made by Burmese cross-border traders with respect to changes needed to be made concerning Burma-China border trade underscore the inefficiency of the so-called open-door market economy and ostentatious legalization of border trade adopted by the Burmese government since 1988:

1.   Only if the door is opened completely, sun rays will shine through, fresh air will enter and the beauty of the outside world can be seen. Because of the fear of harmful odor and mosquitoes entering, the door is not completely opened. If the door is opened only slightly to guard against this possibility, the benefits of opening the door widely cannot be reaped and bad odor and mosquitoes can still creep through. A Chinese official in charge of border areas told us that his country adopted a similar policy of opening the door slightly like Burma in the past with disastrous consequences.[61]

2.   Instead of having to cross over the border to sell, we want to sell our goods in our own land. But there are too many restrictions on our side. In a market

system, if there are too many restrictions businesses cannot succeed. Restrictions tend to generate corruption and make people take bribes.[62]

3. When we examine the state of border trade we find it to be discouraging. Those who are benefiting the most from the border trade are the ones the state gave special privileges and the ones with large capital. Chinese merchants at the Chinese border and the Indian merchants at the Indian border dominate and control the border trade. The medium-and small-sized Burmese traders cannot compete with them. Traders with small capital have to abandon their unprofitable businesses and are forced to work as laborers for big companies.[63]

4. Government decreed that only dollars must be accepted for sale. My opinion is that we should accept whatever foreign exchange for payments: yuan, baht, etc. If we want to attract more tourists and be successful in tourism we need to abolish the dollar-exchange requirement regulation.[64]

NOTES

1. Robert Slater, *Guns through Arcadia* (Madras: Diocesan Press, 1943), p. 139.

2. Ibid., p. 164.

3. See Bertil Lintner, "Triangular Ties," *Far Eastern Economic Review* (March 28, 1991): 22–26. Also, "Rangoon's Rubicon: Infrastructure Aid Tightens Peking's Control," *Far Eastern Economic Review* (February 11, 1993): 28.

4. *The New Light of Myanmar*, Yangon, March 27, 1993.

5. See André Et Louis Boucaud, "Pékin-Rangoun, nouvel axe asiatique," *Le Monde Diplomatique* (May 16, 1993).

6. See Kyaw Yin Myint, "Border Trade" in Burmese, *Dana*, Special Issue, Vol.4, No. 7 (December/January 1994/95): 18–27.

7. See Economist Intelligence Unit (EIU), *Thailand and Myanmar (Burma), no 3 1993* (London: EIU, 1993).

8. See *Bangkok Post*, July 7, 1993.

9. *The New Light of Myanmar,* July 9, 1993, p. 1.

10. *The New Light of Myanmar*, July 30, 1993, p. 1.

11. *The New Light of Myanmar*, September 25, 1993, p. 1.

12. "Myanmar Boosts Naval Power with Frigates," *Jane's Defense Weekly* (August 20, 1994).

13. "Chinese Ships with Burmese Flags Caught in the Indian Water," no. 28 (in Burmese), *Radio Burma Weekly*, August 29, 1994.

14. Economist Intelligence Unit (EIU), *Cambodia, Laos, Myanmar, 3rd Quarter 1995* (London: EIU, 1995), p. 35.

15. Nate Thayer, "Diverted Traffic: Indochina Supplants Thailand Conduit for Burma's Drugs," *Far Eastern Economic Review* (October 1, 1992): 94.

16. Keith B. Richburg, "In China's Wild West, Heroin Grips a Town: Crime, Disease, Prostitution Plague Drug Route," *Washington Post*, July 26, 1996, p. A 29.

17. Testimony of DEA Administrator, Thomas Constantine, to the US Congress Subcommittee on National Security on September 19, 1996.

18. William H. Overbolt, "Dateline Drug Wars: Burma, The Wrong Enemy," *Foreign Policy* (Winter 1991): 177.

19. See Doug J Porter, "A Note on United Nations Involvement in the Border Area Development Program," *Thai-Yunan Project Newsletter,* no. 18 (September 1992): 7.

20. Bertil Lintner, *Burma in Revolt* (Boulder, CO: Westview Press, 1994), p. 317.

21. Ibid., p. 318.

22. Chao-Tzang Yawnghwe, "Politics and the Informal Economy of the Opium/Heroin Trade: Impact and Implications for Shan State of Burma," *Journal of Contemporary Asia,* vol. 23, no. 3 (Manila, 1993): 318.

23. US State Department, *International Narcotics Control Strategy Report (INCSR): Burma 1996* (Washington, DC: US State Department, March 1996), p. 1.

24. See for detail Open Society Institute, *Burma Debate,* vol.3, no. 2 (March–April 1996): pp. 26–27.

25. The US Department of Justice, Drug Enforcement Administration (DEA), The National Narcotics Intelligence Consumer Committee, *The NICC Report 1995* (Washington, DC: DEA, 1996), p. 38.

26. Ibid., p. ix.

27. Ibid.

28. "Burma: Drug Buddies," *Far Eastern Economic Review* (November 14, 1996): 37.

29. Robert S. Gelbard, "SLORC's Drug Links," *Far Eastern Economic Review* (November 21, 1996): 35.

30. US Department of Justice, Drug Enforcement Administration (DEA), *Asian Money Movement Methods, Drug Intelligence Report* (Washington, DC: DEA, July 1994), p. 1.

31. Ibid., p. 3.

32. US Department of Justice, Drug Enforcement Administration (DEA), *Heroin Trafficking Proceeds, Drug Intelligence Bulletin* (Washington, DC: DEA Intelligence Division, DEA-94044, April 1994), p. 1.

33. US Department of Justice, Drug Enforcement Administration (DEA), *Southeast Asian Heroin Trafficking: Emerging Trends* (Washington, DC: DEA-94049, May 1994), p. 1.

34. Ibid., pp. 14–15.

35. Ibid., p. 17.

36. Dennis Bernstein and Leslie Kean, "People of the Opiate: Burma's Dictatorship of Drugs," *The Nation* (December 16, 1996): 14.

37. Ibid., pp. 13–14.

38. Ibid., p. 14.

39. Ibid. See also Harn Yawnghwe, *Burma Alert,* Vol. 7, No. 11 (November 1996): 6.

40. Gelbard, "Slorc's Drug Links," p. 35.

41. Chao Tzang Yawnghwe, *The Shan of Burma: Memoirs of a Shan Exile* (Singapore: Institute of Southeast Asian Studies, 1987), p. 205.

42. Gordon Fairciough, "Good Connections: Firms Linked to Junta Draw Lion's Share of Business," *Far Eastern Economic Review* (August 15, 1996): 67.

43. "SDP: Is Government Linked to Myanmar Drug Warlord?, *Straits Times*, November 1, 1996.

44. *Insight Guides: Burma* (Hong Kong: Apa Productions, 1982), p. 273.

45. Timothy Green, "Jade Is Special, As Are the Risks in Bringing It from Mine to Market" *Smithsonian Magazine* (July 1986): 30.

46. Ibid.

47. Kyaw Yin Myint, "Walk to the East and Look Back to the West: 1993 Border Trade" (in Burmese), *Dana*, Special Issue, vol. 4, no. 7 (Februrary 1994): 22–23.

48. Ibid. p. 23.

49. E. C. Chapman, Peter Hinton, and Jingrong Tan, "Cross-Border Trade between Yunan and Burma, and the Emerging Mekong Corridor," *Thai-Yunan Project Newsletter*, no. 19, (December 1992): 17.

50. Zin Thant, "Myanmah Pyi's or Burma's Northeastern Gateway" (in Burmese), *Dana* (June 1991): p.53.

51. Ibid.

52. See*Far Eastern Economic Review,* Hong Kong, Oct.1, 1992.

53. *Living Color* (Burmese Magazine), (September 1997): 46.

54. Thant, "Myanmah Pyi's," p. 44.

55. Myint, "Walk to the East," p. 18.

56. Ibid., p. 23.

57. Ibid., p. 24.

58. Ibid., pp. 26–27.

59. Ibid., p. 27.

60. Ibid., p. 25.

61. Ibid., p. 27.

62. Ibid.

63. Ibid.

64. Ibid.

8

Human Development under Military Rule: Education, Health, and Welfare

Four Social Objectives of the SLORC:

1. Uplift of the morale and morality of the entire nation;

2. Uplift of national prestige and integrity and preservation and safeguarding of cultural heritage and national character;

3. Uplift of dynamism of patriotic spirit;

4. Uplift of health, fitness and education standards of the entire nation.

In this chapter, the four social objectives of the SLORC printed in bold letters on the front page of The *New Light of Myanmar* since 1996 are scrutinized in light of various social development programs, policies and human development indices of Burma under the military management. Specifically, the fourth objective of the SLORC, uplift of health, fitness and education of the entire nation is dealt with, since the failures of achieving the other three social objectives have been extensively shown in the previous chapters.

EDUCATION

The Mingala Sutra, the classic Burmese Buddhist Thirty-Eight Noble Codes of Conduct or Blessed Codes of Conduct, opens with the question to Buddha: "What many men and deities, Desiring Bliss have sought to find—Come tell me Master, What it is that brings most blessing to mankind?" The answer given in the very first code of conduct prescribed by the Sutra is: "To quit the fools, to court the wise, This is the highest Paradise; To pay respect where it is due, So shall true Blessing wait for you."[1] That is, for a true blessing of life, apart from quitting the fools, a person should "befriend and depend upon the wise and pay respect to those who deserve to be respected," *panditah ninsa thaiwanah* and *puza-hsa puza naiyahnan* in Pali.[2]

There is a saying in the United States: "A mind is a terrible thing to waste." The waste of mind occurs in a particular setting of socioeconomic and political order under a national educational policy adopted and implemented by the government and how the government treats its educated members. In Burma, for more than three decades not only the mind but also the body and the soul of the nation represented by young people and intellectuals have been wasted under the rule of force, on one hand and, on the other, the politically motivated national policy of rewarding "the good-and-loyal" over "the able and educated persons," *lukawn lutaw* in Burmese. This policy is contrary to the policy and practice of not only modern societies but also the Burmese traditional values and standards of conduct, which call for dependency on and respect for the able-and-learned or the wise and not to cut up the face of the country, metaphorically represented by the young children and students, thereby reducing the social capability of Burma for development into a free and prosperous modern society.

The *UN Human Development Report, 1995* states that "the real wealth of a nation is its people–both women and men. And the purpose of development is to create an enabling environment for people to enjoy long, healthy and creative lives. This simple but powerful truth is too often forgotten in the pursuit of material and financial wealth."[3] Creativity of the people requires a social and political climate that permits freedom of expression, thought, and information. It should be added that the real wealth and future development of a nation lie especially in the nurturing of, and investing in, the education of the children and rewarding the educated according to ability, diligence, and performance.

Improvement in the state of technology or increased social capability to generate economic growth calls for investment in education and "the spread and level of modern education and the industrial and commercial experience of people."[4] Specifically, the growth rate of real per capita GDP positively relates to the augmentation of initial human capital (proxied by historical school-enrollment rate).[5] From a historical perspective, Burma's inability to transform itself into a modern state has been singularly due to its inability to provide adequate education to its population and improve the quality of labor force. This fact was observed by J. S. Furnivall considered as the most renowned authority on the impact of British colonial policy and practice on Burma:

Under Burmese rule all the boys were sent to monastic schools because there was a social demand for education; but primary vernacular instruction provided little opportunity for material advancement, and when under British rule, education came to be valued solely as an economic asset, "the difficulty was to create a demand for school, and primary instruction languished.[6]

Between 1900 and 1930, Furnivall observed that although the number of pupils, attending in general, showed a great advance, "of the pupils in the registered schools, 75 percent did not go beyond Standard I or First Grade and 88% failed to complete Standard IV or 4th Grade, which is regarded as the minimum for permanent literacy."[7] However, the number of pupils in the middle standards, from grades 5–12, and higher standards, from grades 8–12, or at secondary and high school level, showed dramatic increases between 1900 and 1937.

Looking purely at the literacy rate and the number of pupils attending schools, the overall impact of the British colonial educational system suggested that there was a great advance. Between 1900 and 1940, the number of students attending schools rose from 3.34 percent to 4.9 percent of the population, mostly due to the remarkable progress in female education. However, Furnivall described the negative progress of education in all its forms in colonial Burma relative to precolonial Burma and neighboring countries during the period 1923 to 1940: "Sixty years ago Upper Burma, under native rule, had far more children at school than any country outside Burma in the tropical Far East; in 1900 Burma as a whole still held the lead, but by 1940 it had sunk to fifth place."[8] According to his statistics, as of 1936–1939 the percentage of population at recognized schools in colonial Burma was 3.92 percent compared with 11.16 percent in Formosa, 10.75 percent in Philippines, 9.69 percent in Thailand and 6.03 percent in Malaysia. He further stated: "But the picture is darker than these figures indicate. It might be claimed sixty years ago that Burma was the best educated in the tropical Far East, with the possible exception of Philippines. It will be difficult to repel the charge that at the time of its separation from India (1937) it was the worst educated."[9] This statement should be modified by adding the phrase "with the exception of Netherlands India or Dutch East India, especially the country now called Indonesia."

EDUCATIONAL SYSTEM AND PROGRESS UNDER THE CIVILIAN GOVERNMENT (1948–1962)

One of the major efforts made by the civilian government of U Nu after Burma gained independence from the British in 1948 was the reform of the deficient colonial educational system with respect to meeting the needs of a modern society and economy. At the time Burma gained independence, there was only one university, Rangoon University, and there were only 250 middle and high schools in the entire country, many of which were run by missionaries. Also, almost one-third of all secondary school pupils were concentrated in Rangoon, indicating that most towns in Burma had no middle and high schools. Under the Pyidawtha Plan (1952–1960), the government launched what is popularly known as "the Mass Education Movement" to achieve five basic goals; a basic education of the three Rs for all citizens, training the requisite number of technicians for the creation of Pyidawtha (A happy and prosperous land), eradication of illiteracy and promotion of five basic Buddhist moral strengths, training of people for responsible citizenship, and training the citizenry for democratic ways of life. To achieve the first goal, a campaign against adult illiteracy was launched by the Mass Educational Council.

The civilian government launched rigorous programs to achieve all of these five educational goals set out in the Pyidawtha Plan, and thousands of primary, middle, and high schools, as well as a limited number of colleges, were opened across the country between 1952 and 1960. Between 1952 and 1960, the number of primary schools increased from 3,557 to 11,557, while the enrollment in the state-sponsored primary, secondary, and high schools nearly tripled, from 666,000 to 1,764,000, and college enrollments more than doubled from less than 6,000 to over 12,000. The overall achievement in the expansion of public education was reflected in the increased percentage of eligible children in primary schools from 31 to 51 percent, in the middle schools from 5 to 9 percent, and in the high schools from 1 to 3 percent.[10]

Technical training in physical sciences and related subjects was established beginning at the middle school level, fifth standard, in which instruction in English as a second language was also introduced. For higher education, Rangoon University and its affiliated colleges were expanded with new buildings, hostels, facilities, and subjects, along with the opening of two-year colleges in major cities, the transformation of Mandalay College into a fully autonomous university, and the accelerated expansion of teachers' training courses and technical training at Insein Technical Institute. In the mid-1950s, with the technical aid of the Russian government, the civilian government of U Nu began the establishment of the Rangoon Institute of Technology (RIT), which opened in 1960 to become the one and only engineering degree-offering college in Burma today.

In order not to exaggerate the achievements in the promotion of basic education and the eradication of illiteracy as well as the expansion of enrollments at all levels of schools, it must be emphasized that such a large-scale drive toward mass education had unfortunate results: poor quality of education and an inability to provide functional or professional education to its native population, which needed to meet the requirements of a modern society and economy. The urban bias of the past colonial educational system continued to persist in that the majority of the native rural population had virtually no economic means and access to modern education and schools. Also, to a large degree the urban population lacked economic means to obtain middle, high school, and college education despite the introduction of a free universal education by the government at all levels. Free public education was free only for tuition and did not cover the costs of school supplies, meals, travel, dormitory expenses, and private tutoring, which became part and parcel of obtaining higher education in Burma as the quality of public education deteriorated.

Although 52 technical and 37 agricultural high schools were created, the government failed to achieve the second goal of training the requisite number of native technicians and professionals for a Pyidawtha domestically due to its bias toward an academic type of education as opposed to technical, vocational, and professional education. As in colonial Burma, a shortage of technical schools, institutes and colleges in agriculture, forestry, engineering, and other professional subjects persisted. However, with the help of bilateral and multi-lateral foreign aid the government embarked upon a rigorous state scholarship program and sent thousands of Burmese students abroad, a majority of them to the United States, for further studies in various fields, including economics, business administration, science, engineering, and technology.

The government also allowed private missionary schools to continue to operate, and English as a subject and medium of instruction in various subjects was also kept at the middle and high school level and at the universities and colleges. Thus, the educational system of the civilian government was relatively free and open with respect to the international flow of ideas and information. The great attention given to investment in education to promote economic growth in the long run may be deemed one of the achievements and appropriate policies of the civilian government. The full realization of the benefits from this investment could not be made due to the overthrow of the democratically elected civilian government of U Nu by General Ne Win and his commanders in 1962, when less and less emphasis was placed on investment in education, and discrimination against the educated and economic retrogression began to transpire in the antiWestern and isolated socialist state of Burma.

THE EDUCATIONAL SYSTEM AND PROGRESS UNDER MILITARY RULE (1962–1988)

Under the military rule of Burma from 1962 to 1988, the human capital stock decreased due to the inward-looking or closed-door policy of isolating the country from the outside world, especially the West, for nearly three decades. Not only was the country physically isolated from the outside world by banning foreign visitors, but also the inflow of news, ideas, information, and knowledge from the West was prohibited by the socialist state of General Ne Win. The rigorous State Scholarship program involving hundreds of state scholars sent each year to Western democratic countries instituted and promoted under the civilian government of the late U Nu was completely halted. Instead, a weak state scholarship program was instituted involving a handful of state scholars who were sent mostly to the Soviet Union and other East European communist countries. Condemning Western education and culture as corrupt, contaminated, and bourgeois, the inflow of English newspapers, books, and journals from the West as well as the use of English as the medium of instruction in schools and colleges were banned.

The consequence of anti-Western educational policy and programs launched under the Burmese Way to Socialism depleted the human capital stock in two ways: a rapid decline in the standard of English and shortage of

Western-trained and educated teachers and scholars whose role was discrimi-nated against and undermined by the state in the functioning of the educational system. In the early 1980s, after the discovery of inadequate English Language comprehension among the brightest Burmese students, reportedly including the daughter of General Ne Win, Sanda Win, who failed foreign language exami-nation, the policy was completely reversed. The use of English as the medium of instruction was introduced at all levels of schools on a national scale, virtu-ally transforming all schools into colonial European code type schools. This policy was doomed to failure since there was a tremendous shortage of native teachers who could teach various subjects in English.

Like all dictators, the basic strategy of Ne Win in protecting his political throne was based upon the political dictum of needing and breeding "loyal" rather than "able" men around him. The Burmese called this method *lukawn lutaw-* good man first and smart man second." In effect, this is analogous to Mao's dichotomy discernible in his writings on "red" versus "expert" cadres. The strategy of rewarding loyalty rather than ability on the societal level has the most damaging impact on the state of technology or technological progress. The ethics of "diligent in work and sober in pleasure" is dissipated in a socialist state where loyalty, connection and party affiliation command greater rewards than ability and diligence. It also caused an enormous brain drain of competent entrepreneurs, professionals, and intellectuals who departed Burma. The dis-crimination against the educated civilians in favor of the uneducated party members, loyal soldiers, and commanders resulted in the massive unemploy-ment of college graduates as well as the decline in the quality of education.

THE DISPARITY OF ECONOMIC DEVELOPMENT AND EDUCATIONAL UNDERDEVELOPMENT

The economic determinant of educational underdevelopment in socialist Burma relates to the regional disparity in economic development: a large gap of living standards (1) between the ruling elite and ordinary people, (2) between the urban and rural communities in central Burma, and (3) between the Bur-mese majority in central Burma and ethnic minorities in peripheral Burma or borderlands. The disparity of income and privilege between the ruling elite and ordinary people generates inequality of access to higher and better education at home and abroad as well as disincentive to learn on the part of low-income and underprivileged, but bright, students. At the primary school level, not all small rural villages of fewer than 100 households have a primary school. The number of primary schools in the small villages ranges from 1 in 5 villages in the pros-perous districts of central Burma, to 1 in 25 villages in the frontier or ethnic minority states. Children from small villages with no primary schools had to travel far to the villages that had state primary schools. After successfully fin-ishing the primary schools, bright youngsters from villages were forced to go to larger villages or faraway towns where there were middle and high schools. Many of them had to drop out because their parents lacked financial means.

At the secondary school level, the state instituted another obstacle for the students by separating "smart science students" from "ordinary arts students" at the 8th grade nationwide examination. Middle school students who failed this examination twice were kicked out of school permanently. They were forced to study privately and take the annual state examination on their own. In the 10th grade, another screening was made by the state by giving nationwide matriculation or college entrance examinations. The same policy of kicking out the students who failed the examination twice was applied to all high school students. Of course, there was black market tutoring, which only the rich and privileged could afford. Hence, by the time young Burmese students took their college entrance or matriculation examinations, many bright but poor as well as average students had fallen by the wayside. The rate of matriculation from among high school students across Burma was kept by the state educational authorities at less than 20 percent. Hence, on one hand, thousands of Burmese youngsters could not obtain a college education, while, on the other, thousands of college graduates could not find employment in totally state controlled and manipulated economic and educational systems of inefficiency and corruption.

The negative impact of the system of weeding out mediocre students or separating talents at the college entrance level was assessed poignantly by a former Burmese educator: "The total annual intake of the higher institutions of learning was less than 20% of the total number of candidates taking the examination (college entrance or matriculation examination), with the result that 4 out of every 5 youths considered themselves as failures at an early stage of their lives."

EDUCATIONAL DISRUPTION AND UNEDUCATED GRADUATES

An additional factor responsible for the exponential decay of Burma's educational system under military rules since 1962 has been the disruption of education or learning by students at all levels of schools. On top of already poor quality of education received by students, the quality of education in Burma suffered from more damage due to regular disruption of learning and discontinuity of the educational process, for the shutting down of schools and colleges to quell unrest and control power by the government has been the ritual in the socialist and present states of Burma. During the 26 years of General Ne Win's rule year, the disruption of education and shutdown of schools and colleges occurred with regularity, with the duration ranging from three months to three years. The cumulative impact of these regular disruptions on the educational system has been an exponential decay in the quality of education.

The shut down of schools and colleges due to sociopolitical unrest, strikes by workers and students, and natural disasters occurred in 1962, 1963, 1967, 1969, 1970, 1974, 1975, 1976, 1987 and 1988. The best known and most recalled incident of shutting down the schools and colleges was the July 1962 student strike, when the Rangoon University Students' Union Building was blown up by the Burmese army soon after the March 1962 military coup. The 1963 shutdown was associated with peace and cessation of civil war demonstrations. The 1967 shutdown occurred in connection with the Sino-Burmese riot and the Sandoway rice riot in Rangoon. The 1969 shutdown occurred in association with the Southeast Asian Games demonstrations. In 1970, there was a student strike at Moulmein, and Moulmein College was shut down. All these shut downs were minor and lasted for three to four months. The major shut downs of schools and colleges across Burma occurred for virtually three years between 1974 and 1976 due to workers' strikes, natural disaster, rice shortages, and the U Thant affair in December. The longest shutdown of schools and colleges transpired in December 1974 in association with the burial issue of U Thant, the ex-secretary general of the United Nations.

THE ECONOMIC ROOT OF STUDENT UNREST AND PROTEST

The stagnation of the educational system of socialist Burma is directly related to the stagnation of the military command economy of inefficiency and corruption. As with basic necessities, the scarcity of modern educational facilities such as notebooks, textbooks, libraries, scientific laboratories, computers, and equipment has been the stark reality of the impoverished socialist economy of Burma. For example, in the 1980s textbooks on various subjects printed and distributed by the government were so scarce they had to be sold by a lottery system to the students. Texts on technical subjects, such as those on engineering, mathematics, sciences and medicine. which were written and had to be taught in English despite the barring of English as a medium of instruction in colleges until 1983, were virtually unavailable except for photostat copies of old texts distributed by certain professors.

The most damaging aspect of the educational system of socialist Burma was the disincentive to learn and attain higher education on the part of all the students. The incentive to learn was severely damaged by a system of rewards based on personal and power connections rather than ability, diligence, and intelligence. High school students who engaged in the lucrative black market trade knew that a college degree meant next to nothing for earning good money and living. College students knew also that those with no college degrees, such as soldiers, ex-military party officials, and black marketeers, earned more money than college graduates and that only if they had personal influence or connections could employment be secured. The economic stagnation and the government's inability to create employment or absorb the successive waves of college graduates into the public sector, the only legal employer of graduates in the socialist economy, created a reserve army of unemployed graduates whose diplomas became worthless to earn a decent living. As a former educator correctly appraised this situation:

Quantitative expansion made sense when the expanding governmental machinery could easily absorb the products in the fifties. Wholesale nationalization of the economy in the sixties further expanding the public sector and shrinking the private sector enhanced the value of educational diplomas. Economic realties (in the 1970s and 1980s) soon changed the circumstances. With the private sector shrinking (except the black market where diplomas are of no value) and the only employer, the governmental administration, now saturated, educated unemployment reared its ugly head. The relative attractiveness of professions, such as the medical, the dental, the engineering, the veterinary, the educational and the economic, in that order gave rise to a kind of elitism for which there was a scramble. With unfavorable teacher-pupil ratio at all levels of education, the race for distinction (as exemplified by Distinctions or "Ds" at government examinations) was run with the aid of outside-class tuition.

In order to prepare their children for passing the national examinations with distinctions to enter the top institutions of learning, parents of well-to-do families and high-ranking government officials paid phenomenal bribes and fees to qualified private tutors who gave special tutorial classes outside the legal public school system. These illegal private tutorial classes were known as the *wine kyushins* in Burmese, or "roundtable tutorial classes" conducted by lowly paid public school teachers and college professors to make extra income. These classes or schools mushroomed throughout Burma, and many of their organizers or entrepreneurs became very wealthy.[11] In the 1980s, even the brightest graduates from the two top professional or technical institutions, medical and engineering institutes, could not find gainful employment in the public sector without political connection. This partially explained why the mass political unrest of 1988 and the most recent December 1996 student protest and demonstration against the government have been associated with students from the Rangoon Institute of Technology as well as the fact that a number of leaders and chairmen of the All Burma Students' Democratic Front (ABSDF) formed during the 1988 political uprising are medical students and doctors.

THE EDUCATIONAL SYSTEM AND PROGRESS UNDER SLORC (1988–)

The exponential decay of the educational system of the past continues to prevail in the present state of Myanmar under SLORC. All the deficiencies and legacies of the past educational system and policies of the socialist state persist. That is, the educational system remains primarily public and in a way more tightly controlled by the state. Since 1988 up to the present, there has not been any attempt to introduce privatization measures of the educational system. The state control of education remains more or less absolute in terms of prohibiting academic freedom on the part of teachers and freedom of speech, thought, and information on the part of the students. The freedom of association with respect to the formation of student unions or clubs is absolutely banned on campuses. Indeed, the central issue in public versus private education in Burma relates to quantity versus quality. In general, a free or low-cost public educational system tends to be low in the quality of education it provides, while a high-cost private educational system tends to be high in the quality of education it provides. The main reason for this is the familiar issue of equity versus efficiency in development. In Burma, the absolute state control of education by banning private schools has had a poor record in the provision of high-quality education.

The system of giving national examinations at the college entrance level or matriculation and weeding out mediocre students or selecting bright students and allocating them to prestigious professional schools, the medical, the dental, and the engineering institutes, on a quota basis has also been kept intact. That is, as in the past, at the 10th grade the students are divided into arts and science groups. This elitist educational system has put a great premium on passing the matriculation examination with top grades or distinctions for the students. Examination questions on various subjects are prepared by professors who are named or selected by the Board of Education of the Department of Education and sequestered by government officials at a designated location under tight security. Securing of these questions from those who have access to them, such as corrupt professors and officials from the Department of Education who are in charge of preparing and printing the examination questions, and selling them to students become a highly lucrative business. Consequently, corruption and cheating continued to proliferate as the leakage of examination questions beforehand occurred.

As before, the poor quality of public education, combined with elitism and low wages of public school teachers and professors, continues to perpetuate private tutorial classes and schools. The participating teachers in these lucrative tutorial classes are lowly paid public high school teachers and college professors many of whom have been forced to resign from their jobs to earn higher wages paid by the owners or organizers of these schools. The average monthly salary of a public high school teacher is around Kt900, while the average monthly salary of an assistant professor at a university is Kt1,200 a month. The average cost of monthly consumption of first-quality rice alone by a Burmese in 1996 is Kt690 (Kt115x6 pyis), which is over 75 percent of the monthly income of a high school teacher and over 57 percent of the monthly salary of an assistant professor. Most of the lucrative private tutorial schools are now owned and organized by wealthy individuals and families with military connections. Although these schools have been allowed to operate, the government imposes regulations, including upper tuition limits per subject per student and per number of subjects taken by a student. As in the past, the organizers of these classes or schools are able to evade government regulations with impunity by bribing government officials. The exorbitant fees charged by these schools have made private tutorial education extremely expensive and beyond the reach of ordinary people. For example, the upper limit of tuition fee set by the government has been Kt30 per subject, whereas the actual or illegal tuition fee charged by these schools was Kt500 in 1989 and went up to over Kt1,000 per subject in 1996.

In addition to the high cost of these private tutorial classes, which became indispensable due to poor quality of public education and the elitism of the educational system, the entrance fees to public or state schools have gone up beyond the means of ordinary people. The following incredible cost of supposedly tuition-free public or state education was reported by the underground student organization of Burma, All Burma Federation of Students' Unions (ABFSU):

It is said that all schools were nationalized since 1962 for the benefit of all. However, schools fees [donations or bribes mandated by the state and collected by school teachers and authorities] for some prestigious schools where only the children of military cronies and wealthy elite attend, are incredibly high. For example, the entrance fees to such schools as Institute of Education Practicing School [Teachers' Training School], Dagon State High School (SHS) 1, Latha SHS 2, Botataung SHS 5, and Bahan SHS 2 in Rangoon, amount to 1 lakh to 2 lakh of (100,000 to 200,000) kyats. The entrance fees to second rate high schools range from 30,000 to 100,000 kyats. The ordinary schools where the majority of students attend require 3,000 to 5,000 kyats for school fees.[12]

It should be noted that the prestigious high schools cited are former Anglo-Vernacular and missionary schools, such as English Methodist, St. John, St. Paul and others in Rangoon that continue to remain highly prestigious for their quality of education despite the change of their names to state high schools after the nationalization all private schools by the military government of Ne Win in 1962.

In addition to the entrance fees, other costs of public education have also escalated with respect to the expenses of textbooks, hostels, transportation, meals, registration, and examination fees. Shortages of textbooks, school supplies, facilities, and qualified teachers in the public school system persist to cause further decline in the quality of education. Moreover, the deeply negative real wages of the parents due to more or less frozen money wages relative to escalating prices of basic necessities have made them unable to send their children to schools. The problem of unaffordable public education due to these costs plagues the poor rural families relatively more than urban families. The dropout rate of students at primary as well as secondary and higher levels of education has accelerated throughout the country. The government continues to open new schools, claiming great advances or achievements made in public education, but the central problem of unemployment for the backlog of college graduates persists as the ostentatious economic reforms of the SLORC have not generated the requisite growth of the economy and the expansion of the private sector to create new employment opportunities.

Under the educational system of the SLORC, high costs and low rate of return from investment in education have accelerated the dropout rate of students at all levels of schools. The following United Nations International Children's Emergency Fund (UNICEF) report best describes the dismal state of educational development and massive dropout rate of primary schools in Burma since 1988:

The primary school network is widespread, with an average of one school for two villages (central Burma only). The qualifications and dedication of teachers are generally good, in spite of the lack of preservice teacher training. However, 39 percent of children never enroll, and only 25 percent of all children complete the five-year cycle of primary education. Drop-out rates seem to be somewhat higher among girls in some areas of the country. Repetition has also been high. Other causes of non-enrollment and drop-out include a curriculum that lacks relevance, insufficient community involvement in primary education, cash costs of poor families, a shortage of text books, and the need for some children to help at home or contribute to the family income. Because the primary school completion is low and there is a shortage of reading materials at the community level for neo-literates, the literacy rate is estimated to have declined to about 55 per cent.[13]

HIGH LITERACY RATE AND LOW ECONOMIC GROWTH

Historically, Burma is acknowledged as a highly literate society richly endowed with natural resources for a great potential of economic development. From precolonial times, through the British colonial period, to the present, the adult literacy rate of Burma has been well above the 20 percent UN benchmark of a least-developed country's human development index. As of 1992, Burma's adult literacy rate was 82 percent.[14] Despite the high literacy rate and richness in natural resources, Burma attained the status of a least-developed country in 1987. On the surface, it seems that the adult literacy rate and level of economic development are directly correlated, as all the industrially developed countries of the West and the newly industrializing countries of Asia, such as Hong Kong, Singapore, South Korea, and Taiwan, have an adult literacy rate of over 90 percent. However, many countries with a very high adult literacy rate like Burma are also found to be economically depressed. This can be observed in the present communist states of Cuba, North Korea, and Vietnam, whose adult literacy rates are 94.9 percent, 95 percent, and 91.9 percent. At the same time, many poor Asian and African countries, such as Bangladesh, Cambodia, Nepal, Pakistan, Ethiopia, Liberia, Mozambique, and Somalia, have a low adult literacy rate of below 40 percent.[15] From these inconsistencies, it must be concluded that the correlation between the high adult literacy rate and high level of income or output is imperfect.

EDUCATIONAL IMBALANCE AND LOW QUALITY OF EDUCATION

The answer to the seeming paradox of why a country with a very high adult literacy rate and rich natural resources like Burma cannot generate high levels of income or output lies in the additional factors of educational development other than the simple factor of adult literacy rate. These factors include the number of students with higher education beyond primary schools, the number of students in technical and scientific fields of studies at home and abroad, investment in education, and above all, the quality of education. For example, for the 1992–1994 period the combined first, second, and third grade level gross enrollment of Burma was 65 percent compared with 98 percent for South Korea, 91 percent for Hong Kong, 80 percent for Malaysia, 80 percent for Indonesia, and 68 percent for Thailand.[16] For the 1988–1991 period, Burma's secondary technical enrollment (as percent of total secondary enrollment) was only 1.2 percent compared with 18.5 percent for Thailand and 12 percent for Indonesia.[17] According to a study of rural poor in Burma by Dapice, "Only 195,000 graduated in 1994/1995 from middle schools and 70,000 from high schools. The size of the yearly age-groups is about 930,000, so just over a fifth of all children get out of middle school and only one in thirteen out of high school. This can be compared to similar data for Indonesia or Vietnam where the ratios are about twice as high."[18]

The ritual of shutting down schools and colleges whenever student unrest and demonstrations occur has also been continuing under the SLORC to depress the quality of education. For example, in central Burma schools and colleges were virtually shut down for three years after the 1988 political uprising as the student protest against the SLORC continued. It continued into the mid-1990s, with the longest shutdown of schools and colleges across Burma occurring in December 1996, when the largest peaceful demonstration by college students against the government since 1988 occurred in Rangoon and other cities. Although primary and secondary schools were reopened in September 1997, colleges remained closed. As in the past, there has been a huge backlog of students at all levels of schools and colleges waiting to finish their education and graduate. It is safe to assume that the practice of giving quick examinations by the state to graduate these students without completing proper course work and studies will continue to make graduation or school and college diplomas empty tokens of educational qualification in Myanmar.

GOVERNMENT EXPENDITURES/INVESTMENT IN EDUCATION

The present educational system continues to deteriorate due to a relatively small amount of state expenditures or investment in education allocated in the state budget. For example, the 1995 government budget shows that the combined expenditures on health, education, and welfare were one-third of the expenditures on defense, which accounted for 60 percent of the total expenditures of the central government. Since 1988, the expenditures on education have been less than 10 percent of the total government expenditures to indicate the continued neglect or rather deliberate undermining of the role of education in favor of military fortification in the development programs of the present military government. According to the *UN Human Development Report*, Burma's expenditures on education declined from 2.2 percent of the GNP in 1960, which remained the same for the decade of the 1970s, to 1.9 percent in the 1980s and 1990s.[19]

Table 8.1 and Figure 8.1 of government expenditures on education versus defense show the preoccupation of the government with military fortification relative to investment in education for the further development of Burma.

Table 8.1

Government Expenditures on Education versus Defense (Billions of kyats)

	1989/90	1990/91	1991/92	1992/93	1993/94	1994/95
Education	2.9	3.8	4.8	4.7	5.6	6.8
Defense (D)	4.1	6.9	8.2	9.1	13.9	14.1
E/D	.70	.55	.58	.51	.40	.48

Source: Ministry of National Planning and Economic Development, *The Union of Myanmar, Review of the Financial, Economic and Social Conditions for 1992/1993, 1994/1995, 1995/1996* and *The SLORC State Budget Law* published between March 30 and April 1 of each year in various issues of the state-run newspaper, *The Working People's Daily* whose name was changed to *The New Light of Myanmar* in 1994.

Figure 8.1

Government Expenditures on Education versus Defense

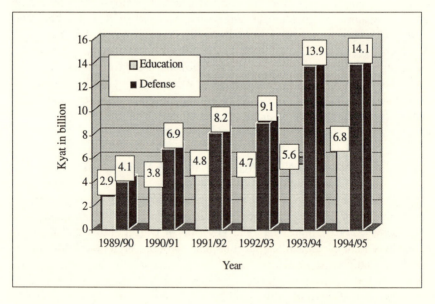

HEALTH AND WELFARE DEVELOPMENT

A poor man may not have enough to eat; being under-fed, his health may be weak; being physically weak, his working capacity is low, which means that he is poor, which in turn means that he will not have enough to eat; and so on.[20]

The preceding passage states a theory known as "the vicious circle of poverty" popular in the economics of development during the 1950s and 1960s. This theory gives a simplistic explanation of why a country like Burma has remained poor for more than three decades of military rule. It has been found that the cross-country causal relationship between poverty reduction or human development, including improvement of the health standard, and economic growth is generally imperfect.[21] Yet, in Burma the causal relationship between the two has been very strong and indisputable.

THE HEALTH SYSTEM AND PROGRESS UNDER THE CIVILIAN GOVERNMENT

At the time Burma gained independence in 1948, Burma's death rate of 30 per 1,000 population was the highest in the world; the infant mortality rate was 195 per 1,000 live births; and the mortality rate of mothers in childbirth was from 5 to 10 times higher than in more advanced countries. The country had only 294 hospitals and dispensaries, with a total of only 8,546 beds—1 bed per 1,980 persons. There were 552 doctors in the medical services of the state and about 700 doctors engaged in private practice for a total of 1,252 doctors serving the population of 17 million—1 doctor per 13,578 persons or .736 doctor per 10,000 persons.[22]

At the end of 1960, there were some 332 government hospitals with a few private hospitals with over 9,600 beds. However, the number of doctors had declined to 1,221 in 1960 compared with 1,252 in 1948 and 1,600 in 1939. In 1960, since the population of Burma was 20.38 million, there was only 1 doctor for every 16,691 persons or .6 doctor per 10,000 persons. However, the number of government-employed midwives, nurses, health visitors, health assistants and vaccinators increased by significant amounts. One of the impressive achievements in health conditions was the government's rigorous antimalaria spraying campaign, which reached 10 million persons in 1960. Overall progress in health standards under these programs was shown in the decline of the infant mortality rate from 221 per 1,000 live births in 1952 to 150 per 1,000 live births in 1960. In the 1950s, government expenditures on health more than tripled to indicate serious attention given to investment in human capital and the promotion of social welfare in the development policy of the civilian government.[23]

THE HEALTH SYSTEM AND PROGRESS UNDER MILITARY RULE
(1962–)

Since the military coup of 1962 up to 1988 the military government of General Ne Win persistently reported an expanding and progressive health system structured on the basis of three sectors: the state, cooperative, and private. Based on government statistical data, the health system in the socialist state of Burma from 1962 to 1988 seemed to have made great advances relative to that of the health system of the civilian government with impressive growth rates in the number of hospitals, dispensaries, and rural health centers. The data in Table 8.2 give this impression.

Table 8.2
Health Facilities and Personnel (1960–1988)

	1959/60*	1987/88	%Growth(1960–1988)
Doctors	1,221	11,076	807
Nurses	1,054	8,238	608
Midwives	1,487	8,187	451
Hospitals and dispensaries	332	763	130
Hospital Beds	9,644	25,759	107
Rural Health Centers	409	1,337	227
Maternity and Child Care	345	348	.8

* In order not to mislead, it is assumed that the year 1959/60 is the de facto culminating year of the
    civilian rule, although the military coup did not occur until 1962. The data for 1960 are assumed
    to be the comparable data for 1962, which are not available.
Sources: Louis J. Walinsky, *Economic Development in Burma 1951–60* (New York: The Twentieth
    Century Fund, 1962), p. 365 and Ministry of Planning and Finance (MPF), *Report to the Pyithu
    Hluttlaw* (Rangoon: MPF, 1987), p. 226.

Between 1960 and 1988, the number of doctors increased from 1,221 to 11,076. Given the population figures of 20.38 million in 1960 and 38.5 million in 1988, the ratio of doctors to population increased from 1 doctor per 16,691 or .6 doctor per 10,000 persons to 1 doctor per 3,476 or 2.876 doctors per 10,000 persons.[24] The number of doctors increased by more than eight times, and nurses by more than six times during the 26 years of General Ne Win's rule. However, the percentage increase in the number of hospitals and dispensaries and hospitals beds was far below the percentage increase in the number of doctors and nurses, indicating a lack of accompanying growth in medical facilities and thus inadequate medical care and services to the general public. The aggregate expansion in the number of hospitals and dispensaries also failed to indicate the fact that most of the expansion was concentrated in urban communities, while health care in rural communities, where the majority of people

resided remained stagnant and neglected without modern hospitals and qualified doctors.

To many outside observers, the government statistical data on hospitals,
doctors and medical facilities gave an impression of a great leap forward in
public health. In reality, there was a large gap between the elite and the masses
with respect to medical supplies and health services throughout Burma. The
best medical facilities, supplies, and doctors were to be found in the military
hospitals established especially for the defense services officers and their families at various bases. In Rangoon, the best-known, ultramodern military hospital has been the Defense Services General Hospital (DSGH) located at Mingla-
don where the Medical College or Medical Institute no. 2 was also located.
Apart from this famous hospital, there are also another modern military or
army hospital known as the Base Military Hospital at U Wisara Road as well as
the Naval Hospital and Air Force Hospital in Rangoon. At major cities where
armed forces bases are located, modern hospitals were established to provide
health care for the military personnel. It should also be mentioned that the new
medical doctors who obtained employment with the state were subject to military draft known as National Service on a lottery basis to serve in the army for
three years.

INFANT MORTALITY RATE REDUCTION

Based solely on growth in the number of doctors, nurses and health assistants and the reduction in the infant mortality rate between 1962 and 1988, the
socialist state of Burma under the military rule of General Ne Win seemed to
have made significant progress in the health system and the provision of health
care, as some Burma observers have suggested.[25] However, a closer scrutiny of
the health system and progress of Burma under rule of General Ne Win and the
SLORC gives a completely opposite picture of Burma's deteriorating health
standards and conditions absolutely and relative to neighboring countries. Table 8.3 and Figure 8.2 show Burma's relatively lower achievement in the reduction of infant mortality compared to the achievement of neighboring countries between 1960 and 1990.

It should also be noted that although the infant mortality rate of Burma was
reduced substantially from 150 per 1,000 live births in 1960 to 67 per 1,000
live births in 1990, Burma's under-five infant mortality rate in 1990 remained
high at 91 per 1,000 live births compared with 30 for Malaysia, 35 for Thailand
and 36 for Sri Lanka.[26]

Table 8.3
Infant Mortality per 1,000 of Live Births (1960–1990)

	1959/60	1989/90	% Reduction
Burma	150	67	55
Vietnam	147	61	58
Sri Lanka	71	27	62
Malaysia	73	23	68
Thailand	103	27	74

Source: United Nations Development Programme (UNDP), *Human Development Reports 1991* and
1996 (New York: Oxford University Press, 1991 and 1996).

Figure 8.2
Infant Mortality Rate in 1960 and 1990

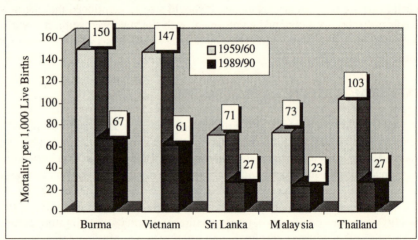

THE HEALTH SYSTEM AND PROGRESS UNDER SLORC (1988–)

The structure and functioning of the health system of Burma under SLORC
have not changed substantively compared to the past socialist state despite a
number of new initiatives with respect to the development of community-based
health care system and organizations, acceptance of certain non-governmental
organizations (NGOs), and increased cooperation with different UN agencies
for upgrading the health standards. As in the past, the health system remains
primarily public, urban-biased, and elitist under the direct control of the Ministry of Health with military commanders, Rear Admiral Than Nyunt as the
minister of health and intelligence chief Lieutenant General Khin Nyunt as the
chairman of the National Health Committee, with no medical training and

knowledge. The three-pronged health system of state, cooperative, and private sectors in the provision of health services is maintained with state and cooperative hospitals, medical services, and personnel quantitatively dominating the health care of the population, while private doctors and medical practitioners continue to play an important role in providing better quality health care to the public. As in the past socialist state, inefficiency and corruption pervade the state sector producing inadequate and poor medical services available to the general public.

THE STATE OF HEALTH OF CHILDREN AND WOMEN IN BURMA

There is a myth about Burma's inexhaustible ability to feed its people reflected in the proud Burmese saying that "the golden fruit, paddy, sprouts profusely from the earth," *myaygyiga shwethee* in Burmese. It instilled a belief among Burmese that no one starves in Burma. This notion is born out of the misconception of the richness of the land as the main determinant of Burma's ability to feed its people. As David Chandler of the World Vision correctly assessed: "This ingrained notion is very difficult to debunk. There is no question that Myanmar is a land of tremendous resources, with great food production capacity. However, the MICS [Multiple Indicator Cluster Survey of the Ministry of Health in collaboration with the UNICEF] data indicating 15.8% of the children are severely malnourished indicates a problem on the scale of national emergency."[27]

Under the SLORC, Burma's infant mortality rate jumped from 67 in 1989 to 105 in 1995, while its under five infant mortality rate jumped from 91 per 1,000 live births in 1989 to 111 per 1,000 live births in 1993 and to 150 per 1,000 live births in 1995.[28] Burma's national infant mortality rate of 105 per 1,000 live births is three to nearly ten times higher than that of its neighboring countries: 34 in Vietnam, 27 in Thailand and 11 in Malaysia. The UNICEF reported: "As the citizens of a 'Least-Developed Country,' the children of Myanmar face a number of problems. For many, even survival is at stake. Children under five account for 40 per cent of all mortality in Myanmar–175,000 die each year."[29] The same report noted that the children of Myanmar suffer from high levels of mortality, malnutrition, and morbidity that are caused by preventable or easily treatable diseases, reflected in an under-five mortality rate of 147 per 1,000 live births, under three moderate and severe malnutrition rates of 36.7 and 40 percent respectively, a low birth weight (2500 grams or less) rate of 23.5 percent, and a goiter rate of 28.2 percent among school children in 1991.[30]

The maternal mortality rate also went up by nearly five times, from 140 per 100,000 live births in 1987 to 580 per 100,000 live births in 1993.[31] Abortion has been identified as "the single greatest cause of maternal mortality, accounting for around 50 percent of all such deaths."[32] The other causes have been various infectious diseases, such as malaria, leprosy, dengue, hemorrhagic fever, and tuberculosis, and unsanitary delivery methods and lack of essential obstetric emergency skills at the first referral level. Indeed, since the fate of the newborn is so critically linked to the mother's health, the infant and maternal mortality rates are inextricably intertwined.

The deteriorating trend of Burma's state of health under SLORC can be seen in the increase of infant mortality and the decline in life expectancy between 1989 and 1995 (Table 8.4).

Table 8.4
Infant Mortality per 1,000 Live Births and Life Expectancy at Birth

	1989	1995
Infant Mortality	67	105
Life Expectancy at Birth	61.3	57.9

Source: United Nations Development Programme (UNDP), *Human Development Reports 1991* and
    1997 (New York: Oxford University Press, 1991 and 1997) and Asian Development Bank
    (ADB), *Economic Report on Myanmar*, (Manila: ADB, November 1995).

The reasons for the phenomenal increase in the infant mortality rate and the decrease in life expectancy during the 1989–1995 period cannot be absolutely specified. According to the data given by the Department of Planning and Statistics of the Ministry of Health, the leading causes responsible for the infant mortality in 1990 were pneumonia, malaria, intestinal infection, debility, malnutrition, and other respiratory diseases, accounting for 24.32 percent, 13.31 percent, 9.98 percent, 9.77 percent, 5.41 percent, and 4.99 percent of total deaths respectively. Based on the very reports of the government, one of the main factors for the increase in the infant mortality rate has been a virtually zero growth in the number of rural health centers and maternity and child care centers or inadequate health services in the rural communities.

As for the decrease in life expectancy, apart from the poor health services as well as the proliferation of infectious diseases and alarming spread of HIV/AIDS infection, an additional reason has been the relentless human rights violations of the Burmese army; such as the use of forced labor, including women and children, portering, forced relocation, and annual military offensives against political and ethnic rebels. These human rights abuses have produced the swelling number of refugees living in makeshift camps under squalid health conditions along and across Burma's borders. As Jesuit Refugee Service (JRS) reported: "Even as 1996 was being promoted as 'Visit Myanmar Year' refugees continued to flee the country making Burma not just the largest country in Southeast Asia [should be mainland Southeast Asia] but also the major refugee producing country of the region."[33] The estimated number of political and economic refugees ranged from 500,000 to 1 million along the Thai border and inside Thailand alone.

HIV/AIDS EPIDEMIC IN BURMA

The report of HIV/AIDS infection of the Burmese people began to receive the attention of the UN World Health Organization (WHO) in 1993 when 261 full-blown AIDS cases and around 7,500 HIV-positive cases were confirmed. The UNICEF reported: "HIV/AIDS has emerged as a major public health problem in Myanmar. According to projections based on the Ministry of Health's sentinel surveillance system, the number of HIV-positive persons could be as high as 400,000 to 500,000 by the end of 1994."[34] In 1996, the WHO, other UN agencies, and independent researchers on Burma's health conditions estimated that around 500,000 out of 45 million Burmese people or 1.1 percent of Burma's population are infected with HIV, although the Burmese Government's National Aids Program (NAP) officially identified only around 14,500 people infected with the disease. The WHO's Global Program on AIDS identified Burma as one of the four Asian countries suffering from the fastest spread of the virus in the world, that is, those with 1 percent or more of its population infected. The three other Asian countries identified are: Cambodia, with 2.8 percent or about 200,000 of its 7 million population infected, India, with 1.7 percent or about 15 million of its 850 million population infected, and Thailand with 1.3 percent or about 800,000 of its 60 million population infected.[35]

Heroin production and trafficking from Burma's Golden Triangle across the borders and the spread of HIV/AIDS inside and outside Burma are directly linked. Many tourists, journalists, and nongovernmental organization (NGO) workers have observed and reported that "Burma is a main conduit of the "AIDS route," which carries infection from Thailand to the border and remote tribal areas of India and China."[36] The drug trafficking routes and the "AIDS route", are inextricably intertwined. Evidence of this can be found in the rising rates of drug addiction and HIV infection among the people in various trading outposts or towns that lie along major contraband trafficking routes of Burma. The most famous contraband trafficking route in northeastern Burma is the Burma Road that traverses the Shan towns of Taungyi, Lashio, Namkhan, and the village of Kyukok and connects with the Chinese border towns of Wanding and Ruili in Yunan province. The other two routes are: the Taungyi-Hopone-Loilem-Namsan-Kentung-Tachilek (the drug capital of Burma) route in southeastern Shan state that connects with the towns of Mai Sai and Chaing Rai in Thailand, and the Monywa-Ye Oo-Kalewa-Kalemyo route in northwestern Burma that connects with the Indian border town of Tamu in the state of Manipur. The streets of these towns, especially those that are located adjacent to the border, are filled with thriving brothels, "tea stalls," and shooting-galleries behind various shops and tea houses where prostitution and the use of heroin proliferate. It has been reported that after the Burmese military junta seized power and legalized cross-border trade with China in 1988, levels of drug addiction in China have increased more than seven times: from 70,000 addicts in

1989 to 500,000 addicts in 1995, accompanied by the spread of HIV among drug users, 70 percent of whom are reported to be in the border town of Ruili in Yunan. A similar rise in the rates of drug addiction and HIV infection has been reported in the three Indian states of Mizoran, Manipur, and Nagaland.[37]

The rising production of opium and heroin under SLORC has not only been shipped abroad but also used inside Burma. The number of opium and heroin addicts not only at the borders but also inside Burma has been reported to have increased at an alarming rate. The increasing availability and use of heroin and other drugs in major cities and on college campuses have been widely observed and reported. It has also been charged that the military government has deliberately ignored or even encouraged the use of illicit drugs by students to divert and subdue their political interest and protest against the government. HIV/AIDS is reportedly not only confined to high-risk groups but has also spread to the general population. Most of the infected and those who are at risk are males of reproductive age working as truck drivers, traders, miners, fishermen, and laborers, as well as young women who are their wives or partners, the majority of whom are associated with the Burma's booming cross-border trade and tourism.

The major mode of transmission of the virus in Burma has been the sharing of needles among heroin users. According to David Chandler of the World Vision: "HIV infection rates among intravenous drug users in various high risk areas are routinely revealed to exceed 90%."[38] An estimated 60 to 70 percent of the intravenous drug users (IDUs) have been reported to have HIV. Possession of drugs and syringes is supposedly illegal in Burma. Syringes are short in supply and are primarily owned by professional drug dealers and injectors who gave injection to the IDUs at "tea stalls" or shooting galleries behind shops and tea houses. Shortage of syringes contributes greatly to the sharing of the needles and "up to 40 people may be injected with the same needle."[39] In particular, there have been reports of an AIDS epidemic among the jade miners in the Kachin state, where the use of drugs and the number of drug addicts have proliferated. The ethnic Kachin Independence Organization (KIO) gave an estimate of some 33,000 opium and heroin addicts in the Kachin state alone.

Another mode of transmission of the disease has been through sexual contact or through other sexually transmitted diseases (STDs). Rural and urban poverty under the "open-door economy of Myanmar" of the government to attract tourists and foreign investors has led to a rapid growth of the sex industry inside Burma and across the border in Thailand where hundreds of thousands of Burmese girls and women have been trafficked to work as prostitutes in hundreds of Thai brothels. In 1992, the estimated number of Burmese girls and women (the majority of whom are ethnic minorities), lured into prostitution in Thailand was around 40,000. It can be assumed that the number has increased greatly in the mid-1990s in light of the increasing poverty, the relentless military campaigns against the ethnic minority rebels, and the forced relocation of the people by the Burmese army.[40] The estimated HIV infection rate among the

Burmese commercial sex workers (CSWs) working in Thailand is around 70 percent.[41]

The most appalling story of Burmese prostitutes infected with HIV relates to their treatment by both Thai and Burmese authorities. According to the Documentation and Research Center of All Burma Students' Democratic Front (ABSDF):

With the collusion of police and military personnel from Burma and Thailand, gangs bring young victims across to Thai border towns like Chaing Mai, Mae Sai, Kanchanaburi, and Ranong where they are sold into forced prostitution for from $100 to $600. Although some have gone willingly for "economic reasons," many have been lured on the false promise of other jobs, while others have been forced into prostitution and brutally beaten if they refuse customers or try to escape.[42]

Equally appalling has been the treatment of the HIV-positive Burmese prostitutes upon their voluntary return or forced deportation by the Thai authorities back to Burma. There have been persistent reports of executing them upon their arrival in Burma by the Burmese authorities, some of them by cyanide injections.[43]

The majority of the prostitutes inside Burma are also found to be infected with the virus. An empirical study of the research team headed by a Burmese woman medical doctor, Daw Khin Thet Wai, projected 64.5 percent of married men who engaged in sex with prostitutes without the use of condoms would be infected with the HIV/AIDS. Consequently, their spouses would be subject to catching the disease. According to the September 1993 report of the Ministry of Health, the percentage of HIV-positive pregnant women in Tachilek, the drug capital of the Shan state, was 12 percent, 2 percent in Kawthaung, 2 percent in Myitkyina, and 1 percent in Moulmein. Their offspring are bound to be infected.[44]

The major contributing factors to the alarming spread of HIV/AIDS in Burma are "the country's ongoing political crisis, mass population movements [due to massive forced relocation, forced labor, and military campaigns of the Burmese army against ethnic minority rebels], poverty, backward medical conditions, and the flood of cheap heroin."[45] All these factors or causes of the spread of the disease are the results of the inept sociopolitical and economic programs and policies of the military regime or the main culprit is what Dr. Cesar Chelala appropriately termed "Burma's Disease-Causing Generals." The denial of the HIV/AIDS epidemic in Burma as a national emergency on the part of government authorities is an additional factor compounding the problem. Typical attitudes and reactions of government officials to the question of the existence and the seriousness of the problem include: the rejection of the alarming spread of the disease reported by outside observers, moral integrity and discipline of the people as a buffer to the disease, confinement of the disease to only high-risk groups such as CSWs and IDUs, foreigners as the cause of the disease, and the ability and competence of the government, Burmese medical doctors, and health workers to prevent and deal with the disease.[46]

Indeed, in light of the booming sex industry, poor health services, facilities and education, increased heroin production and trafficking with the complicity of Burmese generals, and the widespread use and drug addiction of people along the borders and inside Burma, and above all, the denial of the existence and seriousness of the problem by the government, the endemic spread of HIV/AIDS to general population is imminent, and the social and economic cost of treating the cases and halting its spread is going to be enormous.

HEALTH FACILITIES AND PERSONNEL (1990–1996)

The overall picture of Burma's primary heath care infrastructure under SLORC is rather bleak. In 1995, UNICEF assessed: "Although Myanmar's primary heath care infrastructure is improving gradually, only about 80 percent of the population is said to have access to some basic health services, principally immunization and maternal care. About 60 percent of the population is believed to have access to a full array of primary health care services."[47] Comparatively, the access of 60 percent of the population of Burma to basic health services is the lowest among its neighbors with the exception of Cambodia: China, Thailand, and Vietnam with 90 percent each, Indonesia with 80 percent, Philippines with 76 percent, Laos with 67 percent, and Cambodia with 53 percent.[48]

The ratio of Burma's population per doctor has been the worst among its neighboring Asian countries with the exception of Cambodia (Table 8.5).

Table 8.5
Population per doctor (1995)*

Burma	3,125
Vietnam	2,857
Philippines	2,083
Indonesia	1,785
Sri Lanka	1,785
Thailand	1,191
Malaysia	602

Sources: The data are derived from United Nations Development Programme (UNDP), *Human Development Report 1996* (New York: Oxford University Press, 1996), pp. 160–161 and *Asiaweek*, March 3, 1995.

Table 8.6 shows the stagnant condition of health facilities and personnel in Burma under SLORC in the 1990s.

Table 8.6

Health Facilities and Personnel in Burma (1990–1996)*

	89/90	90/91	91/92	92/93	93/94	94/95	95/96
Doctors	12,427	12,427	12,066	11,872	12,340	12,464	12,950
Nurses	8,434	8,811	9,023	7,900	8,264	8,986	9,851
Hospitals	643	661	689	693	698	703	737
Hospital Beds per 10,000 persons	6.37	6.38	6.57	6.46	6.42	6.34	6.34
Rural Health Centers	1,338	1,373	1,375	1,375	1,376	1,377	1,427
Maternity & Child Health Centers	348	348	348	348	348	348	358
Population per Doctor	3,221	3,283	3,444	3,508	3,494	3,528	3,328

* The figures for 1994/1995 are provisional actual and for 1995/1996 are provisional.
Source: Ministry of National Planning and Economic Development (MNPED), *The Union of Myanmar, Review of the Financial, Economic and Social Conditions for 1992/1993 and 1995/1996* (Yangon: MNPED, 1993 and 1996).

Using the relatively more reliable provisional actual figure of the number of doctors given for 1994/1995 rather than the provisional or projected figure of 1995/1996 which is more often than not inaccurate, the annual growth rate of doctors between 1990 and 1995 was only .06 percent relative to the annual population growth of 1.88 percent reported by the government. The growth in the number of hospitals was 1.8 percent, which is roughly the same as the population growth rate. The number of hospital beds available for the population, as well as the growth rate in the number of rural health centers and maternity and child health care centers, remained virtually zero between 1990 and 1995. The ratio of population per doctor went up by 9.5 percent from 3,221 in 1990 to 3,528 in 1995, reflecting an increase in the shortage of doctors. This shortage has been due to the public educational system's inability to produce more medical school graduates and qualified doctors, on one hand, and the exodus of many doctors out of Burma to seek better economic opportunities in more prosperous neighboring countries and the West, on the other. Indeed, in 1994 the government was forced to pass a law prohibiting the newly graduated medical doctors from leaving the country before five years of service.

Other evidence of Burma's poor health standard and inadequate health services provided by the government can be seen in the relatively low percentage of population with access to health services, safe water and sanitation compared with that of the neighboring countries (Table 8.7).

Table 8.7
**Percentage of Population with Access to Health Services, Safe Water, and
Sanitation (1985–1995)**

	Health Services (1985–1995)	Safe Water (1990–1995)	Sanitation (1990–1995)
Burma	60	38	36
Indonesia	80	62	51
Vietnam	90	36	22
Sri Lanka	93	53	61
Malaysia	n.a.	78	94
Thailand	90	86	74

Source: United Nations Development Programme (UNDP), *Human Development Report 1996* (New
    York: Oxford University Press, 1996), pp. 144–145.

The percentage of Burma's population's access to all three important determinants of good health standards is far below that of its neighboring countries, with the exception of Vietnam, which has lower percentages of its population's access to safe water and sanitation than Burma. According to UNICEF:
"Water-borne diseases such as hepatitis, cholera, and diarrhea are problems in
various areas of the country" since "only 19 per cent of families had access to
safe drinking water and 41 per cent to sanitary latrines in 1993."[49] Ultimately,
Burma's 9.4 million malnourished children under age five were the largest
number compared with 8.77 million for Indonesia, 4.4 million for Vietnam, 1.4
million for Thailand, .688 million for Sri Lanka, and .665 million for Malaysia
in the 1985–1995 decade.[50] Based on these data, it seems that the health standards and conditions in Burma under SLORC have not only not improved but
worsened.

INEFFICIENCY, INEQUITY, AND POOR QUALITY OF PUBLIC
HEALTH SYSTEM

Like the educational system, the health system of Burma under military
management was urban-biased and elitist, with extreme disparity in the availability of modern medical facilities and services between the urban and rural
communities, between central Burma and peripheral ethnic minorities states,
and between the ruling elite and ordinary people. A majority of state hospitals
and qualified doctors were concentrated in the district cities and towns. In the
rural communities, where more than 75 percent of the population lived and
worked, there were virtually no modern hospitals. Although the number of rural health centers increased by 227 percent, there were only three more maternity and child care centers created between 1960 and 1988. The government

dispensaries in the rural communities were run by poorly educated and trained government health assistants from the Department of Health with two years of medical education. Consequently, as in the past the major providers of health care in the rural areas in central Burma and ethnic minority borderland remain the traditional medicine men and midwives with no modern medical knowledge. For the decade 1985–1995, the rural-urban disparity in health services of Burma was 35, or the rural population received only 35 percent of the health services received by the urban population. By contrast, for the same period the figures for Thailand, Philippines, and Vietnam were 100, 88, and 80 respectively, indicating the extreme rural-urban health services disparity of Burma.[51]

Like the past health system, the present public health system under SLORC is nominally structured with three sectors: the government, cooperative, and private. However, the cooperative sector is now almost defunct, and the private sector became the dominant sector superseding the stagnating public sector. The size and role of the private sector, which used to be relatively small in the past socialist state, have now greatly enlarged with the rapid deterioration in the quality of public health system and services. The public health system has become highly inefficient and more corrupt due to the government policy of keeping the wages of government employees, including doctors, more or less frozen relative to the escalating cost of living. The average monthly wage of a medical doctor in the public sector is around Kt1,500 ($12.5 at the black market exchange rate in 1996), which did not even cover the cost of monthly consumption of rice, the Burmese main staple, in 1996. Consequently, many well-trained doctors who wish to remain in Burma have been forced to leave the public sector. As the London-based research organization Article 19 observed:

As a result, over the years there has been a constant exodus of qualified doctors from the public sector—either to go abroad or, more recently, into other occupations or into private medical practice in Burma. Throughout the country, despite a general expansion in primary medical care over the past decade, there are huge gaps and constant interruptions in medical provisions, making it difficult to sustain community health programmes.[52]

The UNICEF reported that in 1993 out of 13,392 qualified doctors in Burma only 4,988, or 37 percent, were recorded as employees in the public sector, while 80 percent of the doctors in the public sector were forced to engage in general practice or join private clinics during or after their regular work at public hospitals to supplement their meager income.[53] Other qualified doctors have been forced to leave the country to find higher-paying overseas jobs.

Most important of all, the state-controlled and–managed health system under SLORC has been facing shortages of medical supplies, essential medicines, and drugs for treatment as the former Burma Pharmaceutical Industry (BPI) has not been able to produce the same amount of supplies as it had done in the past. A shortage of raw materials and energy to operate all factories of state enterprises, including the BPI, has caused a greater reliance on the import of medical supplies and drugs, especially Chinese products. The net consequence has been the rising cost of health care as public hospitals and dispensaries can no longer provide adequate medicines and drugs produced by the BPI. It has been reported that, as in the socialist era, patients have to purchase and bring the necessary medicines and medical supplies themselves, bought in the open market, for treatment at state hospitals. The shortage of funds or revenues also led the government to introduce a cost-sharing program at public hospitals whereby patients who can afford to pay are required to pay for private rooms and medical services. It has also been reported that those patients who cannot pay or share the cost receive little or no proper medical care. The cost-sharing program was doomed to failure due to the fact that, to begin with, most patients who go to the public hospitals are low-income and poor families who cannot pay, or those who can pay choose to go to private polyclinics for better medical services. As a Burmese satirically and aptly remarked: "In Myanmar today, you can pay you live; if you cannot pay you die."

As the quality of public medical care has deteriorated rapidly, the demand for private medical care has risen and a number of privately owned and private-government joint venture polyclinics, *sayguns* in Burmese, have sprung up in a few cities, mostly in the capital city of Rangoon. There are two types of these polyclinics: (1) those owned and run by doctors who lease building and state of the art medical equipment, such as ultrasound and X-ray machines, laser surgical tools, nuclear magnetic resonance machines, CAT scans and so on, from private businessmen and importers and (2) those owned by private families or businesses that engage well-known private doctors and specialists to work for them on a commission basis by visiting or rotating among different polyclinics on different days of the week. It has been reported that the top polyclinics have charged their medical service fees for the use of these machines in US dollars or dollar-denominated foreign exchange certificates (FECs). As of 1996, the 16 polyclinics that provide inpatient services in Rangoon are Aung, Aung Hpe, Aye Nyeinthah, Bahosi, Charnmyaie Thahyah, Kanthahyah (also known as Joint Venture No. 7), Kyel Koepwint, Lin, Moethee, Moethidah, Mya Yadanah, Nilah, Paragu, Shin Pahgu, Thara-hpi, and Tawwin Sayguns or Polyclinics.[54] A majority of these well-known private polyclinics are financed and owned by rich businessmen, doctors, and families with military connections.

The following data on the fees or costs of obstetrical and gynecological care at these poly-clinics in Rangoon highlight the high cost of private medical care in Burma today. The fees charged at these poly-clinics range widely from Kt300 to Kt2,500 for different qualities of private rooms per day, and from Kt3,500 to Kt10,000 for obstetrician fees based on the type and quality of medical care and service plus Kt1,000 fee for the second health assistant, and Kt1,500 fee for the first assistant to the main obstetrician, and from Kt700 for the use of ordinary delivery room to Kt1,000 for the use of a cesarean delivery room. The obstetrician fee for the immediate examination and care of the newborn baby is Kt1,500, and the fee for maternal and child care after the birth is

Kt200 per visit.[55] Based on these data and assuming five days of stay at a poly-clinic, the total cost of normal delivery and care for the child and mother after birth would range between Kt10,500 for the least expensive and Kt28,000 for the most expensive or best medical service. These two costs represent almost one and one-half times the Kt7,200 annual salary of the lowest-ranked govern-ment employee and 93 percent of the Kt30,000 annual salary of the highest-ranked government employee.

The preceding nominal data on the total cost of normal child delivery do not include the real and undisclosed cost of obtaining the best medical care from a reputable private doctor. The securing the service of such a doctor is highly private and personal. It is a matter of private contract between the pa-tient and the doctor covering the period of pregnancy before the actual delivery is made at the poly-clinic. The patient must personally contact the doctor be-forehand and pay in advance what the Burmese termed *gadawt kha* , or homage fee in cash or kind. It must be pointed out that the payment of this money does not guarantee the delivery service of the doctor at a polyclinic due to his posi-tion or ability to take quasi rent from patients in the highly inefficient and cor-rupt economic system. This de facto bribery is similar to the "tea money" or "cake money" given to high-ranking government officials to obtain certain fa-vors[56] dating back to the days of the Burmese kingdom and British colonial rule. This custom has persisted throughout the history of independent Burma and proliferated greatly under the past and present military rule as the economy has continued to decline and real wages of government employees have become deeply negative in light of the sustained accelerated inflation and frozen wages. The amount of bribe paid varies depending on the name and prestige of the doctor. It may be several times higher than the normal or stated costs posted and advertised by a polyclinic. It has been reported that the cost of normal child delivery and maternal care ranges from Kt20,000 to Kt50,000, while the cost of special medical services provided by a top obstetrician, surgeon, or specialist with a foreign medical degree at a private polyclinic can be as high as Kt300,000.

From these data, it is obvious that the cost of health care at these polyclin-ics is so exorbitant that it is beyond the reach of ordinary people. The following account of the incredibly high cost of health service at a private polyclinic in Rangoon was given by a Burmese doctor who works for a foreign nongovern-mental health organization:

A pregnant woman of a very wealthy family entered a polyclinic in Rangoon for five days for the delivery of her baby at a cost of Kt2,500 per night of stay. The fee, includ-ing the bribe money, paid to the obstetrician for complete delivery and medical care was Kt100,000. The woman developed a complication during the labor and went into shock, needing desperately a blood transfusion. The poly clinic would not give the blood trans-fusion unless an additional Kt4,000 was paid upfront by the family. After paying and the transfusion was done, the delivery continued and the baby died. Although the woman recovered from the shock, she continued to suffer from further complications.

She had to be rushed to the emergency ward of the government Central Women's Hospital (WCH), formerly the famous Duffrin Women's Hospital of the British colonial era. The reason for this was that the poly-clinic has no facilities for emergency surgical services. Fortunately, the woman recovered after the emergency treatment was performed at the WCH at an additional cost of Kt25,000.

The total cost of delivery and medical treatment at the polyclinic after five days of life and death struggle amounted to Kt150,000 or about $1,000 at the prevalent black market exchange rate of Kt150 to US$1 in early 1997. This dollar cost may seem reasonable according to modern Western standards, but in Burma, it amounts to five times the annual income of Kt30,000 earned by the highest-ranked government official. This case is direct evidence of the development of a highly expensive and inequitable health system in the so-called market-oriented economy of Myanmar, in which only a handful of the rich can afford to pay for the abnormally high cost of modern medical services. It also seems that "even if one can pay, one may die" due to corrupt and inefficient medical services.

THE MILITARY SECTOR AND ITS DOMINANCE OVER THE HEALTH SYSTEM

As in the past socialist state, the military sector of the public health system sector continues to be the most advanced and privileged sector. As pointed out before, the defense services have several modern hospitals at various bases in Rangoon and other major cities, along with an ample supply of medical doctors drafted to serve in the armed services medical corps for three years. Although there are no exact statistical data available, the per capita doctor and hospital ratio in the military sector with some 300,000 persons can be assumed to be several times higher or better than that of the civilian population of some 45 million. In the post-1988 period, the military sector began to face a shortage of doctors. The reason is that many military medical doctors who were involved in the 1988 mass demonstration were purged, and those who were drafted into the military medical corps no longer wished to continue to join and serve in the army. To solve this problem, in 1993, the SLORC established a military medical college or institute in addition to the three existing civilian medical colleges or institutes. It was named the Defense Services Institute of Medicine (DSIM) in Rangoon, similar to the Defense Services Academy at Maymyo, to train and graduate cadets as medical doctors for high-ranking military personnel and their families. It should be noted that modern medical services or health facilities provided by the military sector are not equitably distributed among defense service personnel. Access to the best health care, domestic and overseas, is confined to military commanders, most of whom have their own personal physicians to take care of their families, while low-ranked officers and soldiers in the ranks have no such access.

An important indicator of the military influence and control over the functioning of the health system has been the personal venture or enterprise of the rich and powerful minister of trade and member of SLORC, Lieutenant General Tun Kyi, to establish various health clinics. In the mid-1990s, the Minister created a health foundation called the *Gayunah*, or Kindness Foundation, in the name of providing health services to low-income or poor families. The minister proclaimed himself as the lifelong or permanent patron, *yahthetpan nahyaka*, of the foundation. This multi-billion dollar foundation was established with donations from wealthy merchants and businessmen who needed and received favor from the Ministry of Trade. The foundation began establishing a number of health clinics in Rangoon, Mandalay, and a number of townships. Private and military medical doctors, health assistants, and nurses are obliged to work for the foundation at low commission for social prestige and political connection. For example, a doctor's consultation fee at one of these clinics is Kt300 compared with between Kt500 and Kt1,000 at other private clinics. These clinics also provide or sell medical products to outpatients more abundantly than do the private clinics, as they are patronized by the minister of trade.

It has been reported that hundreds of patients have been flocking to these clinics in light of the deteriorating health services and high costs in government hospitals. These clinics de facto replaced former cooperative health centers to provide outpatient medical services at low cost subsidized by the government. The allowance of such a personal venture and political patronage of a high-ranking military minister to set up health clinics reflects a lack of comprehensive, cohesive and coordinated national health policy and programs since the SLORC came to power. In fact, the development of the national public health system headed by the minister of health, Rear Admiral Than Nyunt, and the chairman of the National Health Committee, intelligence chief Lieutenant General Khin Nyunt, has been undermined by the minister of trade, Lieutenant General Tun Kyi, who has successfully used his *Gayunah* Foundation health clinics for political fame and prominence. It is a well-known fact among Burmese that there is an intense rivalry for political prominence and power between Tun Kyi and Khin Nyunt. Apart from the chairmanship of the National Health Committee, Khin Nyunt, like an ancient Burmese king, carries multiple titles of Secretary No. 1 of SLORC, chief of intelligence, and chairman of a number of national committees, including the Educational Committee, the Border Areas Development Committee and the People's Police Forces Committee, while Tun Kyi, who came to fame as the lord and ruler of Mandalay in Upper Burma responsible for developing and transforming the ancient city of Mandalay into a thriving modern metropolis, holds the powerful and prestigious positions and titles of minister of trade and permanent patron of the *Gayunah* Foundation.

On November 15, 1997, the SLORC was dissolved and replaced by the new nineteen-member military junta with the name of the State Peace and Development Council (SPDC). It may be seen as an act of purging the fourteen members of the SLORC, many of whom have become overtly corrupt, wealthy, and powerful as ministers of certain key ministries, by the living dictator, General Ne Win. The most conspicuous among them was trade minister Tun Kyi. With the removal of Tun Kyi from his cabinet post, his control and sponsorship of various business enterprises, public joint-ventures, and *Gayunah* health clinics came to an abrupt end. With the downfall of Tun Kyi, the closest and favorite crony of General Win, the military intelligence chief Khin Nyunt remained the most powerful among the ruling Burmese generals by occupying the position of the Secretary No. 1 of the SPDC and retaining the chairmanship of multiple committees, including the chairmanship of National Health.

Like the economic system, the present health system of Burma is in disarray and has been functioning with ad hoc committees with no specific privatization programs and reforms of the public health system. In economic terms, the preceding developments have caused a proliferation of corruption, relative price and cost distortions of medical services, and a tremendous misallocation of doctors and health personnel with quasi rents accruing to a handful of foreign—educated and—trained famous doctors or specialists and private polyclinics, resulting in the decline of national health standards. In short, there is no horizontal and vertical integration or coordination in the present national health system of Burma with respect to policy formulation and the implementation of the health programs between the private sector and the public sector and within the public sector itself.

The most important determinant of the deteriorating heath conditions in Burma has been the large ratio of government expenditures on defense to expenditures on health. In the 1990s, the ratio has averaged over 5 to 1 (Table 8.8).

Table 8.8

Total Government Expenditures on Defense versus Health (Billions of kyats)

	1989/90	1990/91	1991/92	1992/93	1993/94	94/95
Defense (D)	4.1	6.9	8.2	9.1	13.9	14.1
Health	.8	1.6	1.9	2.1	1.9	2.1
D/H	5.1	4.3	4.3	4.3	7.3	6.7

Sources: Ministry of National Planning and Economic Development (MNPED), *The Union of Myanmar, Review of the Financial, Economic and Social Conditions for 1995/1996* (Yangon: MNPED, 1996), p. 212 and *The SLORC State Budget Law* published between March 30 and April 1 of each year in the state-owned newspaper, *The Working People's Daily* whose name was changed to *The New Light of Myanmar* in 1994.

It must be emphasized that the data presented in Table 8.8 came directly from the government sources, which seem to reveal the military government's absolute determination and priority given to military fortification over and above improving the health standards and conditions of the country. International sources of information on government's defense expenditures also confirm this fact. In the 1990s, government expenditures on health as a percentage of Burma's GDP averaged .75 percent, whereas defense expenditures, ranging from $900 million to $2.6 billion in 1994, have been estimated to be between 3 and 6 percent of GDP by various international monitoring groups on Burma's defense services and arms procurement, such as the Sweden Stockholm International Peace Research Institute, the US Arms Control and Disarmament Agency, and the U.K. International Institute for Strategic Studies. According to UNDP, in 1995 defense expenditures accounted for 6.2 percent of GDP, while the ratio of military expenditures to combined education and health expenditure was 2.2 to 1.[57]

THE ROLE OF UN AGENCIES AND NONGOVERNMENTAL ORGANIZATIONS IN THE HUMAN DEVELOPMENT OF BURMA

Various UN agencies dealing with both economic and human development maintained their presence in Burma and provided financial and technical aid to the socialist state of Ne Win's Burma. Only after 1988, the agencies dealing with economic development, such as the World Bank, the International Monetary Fund, and the Asian Development, suspended economic aid to Burma. Their cessation of aid and loans to Burma was directly linked to the US government's pressure and a decision to stop all forms of economic aid, with the exception of humanitarian aid, to Burma after the brutal massacre of thousands of unarmed prodemocracy demonstrators by the Burmese army in 1988. Despite this stoppage of multilateral economic aid, due to the fact that Burma remains a member of the United Nations and its auxiliary institutions, they continue to maintain a presence in Burma and have a relationship with the SLORC in terms of reciprocal exchange of missions. All three economic agencies have conducted studies and published confidential reports on recent economic conditions and developments in Burma since 1990. Despite the laborious attempt and request of the Burmese government, they have so far not resumed aid and loans to Burma.

The UN agencies dealing with human development, drug control and refugees, such as the United Nations Development Programme (UNDP), UNICEF, UN Capital Development Fund (UNCDF), UN Drug Control Programme (UNDCP), United Nations Education, Scientific, and Cultural Organization (UNESCO), World Health Organization (WHO), Food and Agricultural Organization (FAO), and the UN High Commissioner for Refugees (UNHCR) and a host of others, continue to have relationship with the SLORC, providing financial and technical aid to both the human development projects of the SLORC and their own projects. All these UN agencies' programs have to be approved or cleared through the Foreign Economic Relations Department of the Ministry of National Planning and Economic Development (MNPED), which coordinates and channels all external resource requirements of various departments and corporations under different ministries of the government.

The human development programs and operations of the preceding UN agencies in Burma are not effectively integrated or coordinated. Although in name the UNDP serves as the coordinator of various UN projects, each agency is autonomous and housed in Rangoon with its own office and representatives. Each of them operates and engages in human development projects with its own budget. Several agencies may fund and participate in one and the same human development project such as educational development, HIV/AIDs prevention, drug control or a maternal and child welfare project in a village or a town targeted and allowed by the SLORC. Each of them may also operate its own project simultaneously with other agencies in the same areas of human development. The Burmese dissidents have also charged these agencies with nepotism and corruption.

The Ministry of Health deals with, and approves, the health development projects of all UN agencies and nongovernmental organizations (NGOs). The Ministry of Health itself is under the direct control and approval of the chairman of the National Health Committee and Foreign Affairs Committee, the intelligence chief, Khin Nyunt. In the early 1990s, in an attempt to capture funds and support of UN agencies, foreign governments, and foreign NGOs, a domestic "nongovernmental organization" with the name Myanmar Maternal and Child Welfare Association (MMCWA) was created under the patronage of the Ministry of Health and UNICEF. It was organized and headed by women medical doctors, most of whom are the wives of high-ranking military rulers. As of 1995, the president of MMCWA was Dr. Kyu Kyu Swe who is the wife of Colonel Pe Thein, the former minister of health and minister of education and one of the ministers of the Prime Minister Office in the SLORC cabinet. The vice president is Dr. Khin Win Shwe, who is the wife of intelligence chief Khin Nyunt and a former medical doctor in the Ministry of Industry No. 1 with no specialty or training in public health or maternal and child care. Another Vice-President is ex-military officer, Captain Kyi Soe with a master degree in public health (MPH). The joint secretary-general is Dr. Nyo Nyo, who is an adviser to the Ministry of Health and the sister of the late Dr. Maung Maung, the civilian president installed during the 1988 political uprising and the lifelong puppet and supporter of General Ne Win. One of many patrons of MMCWA is Dr. Nun Oo, the wife of Vice Admiral Maung Maung Khin, the deputy prime minister and chairman of Myanmar Investment Commission. Another patron is Daw Khin Khin, the wife of an ex-military commander U Ko Lay, the powerful Mayor of Rangoon. The MMCWA has many chapters, such as Rangoon, Mandalay, Moulmein, and other townships whose officers are either the wives of military commanders or linked to the military elite. The organization is well funded by private donations due to the patronage of the wives of high-profile military commanders.

It should also be noted that the address of the MMCWA is 36 Theinbyu Street, Yangon, which is also the address of the Ministry of Health. Apparently, the twin ulterior motives of establishing this so-called nongovernmental organization for maternal and child welfare are to avoid international criticisms of funding a government with ruthless human rights violations records and to capture funds and support from various UN human development agencies, foreign governments, and foreign NGOs. Indeed, any maternal and child care projects of the UN agencies, such as WHO, UNDP, UNICEF, and UN Population Fund, and foreign NGOs, such as the US World Vision, the Netherlands Médcine Sans Frontiere, and the Australian Care International, have to be approved by the Ministry of Health and implemented in association with the MMCWA.

Apart from the so-called nongovernmental organization of MMCWA, there are three other domestic NGOs favored, sponsored and controlled by the SLORC: the Myanmar Medical Association (MMA), the Myanmar Red Cross Society (MRCS), and the latest Union Solidarity and Development Association (USDA). Although there are many dedicated medical doctors, health workers, and volunteers in these organizations, most of the leaders and members of these NGOs are linked with the government and the Ministry of Health. The MMA is the oldest NGO, which was founded in 1949 and was absorbed into the Burma Socialist Programme Party (BSPP) when the senior officials of the Ministry of Health assumed and controlled its leadership. Despite the dissolution of the BSPP in 1988, the leadership of MMA remains in the hands of these officials. The next important NGO is MRCS, which is funded by private donations and the government with an ex-military commander, Dr. Hla Bu, as its president. In fact, MRCS was reportedly involved in the crackdown and forced repatriation of runaway student refugees from the Thai border in 1989 in collaboration with the Military Intelligence (MI) officers who were planted in MRCS.[58] Since 1988, the military government has not allowed the International Committee of the Red Cross (ICRC) to independently operate, monitor and help the plight of political dissidents and refugees. Lastly, the USDA, which was created by the SLORC in the name of national solidarity and development in 1993 with Senior General Than Shwe as its patron, has been ostensibly claimed as a nonpolitical organization and used as an NGO to engage in various domestic and international human development projects.

In terms of extensive engagement with the SLORC and funding of various human development projects, the UNDP, UNICEF, and UNDCP have been the most prominent. Of these three UN agencies, the operation and funding of the UNDP have been the largest. The UNDP had its resident representative in Burma ever since its inception in 1966. It has provided both technical and financial assistance to various development projects of the consecutive military regimes of General Ne Win and the SLORC. During the two decades of Ne Win's rule over Burma from 1966 to 1986, the UNDP funded a total of $120.2 million, or an average of $6 million a year.[59] Between 1987 and 1990, the annual average funding of development projects by the UNDP almost doubled to $11 million a year. For the same period, the annual average aid provided by the UNICEF amounted to $10 million a year.[60]

In the 1990s, the UNDP has increased its funding to even larger amounts under two development assistance programs, the Human Development Initiative (HDI) and the Human Development Initiative Extension (HDI-E). It allocated a total expenditure of $25.5 million for 18 months between 1993 and 1994 or $17 million a year, which is almost three times the average annual assistance given to Burma prior to 1986.[61] Under the HDI-E program (1996–1998), the UNDP conceived and developed 10 more new development projects, dealing with humanitarian development and needs, environment and food security and three-intersectoral projects with emphasis on improving "community-based participation at the grass-roots level" and maintaining the same level of funding at $17 million a year."[62] In 1996, the UNDP sent "an independent HDI mission" made up of four experts to Burma to evaluate the HDI and HDI-E projects. According to this mission: "The HDI projects have been able to carry forward grassroots-focused development strategy as mandated by the UNDP Governing Council/ Executive Board. The achievements of the HDI are impressive given the very short time-frame and other constraints under which they have been operating."[63] Based on the positive findings of these experts, the UNDP concluded that "HDI had in large measure met its objectives" of human development at the grassroots level.[64] However, it should be pointed out that neither the independent expert mission nor the UNDP provided quantitative data and documentation on the achievement of human development or the alleviation of poverty under these projects.

The finding of the independent HDI mission on the impressive achievements of the UNDP's HDI and HDI-E projects is subject to controversy and debate. Specifically, human development at the grassroots level and income-generating activities of the HDI projects for the poor and helpless population of Burma have been challenged. This point was poignantly raised by the opposition leader to the SLORC, Daw Suu Kyi, in her letter written on behalf of the NLD for the urgent attention of the UNDP administrator, Gustav Speth:

It is the firm conviction of the NLD that *humanitarian* aid should be granted in such a way that it reaches the right people in the right way. By the "right people" we mean "the poorest, the vulnerable, and the disadvantaged," who are also seen by the UNDP as those who should be the "primary beneficiaries" of the Human Development Initiative. By "the right way" we mean that aid should be granted in such a way to make it obvious that access to it is not dependent upon factors extraneous to the needs of potential beneficiaries. In the context of Burma today, we would like to ensure that access to aid is not reserved for those who stand in favor with the authorities.[65]

By citing specific examples, she went on to point out not only that the HDI and HDI-E projects of the UNDP are closely scrutinized and controlled by the Township Law and Order Restoration Councils (TLORCs), whose chairman is a military commander, but also that most of the contracts of the two projects are secured by members of TLORCs. In essence, her argument is the same as that of Harberger, who suggested:

Far too often financial or other aid that was motivated by humanitarian values has ended up being creamed off by governmental elites or other power groups whose living standards were not much different from those of legislators and bureaucrats in the industrialized (developed) countries. Humanitarian aid, when given, should find its way to those groups and classes in society by whose position or plight it was motivated.[66]

The main argument against the UN constructive engagement policy for human development, like the argument against the constructive engagement for economic growth of the ASEAN, is that it produces little or no benefit for the majority of the people who desperately need help, namely, hundreds of thousands of forcefully relocated people in central Burma and dislocated refugees in the ethnic minority states and borderlands.

The appropriate policy for UN agencies to pursue in advancing human development aid to a less-developed country ought to be what the UNDP itself has recommended for donor countries: "For countries keen on advancing human development, the way could be open to a new and productive era for official development assistance—one based on a mutual commitment to human development. Request for aid should include plans to cut back military budgets and to increase the human expenditure ratios."[67] It seems that the UNDP and other UN agencies have not followed this recommendation in aiding Burma ,whose government has shown neither a real commitment to human development nor intention of cutting back military budgets and increasing human development expenditure ratios.

As presented in the chapter on fiscal policy, since 1990 the Burmese government's ratio of defense expenditures to expenditures on social services has steadily climbed upward to more than two in 1995/1996 (the projected Kt21.9 billion defense expenditures compared with Kt9.6 billion expenditures on social services). Given this irrefutable fact, it will be argued that the sustained engagement with the SLORC and aid provided by the UN agencies have been counterproductive to human development and democratization of Burma. Instead, UN aid has given strength and legitimacy to a government that has been governing the country against the will of the people. As a dissident Burmese medical doctor put it:

But it is even more important to remember that Burma's military government for years has tried to shore up its legitimacy by surrounding itself with UN workers. This has become especially important today when the legitimacy of the regime has been questioned even in the General Assembly of the UN itself. As every Burmese knows, the military couldn't care less about actual development or welfare of the people. Getting the UN involved is for them a propaganda show: to give legitimacy to a totally illegitimate government."[68]

Madeleine Albright, when she was the US permanent representative to the UN, aptly observed after her visit to Burma in 1995: "For years, controversies surrounded programs conducted within Burma by United Nations agencies, including UNICEF and the UNDP. Their efforts raised a classic dilemma: how to help people living under despotism without helping the despots themselves."[69] This classic dilemma was raised by political scientists and economists with respect to the unintended impact of the World Bank's loans and multilateral aid that resulted in the strengthening and perpetuation of socialist and other dictatorial regimes during the Cold War period. It can be solved only by linking all UN human development aid to the stoppage of human rights abuses or the condition of specific steps of human development and democratization to be taken by the military regime in Burma. However, the prospect for enforcing this linkage seems unlikely in light of the fact that, like the ASEAN, many UN development agencies tend to argue that the goals and functions of their programs are humanitarian and apolitical.

NOTES

1 Robert Slater, *Guns through Arcadia* (Madras: Diocesan Press, 1943), p. 40.

2. Salin Sayadaw, *Hanthahwaddy Payatekyee Neet-thaya* (in Burmese) (Rangoon: Hanthahwaddy Pitaka Press, 1958), p. 78.

3. UNDP, *Human Development Report 1995* (New York: Oxford University Press, 1995), p. 11.

4. Arnold C. Harberger, *Economic Policy and Economic Growth* (San Francisco: Institute for Contemporary Studies, 1985), p. 2.

5. See Robert J. Barro, "Economic Growth in a Cross Section of Countries," *Quarterly Journal of Economics* (May, 1991): 407.

6. J. S. Furnivall, *Colonial Policy and Practice* (New York: New York University Press, 1956), p. 204.

7. Ibid., p. 203.

8. Ibid.

9. Ibid., p. 211.

10. Louis J. Walinsky, *Economic Development in Burma* (New York: Twentieth Century Fund, 1962), pp. 365–366.

11. See for detail Mya Maung, *The Burma Road to Poverty* (New York: Praeger, 1991), pp. 182–185.

12. All Burma Federation of Students' Union (ABFS) Information and Documentation Committee, , *An Overview of the Current Education Situation in Burma,* privately published paper, December 1997: p. 3.

13. UNICEF, *Myanmar-UNICEF Country Programme of Cooperation 1996–2000: Master Plan of Operations* (New York: UNICEF, October 1995), p. 3.

14. UNDP, *Human Development Report 1995,* p. 157.

15. Ibid., pp. 155–157.

16. UNDP, *Human Development Report 1997* (New York: Oxford University Press, 1997), pp. 164–165.

17. Ibid., pp. 180–181.

18. David Dapice, *Accelerating Progress Among the Rural Poor in Myanmar, Accelerating Progress Among the Rural Poor in Myanmar,* A Report to the United Nations Development Programme (New York: UNDP, September 15, 1995), p. 13.

19. UNDP, *Human Development Report 1996* (New York: Oxford University Press, 1996), p. 175.

20. Ragnar Nurkse, *Problems of Capital Formation in Underdeveloped Countries* (Oxford: Basil Blackwell, 1957), p. 4.

21. UNDP, *Human Development Report 1997* (New York: Oxford University Press, 1997), p. 71.

22. Ibid., pp. 38–39.

23. Ibid.

24. Ministry of Planning and Finance (MPF), *The Socialist Republic of the Union of Burma: Report to the Pyithu Hluttaw on the Financial, Economic and Social Conditions, 1988/89* (Rangoon: MPF, 1989), p. 226.

25. See Robert Talyor, *The State of Burma* (Honolulu: University of Hawaii Press, 1987), pp. 359–60.

26. UNDP, *Human Development Report 1996*, pp. 126–127.

27 David Chandler, *Health in Myanmar*, a paper presented at the HIID Conference, December 5–7, 1996, p. 5.

28. UNDP, *Human Development Report 1997*, p. 175 and UNICEF, *Myanmar-UNICEF*, p. 2.

29. UNICEF, *Myanmar-UNICEF*, Ibid.

30. Ibid., 23.

31. Ibid.

32. Ibid., p. 49.

33. Jesuit Refugee Service Asia Pacific, *Diakonia*, Special Annual Report Edition (February 1996): 2.

34. UNICEF, *Myanmar-UNICEF*, p. 56.

35. See Dr. Cesar Chelala, "Burma's Disease-Causing Generals," *The Asian Wall Street Journal* (July 11, 1997).

36. "Out of Bounds: HIV/AIDS at Burma's Borders," *Burma Issues* (October, 1997): p. 5.

37. Ibid

38. David A. Chandler, "HIV/AIDS in Myanmar: Determining the Risk of Transmission and Rate of Infection," *The Role of NGOs in Burma* (Washington DC: World Vision, Practical Christian Caring, June 6, 1995), p. 24.

39. "HIV/AIDS in Burma: an overview," *Burma Issues* (October, 1997) p. 4.

40. "Out of Bounds," Ibid.

41. ABSDF, *Burma and the Role of Women* (Bangkok: ABSDF, March 13, 1997), p. 41.

42. Ibid., p. 41–42.

43. Ibid., p. 44.

44. See Tin Maung Than, "AIDS, How Many have been infected and How many will be infected in Myanmar?," *Thint Bawa* or Your Life (in Burmese) (July 1995): pp. 30–31.

45. "HIV/AIDS in Burma," Ibid.

46. See Chandler, "HIV/AIDS in Myanmar," p. 42.

47. UNICEF, *Myanmar-UNICEF*, p.2.

48. See Chandler, *Health in Myanmar*, p, 11.

49. UNICEF, *Myanmar-UNICEF*, p. 3.

50. UNDP, *Human Development Report 1997*, pp. 146–147.

51. Ibid., pp. 152-153.

52. Article 19, *Fatal Silence? Freedom of Expression and the Right to Health in Burma* (London: Article 19, July, 1996), p. 22.

53. Ibid.

54. See "Costs of Health Care at Private Poly-Clinics" (in Burmese), *Living Color Magazine* (February 1996): 111–113.

55. Ibid.

56. See Chap. 3 of this book.

57. UNDP, *Human Development Report 1997*, p. 189.

58. Article 19, *Fatal Silence?*, pp. 50–51.

59. Soe Saing, *United Nations Technical Aid in Burma: A Short Survey* (Singapore: ISEAS, 1990), p. 66.

60. See Harn Yawnghwe, *Burma Alert*, Vol. 2. No. 8 (August 1991).

61. Executive Board of the UNDP and the UN Population Fund, *Country Programme and Related Matters: Assistance to Myanmar*, DP/1996/4 (New York: United Nations, November 20, 1995), p. 8.

62. Executive Board of the UNDP and the UN Population Fund, *Country Cooperation Framework and Related Matters: Assistance to Myanmar*, DP/1997/4 (New York: United Nations, November 4, 1996), p. 5.

63. *UNDP Human Development Initiative Myanmar: Assessment Report*, Prepared for UNDP by a team of independent experts, September 1996, p. 5.

64. Executive Board of the UNDP, Country Programme, p. 1.

65. Aung San Suu Kyi, *Letter to Mr. Gustav Speth*, Rangoon, January 14, 1996, p. 2.

66. Harberger, *Economic Policy*, p. 44.

67. UNDP, *Human Development Report 1991* (New York: Oxford University Press, 1991), p. 10.

68. Min Naing, "UN Needs to Check on Staff in Burma," *Bangkok Post*, May 1, 1991.

69. Madeleine Albright, "The Burma Daze," *New Republic* (December 4, 1995): p. 1.

Conclusion

Old fashioned authoritarianism is neither petty nor benign. It was the peace that tyrants brought after all, that was once called the peace of the grave.[1] "Mark! where his carnage and his conquests cease! He makes a solitude and calls it—peace."[2]

The military regime of Burma, the State Law and Order Restoration Council (SLORC) whose name was changed to the State Peace and Development Council (SPDC) in November 1997, has resurrected the ancient tyrannical state administered by military commanders serving as chairmen of the regional, district, and township law and order restoration councils, tormenting, taxing, taking, enforcing draconian laws, and conscripting corveé or slave labor for the construction of roads, bridges, hotels, pagodas, and infrastructure. Replicating the ritual of malevolent Burmese kings, the SLORC has been forcefully relocating people across the country and mounting relentless military campaigns against the ethnic minorities of peripheral states that have produced in their wake massive flows of refugees across Burma's borders, as well as death and desolation of hundreds of thousands of people and villages.

In the context of modern times, the Burmese polity is an authoritarian regime or a pure military dictatorship comparable to what existed for decades in various countries across the world. It is a brutal and illegitimate government that has been governing the country without the consent of the governed in direct violation of Article 21, which mandates "the will of the people shall be the basis of the authority of government," and virtually all other articles of the UN Universal Declaration of Human Rights. Despite the SLORC's claim and justification of its human rights abuses in the name of fundamental differences between the Asian or Burmese and Western standards of human rights, this study has shown that the Burmese military regime's actions violate not only Western but also traditional Burmese Buddhist cultural standards and values, especially the mandate of absolute sanctity of life in all forms.

Burma under the SLORC is a mirror image of the Orwellian nightmare state of Oceania where "War is Peace, Freedom is Slavery and Ignorance is Strength."[3] The world has seen such a state at different times in various countries on different continents in the twentieth century: Hitler's Germany, Stalin's Russia, Ceausescu's Rumania, Castro's Cuba, Duvalier's Haiti, Pinochet's Chile, Mao's China, Pol Pot's Cambodia, Kim Il Sung's North Korea, Sukarno's Indonesia, Hussein's Iraq, Abacha's Nigeria, and Mobutu's Zaire. The common characteristics of these nightmare states are intimidation, arrest, torture, murder, disappearances, arbitrary trials and sentencing, extrajudicial execution, and mass slaughter at the dictate of the "Great Leader" or "Great Father," *A-hpai Gyi* in Burmese.

ECONOMIC GROWTH VERSUS DEMOCRACY

Convincing historical evidence exists that abuses of human rights by various authoritarian and totalitarian regimes lead neither to prosperity for the general populace nor the establishment of an equitable society. The "East Asian model or approach to development" ignores this evidence to advance and extol "developmental authoritarianism" for Third World countries to follow. This new theory of development maintains that economic growth supersedes the value of democratic reforms and human rights to justify a role for "the strong or hard state" to control, regulate, and manage the economy and functioning of the market. The strong state has been rationalized by the spectacular economic success of authoritarian regimes of one form or another in the newly industrialized counties (NICs) of Asia or Asian Tigers (Hong Kong, South Korea, Singapore, and Taiwan) and other rapidly developing countries of the ASEAN (Brunei, Indonesia, Malaysia, and Thailand). Further support of developmental authoritarianism comes from the traumatic experience of former communist countries that undertook democratization prior to or simultaneously with macroeconomic liberalization measures that led to sociopolitical instability and economic crises.

The 1997 financial debacle encountered in the Asian miracle economies, especially in South Korea, and in the rapidly developing ASEAN economies, Indonesia, Malaysia, and Thailand, shattered the theory of developmental authoritarianism. This unexpected Asian debacle reaffirms the superior power and performance of Adam Smith's market-guiding "invisible hand" over the "visible hand" of the self-interested regulators of the "strong state." The fundamental weakness of subjecting an economic system to tight control, regulation, and management by powerful ministers is that the ministers are not accountable for improper risk-taking or collusion with unmonitored managers of financial institutions and business enterprises. The problem is one of information asymmetry and nontransparency.

The common feature of Asian economies with opaque information and un-accountable governments is moral co-optation forced upon the ruled by corrupt rulers. In such a system, poorly disciplined regulators with incentive conflicts are lured by opportunistic counterparties by offering incentive-based compensation in exchange for compromises in fiduciary responsibility. Incentive conflict may be deemed as one of the underlying causes of the Asian financial debacle. As Edward Kane put it: "Where misrepresentation and incentive conflicts are not appropriately disciplined by well-informed competition, regulators have an incentive to offer a socially suboptimal menu of regulatory services."[4] The regional financial and economic crisis of Asia underscores how authoritarian states are inevitably less efficient or resilient and more vulnerable to economic crisis than democracies.

THE INVERSE RELATIONSHIP BETWEEN "STABILITY AND DISCIPLINE" AND ECONOMIC GROWTH OF BURMA UNDER THE SLORC

Based on the facts presented in this book, one can conclude that the postulates and presumptions of developmental authoritarianism do not hold true in the Burmese case. Even if one accepts the positive correlation between political stability and economic growth, the type of "stability and discipline" enforced by the SLORC under the rule of terror and force must be deemed inversely related to economic growth. Such an inverse relationship is unequivocally supported by the historical experience of the Sino-Soviet world. That is, the political stability needed to promote economic growth and achieve optimal social welfare must be established under the rule of law by a government according to the wishes and needs of the people. As Daw Aung San Suu Kyi believed, "Democracy as a political system which aims at empowering the people is essential if sustained human development, which is 'development of the people, for the people and by the people,' is to be achieved."[5]

That is not to say that Suu Kyi or the author believes in a wholesale adoption or transplantation of Western liberal democracy for the economic development of Burma. Rather, it is an affirmation of the essence of democracy contained in the Greek word *demokratia*, the empowerment, *kratia*, of the people, *demos*. In order to be successful and sustainable, development policies need to recognize the needs and sufficient empowerment of the "people." It will be concluded that the SLORC's human rights abuses and strategy of seeking a military solution to the complex political problem of building a stable and unified Burma, which has perhaps the largest number of ethnic minority groups in the world, cannot and will not generate the real peace and stability needed to promote and sustain economic growth.

The excruciating dilemma faced by Burma in building a stable and unified Burma is that it needs a strong role of the army to establish the rule of law and maintain order and peace. The methods used so far by the SLORC in establishing "law and order" by violating the fundamental human rights of the people, forcefully subduing the opposition, and instilling fear into the hearts of the helpless people, as well as entering bilateral and not multilateral cease fire agreements with ethnic minority rebel groups to divide and rule have not been effective in accomplishing this task. Until and unless the sharing of power with the civilian political leaders and demilitarization of Burmese polity occur with the willing cooperation of the new breed of democratically minded Burmese military leaders, the real peace and stability needed for economic growth cannot be attained.

The fundamental weakness and fragmentation within and among various opposition groups to the military rule have been a major problem, signaling potential political chaos and instability for Burma. Even if political leadership and power are transferred to the foremost opposition leader, Daw Aung San Suu Kyi, and her party, the NLD, the backing of the army is indispensable for successful democratization and development of Burma. From what was presented in this study, it is more than obvious that the Burmese junta's resolve to marginalize the formidable opposition leader Suu Kyi and hold on to power and rule Burma is absolute and unshakable. There are some speculations among a number of Burma watchers and reporters with respect to the rift and power struggle among the Burmese generals, even considering the intelligence chief Khin Nyint, whom the Burmese dissidents labeled the "Prince of Darkness," as a soft-liner. Even though there may be personal feud and rivalry among the ruling Burmese generals, the threat of retribution for their crimes committed against the people and the potential loss of power and enormous wealth they have accumulated may be deemed the main solidifying force of their unity and consolidation against the democratic opposition. Contrary to the claim of the ruling generals and the belief of some Burma watchers that the living dictator, General Ne Win, has retired from politics, the reality of Burmese political drama seems to indicate that the old dictator has not simply faded away in shaping and controlling the political destiny of Burma. Hence, the rule of force and political impasse of democratization will continue with no immediate prospects for the military junta to give up power and install civilian rule over Burma.

THE BURMA ROAD TO CAPITALISM: AN EXTREMELY INEQUITABLE ECONOMY

This study has shown that the Burmese Way to Capitalism is de facto state capitalism of a dictatorial regime cloaked under the garb of an "open-door market-oriented economy." The Burmese road to capitalism has been paved with unjust takings from the people by the "strong or hard state." The net consequence has been the insecurity of the oppressed people of Burma with respect to life, liberty, and property with little or no incentives to produce, save, and invest and, in tandem, low and unsustainable growth of the economy. The practice of taking from the subjects and rewarding the loyal servants with privileges and wealth by the military rulers is satirically termed by the Burmese as *waisar*, which literally means divide or distribute (*wai*) and eat (*sar*) the wealth. This common practice of rewarding loyal followers by modern dictators to muster support and safeguard power, or what Galbraith termed the use of "compensatory power,"[6] dates back to the days of the Burmese kings who rewarded loyal princes and bureaucrats with power to tax and rule villages, townships, and districts, bestowing upon them the titles of "eaters" of village, township, and district, *ywah-sar, myoe-sar,* and *nel-sar* in Burmese.

With respect to the negative impact of authoritarian military rule on development, it was shown that Burmese military rulers have been prone to extravagance and waste, inhibiting development. Like dictators all over the world, Burmese military rulers manage to delude themselves that roads, bridges, hotels, homes, pagodas, and monuments, which are built with slave labor and forced donations to accommodate foreign tourists and investors to amass foreign exchange and wealth for themselves, are really gifts to posterity, equating personal indulgence with social glory and progress. The net consequence of ruthless "takings" from the people by the consummate state in Burma has been an enormous inequality of living standard, income, and wealth between a handful of the ruling military elite and its supporters and a substantial majority of the disadvantaged population.

Apart from basic necessities, the elite have easy access to modern living standards such as better housing, automobiles, the best health care with private physicians, the best domestic and foreign education for their children with private tutors, foreign travel, golf, tennis, foreign liquor, television, stereo, videos, satellite dishes and so on. Modern lifestyles and ultramodern homes of the military elite and their supporters living at former colonial residential quarters and newly constructed modern quarters in Rangoon, Mandalay and other cities as well as in new satellite towns, all conspicuously symbolize the abodes of what the Burmese called *Lawki Nateban* or modern Nirvana.

Examples of these heavenly homes and estates of the military elite in metropolitan Rangoon are the most famous *Ady Road* or *Maykha Yatethah* (the home and well-fortified villa of General Ne Win); *Bogyoke Ywah* or General's Village, also known as *Shwe Wut Mhon* at *Chinchawn Chan* or *Kanbawza Estate*, which was the home of the first president of the Union of Burma, Saw Shwe Thaike (the well-fortified villas and homes of the former president of socialist Burma, the late San Yu, and present intelligence chief Khin Nyunt), *Parami* (the luxurious homes of former military ministers, commanders, and BSPP apparatchiks), and *Nawarat Yatethah* (modern apartment complexes of high-ranked defense service personnel). Other rich quarters and estates of both the military and civilian elite in Rangoon are *Inyar Myaing, Shwetaung Kyar* (formerly Golden Valley) No. 1 and No. 2, and *Shwegontaing Ban Yatethah*. Rich homes and estates of military elite and high-ranked civilian government officials can also be found in the exclusive sections of several new satellite towns around Rangoon; *Ngwe Kyah Yan, Koan Myint Thayah, Palell Myothit, Padamyar Myothit, Shwe Pauk Kan* or *Second Dagon Myothit,* and *Thuwana Myothit.*

In contrast to these heavenly homes and estates of the elite, a great majority of the urban population live in traditional homes made of thatch and bamboo in the poor sections of Rangoon, other cities, and new satellite towns with little or no access to electricity, safe water, sanitation, and health services. The absolute and relative poverty of the urban population is immediately visible beyond the centers and townships in the outskirts of a major city such as Rangoon and Mandalay. As David Chandler of the World Vision observed:

The reality of 95% Myanmar is very different from the quaint reality of Yangon, Mandalay or Pagan. Just two miles from the city centre of Yangon is one urban township where the daily struggle for survival is as dire and desperate as any urban slum in India or Bangladesh.[7]

The same author noted the abject poverty of most urban families in Burma:

Families in World Vision townships share that they do not have enough to eat. They will drink rice water (boiled rice water) for nutrition, and drink tea to stave off hunger pangs. It is not uncommon for families to eat meat only two times per week. There are ample data indicating that most families in Myanmar have limited socio-economic opportunities, and they are experiencing great pressure in meeting their basic survival needs."[8]

These desperate conditions reflect the emergence of the "new poor" in urban areas of Burma. It has been brought on by the government's policy of property and land development to attract foreign tourists and investors and the accompanying massive eviction of the urban population to new satellite towns with poor infrastructure, creating a trend in Rangoon and in other major cities of what Burmese observed as "the elimination of the middle class." The standard of living of the former middle class of socialist Burma represented by government officials, medical doctors, teachers, and other employees has fallen below the subsistence level because of the escalating prices of basic necessities relative to more or less frozen wages. The deeply negative real wage or income has forced them to sell or lease their property and land cheaply to a handful of wealthy developers and foreign investors, thus depleting their accumulated assets. Consequently, a handful of wealthy developers and businessmen with connections, power, and the opportunity to collect economic rents came to claim a disproportionate percentage of income and wealth in urban Burma.

Poverty is also pervasive in rural areas, where a majority of farmers and laborers are in debt and landless. It is the product of the fleecing of farmers by the state through the quota system of paddy delivery at unfair procurement prices, state monopoly of rice exports, forced donation of labor and cash, the escalating cost of farming relative to income, and exorbitant "real" interest rates on loans charged by private moneylenders and state agricultural banks.

Although there are no exact statistical data available, the extent of rural poverty may be deemed larger than that of urban poverty in light of the extreme rural-urban disparity in central Burma and the disparity between central and peripheral minority states of Burma presented in this study with respect to meeting the basic survival needs, such as nutrition, safe water, sanitation, medicine, and health facilities.

Poverty has been so ubiquitous that UNICEF considers the Burmese general population to be facing "Silent Emergency" in meeting their basic survival needs. This emergency is reflected in the galloping inflation, shortages of basic necessities, and deteriorating heath conditions with the alarming and rising national infant mortality rate that jumped from 67 per 1,000 live births in 1989 to 105 per 1,000 live births in 1995, compared with the infant mortality rates of 34 in Vietnam, 27 in Thailand and 11 in Malaysia. Other indicators of decrepit health conditions include: a phenomenally high maternal mortality rate of 580 per 100,000 live births, compared with 200 in Thailand, 160 in Vietnam and 80 in Malyasia, some 500,000 people infected with HIV/AIDS virus; and thousands of refugees living under sub-human conditions in various makeshift camps all along Burma's borders. In economic terms, the SLORC's development policies and actions have produced a highly inefficient economy operating below the maximum production possibility curve and an extremely inequitable social welfare condition by "making a small group of citizens (the military elite and its followers) appreciably better off with a substantial majority or groups of citizens worse off."[9]

POOR ECONOMIC PERFORMANCE AND UNSUSTAINABLE GROWTH

Contrary to the "positive economic performance of Myanmar" reported by the junta and its lobbyists, the Burmese economy remains in shambles with a low growth rate, galloping inflation, financial distress, chronic trade deficit averaging over $400 million a year since 1988, and a huge outstanding foreign debt of nearly $6 billion in 1996. The phenomenal average real GDP growth rates of over 8 percent between 1992 and 1996 and an incredible claim of a 10.9 percent growth rate (later revised down to 9.8 percent) in 1993 and 9.8 percent for 1995/1996, reported by the military government of Burma, are suspect due to the unreliability of statistical data, on one hand, and the manipulation and distortion of the data for political purposes, on the other. Based on the privately estimated inflation rate of between 40 and 60 percent compared with less than 25 percent reported by the government, it will be concluded that the average real GDP growth rate of Burma since 1988 is less than 3 percent, with dismal prospects of growth for the rest of the 1990s. At any rate, the reality of Burma's macroeconomic performance under the management of the SLORC is that it ranked 132d in human development out of 173 countries with an estimated 40 percent of the population living below the poverty line.[10]

Two major factors that signal a gloomy prospect for sustainable growth and even a potential collapse of the Burmese economy in the near future are the 1997 flood and the Asian financial debacle. Both of them have negatively impacted on the performance of the Burmese economy and foreign exchange market. Due to the devastating flood, rice exports have been reported to have declined from an average of 300,000 tons a year since 1991 to an unprecedented level of 15,000 metric tons with foreign exchange earnings from rice exports plunging downward from an average of $400 million a year to a mere $3 million in the first 10 months of the fiscal year 1997/1998. It is more than likely that rice exports will not exceed 30,000 metric tons for the entire fiscal year 1997/1998.

The growth rate of agricultural output, which accounts for more than 50 percent of Burma's real GDP and 45 percent of current GDP, is reported to be less than 2 percent.[11] The real GDP growth rate for the fiscal year 1997/1998 has been already revised downward to 5.8 percent from the target of 6.4 percent by the government. This revision is still exaggerated and it has been projected that it will be well below 5 percent.[12] The Asian financial debacle has also accelerated the depreciation of the Burmese kyat as the price of the US dollar in the unofficial foreign exchange market soared by more than 100 percent, from Kt185=US$1 in early 1997 to Kt385=US$1 in late 1997. It is more than likely that the unofficial or black market price of the US dollar will climb above Kt400 to US$1 during 1998.

This study has shown that the so-called open-door, market-oriented economy of Myanmar is not truly open and market-oriented since the government continues to maintain both trade and foreign exchange regimes and a monopolistic governmental regulatory system. The net consequence has been the perpetuation of the cancerous dual command economy of the past socialist state with a formal/legal economy and an informal/illegal economy that seethes with inefficiency, corruption, and market distortions. The exact size of the informal/illegal economy is not known, but it is made up of illicit drug and other contraband whose value and volume of output and transactions are substantially greater than those of the formal/legal economy.

The worst consequence of the dual command economy of Burma is the moral co-optation or corruption forced upon the people, including Buddhist clergymen, by the praetorian state, creating a morally bankrupt society in which individual survival, greed, and material wealth supersede any other human values. In Buddhist terms, *lawba, dawtha,* and *mawha*—greed, anger, and delusion—become the dominant forces of Burmese life infested with corruption, *a-gati*. The primary cause for the corruption is according to Burma's symbol of "Freedom from Fear," Daw Aung San Suu Kyi, who asserted: "It is not power that corrupts but fear. Fear of losing power corrupts those who are subject to it."[13] It will be added that while fear of losing power corrupts those with power (the Burmese military rulers), fear of losing life and property forces the powerless (ordinary Burmese citizens) to morally co-opt for survival.

With respect to the ineffective and incomprehensive economic reform measures undertaken by the military regime and the deep-seated economic problems of Burma, the Asian Development Bank (ADB) observed in 1995:

Although further efforts at economic reforms were made in 1992, these were insufficient to deal with Myammar's deep-seated economic problems. In particular, liberalization measures to transform the economy toward a market-oriented system have been fragmentary and far from comprehensive. Major economic problems that persist include inefficient state enterprises, energy and foreign exchange shortages, high trade and budget deficits, rising inflation, continued suspension of foreign assistance and accumulating external debt.[14]

The ADB further assessed:

In recent years, Myanmar has continued its efforts towards liberalizing and opening up the economy. However, the economy remains subject to substantial economic regulations, and sustaining economic growth in the future will require not only improvements in macroeconomic management but also more pervasive structural reforms that allow greater scope for market-determined resource allocation.[15]

The World Bank also concurred with this appraisal: "The current reform efforts are, therefore, unlikely to push the Myanmar economy to a higher growth path on which the bulk of the population would enjoy substantially better living standards."[16]

POOR NATIONAL ECONOMIC MANAGEMENT

Although these observations point to inadequate economic reforms undertaken by the SLORC, none of them emphasize what this author wishes to stress that the root cause of the deep-seated economic problems and of the bleak prospects for sustainable economic growth of Burma lies in the human factor of management of the economy by incompetent and lowly educated military managers. The poor quality of national economic management is apparent at once in looking at the average educational qualifications of decision makers and national managers–members of the military junta and military cabinet ministers. For example, only 2 out of 21 members of the SLORC, General Maung Aye and Lieutenant General Tun Kyi, hold a degree equivalent to the B.A. from the Defense Services Academy (DSA), while the powerful intelligence chief and secretary no. 1 of the SLORC is a university dropout. Except for the trade minister, Tun Kyi, all key military cabinet ministers who also happened to be the members of the SLORC hold no undergraduate college degree, let alone graduate degrees. By contrast, all the top executive council members of the opposition party, the NLD, and 41 percent of its 27-member central committee are college graduates.[17] This fact alone may be considered sufficient explanation for the poor national economic management in Burma, for in all rapidly developing and industrializing Asian countries, one can see that many political leaders, cabinet members, and public administrators are highly educated persons with college degrees, including advanced graduate degrees from prestigious Western colleges and universities, as in the cases of South Korea, Hong Kong, Malaysia, Singapore, Taiwan, Thailand, and even Indonesia.

The policy followed by the military rulers of intimidating, discriminating against and repressing able and educated persons in favor of uneducated and loyal persons has been the main depressant of the social capability of Burma for development. The net impact of this policy and of the wasting of the human capital of Burma by the SLORC is apparent in that 39 percent of children never enrolling and only 25 percent of all children complete the five-year cycle of primary education, while the literacy rate has been estimated to have declined to about 55 percent.[18] In economic terms, the high dropout rate of students at various levels of schools has been the key detriment to the present and future economic growth of Burma, for the higher the dropout rate or the fewer the number of years of school completed by the students, the lower the labor force participation rate and the lower the per capita output.[19]

This policy also flagrantly violates the traditional Burmese cultural value and standard set by the sacred Mingla Sutra of Burmese Buddhism, which mandates to befriend and depend on the wise and learned persons, *panditah ninsa thaiwanah* in Pali. Other traditional advice given to a malevolent and weak Burmese king of the thirteenth century Pagan dynasty, King *Narathihapati* who was nicknamed the *Tayokepyay Min,* "the Runaway King from the Chinese Invaders," by his wise Chief Queen, *Mipayar Saw,* in how to save his throne and kingdom from collapsing was:

Fell not thy country's banner—that is wax not wroth nor rage blindly against the wise men, monks and hermits, who are as thy country's banner. Pluck not out thy country's eyes—that is, be not wroth and furious as a devil, without let or thwarting of thine anger, against thy wise chaplains learned in the Pitikas and Vedas, who are as thy country's eyes. Sully not thy country's face—that is take not by force another's children who are as mirrors of their parents, their husbands, or sons, for such are thy country's face.[20]

The military rulers have sinned against these traditional moral codes of conduct in relentlessly intimidating and repressing the educated and even killing children, young students, and Buddhist monks in the 1988 political uprising. In economic terms, the anti-intellectual policy followed by the SLORC misused and destroyed the human capital that Burma needs to develop into a modern nation. The resulting social deadweight loss underscores the SLORC's failure "to direct society's resources to an allocative pattern capable of achieving optimum social welfare."[21]

MILITARY FORTIFICATION AND SINONIZATION OF BURMA

The policies and actions of Burmese military rulers have a single most The policies and actions of Burmese military rulers have a single most overriding objective—the stranglehold on power. This goal has led the SLORC to consolidate and expand the military might, resulting in excessive and conspicuous public or government consumption, especially the increasing mammoth military expenditures, which accounts for more than 50 percent of the central government budget and 7 percent of Burma's GDP, resulting in the mounting government deficit, which has been financed primarily by printing banknotes. This, in turn, has led to an accelerated growth of money supply and velocity of circulation, resulting in uncontrollable galloping inflation, financial distress, and a host of market distortions and missignals that are inversely related to the growth of the economy.

The perilous consequence of the fortification of military might by the SLORC through the enlargement of its armed forces from some 180,000 men in 1988 to over 300,000 men in 1996 equipped with arms mostly procured from China and the establishment of symbiotic military and economic ties, *swemyo pauk hpaw* in Burmese, with the giant neighbor, has been the Sinonization of the Burmese polity and economy, thus making Burma a virtual satellite of China. The overall development policies and programs of the SLORC indicate a failure to observe the classic economic principle of opportunity cost or trade-off in the allocation of the given resources of Burma between guns and butter or between the build up of military might and human development. The ultimate cost of this policy failure has been and will be sociopolitical instability and reduced social capabilities for sustainable economic growth of Burma in the long run.

THE CONTROL OF THREE POWER BASES: INFORMATION, ECONOMY, AND FINANCE

To keep the stranglehold on political power, the SLORC tightly controls the three basic substructures or foundations of power: information or knowledge, economy or production and distribution of goods and services, and finance. The control of information necessitates repression and control of press, students, teachers, intellectuals, or the educated in general which result in a severe damage to human capital. The need to control the economy led to the establishment of a trade regime, state regulations, interventions, and monopoly of key enterprises and industries, causing inefficiency, inequity, corruption, disincentives, and market distortions. The single most important source of power for the SLORC has been its ability to control and derive foreign exchange from opium production and heroin export, which have steadily grown since it seized power in 1988. The estimated dollar value of heroin export of over 200 tons a year in the 1990s represents nearly 50 percent of Burma's $70 billion legal GDP at the black market exchange rate in 1995. Amid all the conquests and cease-fire agreements of the SLORC with various armed ethnic rebel groups, the reality of Burmese politics and the power base of the SLORC lie in the "politics of heroin" and the complicity of the Burmese generals in the laundering of what is termed "narcodollars" by drug warlords with impunity.

The control of finance necessitates the adoption of various policies of financial repression, such as a centralized state banking system, regulations of interest rates, financial markets and institutions, price and wage controls, and, especially, the maintenance of a foreign exchange regime and an unrealistic foreign exchange rate. The maintenance of an unrealistic official foreign exchange rate that is overvalued more than 20 times, recently more than 30 times, the unofficial/black market rate has been the main cause of the devaluation of the local currency, kyat, in the black market and absolute and relative wage or income differences between Burma and relatively more prosperous neighboring countries. The phenomenal premia of black market exchange rates of various foreign currencies, US dollars in particular, have been causing the dollarization of the economy and a massive exodus of people out of Burma in search of overseas jobs to earn foreign exchange, the job of a seaman on foreign ships being the most popular and coveted one.

For example, there are more than 100 well-qualified, English-speaking Burmese teachers' of various subjects at the Assumption University in Bangkok and hundreds more in various other countries, while 500,000 to 1 million Burmese migrant workers are estimated to be living and working for various Thai business firms at cheap wages along the border in Ranong, Tak, Kanchanaburi, Ratchaburi, Mae Hong Song, Chumphon, Chiang Rai, Chiang Mai, Mae Sai, and other border towns inside Thailand. The estimated Burmese population in Singapore is around 50,000, more than 50 percent of which are reportedly illegal immigrants. Although the exact number of Burmese population is not known, there are reportedly over 100,000 legal and illegal Burmese immigrants working in Malaysia. A few thousand more Burmese are living and working in Japan and South Korea. There are also more than 3,000 Burmese medical doctors working and living in the United Kingdom and United States.

In other words, the military rulers have transformed Burma into "an unworthy land to dwell." According to Buddhist texts, Akkhana Sutra and Mingala Sutra for example, there are eight unworthy places or lands for human beings to dwell known as *yartpyit shitpar*. Among them, *Akkhana, Arpatiyupa* and *Pyitsandarit Detha* or *Desa* in Pali are most well-known. In spiritual term, *Akkhana* refers to an abode of existence devoid of proper Buddhist teachings or scriptures whose inhabitants with wrong thinking and feeble intellect cannot attain enlightenment or become Buddha. *Arpatiyupa Detha* is the antithesis of *Patiyupa Detha*. According to the fourth verse of Mingala Sutra, *Patiyupa Detha* is "a blessed place one should dwell" where the Three Gems of Life (*Yadana Thonepar* in Burmese), the Lord–*Hpayar*, the Law–*Tayar*, and the Order–*Thangha*, are eminent and omnipresent."[22]

Pyitsandarit refers to a remote and undeveloped peripheral place or hinterland that lies outside the boundary of the Central Land, *Myitsima Detha*, with the sacred city of Bodha Gaya at the center, where the Bodhi tree under which Buddha attained enlightenment grows, surrounded by 900 prosperous cities or states of ancient Inida. The mundane characteristics of "an unworthy land to dwell" is described by *Satu Ringabala Amartkyee*, or Caturingabala, a Burmese scholar and royal minister of the fourteenth century Pinya dynasty, as "A land where there are no rich tradesmen and merchants with freedom to pursue profitable trades and businesses, no sages and teachers with knowledge of spiritual and mundane worlds for counsel and instruction, no kings who govern the land according to law, no rivers and ports for travel, and no physicians for cure of diseases."[23]

CONSTRUCTIVE ENGAGEMENT: FOREIGN DIRECT INVESTMENT AND ECONOMIC GROWTH OF BURMA

Exogenously, the most important factor that has helped the Burmese junta to legitimize its rule against the will of the Burmese people has been the willingness of nations from around the world to invest, trade, and establish economic ties with Burma. Whatever little economic growth Burma has experienced since 1988 has largely been attributed to the inflow of foreign direct investments from the outside world. To many outside observers and proponents of investment and trade with an authoritarian regime to promote growth and democratization, the so-called constructive engagement of the ASEAN has given the illusion of an economic boom in Burma and created the delusion of the ruling military junta to initiate and sustain economic growth by means of incremental foreign direct investments. However, the recent Asian financial debacle seems to have shattered this delusion.

Like its predecessor SLORC, the new military junta, SPDC, has been boasting about the real and potential increase in the inflow of foreign direct investments into Burma. The reality of the Asian financial debacle is that the ASEAN economies, with their own financial and economic crises, will not be able to finance their committed investment projects in Burma, let alone make new investments. With the exception of Singapore, the rest of the financially distressed members of ASEAN can be expected to halt or even withdraw their investments in Burma. The evidence of the ASEAN disengagement with Burma to save their own economies can be seen in the launching of massive deportation programs of Burmese workers by Thailand and Malaysia to alleviate their own unemployment problem under the impact of the Asian financial debacle. The involuntary return of these workers to Burma is going to magnify the problems of pervasive poverty and mass unemployment of Burma, signaling a potential sociopolitical unrest.

The trend of disengagement spearheaded by the US government in imposing sanctions against new investments in Burma seems to be occurring with a different twist as the ASEAN find themselves in desperate need of halting the flight of foreign capital, attracting foreign investments, and securing financial aid from the West and international financial institutions to ward off a potential collapse of their economies. Unlike the Asian countries that have close relationships with the United States, such as Thailand and Indonesia, Burma's external sources of funds have been greatly hampered by the cessation of Western bilateral and multilateral aid since the massive political uprising of 1988. In addition to no new investments or inflow of external capital from the United Sates, there is a possibility of withdrawal and liquidation of investments in Burma by United States and other Western multinational corporations as they have done in the cases of Thailand and Indonesia.

Texaco's withdrawal from the Yadagun natural gas project in 1997 and Arco's revelation of its intention to liquidate its newly acquired natural gas exploration project in the Bay of Martaban signal a potential liquidation of Western investment in the most critical sector of the Burmese economy with the largest foreign exchange earning power, the energy sector. The controversial billion-dollar Yadana natural gas project, a joint venture of American Unocal, French Total, and Thai PTTE and the MOGE of the Burmese government, also seems to be in a state of trouble with legal disputes and a sit-in protest by conservationists inside Thailand against the PTTE's pipeline project to ship the natural gas. It has resulted in intervention by the new Thai prime minister, Chuan Leekpai, who sent troops to quell the protest and suspended the pipeline project for four days in the second week of January 1998.

In addition to these feuds that raise the question of whether or not the construction of the natural gas pipeline will be successfully completed, border conflicts between Burma and Thailand have led to the stoppage of cross-border trade to deepen the ongoing economic and financial crisis of Burma. Despite these feuds and troubles, the two major natural gas projects, Yategun and Yadana, are not likely to be abandoned by Thailand and its Western partners, the UK Premier, Nippon Oil, France's Total, and US Unocal, which have heavily invested in the two projects. That is, the economic lifeline of the Burmese military regime in terms of earning foreign exchange from foreign investment in the energy sector seems not likely to be severed.

The two countries from which Burma can hope to secure funds to remain afloat amid the Asian financial and economic crisis are Japan, historically the largest creditor and supporter of the military regime of Burma, and China, Burma's greatest ally since 1988. It is more than likely that the two countries will continue to provide aid and concessional loans to Burma for both economic and political reasons. Two-thirds of Burma's outstanding external debt of over $6 billion is owed to Japan. China has provided aid and concessionary loans far greater in value than that of Japan to finance Burma's various infrastructure projects, especially the construction of new roads and bridges and refurbishment of the old ones that link the two countries to develop export markets and reap loft-sided economic benefits from the booming Burma-China border trade. China's vested political interest in providing aid and loans to Burma since 1988 has been to expand its naval power and presence in the Indian ocean via Burmese lands and waters. Hence, China will continue to maintain its close ties with Burma and provide economic and military aid to rescue Burma, or rather the Burmese junta, from its severe economic and financial crisis. The political implication for Burma, which is already a virtual satellite of China, is that it will become an absolute dependent or colony of China.

Thus, it seems that despite the negative impact of Asian financial debacle, the safety net of obtaining bilateral aids from Japan and China for the Burmese junta to stay in power seems to be in place. It must be emphasized though that the real financial safety net of the Burmese junta is not the inflow of legal foreign exchange, but the inflow of illegal drug money and money laundering with impunity by Burma's infamous drug kingpins such as Khun Sa and Lo Hsing Han in complicity with Burmese generals. However, the Burmese economy under the gross mismanagement of incompetent military rulers is in a downward spiral with escalating inflation, shortages of rice and other basic necessities, rampant corruption, pervasive poverty, and the threat of another massive and violent political convulsion like the 1988 political uprising.

In repudiation of the presumption or theory of those who advocate "engagement " or "constructive engagement" with Burma, especially the ASEAN and the chief executive officers (CEOs) of the multinational corporations, that trade and investment promote economic growth and, in tandem, promote democratization, it will be argued as Schumpeter argued: "By 'development,' therefore, we shall understand only such changes in economic life as are not forced upon it from without but arise by its own initiative, from within."[24] Indeed, "When we say that a culture or institution or nation 'grows' or 'develops,' we are not referring to random and adventitious changes, to changes induced by some external deity or other beings. We are referring to change that is intrinsic to the entity."[25] No such changes from within or changes intrinsic to Burma have transpired as a result of the constructive engagement or the inflow of foreign direct investment that has been claimed and propagandized by the SLORC as the impetus and signal for the turning point of the Burmese economy to leap forward.

As F. Tennyson Jesse, the famed historical writer on ancient and British colonial Burma, wrote with respect to the impact of British investment on colonial Burma:

Meanwhile, in this betwixt-and-between state in which Burma found herself after the Annexation, the profits of industry left the country. Businessmen are not a race of philanthropists and expect some return from their capital. This is not confined to Burma, for though potentially she may be a rich country, it must be remembered that the riches of a country are not only in what she produces, but in her capacity to use her own products, and in this latter form of wealth Burma has fallen.[26]

This story of colonial Burma told by Jesse seems to be recurring in Burma today as Burma's capacity to produce and use its own products seems to have not increased to enrich the people and the country, despite the incremental direct foreign investments made by Asian and Western companies. The macroeconomic evidence of this is reflected in the absolute and increasing dependency on imported foreign goods relative to declining exports, resulting in chronic trade and current account deficits, as well as high unemployment and low savings and investments of Burma. The negative impact of unrestrained foreign direct investment on Burma has been an irreversible destruction of not only natural resource bases and ecological damage to the environment but also the cultural decline and moral decay of the people.

It is appropriate to conclude this study by citing the allegorical article written by a young dissident Burmese Buddhist monk, U Uttara, using the pen name of Ashin Myittah Nanda, "The Time for *Atesah Thaya Owe* (Magic Pot for All Wishes) to Burst Is Near, "[27] which underscores the gross mismanagement of resource-rich Burma by incompetent and corrupt military managers:

Young man: Please tell the story of how the magic pot got into the hands of a bad person.

Aba Toat: In the ancient city of *Bayah-nathi*, Banaris of ancient India, there lived a *Boddithadapa (Boddhisattava),* Buddha-to-be, as a wealthy man. He was a highly devout man and performed deeds of merit daily. He also had a reckless and irresponsible son. When he died, he ascended to heaven and became the King of Angels, *Thagyar Min*. After inheriting the wealth from the father, the son lived lavishly, entertaining friends, drinking, eating, and womanizing. As time passed, the riches he inherited were wasted, cheated, and robbed by pretentious friends around him. He had to sell everything he owned–the house, the land, the clothes and the furniture–making him a destitute person. His father from heaven above was aware of his son's plight and came down to earth and helped him by giving him the magic pot, *Atesah Thaya Owe,* which could fulfill any wish. However, the father warned the son to take good care of the pot so that it would not break. The son kept on living the same lifestyle as before, drinking, gambling, inflicting sufferings upon people, and committing adultery and other misdeeds without remembering or repenting the time when he was poor. One day, he got drunk and forgetting the advice of his father, he began to play with the magic pot by tossing it to the sky and catching it. After a few tosses, he could not catch the fallen pot and it was broken into pieces. Isn't our country so rich in natural resources like the *Atesah Thaya Owe* (Magic Pot for all Wishes)? But because those who are governing the country are bad and reckless, they took out the wealth from the magic pot to buy arms, wasting time and energy needed to develop the economy and dividing the people by blaming this and that ethnic group. Isn't it like playing with the magic pot by tossing it to the sky? Therefore, before the magic pot falls from the sky and breaks into pieces, we must protect it by removing it from the possession of irresponsible military rulers and try to transfer it into the hands of patriotic democratic leaders.

NOTES

1. Michael Walzer, "On Failed Totalitarianism," in Irving Howe, ed., *1984 Revisited: Totalitarianism in Our Century* (New York: Harper and Row, 1988), p. 110.

2. Lord Byron, *The Bride of Abydos*, I:20, cited by Walzer, ibid.

3. George Orwell, *1984* (New York: Nal Penguin, 1961), p. 7.

4. Edward J. Kane, "Ethical Foundation of Financial Regulation," *Journal of Financial Services Research* (January 1, 1997): 52.

5. Aung San Suu Kyi, *Empowerment for a Culture of Peace and Development*, address to a meeting of World Commission on Culture and Development delivered by Corazon Aquino, Manila, 21 November, 1994 p. 5.

6. John Kenneth Galbraith, *The Anatomy of Power* (Boston: Houghton Mifflin, 1983), p. 5.

7. David A. Chandler, "Introduction," *The Role of NGOs in Burma*, World Vision, Practical Christian Caring (Washington DC: World Vision, June 6, 1995), p. 7.

8. David A. Chandler, *"Health in Myanmar,"* a paper presented at an HIID conference December 5-7, 1996, Cambridge, MA, December 3, 1996.

9. J. E. Meade, *Trade and Welfare* (New York: Oxford University Press, 1955), p. 68.

10. Asian Development Bank (ADB), *Economic Development Report on Myanmar* (Manila: ADB, November 1995), p. vi.

11 See Economist Intelligence Unit (EIU), *Country Report, Myanmar (Burma),* 3rd Quarter, 1997 (London; EIU, 1997), p. 8.

12. Ibid.

13. Aung San Suu Kyi, "Freedom from Fear," in Michael Aris, ed., *Freedom from Fear and Other Writings* (New York: Penguin Group, 1991), p. 180.

14. Ibid., p. 145.

15. Asian Development Bank (ADB), *Asian Development Outlook, Myanmar 1995* (Manila: ADB, 1995), p. 147.

16. The World Bank, *Myanmar, Policies for Sustaining Economic Reform* (Washington, DC: The World Bank, October, 1995), p. xiv.

17. See Nemoto Kei, "Aung San Suu Kyi: Her Position in the Present and Future Burma," paper presented at the Colloquium on Burma Studies, Center for Burma Studies, Northern Illinois University, Decalb, October 25–27, 1996, p. 8.

18. UNICEF, *Myanmar-UNICEF Country Programme of Cooperation 1996-2000:Master Plan of Operations* (New York: UNICEF, October 1995), p. 3.

19. See Fritiz Machlup, *Education and Economic Growth* (Lincoln: University of Nebraska Press, 1970), pp. 6–7.

20. U Pe Maung Tin and G. H. Luce, trans., *The Glass Palace Chronicle of the Kings of Burma* (Rangoon: Burma Research Society, 1910), p. 178.

21. Kane, "Ethical Foundation of Financial Regulation," p. 53.

22. See Salin Sayadaw, *Hanthahwaddy Payatekyee Neet-thaya* (in Burmese) (Rangoon: Hanthahwaddy Pidaka Press, 1958), p. 51.

23. Satu Ringabala, "Lawka Niti Pyoe," *Myanma Swel Soan Kyan,* no. 3, vol. 3 (in Burmese) (Rangoon: Sarpai Beikman Press, 1956). See for a short version of this quote *Loka Niti (A Guide to Good Living)* (Yangon: Ministry of Trade, January 1995), p. 94.

24. Jospeh A. Schumpeter, *The Theory of Economic Development* (Cambridge: Harvard University Press, 1951), p. 63.

25. R. A. Nisbet, *Social Change and History: Aspects of the Western Theory of Development* (New York: Oxford University Press, 1969), p. 7.

26. F. Tennyson Jesse, *The Story of Burma* (London: Macmillan, 1946), p. 141.

27. Ashin Myittah Nanda, "The Time for *Atesah Thaya Owe* (Magic Pot for All Wishes) to Burst Is Near" (in Burmese), *The New Era Journal* (March, 1994).

Bibliography

BOOKS AND ARTICLES

Abramovitz, Moses "The Elements of Social Capability" In Ben Ho Kooabd Dwight H. Perkins, eds., *Social Capability and Long-Term Economic Growth.* New York: St. Martin's Press, 1995.

Agénor, Pierre-Richard "Parallel Currency Markets in Developing Countries: Theory, Evidence, and Policy Implications" *Essays in International Finance,* no. 188 (Princeton University, International Finance Section, November 1992).

Albright, Madeleine "The Burma Daze" *The New Republic,* December 4, 1995.

Alesina, Alberto, and Roberto Peroti "The Political Economy of Growth: A Critical Survey of the Recent Literature" *The World Bank Economic Review,* no. 3 (September 1994).

Berfield, Susan "Myanmar Takes a Circuitous, Rocky Route toward Prosperity" *Asiaweek* (January, 5 1996).

Barro, Robert J. "Economic Growth in a Cross Section of Countries" *Quarterly Journal of Economics* (May 1991).

Bernstein, Dennis, and Leslie Kean "People of the Opiate: Burma's Dictatorship of Drugs" *The Nation* (December 16, 1996).

Boucaud, André Et Louis "Pékin-Rangoun, nouvel axe asiatique" *Le Monde Diplomatique,* (May 16 1993).

Bhagwati, Jagdish "The New Thinking on Development" *Journal of Democracy* (October 1995).

Bradley, Barbara "Under Burmese Junta Tourist Dollars Rule" *Christian Science Monitor,* December 29, 1994.

Brenner, Reuven "The Pursuit of Poverty" *The Wall Street Journal,* November 14, 1995.

Byron, Lord *The Bride of Abydos,* I:20.

Chaipipat, Kulachada "ASEAN Stuns West with Plan to Review Rights," *The Nation*, (July 30, 1997).

Chandler, David A. *"Health in Myanmar" A Paper presented at an HIID Conference, December 5–7, 1996*, Cambridge, Massachusetts, December 3, 1996.

———"Introduction" *The Role of NGOs in Burma* World Vision, Practical Christian Caring, June 6, 1995.

Chapman, E. C., Peter Hinton, and Jingrong Tan "Cross-Border Trade between Yunan and Burma, and the Emerging Mekong Corridor" *Thai-Yunan Project Newsletter*, no. 19, Australian National University, December 1992.

Chew, Melanie "Human Rights in Singapore: Perceptions and Problems" *Asian Survey* 34 no. 11 (November 1994).

Clements, Alan *Burma: The Next Killing Fields?* CA: Odonian Press, 1992.

Cockburn, Andrew "Dilemma on the Irrawaddy" *Condé Nast Traveler*, (June 1995).

Dahn, Henrich "The Hotel and Tourism Industry in Myanmar" *Standard Charter Indochina Monitor,* June 1995.

Dapice, David *Landlessness, Poverty, and the Environment in Myanmar: Can Grass Roots Initiatives Create Sustainable Progress?, A Report to the United Nations Development Programme* (Cambridge: Harvard Institute of International Development (HIID), February 10, 1995).

Dapice, David, *Accelerating Progress among the Rural Poor in Myanmar, a Report to the United Nations Development Programme*, (New York: UNDP, September 15, 1995)

Diller, Janelle M. *The National Convention in Burma (Myanmar): An Impediment to the Restoration of Democracy.* New York: International League for Human Rights, 1996.

Fairciough, Gordon "Good Connections: Firms Linked to Junta Draw Lion's Share of Business" *Far Eastern Economic Review* (August 15, 1996).

Forbes, C.J.F.S. *British Burma and Its People: Native Manners, Customs, and Religion.* London: Spottswood, 1878.

Fry, Maxwell J. *Foreign Direct Investment in Southeast Asia.* Singapore: Institute of Southeast Asian Studies, 1993.

Furnivall, J. S. *Colonial Policy and Practice.* New York: New York University Press, 1956.

Galbraith, John Kenneth *The Anatomy of Power.* Boston: Houghton Mifflin, Co. 1983.

Ghai, Yaslt *Human Rights and Governance: The Asia Debate* Asia Foundation's Center for Asian Pacific Affairs, Occasional Paper No. 4, November 1994.

Gelbard, Robert S. "SLORC's Drug Links" *Far Eastern Economic Review*, (November 21, 1996).

Green, Timothy "Jade Is Special, As Are the Risks in Bringing It from Mine to Market" *Smithsonian Magazine* (July 1986).

Gyaw, Ohn *Statement by His Excellency U Ohn Gyaw, Minister of Foreign Affairs and Chairman of the Delegation of the Union of Myanma.* New York: Permanent Mission of the Union of Myanmar to the UN, September 17, 1996.

Hagen, Everet E. *The Economics of Development*, 4th ed. Homewood, Il: Irwin, 1986.

Hall, D.G.E. *Europe and Burma: A Study of European Relations with Burma to the Annexation of Thibaw's Kingdom 1886.* New York: Oxford University Press, 1945.

Harberger, Arnold C. *Economic Policy and Economic Growth.* San Francisco: Institute for Contemporary Studies, 1985.

Hitchcock, David I. *Asian Values and the U.S.: How Much Conflict?,* Monograph Washington, DC: Center for Strategic International Studies, 1995.

Huntington, Samuel P. *Foreign Affairs* 72, no. 3 (Summer 1993).

Ibrahim, Datuk Seri Anwar "Asian Democracy," excerpt from the speech delivered at the Philippine's Centennial Conference of 1896 Revolution, Manila, July 26, 1996, in Harn Yawnghwe, *Burma Alert,* 7, no. 9 (September 1996).

Ifsley, Spencer "Let's Not Visit Myanmar Year '94" *Dawn News Bulletin,* Bangkok: (May/June 1994).

James, William E., Seiji Naya & Gerald M. Meier, *Asian Development: Economic Success and Lessons* (Madison: University of Wisconsin Press, 1989).

Jesse, F. Tennyson, *The Story of Burma* (London: MacMillan & Co. Ltd., 1946).

Jung, Kim Dae "Is Culture Destiny? The Myth of Asia's Anti-Democratic Values" *Foreign Affairs* 73, no. 6 (November/December 1994).

Kamm, Henry "Socialist Burma: Pervasive Poverty, Indifferent Military Rule" *New York Times,* June 25, 1975.

Kane, Edward J. "Ethical Foundation of Financial Regulation," *Journal of Financial Services Research* January 1, 1997.

Kausikan, Bilahari "Asia's Different Standards" *Foreign Policy,* no. 92 (Fall, 1993).

Kei, Nemoto, "Aung San Suu Kyi: Her Position in the Present and Future Burma" Paper presented at the Colloquium on Burma Studies, Center for Burma Studies, Northern Illinois University, Dekalb, October 25–27, 1996.

Kiryu, Minoru *Immediate Measures for Price Stabilization and Achievement of Broad-Based, Consistent Growth Rate in Myanmar Naing-gan* Report to the UNDP Privately published, 1992.

Kyaw, U Wint "1994 Private Banking" (in Burmese) *Dana: 1994 Private Enterprises Yearbook.* Yangon: U Kyaw Kyaw Wai, January 1995.

Kyi, Aung San Suu "In Quest of Democracy" In Michael Aris, ed.,*Freedom from Fear and Other Writings.* New York: Penguin Group, 1991.

——*Towards a True Refuge.* Oxford: Perpetua Press, 1993.

——"Empowerment for a Culture of Peace and Development" Address to a meeting of World Commission on Culture and Development delivered by Corazon Aquino, Manila, November 21, 1994.

——*Letter to Mr. Gustav Speth,* Rangoon, January 14, 1996.

Kyi, Khin Maung "Myanmar: Will Forever Flow the Ayeyarwady?" *Southeast Asian Affairs,* Singapore (1994).

Lim, Linda, Pang Eng Fong, and Ronald Findlay, "Singapore" Ronald Findlay and Stanislaw Wellisz eds., *The Political Economy of Poverty, Equity, and Growth: Five Small Open Economies.* New York: Oxford University Press, 1993.

Lintner, B., *Burma in Revolt.* Boulder, CO: Westview Press, 1994.

——"Triangular Ties" *Far Eastern Economic* (March 28, 1991)

——"Rangoon's Rubicon: Infrastructure Aid Tightens Peking's Control" *Far Eastern Economic Review* February 11, 1993.

Machlup, Fritz *Education and Economic Growth.* Lincoln: University of Nebraska Press, 1970.

MacSwan, Angus "Some Get Rich on the Road to Mandalay" *Burma Monitor*, (March 1933).

Mahnnun Yahzawintaw *Gyi* (The Great Glass Palace History of Kings in Burmese). Mandalay: Daw Hpwar Khin U Hla Aung, 1957.

Maung, Mya "On the Road to Mandalay: A Case Study of Sinonization of Upper Burma" *Asian Survey* 34 no. 5 (May 1994).

——*Burma and Pakistan: A Comparative Study of Development.* New York: Praeger, 1971.

——*The Burma Road to Poverty.* New York: Praeger, 1991.

——*Totalitarianism in Burma: Prospects for Economic Development.* New York: Paragon House, 1992.

Meade, J. E., *Trade and Welfare.* New York: Oxford University Press, 1955.

Meier, Gerald M., and Robert E. Baldwin *Economic Development: Theory, History, Policy.* New York, John-Wiley Sons, 1963.

Metteya, Bhikkhu Ananda *The Religion of Burma.* Madras: Theosophical Publishing House, 1929.

Mohamad, Mahathir bin "Mahathir Hits Spendthrift West" Excerpt from the speech delivered at the Europe/Asia Economic Forum, Tokyo, *Japan Times*, October 26, 1992.

Myint, Dagon U Tun *Ten Great Stories* (in Burmese). Rangoon: Baho Press, 1989.

Myint, Kyaw Yin "Walk to the East and Look Back to the West: 1993 Border Trade" *Dana* (Wealth in Burmese), Special Issue 4, no. 7 (December/January 1994).

——"The 1993 Model Mandalay." *Dana* (Wealth in Burmese) 3, no 9, (December/January, February 1993).

Myint, Zaw Tun "'94 Gold and Gem Market" *Dana* (Wealth in Burmese) 5, no. 6, (January 1995).

Naing, Min "UN Needs to Check on Staff in Burma" *Bangkok Post*, May 1, 1991.

Nanda, Ashin Myittah "The Time for *Atesah Thaya Owe* (Magic Pot for All Wishes) to Burst Is Near" (in Burmese) *The New Era Journal* (March, 1994).

Nisbet, R. A. *Social Change and History: Aspects of the Western Theory of Development.* New York: Oxford University Press, 1969.

Nurkse, Ragnar *Problems of Capital Formation in Underdeveloped Countries.* Oxford: Basil Blackwell, 1957.

Nyunt, Britishat Burma U *Hanthahwaddy Payatekyee Nethaya* (in Burmese). Rangoon: Hanthahwaddy Pitaka Press, 1958.

Oo, Win Naing *Cries from Insein: A Report on Conditions for Political Prisoners in Burma's Infamous Insein Jail* Bangkok: All Burma Students' Democratic Front (ABSDF), 1996.

Orwell, George *1984.* New York: Nal Penguin, 1961.

Overbolt, William H. "Dateline Drug Wars: Burma: The Wrong Enemy" *Foreign Policy* (Winter 1989).

Porter, Doug J. "A Note on United Nations Involvement in the Border Area Development Program" *Thai-Yunan Project Newsletter,* no. 18, September 1992.

Pyin, Maung Thet "Where to Go in 1997" *Myanma Dana* (Burmese Wealth in Burmese) (January 1997).

Richburg, Keith B. "In China's Wild West, Heroin Grips a Town: Crime, Disease, Prostitution Plague Drug Route" *Washington Post*, July 26, 1996.

Ringabala, Satu "Lawka Niti Pyoe" *Myanma Swel Soan Kyan* 3 no. 3, Volume 3 (in Burmese) (1956).

Saing, Soe *United Nations Technical Aid in Burma: A Short Survey.* Singapore: Insitute of Southeast Asian Studies, 1990.

Sarel, Michael *Growth in Asia, What We Can and What We Cannot Infer, Economic Issues.* Washington DC: International Monetary Fund, 1996, p. 10.

Sarkisyanz, E. *Buddhist Backgrounds of the Burmese Revolution.* The Hague: Martinus Nijhoff, 1965.

Schumpeter, Jospeh A. *The Theory of Economic Development.* Cambridge: Harvard University Press, 1951.

Scott, J. G., *Burma: From the Earliest Time to the Present Day.* London: T. Fisher Unwin, 1924.

Selth, Andrew "Burma's Arms Procurement Programme" Working paper no. 289. Camberra,: Australian National University, 1995.

Sen, Amartya "Freedoms and Needs," *The New Republic* (January 10, 17, 1994).

Shaing, U Tin, ed. *The Glass Palace Chronicle* (in Burmese). Rangoon: Pyigyi Munnaing Pitaka Press, 1963.

Shenon, Philip "Law Maker Meets again with Burmese Dissident" *New York Times,* February, 16, 1994.

Shenon, Philip, "On the Road to Mandalay" *New York Times,* April 14, 1994.

Shin, Mya Saw, trans. *The Constitution (The Fundamental Law) of the Socialist Republic of the Union of Burma.* Washington, DC: Library of Congress, Law Library, June 1975.

Shin, Mya Saw, Alison Krupnick, and Tom L. Wilson, *"Burma" or "Myanma": U.S. Policy at the Crossroads.* Washington, DC: Bureau of Asian Research, October 1995.

Silverstein, Joseph "Some Thoughts upon and Recommendations for a U.S. Policy toward Burma (Myanmar)" A Paper prepared and presented for the U.S. House of Representatives Committee on Foreign Affairs Hearing on US Policy toward Burma and Southeast Asia, Washington, DC, March 25, 1993.

——"Burma's Uneven Struggle" *Journal of Democracy* 7, no. 4, (October 1996).

Slater, Robert *Guns through Arcadia.* Madras: Diocesan Press, 1943.

Smith-Forbes, Charles J. F., *British Burma and Its People: Native Manners, Customs, and Religion.* London: Spottswood & Co., 1878.

Strachan, Paul, "Burma: To Go or Not to Go?" *Burma Debate* 2, no. 5, (November/December, 1995).

Talyor, Robert *The State of Burma.* Honolulu: University of Hawaii Press, 1987.

Than, Mya "Growth Pattern of Burmese Agriculture: A Productivity Approach," Occasional paper no. 81 Institute of Southeast Asian Studies, Singapore 1988.

——"Agriculture in Myanmar: What Has Happened to Asia's Rice Bowl?" *Southeast Asian Affairs,* Singapore, (1990).

——*Myanmar's External Trade: An Overview in the Southeast Asian Context.* Singapore: Institute of Southeast Asian Studies, 1992.

Than, Tin Maung "AIDS, How Many have Been Infected and How Many Will Be Infected in Myanmar?" *Thint Bawa* (Your Life) (in Burmese) (July 1995).

Thayer, Nate "Diverted Traffic: Indochina Supplants Thailand Conduit for Burma's Drug" *Far Eastern Economic Review* (October 1, 1992).

Thittila, U "The Meaning of Buddhism" *The Atlantic Monthly,* February 1958.

Tin, U Pe Maung and G. H. Luce *The Glass Palace Chronicle of the Kings of Burma.* Rangoon: Rangoon University Press, 1960.

Tinker, H. *The Union of Burma.* London: Oxford University Press, 1961.

Tun, U Than *Ancient Burmese History: Studies in Burmese History No. 1* (in Burmese). Rangoon: Mahah Dagon Press, 1964.

Walinsky, L .J. *Economic Development in Burma 1951–60.* New York: Twentieth Century Fund, 1962.

Walzer, Michael "On Failed Totalitarianism" Irving Howe, ed., *1984 Revisited: Totalitarianism in Our Century* (New York: Harper and Row Publishers, 1988).

Werhane, Patricia H. *Adam Smith and His Legacy for Modern Capitalism.* New York: Oxford University Press, 1991.

Win, Aye Aye "Suu Kyi Accuses Junta of Forcing Opposition to Quit" *Bangkok Post,* July 1,1996.

Wong, John "The Relevance of and Lessons of the Early Development Experience of Newly Industrializing Economies with Special Reference to Laos and Myanmar" *Paper prepared for the United Nations by the Director of Institute of East Asian Political Economy,* Singapore, 1995.

Yammazaki, Masakazu "Asia, a Civilization in the Making" *Foreign Affairs* 75, no. 4 (July/August 1996).

Yawnghwe, Chao-Tzang *The Shan of Burma: Memoirs of a Shan Exile.* Singapore: Institute of Southeast Asian Studies, 1987.

——"Politics and the Informal Economy of the Opium/Heroin Trade: Impact and Implications for Shan State of Burma" *Journal of Contemporary Asia* 23, no. 3 (1993).

Yew, Lee Kwan "Democracy and Human Rights" *Australia and World Affairs,* no. 16 (Autumn 1993).

Zaung, Kachin Land Thant "To the Tamah Khan Land Jade Joint Ventures" *Myanma Dana* (Burmese Wealth in Burmese), no. 70, (April 1996).

DOCUMENTS AND NEWSPAPERS

All Burma Federation of Students' Unions (ABFSU), Information and Documentation Committee, *An Overview of the Current Education Situation in Burma,* privately published paper, December 1997.

All Burma Student Democratic Front (ABSDF), Central Committee *The Scrutiny of the National Convention,* Down Gwin, 1994.

——*Dawn News Bulletin,* May/June 1994.

——*The Dawn Star,* February 2, 1996.

——*Pleading not Guilty in Insein,* Down Gwin, January 1997.

Amnesty International, *Myanmar: Prisoner of Conscience, Torture, Extrajudicial Executions* New York, August 1988.

——*"No Law at All,"* Human Rights Violations under Military Rule New York, October 1992.

Article 19 Country Report. *State of Fear: Censorship in Burma.* London: December 10, 1991.

——*Fatal Silence? Freedom of Expression and the Right to Health in Burma.* London, July 1996.

Asia Watch *News from Asia Watch* Washington DC, September 15, 1989, August 14, 1990.

Asia Week.

Asian Development Bank *Asian Development Outlook, Myanmar* Manila, 1993, 1996.

——*Economic Development Report on Myanmar* Manila, November 1995.

Bangkok Post.

Burma Debate "An Interview with Aung San Suu Kyi" New York, 1995.

Burma Information Group *Heroes inside the Jails of SLORC* Bangkok, November 1994.

Burma Issues A Special Report, Bangkok, April 1997.

Burma Underground Rights Movement for Action (BURMA), *Life in Burma's "New Town,"* Bangkok, August 1990.

Corporate Social Issues Reporter Washington, DC, IRRC, April–May 1996.

Dawn News Bulletin Bangkok, ABSDF, May/June 1994.

Earth Rights International News 1, no. 2, (April 1996).

The Dawn Star Bangkok, ABSDF, February 2, 1996.

Economist London, January 1996.

Encyclopaedia Britannica London, 1980.

European Intelligence Unit *Country Report: Myanmar (Burma),* London, 1993–1997.

Fareastern Economic Review (Hong Kong).

Foreign Broadcasting Information Service (FBIS) *Burma,* Washington, DC, 1991–1993.

Government of Australia, Department of Foreign Affairs and Trade, *Burma, (Myanmar), May 1997,* Canberra, 1997.

Government of the Union of Myanmar. Ministry of National Planning and Economic Development (MNPED) *The Union of Myanmar, Review of the Financial, Economic and Social Conditions for 1992/1993, 1994/1995 and 1995/1996.* Yangon : MNPED 1993, 1995, 1996.

——Ministry of National Planning and Economic Development, Central Statistical Organization (CSO), Selected Monthly Economic Indicators Yangon: CSO, July-August, 1997.

——Ministry of Planning and Finance (MPF) *The Socialist Republic of the Union of Burma: Report to the Pyithu Hluttaw on the Financial, Economic and Social Conditions, 1988/89.* Rangoon: MPF, 1989.

——Myanma Oil and Gas Enterprise (MOGE) *Prospect, Trend, Opportunities and Types of PSC (Production Sharing Contract) for Oil and Gas Exploration,* Yangon, February 1992.

——State Law and Order Restoration Council *Myanmar,the Nation-Building Activities; The Historical Chronicle of the Works of SLORC from 1988 to 1991* (in Burmese). Rangoon: Ministry of Information, December 20, 1991.

——*Myanmar Export/Import Rules and Regulations for Private Business Enterprises (1994.)* Yangon: Directorate of Trade, July 1994.

——Ministry of Trade Lawka Niti, Guide to Good Living. January 1995.

Green, Number 32, August–September 1993, Bochum, Germany, December 1993.

Human Rights Watch/Asia, *Burma,* New York, March 1, 1996.

Human Rights Watch/Asia, *Burma: Children's Rights and the Rule of Law,* vol. 9, no. 1 (C), New York, January 1997.

International Human Rights Law Group (THRLG). *Report on the Myanmar Election.* Washington, DC: May 19, 1990.

International Labor Organization (ILO), International Labor Conference *Provisional Record, Eighty-Third Session, Report of the Committee on the Application of Standards,* no. 14, Geneva, June 20, 1996.

International Monetary Fund *Myanmar, Recent Economic Developments,* Washington, DC: 1996, 1997.

Investor Responsibility Research Center (IRRC), *Corporate Social Issues Reporter,* Washington, DC: April-May, 1996.

Jane's Defense Weekly.

Jesuit Refugee Service Asia/Pacific *Burma Update,* Bangkok, June 22, 1992, August 10, 1993, April 1997.

Lawyers Committee for Human Rights (LCHR) *Summary Injustice: Military Tribunals in Burma* New York: 1991.

Living Color Magazine (in Burmese) (February 1996).

Multinational Monitor Washington DC: January/February 1995, October 1996.

The Nation.

The National Coalition Government of the Union of Burma (NCGUB) *Human Rights Year Book 1996: Burma* Washington DC: NCGUB, July 1997).

The New Light of Myanmar.

The New York Times.

News International "Icon of Hope," London, June, 1996..

UNICEF, Myanmar-UNICEF *Country Programme of Cooperation 1996–2000:Master Plan of Operations.* New York: UNICEF, October 1995.

United Nations *Human Rights Situations and Reports of Special Rapporteurs and Representatives*, A/50/568 New York, October 16, 1995.

——Report of the Special Rapporteur, Rajsoomer Lallah *Human Rights Questions: Human Rights Situations and Reports of Special Rapporteurs and Representatives* New York, General Assembly Fifty-First Session, October 8, 1996.

United Nations Development Programme (UNDP) *Human Development Reports.* New York: Oxford University Press, 1993–1997).

——*UNDP, Human Development Initiative Myanmar: Assessment Report* Prepared for UNDP by a team of independent experts, September 1996.

——*Country Cooperation Framework and Related Matters: Assistance to Myanmar*, DP/1997/4. New York: United Nations, November 4, 1996.

——Executive Board of the UNDP and the UN Population Fund.*Country Programme and Related Matters: Assistance to Myanmar*, DP/1996/4. New York: United Nations, November 20, 1995.

U.S. Government, Department of Justice, Drug Enforcement Administration (DEA) *Heroin Trafficking Proceeds, Drug Intelligence Bulletin.* Washington DC: DEA Intelligence Division, DEA-94044, April 1994.

——*Southeast Asian Heroin Trafficking: Emerging Trends.* Washington DC: DEA 94049, May 1994.

——*Asian Money Movement Methods, Drug Intelligence Report.* Washington DC: DEA, July 1994.

——The National Narcotics Intelligence Consumer Committee *The NICC Report 1996.* Washington, DC: DEA, 1996.

——Department of State *Burma Report on Human Rights Practices.* Washington DC: Bureau of Democracy, Human Rights and Labor, January 30, 1997.

——US Embassy *Burma, Country Commercial Guide.* Rangoon: US Embassy, July 1996.

——US Embassy, *Foreign Economic Trend, Burma 1995* Rangoon: US Embassy, 1996.

Wall Street Journal.

Washington Post.

The Working People's Daily.

The World Bank. *Myanmar, CEM Update.* Washington,DC: World Bank, September 13, 1990.

——*Myanmar, Policies for Sustaining Economic Reform, Report No. 14062-BA.* Washington, DC: World Bank, October, 1995.

Yawnghwe, Harn *Burma Alert* August 1991, February 1995, June 1996.

Index

About the Author

MYA MAUNG is Professor of Finance in the Wallace E. Carroll School of Management at Boston College. He has done extensive empirical research and written several articles on Burma and other developing countries. He is the author of *The Burma Road to Poverty* (Praeger, 1991) and *Totalitarianism in Burma: Prospects for Economic Development* (1992).